IRONY IN THE MATTHEAN PASSION NARRATIVE

IRONY IN THE MATTHEAN PASSION NARRATIVE

INHEE C. BERG

Fortress Press
Minneapolis

IRONY IN THE MATTHEAN PASSION NARRATIVE

Copyright © 2014 Fortress Press. All rights reserved. Except for brief quotations in critical articles or reviews, no part of this book may be reproduced in any manner without prior written permission from the publisher. Visit http://www.augsburgfortress.org/copyrights/ or write to Permissions, Augsburg Fortress, Box 1209, Minneapolis, MN 55440.

Scripture quotations are from the New Revised Standard Version Bible, copyright © 1989 by the Division of Christian Education of the National Council of the Churches of Christ in the USA. Used by permission. All rights reserved.

Cover design: Tory Herman

Cover image: © Cameraphoto Arte, Venice / Art Resource, NY

Library of Congress Cataloging-in-Publication Data is available

Print ISBN: 978-1-4514-7033-8

eBook ISBN: 978-1-4514-8432-8

The paper used in this publication meets the minimum requirements of American National Standard for Information Sciences — Permanence of Paper for Printed Library Materials, ANSI Z329.48-1984.

Manufactured in the U.S.A.

This book was produced using PressBooks.com, and PDF rendering was done by PrinceXML.

Fiat voluntas tua in terris sicut in coelis.
This work is gratefully dedicated to my beloved mother.

CONTENTS

Preface	ix
Abbreviations	xi
1. Irony and the Matthean Passion Narrative	1
2. A General Overview of Irony	25
3. Conventional Ironies	79
4. Irony of the Matthean Passion Narrative	101
5. Theology of the Matthean Passion Narrative: The Meaning of the Death of Jesus through the Lens of Irony	193
Bibliography	209
Index of Names	225
Index of Subjects	229

Preface

The Gospel of Matthew consists of a story featuring Jesus from his birth to death. As the meaning of the name Jesus (1:21) prophetically foresees, his life is geared for a specific goal to achieve God's saving will for his people. It is the Gospel's testimony that God's will is to save his people through his Son, Jesus, and this is the *raison d'être* of the story. God wills to gather and save his people who are like lost sheep without a shepherd (9:36; 10:6; 15:24) and Jesus, the Son of God, carries out this divinely willed salvation as the shepherd of the people (18:12; 25:32f; 26:31). God not only wills human salvation but also has a specific will concerning the way it is achieved. For this reason, Jesus describes his passion as the "cup" (26:39) associated with the saving will of God (26:42, 53-56) which only the Son of God can "drink."

The climax of Jesus' story is found in the Matthean passion narrative (26:1—27:66), where the entire narrative of the Gospel finally reaches fulfillment. The Matthean passion narrative encapsulates the central themes of the Gospel: Jesus, the Christ Savior, gives his life as a ransom for many (20:28; 26:28) and he accomplishes the divinely-willed salvation through his innocent suffering and death, which the Gospel's implied author emphatically equates with the "innocent blood" of Jesus (27:4, 19, 24). As the innocence of Jesus and the penalty of the cross which he bears are in binary opposition, the way in which God's salvation is achieved through the ultimate sacrifice of Jesus-the-innocent is ironic.

The implied author of the Matthean passion narrative assumes the role of an ironist and reports the circumstances involving in Jesus' death and its theological significance through the kaleidoscopic lens of irony. Nevertheless, the Gospel author's dexterous use of irony as his rhetorical device has not yet received full scholarly appreciation. Therefore, this book focuses on the ways in which the Matthean passion narrative uses irony in its narration and employs it to communicate the significance of the meaning of the death of Jesus.

Irony operates using the phenomenon of a dualistic story. The ironist carefully presents the two worlds of the story in dynamic juxtaposition. In contrast to the lower level of story, which is inferior and false, the upper level of story is superior and true. There is more than meets the eye. This situation creates an irreconcilable incongruity between these two worlds—what appears to be versus what really is—which produces the conflict to be resolved. The greater the incompatibility of appearance and substance, the more critically revealing the irony that is present.

The Matthean passion narrative is the very seat of revelatory irony within the Gospel of Matthew because the ironic dimension of the Matthean passion narrative reaches its greatest depth in Jesus' death on the cross. The Son of God saves his people by shedding his innocent blood. There exists a profoundly inescapable contrast between the nature of Jesus, as the Christ and the Son of God, and the nature of the cross, known as slavish punishment and dejection (*supplicium servile*), which he bore. Since the *locus* of divine salvation is the very *locus* of humiliation—the most unlikely place for divine activity—the Matthean passion narrative demands that the reader take an ironic view of the cross in order to perceive the salutary impacts of Jesus' death unfolded through it.

Irony is inherent in the nature of the cross that is not only incompatible with but also repellent to the profoundly majestic figure of Jesus Christ. Given the fact that the Christian faith tradition is built upon the Christ-event, irony becomes a way of looking into the heart of Christianity which not only feeds on the saving effect of the innocent blood of Jesus (26:28) but also proclaims it (26:13).

Abbreviations

ABRL	Anchor Bible Reference Library
AsSeign	*Assemblées du Seigneur*
AsTJ	*Asbury Theological Journal*
ATR	*Anglican Theological Review*
BAGD	Bauer, W., W. F. Arndt, F. W. Gingrich, and F. W. Danker. *Greek-English Lexicon of the New Testament and Other Early Christian Literature*. 2d ed. Chicago, 1979
BETL	Bibliotheca ephemeridum theologicarum lovaniensium
BEvT	Beiträge zur evangelischen Theologie
Bib	*Biblica*
Bijdr	*Bijdragen: Tijdschrift voor filosofie en theologie*
BJRL	*Bulletin of the John Rylands University Library of Manchester*
BR	*Biblical Research*
BSac	*Bibliotheca sacra*
CBQ	*Catholic Biblical Quarterly*
ChrLit	*Christianity and Literature*
CJ	*Classical Journal*
ConBNT	Coniectanea neotestamentica or Coniectanea biblica: New Testament Series
CQ	*Classical Quarterly*
CTM	*Concordia Theological Monthly*
CurTM	*Currents in Theology and Mission*
DRev	*Downside Review*
DunRev	*Dunwoodie Review*
Enc	*Encounter*
EstBib	*Estudios bíblicos*
ETL	*Ephemerides theologicae lovanienses*
ETR	*Etudes théologiques et religieuses*
EvT	*Evangelische Theologie*
EWNT	Eternal word television network
ExpTim	*Expository Times*
GBS	Guides to Biblical Scholarship
GR	*Georgia Review*
HBT	*Horizons in Biblical Theology*
HibJ	*Hibbert Journal*

HNTC	Harper's New Testament Commentaries
IBS	*Irish Biblical Studies*
ICC	International Critical Commentary
IDB	*The Interpreter's Dictionary of the Bible*. Edited by G. A. Buttrick. 4 vols. Nashville, 1962
IJT	*Indian Journal of Theology*
Int	*Interpretation*
Imm	*Immanuel*
JAAR	*Journal of the American Academy of Religion*
JBL	*Journal of Biblical Literature*
JES	*Journal of Ecumenical Studies*
JETS	*Journal of the Evangelical Theological Society*
JHI	*Journal of the History of Ideas*
JLS	*Journal of Literary Semantics*
JR	*Journal of Religion*
JRS	*Journal of Roman Studies*
JSNT	*Journal for the Study of the New Testament*
JSNTSup	Journal for the Study of the New Testament: Supplement Series
JSOT	*Journal for the Study of the Old Testament*
JSOTSup	Journal for the Study of the Old Testament: Supplement Series
JTS	*Journal of Theological Studies*
List	*Listening: Journal of Religion and Culture*
Neot	*Neotestamentica*
NHL	*Nag Hammadi Library in English*. Edited by J. M. Robinson. 4th rev. ed. Leiden, 1996
NIBCNT	New International Biblical Commentary on the New Testament
NIGTC	New International Greek Testament Commentary
NovT	*Novum Testamentum*
NovTSup	Supplements to Novum Testamentum
NRTh	*La nouvelle revue théologique*
NTAbh	Neutestamentliche Abhandlungen
NTS	*New Testament Studies*
NTT	*Norsk Teologisk Tidsskrift*
PerTeol	*Perspectiva teológica*
PRSt	*Perspectives in Religious Studies*
QJS	*Quarterly Journal of Speech*
RB	*Revue biblique*
RechBib	Recherches bibliques
RQ	*Römische Quartalschrift für christliche Altertumskunde und Kirchengeschichte*

SBL	Society of Biblical Literature
SBLDS	Society of Biblical Literature Dissertation Series
SBT	Studies in Biblical Theology
Scr	*Scripture*
SE	*Studia evangelica I, II, III* (= TU 73 [1959], 87 [1964], 88 [1964]. etc.)
SEL	*Studies in English Literature*
SNTSMS	Society for New Testament Studies Monograph Series
SP	*Sacra pagina*
TD	*Theology Digest*
TDNT	*Theological Dictionary of the New Testament*. Edited by G. Kittel and G. Friedrich. Translated by G. W. Bromiley. 10 vols. Grand Rapids, 1964–1976
TS	*Theological Studies*
TynBul	*Tyndale Bulletin*
VT	*Vetus Testamentum*
WBC	Word Biblical Commentary
WW	*Word and World*
ZNW	*Zeitschrift für die neutestamentliche Wissenschaft unt die Kunde der älteren Kirche*

1

Irony and the Matthean Passion Narrative

Purpose

Irony (εἰρωνεία, *eirōneia*) is a literary-rhetorical device of the implied author by which he reveals *what is hidden* (reality) behind *what is seen* (appearance). The reading of irony must parse both of these dimensions of meaning. Irony defies one-dimensional reading and underlines the complexity of reality. In the story world, the implied reader cannot perceive the deeper meaning of the ironic words, situations or character dynamics merely through a surface level reading but only through a "delightful leap of intuition,"[1] which is a result of persuasion based on the so-called "implicit flattery"[2] between the ironist, the implied author, and his reader. As result, irony offers its reader a superior understanding through which he is able to perceive the distinction between the reality and its shadow.

In the story world of the First Gospel, irony is well observed. The Matthean implied author shapes the narrative in an ironic fashion by embedding crucial information through a strategic choice of words, an intentional arrangement of the story and a revealing characterization. He employs irony within his narrative in an omniscient manner and intends his implied reader, whom he believes capable of understanding irony, to detect his literary technique so that the reader may arrive at an ideal understanding of the story's reality. At the beginning of Matthew, the implied author provides his reader with a particular divine perspective as the norm of the story that Jesus will save his people from their sins (1:21). The fact that this divine perspective on the

---

1. Wayne C. Booth, *A Rhetoric of Irony* (Chicago: University of Chicago Press, 1974), 12.
2. Seymour Chatman, *Story and Discourse: Narrative Structure in Fiction and Film* (Ithaca: Cornell University Press, 1978), 229. Also, Robert Fowler, *Loaves and Fishes: The Function of the Feeding Stories in the Gospel of Mark* (SBLDS no. 54; Chico: Scholars, 1981), 161 says it "winks at the reader."

person of Jesus is hidden from the characters within the story world but is only revealed to the reader inevitably produces a dualistic story phenomenon and conflict between the characters which are the fundamental elements of irony. This book examines how the Matthean implied author moves the story of Jesus on the course of ironic path and how he molds his story with a view toward communicating the ironic significance of Jesus' death.

The Matthean Passion Narrative (26:1–27:66), beginning with the story of the anointing of Jesus by a woman in Bethany, is the Gospel's most pregnant unit of irony. The theological message of Matthew, in which a rejected, crucified Messiah saves his people from their sins (1:21), is ironic by its nature since so few who witness the divine act of salvation realize what is actually happening. Likewise, David Rhoads and Donald Michie convey that irony is rooted in the theme of the death of Jesus by recapitulating the idea that God saves and rules in ways that people do not expect.[3] Under the same observation, both David B. Howell and Mark A. Powell suggest that the passion account displays the evangelist's frequent and intensified use of irony.[4] The ironic dimension of the Matthean passion narrative reaches its highest level of intensity in Jesus' death on the cross—the goal of the life and ministry of Jesus. Thereby, the Matthean passion narrative is the very seat of revelatory irony where the divinely-willed salvation is disclosed through means of irony and its reversal effect.[5]

Irony, known by intellects from different social classes, including the ancient dramatists, philosophers, and rhetoricians, is not an easy tool to employ without drawing proper limits. In addition to its old and complex history, contemporary understandings of irony not only abound but also often produce different results than the traditional rendering of irony. This diversity can yield great confusion as critics search out the meaning and ramifications of particular instances of irony. Nevertheless, observations of selected literary and biblical sources argue for a consistent tradition of what this book groups together as "conventional irony"—a combination of verbal, dramatic, and character ironies. Under this premise, this current work narrows the scope of its investigation

---

3. David M. Rhoads and Donald M. Michie, *Mark as Story: An Introduction to the Narrative of a Gospel* (Philadelphia: Fortress Press, 1982), 60. Further see R. Alan Culpepper, *Anatomy of the Fourth Gospel: A Study in Literary Design* (Philadelphia: Fortress Press, 1983), 169–75; Powell, *Narrative*, 31.

4. David B. Howell, *Matthew's Inclusive Story: A Study in the Narrative Rhetoric of the First Gospel* (Sheffield: Sheffield Academic, 1990), 150; Powell, *Narrative*, 49.

5. Garnett G. Sedgewick, *Of Irony: Especially in the Drama* (Toronto: University of Toronto Press, 1935), 59 suggests, based on Aristotle's theory of tragedy in *Poetica*, XI, that irony implies the principle of a reversal of fortune.

of irony so that it only attends to these three types of irony through which the author-ironist of the Matthean passion narrative presents the intended but covert meaning of Jesus' death.

The goal of this book is to show how the Matthean passion narrative's conventional irony functions as the effective rhetorical device through which the theological significance of Jesus' death is unveiled. To achieve this specific purpose, several preliminary subjects will be examined. These include irony as a means of persuasive communication, the implied author of the Matthean passion narrative as the divine ironist, and the previously unanswered need for an examination of the Matthean passion narrative's irony, a need as yet not met in the current biblical scholarship.

The message of the cross is not only the climax of Jesus' earthly ministry but also the goal of his life. The Matthean passion narrative's implied author delivers this core message of the Gospel by employing irony, one of the rhetorical figures, more commonly called figures of speech. The classic treatment which has been done on this topic is the work of the Roman rhetorician Quintilian (c. 35–100 CE), in his *Institutio oratoria* on which modern classifications and analyses are based. According to him, a figure of speech is a word or phrase that diverges from straightforward, literal expression.[6] It is crafted for emphasis, intelligibility or stylish delivery of meaning. Quintilian has divided figures of speech into two main categories: tropes (from the Greek verb, τροπόω, "make to turn") and schemes (from the Greek noun, τό σχῆμα, "form, shape, figure").[7] Tropes and schemes are collectively known as figures of speech "in which the actual intent is expressed in words which carry the opposite meaning."[8] The former operates through changing or modifying the general meaning of a term to provide ornament to meaning,[9] while the latter involves a deviation from the ordinary or regular pattern of words.[10] Based on Quintilian's theory, irony is uniquely not only a trope (*tropos*) but also a figure (*schema* or

---

6. Quintilian, *Institutio oratoria*, 9.1.2.

7. Ibid., 8.5.35, 9.1.1.

8. William Flint Thrall and Addison Hibbard, *A Handbook to Literature* (rev. C. H. Holman; New York: Odyssey, 1960), 248.

9. Quintilian, *Inst.*, 8.6.1, "A trope is a shift of a word or phrase from its meaning to another with a positive stroke . . . A trope, then, is language transferred from its original and principal meaning to another for the sake of decoration of speech" (*tropos est verbi vel sermonis a propria significatione in aliam cum virtute mutation . . . Est igtur tropos sermo a naturali et pricipali significatione tralatus ad aliam ornandae orationis gratia*). Translation is mine.

10. Ibid., 9.1.4, "A figure, as its very name reveals, is a configuration of a certain speech distinct from the common and immediately principal form" (*'figura,' sicut nomine ipso patet, conformation quaedam orationis remota a communi et primum se offerente ratione*). Translation is mine.

figura).[11] It belongs to the category of tropes because it uses words in a way that conveys a meaning opposite to their ordinary and expected significance.[12] It is a scheme as well because irony represents the complexity of the whole passage and concerns the total shape of the theme.[13]

Irony as a part of classical Western rhetoric is fundamentally the art of persuasion.[14] Aristotle (384–322 BCE), the epitome figure for the development of rhetoric, explains in his book, *Ars rhetorica*,[15] that rhetoric as the art of persuasion concerns itself with "proofs" (αἱ πίστεις) for persuasion.[16] Wayne C. Booth, a prominent student of irony in modern times, extensively expresses a special interest in the rhetorical use of irony in literature. Though he acknowledges irony as an elusive subject to define, he values most the rhetorical function of irony. Booth considers irony as a means of communication and expresses that the prime function of irony is uniting or dividing authors and readers.[17]

Furthermore, irony has been frequently used to characterize the relationship between the infinite and the finite. Irony serves a staple ingredient in ancient stories of divine dealings with human beings. Religious man appreciates the idea of a being(s) superior to himself. Mercea Eliade, following Rudolf Otto, terms the divine or the sacred as *the Holy* or *the Wholly Other* (*ganz andere*) who breaks into human experience through hierophany.[18] *Homo Religiosus* takes this revelation as the object of its religious inquiry, a task which encompasses both the religious appreciation of *the sacred* and subjection to it. Man's encounter with *the Holy* inevitably discloses the different realities of God and man or the two discrete worlds to which each respectively belongs. The relationship of these two worlds of God and man is not necessarily one of hostility but destined to be one of a hierarchical order in which man's world

11. Ibid., 9.1.7.

12. David Holdcroft, "Irony as a Trope and Irony as Discourse," *Poetics Today* 4 (1983): 493–511 treats irony as a trope based on J. L. Austin's theory of speech acts.

13. Quintilian, *Inst.*, 9.2.46.

14. Kenneth Burke, *Language as Symbolic Action* (University of California Press, 1968), 28, suggests that rhetoric induces cooperation by persuasion and discussion.

15. Aristotle's the "Art of Rhetoric" (Ἡ Τέχνη Ῥητορική), in Latin *Ars rhetorica*, is the fifth century (BCE) treatise on the art of persuasion.

16. Aristotle, *Rhet.*, I.ii.2, "Rhetoric is the power of discovering all the persuasive elements in a speech" (ἔστω δὴ ῥητορικὴ δύναμις περὶ ἕκαστον τοῦ θεωρῆσαι τὸ ἐνδεχόμενον πιθανόν). Translation is mine.

17. Booth, *Rhetoric*, ix, 204–05, 217.

18. Rudolf Otto, *The Idea of the Holy: An Inquiry into the Non-Traditional Factor in the Idea of the Divine and its Relation to the Rational*, trans. John W. Harvey (New York: Oxford University Press, 1950), 25–30; Mercea Eliade, *The Sacred and the Profane: The Nature of Religion* (New York: Harcourt, Brace, 1959), 11.

and its perspective should be subject to the divine world and its governing perspective. Ancient literature testifies to divine dealings with humanity and attests that the economy of divine justice often points to a discrepancy between the ways in which the gods and human beings perceive reality.[19] In a similar way, the Scriptures identify essentially different operational principles of the two entities, God and man, and thus the ironic dynamics produced by their interactions. For example, the author of the Gospel of John employs an adverb, ἄνωθεν (from above) to express the distance between the divine value and the human value. The author explains that all the misconceptions and the oppositions against the protagonist Jesus, the sole carrier of the divine reality, are due to the fundamental difference of the origin between Jesus, whose reality is from "above," and humanity, whose being is anchored "below." The uniquely Johannine phrase, "You must be born from above" (δεῖ ὑμᾶς γεννηθῆναι ἄνωθεν, John 3:7) corresponds to the idea that the believer is none other than the one who adopts the divine perspective revealed through Jesus so that he may "see the kingdom of God" (ἰδεῖν τὴν βασιλείαν τοῦ θεοῦ, John 3:3b).

In ancient narratives including religious texts such as biblical writings, irony is predominantly a tool for communicating the divine, or the higher power, beyond human reach.[20] In this sense, irony is a revelatory language.[21] Glenn S. Holland defines such a revelatory function of irony as a religious use of irony and expresses it as follows.

> The language that scholars use to describe the ironic perspective is filled with terminology that applies equally well to the divine perspective: it is detached, it is superior, it sees things from above, it reveals the true meaning of things, it sees the present in the light of knowledge about the future.[22]

---

19. For example, the *Epic of Gilgamesh,* the Greek tragedies, and the prophetic literature among various religions can represent this type of literature.

20. For example, Aida Besançon Spencer, Gail R. O'Day, Jerry C. Hogatt, Glenn S. Holland, and Walter Brueggemann consider irony as a useful rhetorical tool used in Scripture. See Spencer, "The Wise Fool (and the Foolish Wise): A Study of Irony in Paul," *NovT* 23 (1981): 351; O'Day, "Narrative Mode and Theological Claim: A Study in the Fourth Gospel," *JBL* 105 (1986): 663; Hoggatt, *Irony in Mark's Gospel: Text and Subtext* (Cambridge/New York: Cambridge University Press, 1992), 57–89; Holland, *Divine Irony* (London: Associated University Presses, 2000), 15–16, 23–25; Brueggemann, *Solomon: Israel's Ironic Icon of Human Achievement* (Columbia: University of South Carolina Press, 2005), xii.

21. O'Day, *Revelation in the Fourth Gospel* (Philadelphia: Fortress Press, 1986), 31, notes irony as "a mode of revelatory language."

22. Holland, *Divine Irony,* 60.

Holland further employs the term "Augustan irony" to name a divine irony which brings about a disclosure of a hidden reality.[23] The ironist of "Augustan irony" accepts divine judgments and perspectives, which create irony, and exhibits godly control over them. Following this line of logic, if irony is a medium for an ironist to reveal the divine cause, this type of irony may be called a divine irony and the one who communicates such irony may be called a divine ironist like the implied author of the Gospel of Matthew.

The presence and activity of divine ironists can be observed within biblical material. James G. Williams notes that the prophets of Israel stand between God and his people as intercessors. He explains that God experiences the *pathos* of the contradiction between his people as they are and as he intends them to be.[24] His people, however, always fall short of the expectation of their calling and this is why God suffers such *pathos*. According to Williams, the prophets then adopt the same divine *pathos* in their message. Even though the prophets are privileged in the sense that they share the divine perspective, they also suffer with God because of the instability and deviation of their generation from the will of God. Williams concludes that the prophets use irony along with lament as the channels through which God communicates divine affection toward his people, and therefore the prophets are divine ironists.

Likewise, in the tradition of ancient philosophy, the watershed figure, Socrates, assumed a similar role as a divine ironist through his action in response to a Delphic oracle regarding his incomparable wisdom. According to Plato's *Apologia* (Apology of Socrates), the core of Socrates' defense at his Athenian trial is the service he has undertaken on behalf of the gods.[25] Socrates says to the jurors (*iudices*) that his friend, Chaerophon, had asked the oracle if there were anyone wiser than Socrates, and in return Chaerephon received an answer saying "no one is wiser." For Socrates, this Delphic oracle sets him on a path of divine service as he interprets the oracle's praise as signifying that Socrates is wiser than anybody because he knows that being free of pretension to wisdom is wisdom. His mission is comprised of freeing men from their pretense of wisdom[26] and exhorting them to care for its actual attainment through perfecting their souls and acquiring the most precious good: virtue (*virtus*).[27] In his performance of this divinely-inspired mission, Socrates was perceived by the

---

23. Ibid., 54.
24. James G. Williams, "Irony and Lament: Clues to Prophetic Consciousness," *Semeia* 8 (1977): 51–71.
25. Plato, *Apologia*, 20e–21a.
26. Ibid., 23b, e, 28e, 38a.
27. Ibid., 29e, 30a, 31b.

Athenians as speaking, questioning, and acting ironically, especially through his pretension of ignorance.

As we have seen through the cases of the prophets of Israel and Socrates, divine ironists are those who adopt the divine perspective and undertake its delivery to the public as their mission. In the same way, the Matthean passion narrative's implied author, who is defined by the reference of the narrative and its voice, takes on the identity of a divine ironist. His perspective on Jesus' death and its theological implication is coherent with the narrative's perspective on the centrality of the cross to the divine plan of salvation. The author-ironist of the Matthean passion narrative arranges the words, the events, and the characters of antagonism surrounding the death of Jesus to reveal how these seemingly tragic happenings eventually achieve God's salvific plan for his people (1:21) which is depicted as the foremost will of God in Matthew.

Prior to modern biblical scholars' critical engagement of irony in the canon, literary critics had developed a tremendous volume of works that illuminate the history, definition, form, and use of irony in ancient and modern literature.[28] Their thorough body of work ranges chronologically from ancient Greek dramas, including the Trilogists of tragedy,[29] via Socrates (470–399 BCE), to modern German Romantic irony and New Criticism. It also ranges geographically from Europe to North America. Although the large quantity and outstanding quality of this scholarship concerning irony serves as a strong basis for a critical reading of the Matthean passion narrative's irony, its excessively elaborate categorizations of irony, both in its definitions and classifications, make the interpretation of irony rather difficult. Discerning use of the materials at hand is therefore necessary.

In contrast to the exhaustive study of irony achieved by its general critics, the expositions of irony within biblical scholarship have been on a much smaller scale, although the fundamental hermeneutical shift occurring since the 1970s has brought with it growing interest in irony.[30] By the early 1970s, literary

---

28. Several founding scholars and their works in this area of study are Otto Ribbeck, "Über den Begriff des eirōn," *Rheinisches Museum* 31 (1876): 381–400; J. A. K. Thomson, *Irony: An Historical Introduction* (London: George Allen and Unwin, 1926); Sedgewick, *Of Irony*; David Worcester, *The Art of Satire* (Cambridge: Harvard University Press, 1940); Alan R. Thompson, *The Dry Mock: A Study of Irony in Drama* (Berkeley: University of California Press, 1948); Robert B. Sharpe, *Irony in the Drama: An Essay on Impersonation, Shock, and Catharsis* (Chapel Hill: University of North Carolina Press, 1959); Edwin M. Good, *Irony in the Old Testament* (Philadelphia: Westminster, 1965); Douglas Colin Muecke, *The Compass of Irony* (London: Methuen, 1969); Thirlwall, "On the Irony of Sophocles," 483–537; Booth, *Rhetoric*; Søren Kierkegaard, *The Concept of Irony with Continual Reference to Socrates* (ed. and trans. Howard V. Hong and Edna H. Hong; Princeton, NJ: Princeton University Press, 1989).

29. Aeschylus (525–456 BCE), Sophocles (495–406 BCE), and Euripides (480–406 BCE).

critics had begun a new era of studying the New Testament as "literature." Under this initiative, biblical scholars such as Norman R. Petersen, David Rhoads, Don Michie, R. Alan Culpepper, Jack D. Kingsbury and Robert C. Tannehill engaged in reading the Gospels with a literary-narrative approach.[31] Through the efforts of these biblical scholars, the Gospels began to be read as stories of Jesus, and the literary features of the Gospels such as plot, character, setting, perspective and other rhetorical techniques of the implied author, such as irony, came under consideration. However, no significant attention has been given to the use of irony as a rhetorical device within Matthew's narrative,[32] particularly the Matthean passion narrative, as an independent subject by any New Testament scholar in a fashion comparable with that of other parts of the canon.[33] At best, one can find rather scattered comments on the ironic utterances, situations, and characters related to parts of Matthew.[34] Partial

---

30. Hoggatt points out that since the 1970s irony has come to be considered a literary phenomenon worthy of exploration in its own right. See Hoggatt, *Irony in Mark's Gospel*, ix.

31. Norman R. Petersen, "Point of View in Mark's Narrative," *Semeia* 12 (1978): 97–121; Petersen, *Literary Criticism for New Testament Critics*. GBS (Philadelphia: Fortress Press, 1978); Rhoads and Michie, *Mark*; David M. Rhoads, "Narrative Criticism and the Gospel of Mark," *JAAR* 50 (1982): 411–34; Jack Dean Kingsbury, *The Christology of Mark's Gospel* (Philadelphia: Fortress Press, 1983); Culpepper, *Anatomy*; Kingsbury, *Matthew as Story* (Philadelphia: Fortress Press, 1988); Robert Tannehill, *The Narrative Unity of Luke—Acts: A Literary Interpretation*, 2 vols. (Philadelphia: Fortress Press, 1986, 1990).

32. In this regard, Dorothy Jean Weaver expresses that "I have not succeeded in locating any major studies, whether essays or monographs, which deal with Matthew's use of irony as a literary technique." See Weaver, "Power and Powerlessness: Matthew's Use of Irony in the Portrayal of Political Leaders," *SBL* 31 (1992): 454.

33. For example, Stanley Hopper, "Irony—the Pathos of the Middle," *Cross Currents* 12 (1962): 31–40; Good, *Irony in the Old Testament*; Jacob Jónsson, *Humor and Irony in the New Testament Illuminated by Parallels in Talmud and Midrash* (Reykjavik: Bókaútgáfa Menningarsjóts, 1965); M. Perry and M. Sternberg, "The King through Ironic Eyes: The Narrator's Devices in the Biblical Story of David and Bathsheba and Two Excurses on the Theory of the Narrative Text," *Hasifrut* 1 (1968): 263–92; M. H. Levine, "Irony and Morality in Bathsheba's Tragedy," *Journal of the Central Conference of American Rabbis* 22 (1975): 69–77; Williams, "Irony and Lament"; S. Bar-Efrat, *The Art of the Biblical Story* (Tel Aviv: Sifriat Hapoalim, 1979); Jerry H. Gill, "Jesus, Irony and the New Quest," *Enc* 41 (1980): 139–51; Adele Berlin, *Poetics and Interpretation of Biblical Narrative* (Sheffield: Almond, 1983); Paul D. Duke, *Irony in the Fourth Gospel* (Atlanta: John Knox, 1985); Robert Alter, *The Art of Biblical Narrative* (New York: Basic Books, 1981); Spencer, "The Wise Fool"; James M. Dawsey, *The Lukan Voice: Confusion and Irony in the Gospel of Luke* (Macon, Ga.: Mercer University Press, 1986); Hoggatt, *Irony in Mark's Gospel*; Brueggemann, *Solomon*.

34. David R. Catchpole, "The Answer of Jesus to Caiaphas (MATT. XXVI. 64)," *NTS* 17 (1970): 213–26; Birger Gerhardsson, "Confession and Denial before Men: Observations on Matt 26:57–27:2," *JSNT* 13 (1981): 46–66; Richard A. Edwards, *Matthew's Story of Jesus* (Philadelphia: Fortress Press, 1985);

exceptions to this state of affairs include contributions by Donald Senior, Mark A. Powell, Timothy B. Cargal, John P. Heil, Dorothy Jean Weaver, and Warren Carter. Senior points out that there is a special use of irony in the activity of Judas and the Jewish religious leaders in the Matthean passion narrative, which reveals the fact that they unwittingly assist in achieving the divine goal, namely the death of Jesus.[35] In his book, *What is Narrative Criticism?* Powell attests to irony as a rhetorical device employed by the Gospel writers which can be detected through a narrative-critical reading. In his analysis of the conflict in the Matthean passion narrative, he succinctly addresses the "great irony of Matthew's Gospel" that Jesus must "lose" his conflicts with the religious leaders and with his own disciples to win the greater conflict with Satan.[36] The works of Cargal and Heil, though rather fragmentarily, both deal with a common theme: the innocent blood of Jesus and its salvific function which is ironically exposed through one of the most troubling statements in the New Testament[37] and the darkest, hardest verse in Matthew's Gospel, 27:25.[38] Both Cargal and Heil consider that this troubling verse challenges the reader to reevaluate the traditional views regarding the intent of Matthew in reporting the cry of the people since the Matthean portrayal of the people's rejection of Jesus is subtler in its intended meaning than it seems on surface.[39] Neither of them, however, describes how this verse works ironically within the Gospel of Matthew which narratologically culminates in the Matthean passion narrative.

Focusing on the characters who are opposite and their characterizations in the Gospel of Matthew, Weaver provides much fuller exposition on irony surrounding the character dynamics in the story world of Matthew. She examines the use of irony in the characterization of the Gospel's political figures—Herod the king (2:1-23), Herod the tetrarch (14:1-12), and Pilate the governor (ch. 27)—and paints the virtual powerlessness of political leaders vis-à-vis the genuine powerfulness of Jesus, the protagonist.[40] From the point of view

David Hill, "Matthew 27:51–53 in the Theology of the Evangelist," *IBS* 7 (1985): 76–87; Timothy B. Cargal, " 'His Blood Be upon Us and upon Our Children': A Matthean Double Entendre?" *NTS* 37 (1991): 101–12; Weaver, "Power and Powerlessness"; Kirk Kilpatrick, *Beautiful Irony, Matthew 21:1–14* (Germantown, Tenn.: Mid-America Baptist Theological Seminary, 1996).

35. Donald Senior, *The Passion of Jesus in the Gospel of Matthew* (Wilmington: Michael Glazier, 1985), 104–6.

36. Powell, *Narrative*, 48.

37. Cargal, "His Blood," 101.

38. Robert H. Smith, "Matthew 27:25: The Hardest Verse in Mathew's Gospel," *CurTM* 17 (1990): 421.

39. Cargal, "His Blood," 111; John P. Heil, "The Blood of Jesus in Matthew: A Narrative-Critical Perspective," *PRSt* 18 (1991): 117–18.

of postcolonial criticism, Carter argues in his book, *Matthew and Empire*, that the Gospel protests Roman imperialism by asserting that God's purposes and will are performed not by the empire and emperor but by Jesus and his community of disciples. Carter establishes Matthew's imperial context by examining Roman imperial ideology through materials present in Antioch, the place from which he believes Matthew was written. Carter pays particular attention to what he perceives to be the Gospel's central irony, namely that in depicting God's ways and purposes, the Gospel employs the very imperial framework that it resists.[41]

Just as literary-critical works concerning the irony of Matthew as a whole are scarce, literary-critical investigations of the Matthean passion narrative's irony as the author's rhetorical device fortifying the meaning of the death of Jesus are likewise scanty. However, despite this relative insufficiency of critical work concerning the irony of Matthew and the Matthean passion narrative, the narrative-critical reading of the First Gospel with emphases on the story's coherency and informing nature points to the potential existence of irony woven therein. In addition to this, the extensive sources for the study of irony provided by both the literary critics in general and the above-mentioned biblical scholars specifically provide helpful examples as we look into the way that irony contributes to the Matthean passion narrative's unique portrait of the death of Jesus and its significance.

Methodology

To examine the theological implications for the meaning of Jesus' death conveyed from the ironic point of view of the Gospel's author-ironist, we adopt the critical tools for the reading of the Matthean passion narrative's conventional irony and its portrayal of the Christ-event: narrative criticism and Wayne C. Booth's "stable irony."

Adopted Principles from Narrative Criticism

To observe the literary-rhetorical use of conventional irony within the Matthean passion narrative, employing some of the principles espoused by narrative criticism is necessary. Several basic assumptions established by narrative criticism are drawn upon such as the presence of the implied author and the implied reader, the organic whole of the narrative under a particular

---

40. Weaver, "Power and Powerlessness," 466.

41. Warren Carter, *Matthew and Empire: Initial Explorations* (Harrisburg: Trinity Press International, 2001), 51, 171.

governing norm of the text and the rhetorical-persuasive function of the narrative.

Narrative criticism allows for the reading of the Matthean passion narrative's irony as intended by its implied author. The implied author is not identical with the real author of the text. The implied reader is a reconstruction of the reader informed and guided by the text itself.[42] In this light all narratives have an implied author, even if the historical author is unknown. The implied author is the important component of the story on several grounds. It is the implied author who invests the story with coherence in its shape which is necessary for a coherent meaning of the book.[43] In other words, a story is not a coincidental happening but an outcome of the author's intentional lay-out. Seymour Chatman explains it that the narrative blocks of a story are arranged by the implied author, creating "a logic of connection and hierarchy."[44] The voice of the implied author, also known as the narrator's voice,[45] represents the perspective or the evaluating point of view from which the story is told.[46] The reader perceives the existence of the implied author and his ideas and values through the narrator's distinctive voice. In Matthew as a whole, the narrator is virtually identical with the implied author whose detached voice in third-person narration characterizes and speaks on behalf of the implied author.[47] The Matthean implied author is reliable[48] since not only does he promote the

---

42. Booth, *The Rhetoric of Fiction* (Chicago: University of Chicago Press, 1961), 66–77; Chatman, *Story and Discourse*, 147–51; Powell, "Toward a Narrative-Critical Understanding of Matthew," *Int* 46 (1992): 342–43.

43. I used the term, the "shape of the story," as identical with the plot of the story. Frank Kermode, *The Sense of an Ending: Studies in the Theory of Fiction* (Oxford: Oxford University Press, 1967), 45 notes that plot is "an organization that humanizes time by giving it form."

44. Chatman, *Story and Discourse*, 52–53.

45. J. D. Kingsbury, T. B. Cargal and Janice C. Anderson observe the close relationships that are virtually indistinguishable between the implied author and the narrator and the implied reader and the narratee. See Kingsbury, "Reflections," 455; Cargal, "His blood," 103; Janice C. Anderson, *Matthew's Narrative Web: Over, and Over, and Over Again* (JSNTSup 91; Sheffield: JSOT, 1994), 48.

46. Powell, *Narrative*, 24 explains the evaluating point of view as "the norms, values, and general worldview that the implied author establishes as operative for the story, by which readers are led to evaluate the events, characters, and setting that comprise the story." The implied reader is requested to adopt authorial perspective to make sense of the text. Also, Boris Uspensky, *A Poetics of Composition: The Structure of the Artistic Text and Typology of a Compositional Form* (trans. V. Zavarin and S. Wittig; Berkeley: University of California Press, 1973), 56 suggests that all other points of view of the narrative must be subordinate to the point of view of the implied author.

47. Cargal, "His blood," 103 opines that in the case of Matthew, as with most ancient literature, there is no need to distinguish between the implied author and the narrator or the implied reader and the narratee since neither narrator nor narratee emerge as characters within the story. Likewise, Anderson,

normative viewpoint of Jesus, the protagonist of the narrative,[49] but his point of view of telling the story is consistent with Jesus' teachings and corresponding actions. In Matthew we hear the narrator telling the story of Jesus' death in an ironic mode and therefore its implied author is best characterized as the divine ironist whose point of view represents the divine *pathos* dealing with his people through the death of Jesus. Since irony requires the discrepancy between a higher or true point of view and a lower or false one, recognition of the implied author's over-arching perspective is a crucial element in identifying the irony in the Matthean passion narrative.

The Matthean passion narrative's implied author, namely, the divine ironist, functions as an undramatized and omniscient-omnipresent narrator.[50] Most distinctively, he has the ability to read the minds of the characters, even Jesus.[51] He knows what Jesus knows and what he is feeling.[52] Virtually no distance exists between the implied author and Jesus the protagonist whose story the narrator, the voice of the implied author of Matthew, narrates. These listed traits of the Matthean passion narrative's implied author are deduced from an analysis of the voice narrating the passion story of Jesus as an observant reporter in an all-seeing, knowledgeable and linguistically proficient manner.[53]

Matthew's Narrative Web, 28–29 says that the undramatized reliable narrator of Matthew is indistinguishable from its implied author.

48. Regarding the reliable narrator of Matthew, see Kingsbury, "The Figure of Jesus in Matthew's Story: A Rejoinder to David Hill," *JSNT* 25 (1985): 65 and Anderson, *Matthew's Narrative Web*, 55. Not every narrator projected in the Gospels has been considered reliable. Dawsey, *The Lukan Voice*, 41, 152 has suggested that Luke does employ a narrator who proves unreliable. However, Tannehill, *Narrative Unity of Luke—Acts*, 7 has discounted this position. Likewise Tannehill, Powell, *Narrative*, 54 regards the narrators of the Gospels as reliable and their evaluative points of view are always true. It is reasonable to see that biblical narratives do not employ an unreliable narrator which is assumed due to the significance and directness of the Gospel message itself unlike modern literature which sometimes employs the device of an unreliable narrator, whose views the reader is expected to question.

49. The Gospel traditions depict Jesus a reliable and normative character, representing the point of view of God, which is a powerful and normative rhetorical device in itself. Jesus' reliability as a character in the Gospel of Matthew was evidenced from the beginning through his genealogy, birth story, baptism, fulfillment quotations, and valid witnesses about him from other characters within the story, the narrator, God, and even Satan.

50. Anderson, *Matthew's Narrative Web*, 70 regards the Matthean implied author as frequently privileged to have inside views of characters, even what Jesus knows and feels. His omniscience and correctness of perception are proved by Jesus.

51. Matt. 9:3, 21; 16:7; 21:25; 26:4, 8, 10, 16, 22, 37, 43, 59-60, 75; 27:1, 3, 14, 18.

52. Matt. 12:15b, 25; 16:8; 22:18; 26:10.

53. Matt. 26:3, 6, 17, 20, 25, 30, 36, 47-51, 57-58, 63-74; 27:1-2, 5-8, 15, 19-20, 33, 46.

As is the case for the implied author, the implied reader is a construct of the text itself.[54] He is the reader whom the implied author had in mind and "in whom the intention of the text to be thought of as always reaching its fulfillment."[55] In narrative-critical terms, the text calls for any real human of any era to become its implied reader, to be formed and guided by the text through the communication process, and be summoned to experience its purposes which reach fulfillment. The importance of the implied reader should not be minimized because, in a nutshell, the goal of narrative criticism is to read the text as the implied reader.[56] Even though the actual responses of real readers are unpredictable, there may be clues within the narrative that indicate an anticipated response from the implied reader.[57] Taking this into account, the formation of an interpretive community between the implied author and the implied reader is inevitable.[58] Most likely this interpretive enterprise generated between these two parties in the story world depends on rhetorical devices, such as irony, at the disposal of the implied author.[59]

When we consider the implied author of the Matthean passion narrative as the divine ironist, employing irony as the means of communication, it is reasonable to consider that his intended counterpart must be a reader who is competent in understanding irony. Therefore, the ideal implied reader of the Matthean passion narrative's irony is one who carefully follows the narrative's plot and the rhetorical patterns of the text,[60] picking up on the clues that the

---

54. Chatman, *Story and Discourse*, 149 notes that "the implied reader is distinct from any real, historical reader in the same way that the implied author is distinct from the real, historical author."

55. Kingsbury, *Matthew as Story*, 38.

56. Powell, *Narrative*, 20. Also, see Powell, "Expected and Unexpected Readings in Matthew: What the Reader Knows," *AsTJ* 48 (1993): 32.

57. Chatman, *Story and Discourse*, 150.

58. Powell, *Narrative*, 28; Richard A. Edwards, "Reading Matthew," *List* 24 (1989): 251–61; Howell, *Matthew's Inclusive Story*, 110–30; Bernard Brandon Scott, "The Birth of the Reader," *Semeia* 52 (1990): 83–102; Powell, "Toward a Narrative," 343 all consider that the implied author must pay attention to the manner in which the implied reader is expected to be educated in the process of reading the narrative to accomplish the goal of the text.

59. Chatman, *Story and Discourse*, 229 refers this communicative interaction between the implied author and his partner, the implied reader, as "implicit flattery," and Duke, *Irony in the Fourth Gospel*, 38–39 notes that "irony rewards its followers with a sense of community." Even though Warren Carter, *Matthew: Storyteller, Interpreter, Evangelist* (Peabody: Hendrickson, 1996), 278–79, expresses his concern for the essentially unrealistic and impossible task to grasp all the complex interrelationships that may occur within a text, it cannot be disregarded that the text provides for the concrete contours of their interactions.

60. H. J. Bernard Combrink, "The Structure of the Gospel of Matthew as Narrative," *TynBul* 34 (1983): 61–90 and Frank J. Matera, "The Plot of Matthew's Gospel," *CBQ* 49 (1987): 233–53 explain that

implied author left for his interpretive partner.[61] He is summoned to be attentive to the character dynamics and the differences in values which each distinctive group of characters upholds. He makes a value judgment on the characters not based on his personal beliefs, but based on the divine point of view, which the implied author suggests as the ultimate norm of the story. It is a task of utmost importance for the implied reader to adopt the governing perspective of the narrative primarily because the implied authors of biblical narratives have made God's evaluative point of view normative for their works.[62] Although the implied reader has the freedom and ability to "draw near" or "distance" himself from any given character(s), he is best described as one privileged and guided by the text for a specific achievement: understanding of the story. In short, the notion of both the implied author and reader espoused by narrative criticism is critically text-centered.

Moving on to the principle concerning coherence of the narrative as a whole, it is necessary to pay attention to the preeminence of the text as an entity full of essential information for the meaningful interpretation of the Matthean passion narrative's irony. The boundary where the interpretive interaction between the implied author and reader occurs is none other than the finished form of the entire text.[63] Livia Polanyi,[64] Louis Mink,[65] and Robert Culley[66] all have pointed out that the narrative must be self-contained, coherent, and

---

narrative criticism is interested in how the story that Matthew tells unfolds for the reader. These scholars consider that paying attention to the plot of the story is equal to looking for the rhetorical patterns of the text which give rise to the story's continuity, i.e. the continuity existing between the episodes.

61. Powell, *Narrative*, 32 puts this as the implied reader's experience of "like-mindedness" with the implied author.

62. Kingsbury, "The Figure of Jesus," 4–7. Based on the notion that the implied author is the defender of the divine perspective, it can be said that the implied author is the foremost believer and the prime example for the reader. In the same vein, Powell, *Narrative*, 88–89 considers that that narrative criticism stands in a close relationship with the believing community since it treats the text in a manner that is consistent with a Christian understanding of the canon and seeks to interpret a given text at its canonical level. He goes further saying that narrative criticism emphasizes that a Christian doctrine of spiritual revelation is considered to be an event that happens now, through an interaction of the reader with the text and through the active role of the Holy Spirit. Also, Powell, *Narrative*, 24–25 points out that the Gospels allow for another way of thinking: a second perspective opposing God's perspective and representing the point of view of Satan. In the Gospel tradition Satan's point of view is always incorrect though he sometimes correctly identifies Jesus as the Son of God.

63. Carter, *Matthew*, 276–77 describes the interactions occurring between the implied author and the implied reader as a game and asserts that it must be enjoyed within the boundary and rule of the text.

64. Livia Polanyi, "What Stories Can Tell Us about Their Teller's World," *Poetics Today* 2.2 (1981): 97–112.

65. Louis Mink, "History and Fiction as Modes of Comprehension," *NLH* 1 (1970): 541–48.

have a single unifying point, which Culley calls the story's "core cliché." Therefore, narrative criticism enables us to see the text of the Gospel of Mathew as thematically coherent document, and at the same time it demands that the reader pursue a coherent and consistent interpretation by relying on the interrelations of the textual elements. The implied reader of the text is supposed to know or believe everything that the Gospel expects him to know or believe.[67] Conversely, he does not know or believe anything that the Gospel does not expect him to know or believe because necessary knowledge and the content of belief are revealed, assumed or implied within the narrative. According to narrative criticism, the text is a unit for meaning. Narrative criticism not only treats the text as an end in itself but also establishes the authority of the text by giving a hermeneutical preference to the word (i.e. voice) of the implied author over its real author since the implied author's point of view through which the story is narrated can be determined without considering anything extrinsic to the narrative. The text presumes authority in the sense that the narrative speaks for itself and that the interpretive key lies within the text itself. In this regard, the narrative "context" is important because all interpretative activities are supposed to occur within the given information of the narrative. Accordingly, the Matthean passion narrative's irony must be read in the whole framework of the Gospel of Matthew as well as in its particular context.[68] As result, a narrative sensitive and close reading of Matthew as an organic whole will show the ironically-ridden Matthean passion narrative positioned at its theological height.

In summary, narrative criticism offers an impetus for fresh interpretation of the biblical story of Jesus because it allows the story to speak to any real reader in ways that enable the reader to become the implied reader. Further, with its emphases on the finished form of the Gospel and its poetic and rhetorical functions of the text, narrative criticism provides the reader an eye to appreciate the implied author's literary-rhetorical devices, such as irony, for the purpose of engaging in persuasive communication.[69] The rhetorical function of irony in challenging the surface meaning of things and thus highlighting the deeper

---

66. Robert Culley, *Studies in the Structure of Hebrew Narrative* (Philadelphia: Fortress Press, 1976), 13–20.

67. Powell, "Expected and Unexpected Readings of Matthew," 32–48.

68. Booth, "Irony and 'Ironic' Poetry," *College English* 9 (1948): 232–33, 237, highlights the importance of the context for the interpretation of irony.

69. Applying it to the Gospel of Matthew, Powell, "Toward a Narrative," 341 points out that "narrative criticism views Matthew's Gospel as a form of communication that cannot be understood without being received and experienced."

level of meaning of the text by appealing to the sensibility of the text corresponds well to the general outlook of narrative criticism. Therefore, attention to irony is indispensable for narrative criticism.

WAYNE C. BOOTH'S "STABLE IRONY"

Wayne C. Booth makes an enduring impact on the history of the study of irony. In particular, Booth's "stable irony" shares many points of contact with the examined principles of narrative criticism, and both together create the ground on which a narrative-critical reading of the Matthean passion narrative's irony can take place. Prior to Booth, Douglas Colin Muecke began pioneering work by classifying irony under several categories.[70] Booth adopted some of his classifications, but also added another important distinction: "stable and unstable irony."[71] Booth identifies "stable irony" as "tamed irony" or a "less savage beast" and "unstable irony" as "untamed irony."[72] A later scholar, Paul D. Duke, explains the essence of "untamed irony," namely, the assumption that irony is everywhere, saying

> Scholars and critics who quest after ironies in a text are prone, once they have caught the thrill of the hunt, to become downright intoxicated, not only bagging their limit so to speak, but opening fire on everything in the text that moves.[73]

Both Booth's self-explanatory phrase "untamed irony" and Duke's description of it indicate that the concept of "untamed irony" exists as a kind of irony that is not rooted so much in explicit textual features as it is in the critic who is "untamed" in his freedom to interact with the text guided chiefly by his own experiences. Contrastingly, Booth's "stable irony" contributes to the study of irony since the theory focuses on a specific type of irony and rejects broad and meaningless extensions of the world "irony" to cover nearly any complex and ambiguous literary statement. Booth's "stable irony" emphasizes that the ironist establishes the relationship to his audience-reader who is highly associative and

70. Muecke, *Compass*, 40–215 provides several classifications of irony such as three grades of irony (overt, covert, private irony), four modes of irony (impersonal, self-disparaging, ingénue, dramatized irony), ironies pertaining to situation (irony of simple incongruity, irony of events, dramatic irony, irony of self-betrayal, irony of dilemma), general irony including cosmic irony, and romantic irony.

71. Booth, *Rhetoric*, 1–27, 233–67.

72. Booth, "The Pleasures and Pitfalls of Irony: or, Why Don't You Say What You Mean?" in *Rhetoric, Philosophy, and Literature: An Exploration*, ed. Don M. Burks (West Lafayette, IN: Purdue University Press, 1978), 5.

73. Duke, *Irony in the Fourth Gospel*, 2.

willing to engage. According to Booth, stable irony occurs when the ironist, whether implicitly or explicitly, provides the reader-audience a firm ground for discerning irony and thus subverting the surface meaning. Unstable irony, on the other hand, offers no fixed standpoint for meaningful reading.

Classical stable irony, the principles of which this study adopts, exhibits four characteristics: (i) it is intended (by the implied author-ironist), (ii) it is covert (having been embedded in the narrative), (iii) it is stable or fixed (not susceptible to further creativity of the reader), and (iv) it is finite in application (having unequivocal meaning). Booth calls these traits "the marks of stable irony."[74] Stable irony is by no means accidental or unconscious but rather deliberately created by the author to be read and understood. It is also hidden in the deep tissue of the text because the implied author seems to intend it "to be reconstructed with meanings different from those on the surface."[75] Further, stable irony is characterized by both its finitude and stability. Stable irony is fixed in the sense that the reader is not allowed to undermine a reconstruction of meaning that has once been made with additional "demolitions and reconstructions."[76] Also, it is finite in application because the reconstructed meanings are bound to a specific context that is textual, immediate and local. Conversely, "unstable irony," which is unintended, overt, and unlimited in its exposition, literally falls to the free disposal of the reader who is limited only by his own reference and imagination.

Booth underlines the inevitable link between the author and stable irony, a so-called intentionality of irony.[77] Such intentionality of irony lies close to the core agenda of the narrative.[78] In other words, it is embedded in the narrative and invites the reader to undertake some interpretative exercise. While Booth calls the reader's interaction with the text a "delightful leap of intuition,"[79] the "intellectual dance"[80] and a "secret communication,"[81] Weaver refers to it as an "act of mental gymnastics."[82] Regardless of the multiple sub-categories of stable and unstable ironies,[83] Booth strongly believes that irony must be

74. Booth, *Rhetoric*, 3–8.
75. Ibid., 6.
76. Ibid.
77. Booth, "The Pleasures and Pitfalls of Irony,"10.
78. Hoggatt, *Irony in Mark's Gospel*, ix says, "irony lies close to the narrative's score."
79. Booth, *Rhetoric*, 12.
80. Booth, "The Empire of Irony," *GR* 37 (1983): 729.
81. Booth, *Rhetoric*, 12.
82. Weaver, "Power and Powerlessness," 454.
83. Booth, *Rhetoric*, 233–77. On the one hand the sub-categories of "stable irony" include stable-covert-local (or definite), stable-overt, and stable-covert-infinite and on the other hand the sub-

discovered by the reader.[84] This notion embraces the possibility that some readers will go astray including the possibility of misinterpretation on the reader's part.[85] Despite the importance of the reader as an interpreter of irony, Booth firmly rejects the practice of "uncritical minds" who call "anything under the sun ironic" when "ironic" means simply "odd" or "interesting."[86] For him, "stable irony" salvages irony from the chaotic manipulations of the free thinker who takes unreserved delight in pursuing the "wild beast," namely an aforementioned "untamed irony." Conclusively, Booth's view of stable irony bespeaks a kind of mutually dependent communication on the part of the implied author requiring the ironically-capable implied reader.

Although irony is an art of "indirection" and "disguise" which distinguishes itself from a direct statement, stable irony represents a definite meaning in that it primarily concerns not the interpretative ingenuity of the reader but authorial intention.[87] For that reason, the recognition of a localized meaning of irony, indebted to the intention of the ironist, is equal to the art of stopping at the right spot rather than of knowing when to start.[88] At this juncture, some may raise the question of how authorial intention is detected. Glenn S. Holland answers this based on two criteria: external and internal.[89] If the "collective experience" of the reader regarding the author's credibility as an ironist serves

---

categories of "unstable irony" consist of unstable-overt-local, unstable-covert-local, unstable-overt-infinite, and unstable-covert-infinite. Booth further distinguishes some shades of "stable irony" so that stable irony can vary in its degree of secretiveness based on the ad hoc purpose of the ironist. For example, when Cicero, *In Catalinam* I.8.19, speaks of his opponent Catiline as "*virum optimum*" (a noble man), both Cicero and his audience-reader understand that the word expressed, "*optimum*" (noble), must mean "*pessimum*" (wicked). For certain, Cicero's remark about the rebel of the state (*patricidia*), Catiline, uses "stable irony." It is intended by the author and is finite in its exposition, yet it is also clearly overt. These multiplications within each genus warn us that not only the definition of irony but also the categorization of irony requires a literary sensitivity, a keen-intellect, and an open mind on account of its difficult nature.

84. Booth, *Rhetoric*, 5–6.

85. Booth, "The Pleasures and Pitfalls of Irony," 5. Also Gregory Vlastos, "Socratic Irony," *CQ* 37 (1987): 79, points that "when irony riddles it risks being misunderstood," and Brenda Austin-Smith, "Into the Heart of Irony," *Canadian Dimension* 27 (1990): 51 notes the possibility mostly embraced by the modern that "irony as product undermines irony as process."

86. Booth, "The Empire of Irony," 721.

87. Maurice Natanson, "The Arts of Indirection" in *Rhetoric, Philosophy and Literature* (ed. Don M. Burks; West Lafayette: Purdue University Press, 1978), 39–40 identifies irony as an "art of indirection" andClaudette Kemper, "Irony Anew, with Occasional Reference to Byron and Browning," *SEL, 1500–1900*, 7 (1967): 705 as "disguise."

88. Booth, "The Pleasures and Pitfalls of Irony," 10.

89. Holland, *Divine Irony*, 39–42.

as an example for an external criterion, the text itself is the prime, internal indication of the author's ironic intention. Holland asserts that the perception of irony by an alert, competent reader is only inspired by the text through its rhetorical persuasion.

Booth suggests four steps for interpretation of irony.[90] As the first step, the reader must reject the literal meaning when he recognizes some incongruity, signaling an unspoken proposition, in statements or events. Booth considers this first step as essential to irony. Next, the reader should try out alternative interpretations or explanations which will in some degree be incongruent with what the surface statement seems to say. Then, the reader moves onto the third step: making decisions about knowledge or beliefs of the implied author, which are found in the work itself, because it is most unlikely that the author could arrange ironic sayings or events in a specific fashion without having intended them as such. When the reader has gone through these three steps in order, though Booth sees that these steps are often virtually simultaneous,[91] the reader can finally try a new meaning that is in synchronization with that which the reader knows or can infer about the implied author's beliefs and intentions.

In summary, the theological exposition of the Matthean passion narrative's conventional irony relies on the principles provided by both narrative criticism and Booth's stable irony. Taken as a whole, the adopted principles of narrative criticism share the core characteristics of stable irony. First, narrative criticism focuses on the internal communication or a bonding process between the implied author (the ironist) and the implied reader (the ironically-capable reader).[92] Second, narrative criticism focuses on the text as a meaningful whole and also on irony as the rhetorical vehicle for an intended implication by the implied author.[93] Just as Booth considers that authorial intention establishes an evaluative point of view essential to the proper perception of irony, a narrative-critical reading prioritizes the textual features in a given narrative which reveal the regulating norm of the implied author, the ironist. Thereby both narrative criticism and Booth's stable irony perceive irony as a stable literary device. Lastly, guided by these premises, the implied reader of the

---

90. Booth, *Rhetoric*, 10–14.

91. Ibid., 12.

92. Booth, "The Empire of Irony," 729 acknowledges that the "intellectual dance" which the reader of irony performs to understand it, brings him into a tight bonding with the ironist by stimulating him to take part in his mental processes. In the same vein, Joseph A. Dane, "The Defense of the Incompetent Reader," *Comparative Literature* 38 (1986): 62 says that Booth's stable irony is "less a fact of a text than a process that occurs between the text and a reader."

93. Powell, *Narrative*, 31 opines that "attention to irony is essential to narrative criticism."

Matthean passion narrative's irony not only yields himself to the authority of the text, but also considers information provided by the text sufficient for meaningful interpretation. Therefore, in the course of reading, when the implied reader encounters a point on which the text is silent, he does not attempt to fill the gap inventively beyond what the narrative supplies him. Both narrative criticism and Booth's stable irony point to priority of the text and its referentiality rather than the reader and his poetical creativity in establishing the referential meaning of the narrative. As far as the reading of the Matthean passion narrative's conventional irony is concerned, it is the reading of the ironically-capable implied reader, whose reading of irony will follow a pattern shaped and governed by the rhetorical rubric of the narrative.

Chapter Layouts

Building upon chapter 1, which introduced the subject matter and the purpose of the study, chapter 2 will present a general overview of irony in two *foci*: one, the history of irony with a suggestion of a working definition of irony, and two, the formal requirements of irony. The first part of chapter 2 will only provide summary of the history of irony since this study is not intended to exhaust the history of irony but only to provide the essentials needed to equip the reader with a basic understanding of irony which is indispensable for a successful reading of the present work. The section about the history of irony will show the argument made by each main critic of irony in antiquity as well as a certain connection between these primary critics' observations on irony. Following after the review of the concept of irony among the early authors, the transitional stage of irony in the Middle Ages and the Renaissance will be described. The use of irony in these eras denotes the fundamental discrepancy regarding the understanding of irony between the ancient and the modern mind. While the ancient mind's concept of irony arises from that which is centered in the belief of the divine, the infinite, and the holy, the modern mind's concept of irony is rooted in human perception of the humane, the finite, and the cynical mistrust of institutions and common truths. Concluding the section on the history of irony, the discussion of irony in the modern times will attend to its noticeable growth and diverse ramifications due to the change within Western European philosophical trends and the critics' autonomy in dealing with the subject.

The second part of chapter 2 will review the formal elements of irony. In some sense, it seems that defining irony precisely is an impossible task. On the other hand, identifying what generally constitutes irony is realistic and identifying the formal requirements of irony can provide interpretative guideposts for the reader of a narrative which operates through irony.

In chapter 3, the form and use of conventional ironies will be reviewed. In this part of the discussion, the definition of verbal, dramatic, and character irony will be explored and select examples pertaining to each category within ancient literature as well as within the biblical narratives will be given. Chosen examples of conventional irony from non-biblical source are ancient dramas such as *Nubes* by Aristophanes (c. 446–388 BCE), *Oedipus Rex* by Sophocles (495–406 BCE), *Bacchae* by Euripides (c. 480–406 BCE), and *Metamorphoses* by Apuleius (c. 123–180 CE). Furthermore, the tradition around Socrates is also included because he is regarded as the founder of "irony" (εἰρωνεία, *eirōneia*). The rationale for examining these ancient sources is that they illustrate the classical examples and rhetorical models of conventional irony within literature and therefore, they are useful to strengthen the reader's understanding of irony. They will not receive a full comparative study, but will assist the reader in acquiring a skill for detecting conventional irony and a deeper familiarity with its definitions, characteristics, and functions so that he can properly decipher conventional irony within a given literary context such as the Matthean passion narrative.

Based on the critical information about irony provided by the earlier chapters, chapter 4 will launch a sequential narrative-critical reading of the Matthean passion narrative's irony. The first half of chapter 4 will define the limits of the literary unit of the Matthean passion narrative (26:1—27:66). The last half will explicate the use of conventional irony within the Matthean passion narrative through the stance of narrative criticism. Instead of lining up cases of irony under each category of conventional irony, the book will expose their occurrences according to the chapter of the Matthean passion narrative in which it is found. In this way, the Matthean passion narrative will be read chronologically not fragmentarily. Also, it will be observed that not every case of conventional irony in the Matthean passion narrative belongs to only one category. In fact, the Matthean passion narrative's conventional irony is so complex that the reader may detect combinations of irony, such as an instance of verbal irony with situational irony, a moment of situational irony in an example of character irony, an occurrence of character irony with a case of verbal irony, or in some cases, all in one.

The concluding chapter 5 will synthesize the data to present the characteristic Matthean theological interpretation on the death of Jesus communicated through the conventional irony of the Matthean passion narrative in four categories: (i) the identity of Jesus, (ii) the saving will of God, the governing norm of the Matthean passion narrative (iii) God's universal salvation, and (iv) *Deus triumphus* (God the victorious) vs. *Satan victus* (Satan the defeated), the outcome of the Christ-event.

First, the Matthean passion narrative's ironic portrait of Jesus' death decidedly answers the most crucial question of "who Jesus is." Throughout the Gospel, the Gospel's implied author-ironist presents the complexity of Jesus' identity and allows his reader to acquire comprehensive knowledge of the person of Jesus by exposing him to direct and indirect statements of Jesus regarding himself and to the testimonies of key witnesses of Jesus. Despite the abundance of information regarding "who Jesus is," the Gospel depicts that the central cause of conflict between Jesus and his antagonists hinges on the issue of Jesus' identity. In the most heated moments of confrontation in the Matthean passion narrative, when Jesus' identity is questioned by the representatives of his people, irony hidden in their accusations and belittlements turns their emphatic denouncement of Jesus into an irrefutable affirmation in spite of their ignorance accompanied by disbelief.

Second, the Matthean passion narrative's irony reveals the will of God (τὸ θέλημά τοῦ θεοῦ, 26:42) as the governing norm of Jesus' entire life and ministry culminating in his passion. Matthew constantly stresses this theme throughout the narrative and considers that God's saving will is fully accomplished in Jesus' death. Jesus drinks "the cup" (τὸ ποτήριον, 26:39), which is a symbolic description of the will of God in the Gospel, and thus embraces his Father's will through his radical obedience that is expressed in his innocent death. As Jesus, the Son of God carried out his Father's will. His disciples are likewise called to bear their own crosses (10:3-39), the tokens of utter submission. The Matthean passion narrative's irony reveals bearing one's cross and following after Jesus in this path as the most desirable pattern for true discipleship, despite the persecution and even "passion" awaiting them (10:24-25).

Third, the Matthean passion narrative's irony pertaining to the irreconcilable conflict between the innocence of Jesus (that is, the innocent blood of Jesus) and the shame of the cross which he endures sums up the core message of Christianity that God's universal salvation is proffered through the death of his Son, Jesus, for both Jews and Gentiles alike. It is particularly important to observe how the Matthean passion narrative's irony exposes the hidden agenda of the death of Jesus in the most controversial scene of the Matthean passion narrative where his people (1:21) makes a collective decision to reject him but yet unwittingly come under the insuperable embrace of God (27:24-25). Although it is apparently tragic that God's people, for whom God sent his Son (1:21; 3:17; 17:5), attempt to sever their tie from that very one who is sent by God, it is the revelation of the Matthean passion narrative's irony that there is no scandal of sin that cannot be overcome by the salvation secured through the death of Jesus. Additionally, God's salvation achieved through Jesus' death is also for the nations beyond the Jewish race, despite the fact that Jesus comes as the Jewish Messiah (1:1) and eventually dies under the charge of being the King of the Jews (27:37). Jesus' entire ministry manifests his equally compelling compassion and care for the "sinners" (9:11-13) and this attests to the universal nature of his saving ministry as he unequivocally explains that the reason for his ordeal is to save "many" (that is, "all", 20:28; 26:28).

Lastly, the reading of the Matthean passion narrative's irony presents the death of Jesus as the most indicative incident revealing the ultimate *Deus triumphus*. The cross of Jesus is the place where the undefeatable God manifests himself in the way he deals with Satan. The literary-critical reading of the First Gospel shows that Satan's activity ironically contributes to what God intends to achieve through his Son, Jesus. Even though Jesus seems to be caught in a mechanism of evil when he is surrounded by the streams of opposition and the growing ferocity of violence, the Matthean passion narrative's irony subtly discloses that the kingdom of Satan is divided and that Jesus' passion is God's checkmate on Satan who is stuck in a dilemma, neither moving forwards nor backwards, while his associates unknowingly act against the aspiration of their head.

2

A General Overview of Irony

Difficulty of Defining Irony

Irony is an ancient concept, probably millennia old.¹ It is a significant part of the legacy of human language and intellectual culture, having a reality of its own well before its definition came into view.² Though its presence has never been doubted throughout the history of literary criticism, the term itself is relatively new. Irony occurs both in everyday communication and literature. It ranges from the most uncomplicated form of utterance to the most complex literary disguise. The most rudimentary form of irony is found in the often-used sarcastic expressions "Yeah, right" or "How nice!" These locutions combine a form of agreement with an implied denial, saying *yes* but meaning *no*, and conveying a very different effect than just a mere negation. In a complex rhetorical arrangement of the author-speaker, irony brings about persuasion in ways that literal speech cannot.³

It is a well-known fact among the literary critics that giving irony a definition is difficult. Lars Elleström compares irony to the famous monster of Dr. Frankenstein which corresponds with Bert O. States' description of irony as "child of Janus, god of beginnings, and, without doubt, the most ill-behaved of all literary tropes."⁴ Like grasping a pervasively spreading fog,⁵

---

1. Garnett G. Sedgewick, *Of Irony: Especially in the Drama* (Toronto: University of Toronto Press, 1935), 5 states that irony "must really be as old as coherent speech."

2. J. A. K. Thomson, *Irony: An Historical Introduction* (London: George Allen and Unwin, 1926), 2 notes that irony existed long before εἰρωνεία (*eirōneia*), the Greek technical term for irony.

3. Booth, "The Empire of Irony," *GR* 37 (1983): 729 notes that irony has engaged us in a way that no straight talk ever could.

4. Lars Elleström, *Divine Madness: On Interpreting Literature, Music and Visual Arts Ironically* (Lewisburg: Bucknell University Press, 2002), 15; Bert O. States, *Irony and Drama: A Poetics* (Ithaca: Cornell University Press, 1971), 3.

5. Booth describes the study of irony as looking at foggy landscapes. Booth, *The Rhetoric of Fiction* (Chicago: University of Chicago Press, 1961), 120 writes, "We have looked for so long at foggy

giving irony either a precise or a satisfactorily comprehensive definition is notoriously slippery. In the same vein, an accomplished literary critic of irony, D. C. Muecke, laments the conceptual fogginess of irony in his opening remark: "Getting to grips with irony seems to have something in common with gathering the mist. There is plenty to take hold of if only one could."[6] Thus, he opined that it is better to list examples of irony rather than define irony exactly because it is difficult to define irony comprehensively.[7]

W. C. Booth actually attempted to accomplish what he had in mind: listing the cases of irony.[8] However, he reached a discouraging conclusion which is similar to a common lament over the concept of irony. In his 1983 article "The Empire of Irony," Booth summarizes his attempt to list cases of irony:

> I begin with a strong temptation not to discuss the empire of irony but to conduct a requiem for the terms "irony," "ironic," and "ironically." A couple of years ago I began to collect written and spoken claims that this or that event or statement was ironic, and the collection became so large, and the various meanings so diverse, that I soon came to suspect that anybody who used the words could not possibly have any precise meaning in mind.[9]

In the same article, Booth focuses on the heart of the problem in discussing the concept of irony that has been created by the critics' uncritical use of the term. He says,

> Obviously, "irony" and "ironic" have become little more than all-purpose, flexible slot-filters, vogue words, useful whenever one does not want to choose stronger clearer terms—or dares not do so because they will be too clear—or whenever one simply has nothing to say and wants to sound educated . . . when "ironic" means simply "odd" or "interesting," uncritical minds can quite literally call anything under the sun ironic.[10]

landscapes in misty mirrors that we have come to *like* fog. Clarity and simplicity are suspect, irony reigns supreme."

6. Douglas C. Muecke, *The Compass of Irony* (London: Methuen, 1969), 3.

7. Ibid., 19.

8. Booth, "The Empire of Irony," 721–22 offers a catalogue of useful synonyms for "irony" in nouns, adjectives, and adverbs as his attempt to serve those who would like to rescue the ironic terms for useful service.

9. Ibid., 719.

10. Ibid., 721.

Accordingly, though "irony" is often used, it is a rather vague term. In addition, its forms and functions are diverse and versatile.[11] Forms of irony may vary widely and be looked at from many different angles, since irony often casts a "veil of absurdity"[12] over the object to be interpreted or communicated. However, even though irony is often associated with deliberate and strategic expressions of falsehood,[13] leaving the audience-reader in the dark is not the goal of irony. Such complexity in irony creates "an aggressively intellectual exercise that fuses fact and value" because it is "coupled with a kind of subtlety that cannot be deciphered or proved simply by looking at the words."[14]

In this section, we do not attempt to exhaust the history of the concept of irony since the issue is bigger than this book's capacity to examine it. Therefore, as essentially as possible, chapter 2 will examine the subject ignited by ancient critics of irony and progressively developed via the medieval age down to its complex transformation during the modern times. To this end, the chapter will provide the reader with a working definition of irony based on which this project will unfold the theological uses of irony within the Matthean passion narrative.

Early examples of irony and reflections upon it occur in Aristophanes (c. 446–388 BCE), Xenophon (c. 431–355 BCE), Plato (c. 427–347 BCE), Aristotle (384–322 BCE), Cicero (106–43 BCE), and Quintilian (c. 35–95 CE). Their notions of irony have been the primary sources for the discussion of the topic, particularly in relation to the definition and nature of irony. Even more, their works guided the following generations' criticism. Each early proponent of irony is indebted to his predecessor's view whether he is aware of his indebtedness or not. Even though these early critics' comments about irony are unsystematic and sporadic, they did develop the essential indicators of irony which are significant criteria for its study to this day. Almost every student of irony refers to these ancient critics one way or another, since they regulate observations of irony and provide a framework for comprehending the wide variety of ironic forms.

---

11. Otto Ribbeck, "Über den Begriff des eirōn," *Rheinisches Museum* 31 (1876): 400 defines irony as "protean" (*proteusartig*).

12. Christopher W. Tindale and James Gough, "The Use of Irony in Argumentation," *Philosophy & Rhetoric* 20 (1987), 1.

13. H. P. Grice, "Logic and Conversation" in *Syntax and Semantics* (ed. Peter Cole and Jerry Morgan; New York: Academic, 1975), 41–58.

14. Booth, *A Rhetoric of Irony* (Chicago: University of Chicago Press, 1974), 44.

Brief History of the Word *Irony*

L. Elleström analyzes the history of irony in two complex streams: the history of the word *irony* and the history of the concepts of irony.[15] Here we will briefly address the former before we get to the main entrée, the history of the concept of irony.

It is commonly accepted that irony, εἰρωνεία, has its root in an Attic Greek verb, εἴρω (to say, tell, or ask). Beyond this basic understanding, there is no general agreement concerning the etymology of the word *irony*.[16] Otherwise, as Muecke expresses, the taxonomy of irony is very nebulous.[17] According to Julius Porkorny, εἴρω originally comes from Indo-European *uer-* or *war-* whose basic meaning is "solemn or ceremonious speech."[18] In this regard, the English *word*, the German *wort*, and the Latin *verbum* all have their origin in this Indo-European etymology.[19] Derivations of the word "irony," such as εἴρων,[20] εἰρωνεία,[21] εἰρωνεύομαι,[22] and εἰρωνικός[23] are connected to the verb εἴρω, signifying that irony primarily works with the word in relation to the speech act.[24] Peter L. Hagen supports this by suggesting that another Greek word ῥῆμα (word) shares the same common ancestor, giving rise to ῥήτωρ (a public speaker, pleader, orator), ῥητορική (rhetoric, oratory, art of speaking), and an adjective ῥητορικός (rhetorical, oratorical).[25] It is helpful to notice that *word, irony* and *rhetoric* all may share the same root, and are thus historically and conceptually related. Later, the Greek terms for irony and its derivates were translated into the Latin: *ironia* or *dissimulatio* for εἰρωνεία, *dissimulator* for εἴρων and *dissimulo* for εἰρωνεύομαι. Dilwyn Knox suggests

---

15. Elleström, *Divine Madness*, 15.
16. Ibid.
17. Muecke, *Compass*, 3.
18. Julius Porkorny, *Indogermanisches Etymologisches Wörterbuch*, (Band I; Bern: Francke, 1959), 1162–1163.
19. Ibid.
20. "εἴρων" is typically translated as an "ironist," "dissembler," "self-deprecator," or "one who *says* less than he thinks."
21. "εἰρωνεία" is typically translated as "irony," "dissimulation" or "assumed ignorance."
22. "εἰρωνεύομαι" (verb) means to "dissemble" or to "feign ignorance."
23. "εἰρωνικός" (adjective) means "dissembling," or "putting on a feigned ignorance."
24. Booth, "The Empire of Irony," 724 notes the primacy of verbal irony which later had further ramifications for other faces of irony. He says that "intended verbal ironies, designed by human speakers who expect them to be seen as ironies, are now only a small branch of the huge family, though once they were the whole clan."
25. Peter L. Hagen, "The Rhetorical Effectiveness of Verbal Irony" (Ph.D. diss., Pennsylvania State University, 1992), 16.

other combinations of irony proposed by medieval and some Renaissance authors. He writes,

> *Ironia* (or *hyronia*, *hironia*, etc.) derived purportedly from a Greek word *iron* (or *hyron*, *yron*, etc.) and *onoma* (i.e. ὄνομα) meaning opposite (*contra*) and term (*nomen*) respectively. Another author derived *yronia* from *yros* meaning opposite (*contra*) and *nois* (i.e. νόος/ νοῦς?) meaning mind (*mens*) because in *yronia* the speaker has in mind the opposite to his literal meaning.[26]

Based on the Greek and the Latin renderings of irony in relation to *word*, it is not surprising that in the Greco-Roman world, as far as the history of irony goes back, it was primarily understood as a kind of dissimulation using *word*. In the course of time, adding more flesh and sinew to this basic skeleton, irony slowly gained its distinctive meaning as a literary-rhetorical device used by the author-speaker within literature.

The Concept of Irony: A Historical Survey

The Greeks primarily developed the concept of irony. Not only the literature of the Greeks but their outlook and attitudes towards life are familiar with irony.[27] The definition of irony, εἰρωνεία (*eirōneia*), historically developed around the concept of the εἴρων (*eirōn*) of Greek theater, the dramatic character of the Old Comedy, and Socrates, who was perceptively identified as the classic image of the εἴρων. Therefore, the study of irony finds its origins in the observation of the ancient Greek dramas and the criticism developed in relation to the figure of Socrates (470–399 BCE).

In Greek Old Comedy,[28] the εἴρων was a comic character who succeeded by making his boastful antagonist, an ἀλαζών (*alazōn*) generally known as an imposter or quack, an object of humor.[29] Together with the ἀλαζών and

---

26. Dilwyn Knox, *Ironia: Medieval and Renaissance Ideas on Irony* (Leiden: E. J. Brill, 1989), 11.
27. Thomson, *Irony*, 2.
28. Hellenistic scholars in Alexandria first established the categorization of Athenian comedy in three stages: Old, Middle and New. One important distinction between Old, Middle and New Comedy is the prominence of the chorus. In Old Comedy (fifth century to the late fourth century BCE), its contrast with the dignity and seriousness of tragedy could not be more marked. Slapstick action, scatological and sexual jokes and just about every other device of humor known to man are found in Old Comedy. Political and social satire, along with literary parody, is also characteristic of Old Comedy. See Roger Dunkle, *The Classical Origins of Western Culture* (New York: Brooklyn College Press, 1986), 81–84.
29. Ribbeck, "*eirōn*," 381–400.

the βωμολόχος (*bōmolochos*) known as a low jester or buffoon, he formed one of the three stock characters of Greek Old Comedy. This earliest Greek identification of irony drawn from the image of the εἴρων mainly has to do with a deceptive mode of behavior.[30] The εἴρων wears the *persona* (character mask) of the seeming simpleton and frequently triumphs over the ἀλαζών by making himself appear less than he actually is. In this sense, the Latin term, *dissimulator* (one who disguises) for the εἴρων can be seen as an accurate rendering. In stark contrast to the εἴρων, the ἀλαζών is one who boasts, exaggerates, and bustles to give an impression of superiority in knowledge and character. Yet, he is the true fool and a man of inferiority. The εἴρων and the ἀλαζών are diametrically opposite characters in their nature and function. The two figures are similar in that each one is something quite different than he appears to be. If the former usually fills the role of a protagonistic and normative figure who sets the standard, challenging other characters of the story to follow, the latter serves as an antagonistic and absurd figure in self-destructive ignorance. These two contrasting figures create a dramatic effect, that is a conflict (ἀγών or ἀγωνία), which moves the plot of the story forward to its conclusion.[31] The main cause of the ἀγών (*agōn*) is furnished by the ἀλαζών because he is blindly confident that his belief or idea is indisputable. His self-sufficiency is the main ingredient of the conflict with the εἴρων.

In short, the paradigm of Greek Old Comedy shows that the best way to understand the εἴρων, and thus its derivative εἰρωνεία, is by observing his relation to his counterpart, the ἀλαζών. In fact, the εἴρων and the ἀλαζών are correlative terms. As Cicero puts it, the former dissimulates (or professes something less) and the latter simulates (or professes something more);[32] each explains the other. Neither is intelligible apart from the other.

In his classical study of irony with a focus on Greek literature of the fifth and fourth centuries BCE, Otto Ribbeck gives a historical review, reporting the appearance of irony as a technical term.[33] According to his observation, the word, εἴρων, meaning "cunning," "wily," "sly," is introduced through comedy, specifically by an Athenian comic poet, Cratinus (c. 520–423 BCE), a six-time winner at the city Dionysia and one of the three great playwrights of the

---

30. David Kaufer, "Irony and Rhetorical Strategy," *Philosophy & Rhetoric* 10 (1977): 103; Sedgewich, *Of Irony*, 6.

31. Northrop Frye, *Anatomy of Criticism* (New Jersey: Princeton University Press, 1957), 33–67; Francis M. Cornford, *The Origin of Attic Comedy* (ed. T. H. Gaster; Ann Arbor: University of Michigan Press, 1993), 20.

32. Cicero, *De officiis*, I.30.

33. Ribbeck, "eirōn," 381–400.

spirited and satirical Athenian Old Comedy along with his contemporaries Aristophanes and Eupolis. However, its derivative, εἰρωνεία, that signifies the nature and the attitude of the εἴρων, occurs for the first time in the work *Nubes* (Clouds), by the Greek comic dramatist, Aristophanes (c. 446–388 BCE).[34] Aristophanes, who is known as the Father of Comedy or the "Prince of Ancient Comedy,"[35] used irony to denote an unscrupulous trickery.[36] Later, another Athenian poet and playwright of the New Comedy, Philemon (c. 362–262 BCE), further defines irony as a fox, contrasting it with "straightforwardness."[37]

The concept of εἰρωνεία, built around its connection to the comic character, εἴρων, is not alone sufficient to explain its subsequent conceptual developments as a rhetorical device as well as a criticism of life. Here, the association of εἰρωνεία with the renowned ancient Greek philosopher Socrates comes into the picture to reveal irony as a way of life. This relationship has had a lasting impact on the history of the concept of irony. Regarding an intimate link between the εἴρων and Socrates, Norman Knox explains,

> The central fact about the history of irony in Greek use is its inseparability from Socrates' personality and influence. But it is essential to remember that neither Socrates nor his friends ever used the word in a serious way to describe the Socratic method, and that the idealization of Socratic dialectic which modern writers have embodied in "Socratic irony" were never attached to the word irony in classical Greek and Latin.[38]

Though we must consider Knox's warning against an overemphasis regarding the attribution of the history of irony to Socrates alone, his assertion contains only a half truth. He is right that the word εἴρων and its derivatives are not often used directly about Socrates by his contemporaries. For example, Xenophon[39]

---

34. Aristophanes' *Nubes*, a satiric comedy winning third prize at the Dionysia of 423 BCE lampoons the sophists, who charge for their services, and the intellectual trends of late fifth-century Athens. The work features Socrates as a head of the thinking-factory (i.e. thoughtery), corrupting youth with twisted logic. The original composition is assumed to be in 423 BCE. An uncompleted revised version from 419–416 BCE survives.

35. E. Cobham Brewer, *The Reader's Handbook of Allusions, References, Plots and Stories* (Philadelphia: J. B. Lippincott Company, 1889), 52; Edward Latham, *A Dictionary of Names, Nicknames and Surnames, of Persons, Places and Things* (New York: E. P. Dutton & Co., 1904), 101.

36. Aristophanes, *Nub.*, 449.

37. Ribbeck, "eirōn," 381–83.

38. Norman Knox, *The Word Irony and Its Context, 1500–1755* (Durham: Duke University Press, 1961), 3.

describes Socrates in terms that conform to some definitions of irony, such as depicting Socrates as a "mocker" and as one who is asking questions when he knows the answers.[40] However, early literates who either use or comment on irony—including Xenophon himself, Aristophanes, Plato, Aristotle, Cicero, and Quintilian—conceptually speak of irony in relation to or in memory of Socrates.

The word εἰρωνεία, has long been attributed to Socrates. Thus, Søren Kierkegaard, in his doctoral dissertation, considers that Socrates was the first to introduce irony.[41] All serious discussions of εἰρωνεία followed upon the association of the word with Socrates, occurring in two contexts: the ethical and the rhetorical. If the Greek critics of irony, mainly philosophers, dominated the former context, the Roman critics, mainly rhetoricians, generated insights in relation to the latter context. Having in mind this basic distinction, the following will describe some important expositions of these prime critics of irony in their own terms.

THE CONCEPT OF IRONY AMONG THE EARLY AUTHORS

I. ARISTOPHANES (C. 446–388 BCE)

Most critics launch their discussion on irony in the late fifth century BCE with Socrates, more precisely with the Platonic Socrates.[42] Yet, this trend curtails the impact of the earliest discussion of irony generated by Aristophanes, an early Greek comic poet. Aristophanes is a figure of significance for the discussion of the history of the concept of irony. He seems to have coined the term εἰρωνεία with the implication of a hostile or deceitful pretense. Gregory Vlastos catalogues the word and its derivatives' first appearances in Aristophanes' comedies: the *Vespae* (Wasps), the *Aves* (Birds) and the *Nubes* (Clouds).[43] Other early critics' discussions in relation to irony are seen to be direct and indirect reactions to Aristophanes' evaluative link between εἰρωνεία and Socrates as the chief sophist from his point of view.

Norman Knox has observed the meaning of εἰρωνεία as sarcastic praise and disingenuous self-deprecation, and the εἴρων as a practitioner of such sarcasm and disingenuousness which later came to be associated with the work and

---

39. Xenophon was an admirer of Socrates and well known for his writings on the sayings of Socrates, such as *Memorabilia* and *Apologia Socratis* and *The life of Greece*.

40. Xenophon, *Memorabilia*, 4.4.9; 1.2.36.

41. Søren Kierkegaard, *The Concept of Irony with Continual Reference to Socrates* (ed. and trans. Howard V. Hong and Edna H. Hong; New Jersey: Princeton University Press, 1989), 6.

42. Joseph A. Dane, *The Critical Mythology of Irony* (Athens: University of Georgia Press, 1991), 21.

43. Gregory Vlastos, "Socratic Irony," *CQ* 37 (1987): 80.

lifestyle of Socrates.[44] Although it is uncertain how Socrates became the central figure in the ancient form of irony as the prototype of the εἴρων, it is likely that Aristophanes served as a chief originator of this viewpoint since the dominant sense of εἰρωνεία, a mocking pretense and deception, made its first appearance in his comedy, the *Nubes* in which Socrates is ridiculed.[45] For example, Socrates is portrayed as floating in the air (wafted in a basket) to suspend his brain and mingle the subtle essence of his mind with the air and contemplates the sun and other portents of the sky. He is aloft, a transcendentalist, "treading the air," and like the water-cress, he thus can penetrate the things of heaven.[46] Careful observation, however, clarifies that Aristophanes depicted Socrates as fitting into the category of ἀλαζών rather than of εἴρων, since he criticized Socrates as one who corrupts youth by teaching them the unjust argument (τὸν ἄδικον τοῦτον λόγον),[47] believes in strange gods, and hatches the ideas in his thinkery or thought factory (φροντιστήριον)[48] that make the worse reason appear to be the better in his pretense of knowledge. Instead, the character Strepsiades, an old and unintelligent rustic who suffers an enormous debt due to the extravagance of his horse-loving son, Phidippides.[49] One scene of the *Nubes* delivers an oddly funny conversation regarding the presence of Zeus and the cause of a meteorological phenomenon such as rain between Strepsiades and Socrates in the roles of the εἴρων and the ἀλαζών.[50] The scene chiefly

44. N. Knox, *The Word Irony*, 3.

45. A brief summary of the *Nubes* is that Strepsiades, an uneducated old man, who is deeply in debt because of the extravagance of his horse-racing son Phidippides, decides call in the aid of the new science taught by Socrates to discourage his creditors with ridiculous logic, but in the end he himself, with his wife, falls prey to his son who has just learned the twisted and absurd logic from Socrates' thoughtery to beat his parents.

46. Aristophanes, *Nub.*, 216–33.

47. Ibid., 89–99, 116.

48. In *Nub.*, 225, Aristophanes views Socrates as a "think-tank" (φροντιστής), and thus his house as a "thoughtery" (φροντιστήριον). These identifications of Socrates and his school were quite derogatory, and were meant to evoke laughter among the Athenian audience.

49. Phidippides is a horse-racing lover as his name attests. Aristophanes, *Nub.*, 58–80 reports Strepsiades' regret over giving the boy the name Phidippides out of many other options. Thus, he blames his wife for their son's name because she insisted on having some reference to a horse in his name.

50. "Strepsiades: Oh! Earth! What august utterances! How sacred! How wondrous! Socrates: That is because there are the only goddesses; all the rest are pure myth. Strepsiades: But by the earth! Is our father, Zeus, the Olympian, not a god? Socrates: Zeus! What Zeus! Are you mad? There is no Zeus. Strepsiades: What are you saying now? Who causes the rain to fall? Answer me that! Socrates: Why, these, and I will prove it. Have you ever seen it raining without clouds? Let Zeus then casus rain with a clear sky and without their presence! Strepsiades: By Apollo! That is powerfully argues! For my own part, I always thought it was Zeus pissing into a sieve." See *Nub.*, 364–373.

exposes the latter, the wise Socrates, defeated in a debate by appearing foolish when Strepsiades comically reduces the debate with Socrates from an erudite issue on the gods' existence to a trifling matter. In his defense and reassertion of the gods, Aristophanes must have written this part of the conversation between Strepsiades, the assumed student, and Socrates, the assumed teacher, to dramatize how this highly regarded atheistic teacher is failing in his theological debate with his meager student. Strepsiades brings Socrates down from the seat of honor reserved for the wise and turns the exchange into a ludicrous conversation, which is rather embarrassing. In the *Nubes*, it seems that Aristophanes employs some versatility in his subversive applications of εἴρων and εἰρωνεία.[51] In the plays of Aristophanes, the εἴρων normally is a cunning and sly figure taking delight in humiliating his opponent, the ἀλαζών, by disclosing his absurdity. He gives the impression of being a fool, but ultimately he triumphs, thanks to his cleverness. However, in the *Nubes*, Aristophanes paints Strepsiades as the εἴρων, yet a less conventional one because this character is by no means clever. In fact, Strepsiades is rather a perplexed fool who is not only outwitted, but also physically abused by his son, Phidippides, in the end. Meanwhile, Aristophanes indirectly connects the word εἰρωνεία to Socrates in a derogatory way, revealing his perception of Socrates as being an intolerable εἴρων.[52] It is perceivable that Aristophanes' sarcastic portrayal of Socrates has a deep connection to his hostile attitude toward sophists and their sophistry in general. His *Nubes* is the best example of where Aristophanes directly identifies Socrates as the sophist who practices its well-known disguise. Sophists were known for their dexterous twists of language, called, δισσοὶ λόγοι (two-fold words).[53] This is a technique of stating one thing by implying another. As Aristophanes perceived, we can see elements in their works and use of words that must have contributed to the later proliferation of irony such. Examples of this include antithesis evident from the μέν . . . δέ construction,[54] and the δισσοὶ

---

51. Alan R. Thompson, *The Dry Mock: A Study of Irony in Drama* (Berkeley: University of California Press, 1948), 27 confirms this view. He notices that in Aristophanes' *Nubes*, the traditional εἴρων–ἀλαζών formula is seldom apparent.

52. In Aristophanes, *Nub.*, 449, εἴρων appears as a term of abuse spoken by Strepsiades, "a supple knave, rascal" (μάσθλης εἴρων). Aristophanes depicts Socrates as such through the words of his character, Strepsiades. In the story world, it is this disreputable type of individual which Strepsiades hopes to become by associating himself with Socrates.

53. W. K. C. Guthrie, *The Sophists* (Cambridge: Cambridge University Press, 1971), 182 says that this doctrine was first attributed to Protagoras.

54. In the *Rhetorica*, III.ix.8, Aristotle opines that the style of antithesis is pleasing, because contraries are easily understood and even more so when placed side by side. An exemplary Sophist writing, Gorgias'

λόγοι. In fact, in the *Sophista*, Plato attests to the word *irony* associated with sophists.[55]

Though Aristophanes ridicules and lampoons the philosophers, specifically the sophists, he was not the first to do so. A century before him, Epicharmus (c. 540–450 BCE), the originator of Sicilian (or Dorian) comedy, likewise satirized philosophers. The intellectual trends of late fifth-century Athens—the growth of non-traditional forms of scientific inquiry and of new pedagogies in the education of youth, specifically rhetorical training—were considered useless, immoral, dangerous, and atheistic to Athens. It is in this context that Aristophanes places Socrates at the center of the *Nubes* as the arch-sophist who runs an educational cult in his derogatory "thinkery" where he misleads young men to run after fame, power, and wealth. It is quite revealing that in Plato's *Apologia*, Socrates is made to say that *Nubes* had deepened the prejudice against him.[56] He refers to a "certain comic poet" who has slandered him,[57] and identifies this poet as Aristophanes.[58] Plato, the pupil of Socrates tries to show the inaccuracy and unfairness of the popular image of his master fueled by comedies like the *Nubes,* that played what he considered the decisive role in Socrates' condemnation on capital charges in Athens in 399 BCE.[59]

In conclusion, we may suggest that Aristophanes contributed to the history of the concept of irony in two important ways. First, in his play, the *Nubes*, the εἴρων and εἰρωνεία made a leap from a comic figure of ancient Greek drama and its faculty to Socrates and his dialectics, and thus he seems to have initiated the following generations' interest in and pursuit of the study of irony in relation to Socrates. Second, Aristophanes establishes the fundamental implication of εἰρωνεία, something base and amoral, in his effort to attribute it to the trickery of Socrates. Aristophanes' *Nubes* serves as a classical source for the history of irony or Socratic irony. It could have been partly responsible for adding further negativity to the growing civic agitation against Socrates

---

Helena begins with the antithesis, "What is becoming to a city is manpower, to a body beauty, to a soul wisdom, to an action virtue, to a speech truth, and the opposite of these are unbecominig."

55. Plato, *Sophista*, 268a–b. Furthermore, in the same book 234c, 235a, 241b and in the *Respublica*, 598d, 602d, Plato calls the Sophist a deceitful magician.

56. The *Apologia* (Apology of Socrates) is Plato's version of Socrates' forensic oratory given in the Athenian court as he defends himself against the charges.

57. Plato, *Apol.*, 18d.

58. Ibid., 19c.

59. The charges against Socrates, such as youth corruptor and atheist, are attested in the following works: Plato, ibid., 24b; Xenophon, *Mem.*, 1.1.1; Diogenes Laertius 2.40. Also, see T. C. Brickhouse and N. D. Smith, *Socrates on Trial* (Oxford: Oxford University Press, 1989), 30–37.

which eventually led him to an execution owing to the fact that Socrates was dramatized as a harmful trickster of idea, corrupting the young.[60] As noted by classicist Jeffrey Henderson, the reader may accept *Nubes* as valid information concerning public thought about Socrates in the Athens of 423–c. 416 BCE.[61]

II. PLATO (C. 427–347 BCE)

The modern notion of the ironic Socrates depends on a number of factors. Among them is the revised image of Socrates produced by Plato. Plato's representative works—*Apologia*, *Respublica*, and *Symposium*—provide the reader with examples of the close association of irony with Socrates by reminiscing of Socrates' speaking and acting ironically. According to Plato, irony was a discourse style well used by his teacher, Socrates. Socrates, in *Apologia*, claims ignorance which contrasts the Delphic oracle given to his friend Chaerophon attesting to Socrates' superior wisdom. Plato, in *Apologia*, recollects that Socrates, filled with the intention of divine service, took the mode of ironic behavior so that he might lead his interlocutors to wisdom.[62] In a stark contrast to his contemporary intellectuals whom he cross-examined, Socrates would rather be as he is, knowing that he knows nothing, than to be inflated by a false conviction of his own great wisdom.[63] Thus, he concludes, he truly is wiser than other men because he knows what he does not know. As a valuable literary source to Socrates' life and ideas, *Apologia* evidences that irony was both the rhetorical tool and the mode of life adopted by Socrates to wield his pedagogical excellence.

The first significant instances of the Greek word εἰρωνεία and other derivates occur throughout the works of Plato, but not always exclusively in relation to Socrates. For Plato, εἰρωνεία no longer meant straightforward lying, as it did for Aristophanes, but an intended dissimulation which the audience was meant to perceive. In the *Apologia*, the use of the word by Socrates implies that irony is characteristic or habitual of him.[64] However, the Socrates of Plato

---

60. There exist fundamental discrepancies, however, between Aristophanes' descriptions of Socrates and Socrates' actual career. For instance, in contrast to the sophists who charge for their service, Socrates never took money from his students in exchange for teaching them philosophy and rhetoric and he himself publicly derided the sophists for their beguilingly crafty arguments and lack of moral scruples.

61. Jeffrey Henderson, *Aristophanes: Clouds, Wasps, Peace* (ed. and trans. Jeffrey Henderson; Cambridge, Mass., London, England: Harvard University Press, 1998), 5.

62. Plato, *Apol.*, 20c–24e.

63. For Socrates, the pursuit of wisdom begins with "knowing yourself," which is equal to intellectual humility.

64. Plato, ibid., 37e, 38a.

shares nothing with the contemptible fraud depicted in Aristophanes' *Nubes*. Developed further in Plato's *Respublica* and *Symposium*, irony comes to refer to a mode of life.[65] In support of this idea is Plato's portrayal of Socrates and his use of irony to defend himself even in court.[66] This tactic can be perilous and self-inflicting since the jury may easily roll their eyes due to their perception of the ironic Socrates as a vexing mocker.[67] Even later, the Roman rhetorician Quintilian confirms that Socrates' tactics were self-damaging in the *Institutio oratoria* stating that,

> Everybody knows that nothing would have contributed more to Socrates' acquittal than if he had used the ordinary judicial method of defense, conciliated the hearts of his juries by a humble tone, and anxiously taken effort to refute the actual charge. [68]

Further, Plato reports in his *Respublica* that Socrates' irritated opponent, Thrasymachus demands Socrates answering instead of asking,[69] and complains, "O lord, this is Socrates' usual irony!" (αὕτη κείνη ἡ εἰςθυῖα εἰρωνεία Σωκράτους).[70] As the case of Thrasymachus shows, for a frustrated interlocutor of Socrates, Socratic irony (in other words, his pretended ignorance), topped with Socrates' seemingly evasive attitude from answering, means at best "mocking pretence," "leg-pulling," "sly-foxery,"[71] or "dry mock."[72] Likewise, Plato's *Phaedo* also testifies to this because the Athenian accusers of Socrates in the court thought that his profession of ignorance and humility was insincere and meant to trick them. Therefore, as J. A. K. Thomson presumes, when his

---

65. Plato, *Resp.*, 337a; Plato, *Symposium*, 216e, 218d.

66. Plato, *Apol.*, 19–20.

67. The irony seems to be a main cause of the anger of his audience, as Socrates declares in Plato, ibid., 21e.

68. Quintilian, *Institutio Oratoria*, 11.1.9, "Nam quis nescit nihil magis profuturum ad absolutionem Socrati fuisse quam si esset usus illo iudiciali genere defensionis et oratione summissa conciliasset iudicum animos sibi crimenque ipsum sollicite redarguisset?" Translation is mine.

69. Socrates frequently assumes his ironic pose and *elenchus*, known as the Socratic dialogue method, in conversation with his younger associates, in order to put them at ease to learn the skills of argument and thinking through playfulness of irony. Socrates, however, employs irony as a means of exposure and confusion particularly when he is involved in discussion with more mature interlocutors, such as sophists, who have an inflated self-image and unwarranted confidence.

70. Plato's *Resp.*,336a.

71. Sedgewick, *Of Irony,* 11 explains that the word, "irony," down to Aristotle, was a term of abuse connoting "sly-foxery" with "a tinge of 'low-bred.' "

72. David Worcester, *The Art of Satire* (Cambridge: Harvard University Press, 1940), 78.

opponents called Socrates ironical, they did not mean to compliment him since they employed εἰρωνεία in the tone of accusation.⁷³

Though the majority of Socrates' contemporaries are reported as regarding the essence of irony as a lack of candor, it is Plato who takes up anew and enriches the concept of the εἴρων without essentially altering the basic concept of opposing appearance and reality. Plato seems to endeavor to render a positive portrait of Socrates who is highly decorated with needless prejudice. This effort is reflected in his fictional narrative of a banquet, *Symposium*, where the opposites come together and these intellectuals *par excellence* engage themselves in the dialogue of love. In *Symposium*, Aristophanes and Socrates are amiably drinking together as guests and friends of a tragic poet, Agathon. Both express their views on the discourses in praise of love spoken by Socrates without contention, though Plato depicts Aristophanes almost comically as he is often hindered when he tries to speak, first by his own hiccups and second by a band of revelers. Reflecting on Plato's portrait of both Socrates and Aristophanes, it seems that Plato subtly makes the point that his teacher was a man of noble character, able to pull his vigorous accuser Aristophanes into a circle of friendship.⁷⁴ In the *Symposium*, Plato further attributes characteristic descriptions of Silenus⁷⁵ and Marsyas, the flute player⁷⁶ to Socrates through the speech of Alchibiades. Silenus' external appearance contrasts with the treasures

---

73. Thomson, *Irony*, 167–68.

74. Additionally, an unknown legend relates an extraordinary incident when Socrates, not being greatly offended by the derision made against him in Aristophanes' *Nubes*, not only attended to the play's first performance (423 BCE) but also stood and waved to the audience at the end of the play.

75. Sileni, as the plural of Silenus, were companions of Dionysus, the Thracian god of wine. They were old, fat, and bold with thick lips and snubbed noses. Later the plural, "sileni," came to refer to one individual named Silenus, the teacher and faithful partner of Dionysus. It is known that Silenus possessed special knowledge and prophesies when intoxicated. Dane, *Mythology of Irony*, 21 comments that "the image of the Silenus and the word irony provide later writers with fixed and stereotypical descriptions of Socrates, even though both the image and the word may be radically reinterpreted." In later generations, accepting the function of *ironia* as a species of *allegoria*, Desiderius Erasmus of the fifteenth century considers Alcibiades' Sileni as an icon of Scripture as well as a code for allegorical interpretation. Interestingly, he defines even Jesus Christ as a certain Silenus in his contrast between body and soul. See Desiderius Erasmus, *Desiderii Erasmi Roterodami Opera Omnia*, (Vol. I ed. Joannes Clericus; Leiden: Petri van der Aa, 1703–1706; repr., Hildesheim: Georg Olms, 1961), 771 writes, "Was not Christ a certain amazing Silenus?" (an non mirificus quidam Sienus fuit Christus). Translation is mine.

76. According to Greek mythology, Marsyas was the son of Heracles. He was a satyr known as an expert player of the aulos, the double-piped reed instrument. He challenged Apollo, the god of music and poetry, also known as the director of the muses, a contest of music. He lost this contest and was flayed alive, losing his hide and life. Since the contest was manipulated to be judged by the muses, his defeat was anticipated.

(ἀγάλματα)—full of tiny golden statues of the gods. In a similar way, Socrates is an ironically fascinating man of superior knowledge and wisdom in spite of his public persona.[77] Similarly Marsyas' repulsiveness contrasts with the beauty and charm of his voice and music. Alchibiades perceives Socrates as producing the same effect with his speech as Marsyas did with his musical instrument because Socrates enchants, mesmerizes and captures the souls and hearts of men. For Plato, irony is used positively by Socrates to elicit an awakening in the mind of his interlocutors through a purposefully beneficial pretense of naivety. In the same vein, Gregory Vlastos opines that Socrates could have deceived without intending to deceive, and suggests that Socratic irony must be free from the notion of "deceit" and is better conceived of as a pretension of ignorance for moral autonomy and seeking for self-knowledge.[78]

III. ARISTOTLE (384–322 BCE)

It is Aristotle who characteristically embellishes the concepts of εἰρωνεία and its opposite, ἀλαζονεία with ethical implications. Aristotle's views on irony, however, are not clear-cut because he seems to present contradictory views of irony.[79] He overtly uses εἰρωνεία in two contexts, the first case in the *Rhetorica* and the second case in the *Ethica nichomachea* (τὰ ἠθικά). In the former, Aristotle's εἰρωνεία is a form of showing contempt (ὀλιγωρία),[80] a means of belittling and mocking "something which appears valueless" (περὶ τὸ μηδενὸς ἄξιον φαινόμενον).[81] In this sense, Irony is disdainful (καταφρονητικόν).[82] Thus, Aristotle classifies the εἴρωνες (dissemblers) with other πανοῦργοι (knaves, villains) who should be feared because of their dissembling nature.[83] Aristotle's εἴρωνες is more to be feared than he who is hot-tempered (οἱ ὀξύθυμοι) and speaks outspokenly (οἱ παρρησιατικοί).[84] Even in the *Rhetorica*, however, in his comparison of εἰρωνεία to βωμολόχια (vulgar buffoonery, ribaldry), Aristotle evaluates irony as more befitting (ἁρμόττειν) a free (noble) man than βωμολόχια by ranking the εἴρων as socially superior to a βωμολόχος (a low jester, buffoon).[85] To him, εἰρωνεία

---

77. Plato, *Symp.*, 215b–d, 216d, 217a, 221d–e, 223d.
78. Vlastos, "Socratic Irony," 79–97.
79. P. W. Gouch, "Socratic Irony and Aristotle's *eiron*: Some Puzzles," *Phoenix* 42 (1987): 95.
80. Aristotle, *Rhet.*, II.ii.3.
81. Ibid.
82. Ibid.
83. Ibid., II.v.11.
84. Ibid.
85. Ibid., III.xviii.7.

as a "gentlemanly" (ἐλεύθερος) sort of jest (γελοῖα) is employed on one's own account, and βωμολόχια on that of another (ὁ μὲν γὰρ αὑτοῦ ἕνεκα ποιεῖ τὸ γελοῖον, ὁ δὲ βωμολόχος ἑτέρου).[86] Thus, though *Rhetorica* does not overturn the general evaluation of εἰρωνεία as a form of deception, it accords it to a higher social status than some forms of direct speech. Joseph A. Dane's assertion that irony became not only a descriptive term but an evaluative one[87] seems to be reflective of Aristotle's perception of irony.

This ambivalent concept of εἰρωνεία associated with Socrates continues in Aristotle's *Ethica nichomachea*, a treatise on virtue and moral characters.[88] It was Aristotle who first attempted to explain irony by contrasting the εἴρων and the ἀλαζών. He summarily describes both parties as follows,

> Concerning the truth then, the middle may be called truthful, and the mean truthfulness; pretence in the form of exaggeration is imposture (ἀλαζονεία), and its possessor an impostor (ἀλαζών); in the form of understatement, self-depreciation (εἰρωνεία), and its possessor the self-depreciator (εἴρων).[89]

Aristotle considers that truth lies between these two opposites, the ἀλαζών and the εἴρων, and that the truthful man belongs to neither of them but stands somewhere in the middle of them. He explains

> It seems then, the impostor (ἀλαζών) is a man who pretends to be apt to claim the things that bring glory that he does not possess, or claim more of them than he has, while conversely the self-depreciator or the mock-modest man (εἴρων) disclaims or belittles what he has. Midway between them is one who calls a thing by its own name, being truthful both in life and in word, and admits what he has without exaggeration or understatement.[90]

---

86. Ibid.
87. Dane, *Mythology of Irony*, 45.
88. Aristotle, *Eth. nic.,* III.viii.6; IV.vii.14; VI.xiii.3.
89. Ibid., II.vii.12, "περὶ μὲν οὖν τὸ ἀληθὲς ὁ μὲν μέσος ἀληθής τις καὶ ἡ μεσότης ἀλήθεια λεγέσθω ἡ δὲ προσποίησις ἡ μὲν ἐπὶ τὸ μεῖζον ἀλαζονεία καὶ ὁ ἔχων αὐτὴν ἀλαζών ἡ δ' ἐπὶ τὸ ἔλαττον εἰρωνεία καὶ εἴρων ὁ ἔχων." Translation is mine.
90. Ibid., IV.vii.2–4, "δοκεῖ δή ὁ μὲν ἀλαζὼν προσποιητικὸς τῶν ἐνδόξων εἶναι καὶ μὴ ὑπαρχόντων καὶ μειζόνων ἢ ὑπάρχει ὁ δὲ εἴρων ἀνάπαλιν ἀρνεῖσθαι τὰ ὑπάρχοντα ἢ ἐλάττω ποιεῖν ὁ δὲ μέσος αὐθέκαστός τις ὢν ἀληθευτικὸς καὶ τῷ βίῳ καὶ τῷ λόγῳ τὰ(ὑπάρχοντα ὁμολογῶν εἶναι περι αὐτόν καὶ οὔτε μείζω οὔτε ἐλάττω." Translation is mine.

Given his doctrine of "the mean," Aristotle does not consider either the εἴρων or the ἀλαζών to be virtuous, thus their traits, neither εἰρωνεία nor ἀλαζονεία, virtues. He sees both as deficiency of truth and vices lying at the opposite poles of truthfulness: the former playing down the truth and the latter playing it up. At best, they are the form of "pretense (προσποίησις),"[91] and two grades of blameworthiness for Aristotle. It is crucial to note that Aristotle judges that both the εἴρων and the ἀλαζών have faults of character and that they are blamed (ψεκτοί) for their love of falsehood (ψεῦδος).[92] Nonetheless, Aristotle specifies that "both insincere men are blamable, but more the ἀλαζών," (οἱ δὲ ψευδόμενοι ἀμφότεροι μὲν ψεκτοί μᾶλλον δ' ὁ ἀλαζών).[93] Here a twist arises. Though Aristotle regarded the εἴρων as neither pernicious nor ideal, he reserves some cautiously guarded positive evaluation for this type of figure. It makes the reader wonder why his harsh evaluation of εἰρωνεία in the *Rhetorica* takes a more moderate tone in the *Ethica nichomachea*. In this latter work, he prefers εἰρωνεία to ἀλαζονεία as if he sets the scales for the ideal behaviors in relation to a truthful man's practice of the truth. According to Aristotle, the truly condemnable is the ἀλαζών, although both the εἴρων and the ἀλαζών are distant from the mean of truthfulness. In this way, Aristotle portrays the real opposite to the truthful person as the ἀλαζών in a paradigm of thought where ἀλαζονεία is worse than εἰρωνεία. The following excerpts all attest to such an Aristotelian view.

> Such a laudable man rather inclines to understate the truth. For, this appears in better taste because the excess (or exaggeration) is offensive (τὸ ἐπαχθεῖς).[94]

> Self-depreciators, who understate things seem of a more refined character (χαριέστερο), for they are thought to say not for gain but to avoid ostentation (τὸ ὀγκηρόν) . . . but those who moderately disguise themselves in understatement and understate about matters not too commonplace and obvious seem attractive. The impostor seems to be the opposite of the truthful man, for he is a worse character than [the mock-modest man].[95]

91. Ibid., IV.vii.1.
92. Ibid.
93. Ibid.
94. Ibid., IV.vii.9, "ὁ δὲ τοιοῦτος ἐπαινετός ἐπὶ τὸ ἔλαττον δὲ μᾶλλον τοῦ ἀληθοῦς ἀποκλίνει· ἐμμελέστερον γὰρ φαίνεται διὰ τὸ ἐπαχθεῖς τὰς ὑπερβολὰς εἶναι." Translation is mine.
95. Ibid., IV.vii.14, 16–17, "οἱ δ' εἴρωνες ἐπὶ τὸ ἔλαττον λέγοντες χαριέστεροι μὲν τὰ ἤθη φαίνονται οὐ γὰρ κέρδους ἕνεκα δοκοῦσι λέγειν ἀλλὰ φεύγοντες τὸ ὀγκηρόν . . . οἱ δὲ μετρίως χρώμενοι τῇ

The contrasting Aristotelian views of irony, which describe irony as a form of deceit not far from the traditional view in his *Rhetoric*, and as positive gentlemanly device in *Ethica nichomachea*, lead to two conclusions: one, εἰρωνεία in Greek literature until the time of Aristotle possessed a negative connotation (that is, a term of abuse),[96] and two, the variety in perspectives between Aristophanes, Plato, and Aristotle show that from early times the concept of εἰρωνεία has not been an easy subject on which to reach a consensus. Nevertheless, we will see major significant changes in the concept of irony in the work of the Roman rhetoricians such as Cicero and Quintilian.

IV. CICERO (106–43 BCE)

The most influential discussions regarding the concept of εἰρωνεία as a literary-rhetorical device are ushered in by the Romans, Marcus Tullius Cicero and Marcus Fabius Quintilian (c. 35–95 CE). These Romans caused a dramatic shift in the history of irony when they focused on the rhetorical significance of irony in contrast to the Greeks' emphasis on the ethical implications of irony. This hermeneutical shift in the dialogue about εἰρωνεία triggered the conceptual rebirth of irony on which the later perspectives on irony greatly depend. Their statements of irony fix the language in which εἰρωνεία would be discussed in Western Europe,[97] and further strengthen the crucial associations of the word with Socrates by excluding the negative connotations of irony. Most importantly, these Roman authors exhibit fundamentally different views from most of the Greeks either on what εἰρωνεία is or on its moral standing. They do not perceive the pretense of εἰρωνεία as deceptive but as a laudable rhetorical skill.

In his renderings of irony, Cicero uses the words *simulator, dissimulator, dissimulatio, urbana dissimulatio* and phrases such as *inversio verborum*,[98] *invertere verba*[99] besides the Greek terms, εἴρων, εἰρωνεία and the infrequent *ironia* from which the English *irony* comes. Cicero attempted to offer transliterated Greek in his mother tongue and fashioned the new Latin word *ironia*. Differently from his Greek predecessors, Cicero was successful at giving clear definitions of irony employing these terms on several occasions.[100] The most well-known phrase

---

εἰρωνεία καὶ περὶ τὰ μὴ λίαν ἐμποδῶν καὶ φανερὰ εἰρωνευόμενοι χαρίεντες φαίνονται ἀντικεῖσθαι δ' ὁ ἀλαζὼν φαίνεται τῷ ἀληθευτικῷ χείρων γάρ." Translation is mine.

96. Sedgewick, *Of Irony*, 11.
97. Dane, *Mythology of Irony*, 47.
98. Cicero, *De oratore*, II.lxv.261.
99. Ibid., II.lxv.262.
100. Ibid., II.lxvi.269, 272; III. 203.

used for irony forged by Cicero is *urbana dissimulatio*.[101] This well sums up his evaluative attitude to εἰρωνεία. Using this formulaic phrase, he defines irony in the *De oratore*.

> *Urbana dissimulatio* (gentlemanly assumed simplicity) is when words are spoken in contrast to their meanings (*cum alia dicuntur ac sentias*).[102]

In the same book, Cicero discusses irony as a part of the general theory of *facetiae* (plural wit), figures of thought,[103] and states at some length the value of wit to the orator.[104] For example, in the *De officiis*, Cicero describes Socrates as an exemplary ironist who knows how to take advantage of humor:

> From the Greeks, we received Socrates delightful and witty, a genial conversationalist in his every speech, whom the Greeks name εἴρων, in contrast to Pythagoras and Pericles who acquired the utmost influence without any cheerfulness.[105]

Regarding irony as wit under the rubric of figures of thought is part of the view of many modern scholars such as Alan R. Thompson,[106] Jakob Jónsson,[107] Kenneth Burke[108] and H. S. Lang,[109] with their emphasis on the comic element as the key feature of irony.[110] Particularly, Burke considers irony to be a

---

101. This can be translated as "gentlemanly assumed simplicity."
102. Ibid., II.lxvii.269, "urbana etiam dissimulatio est, cum alia dicuntur ac sentias." Translation is mine.
103. Ibid., II.liv.218.
104. Ibid., II.liv.216–290, especially 236.
105. Ibid., I.xxx.108, "de Graecis autem dulcem et facetum festivique sermonis atque in omni oratione simulatorem, quem εἴρων Graeci nominarunt, Socratem accepimus, contra Pythagoram et Periclem summam auctoritatem consecutos sine ulla hilaritate." Translation of "festivique sermonis atque in omni oratione simulatorem" as "a genial conversationalist in his every speech" is borrowed from Walter Miller's translation. See Cicero, *De Officiis* (trans. W. Miller; London: William Heinemann LTD, 1928), 111.
106. Thompson, *The Dry Mock*.
107. Jakob Jónsson, *Humor and Irony in the New Testament Illuminated by Parallels in Talmud and Midrash* (Reykjavik: Bókaútgáfa Menningarsjóts, 1965).
108. Kenneth Burke, *A Grammar of Motives* (2d ed.1955; repr., Berkeley: University of California Press, 1969).
109. Candace D. Lang, *Irony/Humor: Critical Paradigms* (Baltimore: Johns Hopkins University Press, 1988).
110. In opposition, scholar Jerry C. Hoggatt, *Irony in Mark's Gospel: Text and Subtext* (New York: Cambridge University Press, 1992), 2–3 especially criticizes Jónsson's obsessive attention to the humor of Jesus, saying it entirely misses the obvious ironies within Jesus' story.

constitutive element of motive and a synonym for comedy. These scholars, including Burke, do not expound on the historical link between irony and humor on which they rely as an essential constituent of irony. It seems, however, likely that the traditional use of irony within the Old Greek Comedy and its use in Cicero, who treats irony as a part of the general theory of the laughable[111] and as one of six main divisions of wit,[112] serve as the primary sources for explaining an etiological relation between irony and humor.

Cicero treats irony in his orations in nearly all its varieties, ranging from bitter sarcasm and invective to light and playful irony. The attention that Cicero shows in his dealing with irony characterizes it as the literary technique that the orator can use masterfully in diverse literary contexts with manifold rhetorical purposes. Beyond his echoing of Aristotle's appropriation of irony being fitting to a freeman's jest,[113] Cicero ties this favorable estimation of irony directly and exclusively to Socrates, something Aristotle avoided in order to preserve his doctrine of "the mean." It is worth noting that the negativity commonly attached to εἰρωνεία by the earlier Greeks seems to disappear in the time of Cicero and instead, a full grown admiration of εἰρωνεία in its association to Socrates comes to the fore. It is clear in the following remark of Cicero:

> *Urbana dissimulatio* is when words are spoken in contrast to their meanings (*cum alia dicuntur ac sentias*) . . . Fannius in his "Annals" reports that Africanus, the one called Aemilianus was distinguished in this kind of speech, and describes him by the Greek word, εἴρων, but upon the evidence of those who know these matters better than I do, I opine that Socrates far surpassed all others for accomplished wit in this strain of irony or assumed simplicity. This is a sort of humor and is blended with seriousness, and is suited to public oration as well as to the speech of gentlemen.[114]

Certainly, Cicero's *ironia* has a very different tone from the Greek, εἰρωνεία. As Vlastos puts it, "Laundered and deodorized, it now betokens the height of urbanity, elegance, and good taste."[115] Cicero not only redeems irony from

---

111. Cicero, *De or.*, II.liii.216–II.lxxi.290.

112. Ibid., II.Lxvi.264–II.lxxi.290.

113. Aristotle, *Rhet.* III.xviii.7.

114. Cicero, *De or.*, II.lxvii.269–70, "urbana etiam dissimulatio est, cum alia dicuntur ac sentias . . . in hoc genere Fannius in Annalibus suis Africanum hunc Aemilianum dicit fuisse egregium et Graeco eum verbo appellat εἴρωνα: sed, uti ferunt qui melius haec norunt, Socratem opinor in hac ironia dissimulantiaque longe lepore et humanitate omnibus praestitisse. Genus est perelegans et cum gravitate salsum, cumque oratoriis dictionibus tum urbanis sermonibus accommodatum." Translation is mine.

its connotations of abuse and mockery, but also upgrades it to a very unique position as *urbana dissimulatio* of *homo ingenuus*.[116] For him, irony is not any more a form of deception, but a courteous, sophisticated, and clever manner of speaking, part of a rhetorical strategy which aims at a particular effect. It seems evident that Cicero's refined concept of irony was clearly related to his deep conviction that Socrates was a great philosopher and teacher,[117] a man of remarkable ethics,[118] a brilliant dialectician with profound meaning in every word,[119] and a man of great and godlike virtues.[120]

It is truly Cicero who changed the course of the criticism of irony, not only by providing εἰρωνεία with a specific definition that the Greeks did not, but also by making frequent use of irony as a figure of thought in his own orations.[121] He indulges in ironically assumed simplicity—*urbana dissiumlatio*—affecting ignorance or lack of ability,[122] of which he deems Socrates the prototype.[123] Thus, he furbishes εἰρωνεία with a new mask as something noble and effective which reflects the ironist's inner motive. His frequent employment of irony in parallel with the former use of Socrates, the renowned yet controversial philosopher and rhetorician, helped to restore to irony a positive value based on its rhetorical quality. Furthermore, with Cicero we also see a significant development of the concept of irony, moving from irony of speech to irony of manner. This tendency we can observe earlier in Plato when he mentions irony as a constituent of Socrates' character.[124] This alludes to Plato's perception that Socrates' characteristic use of ironic speech would originate from a deeper origin, his ironic lifestyle.[125] Aristotle also describes irony as both a verbal device and a character trait. Surpassing the

---

115. Vlastos, "Socratic Irony," 84.

116. Cicero, *De or.*, I.xxx.137. *Homo ingenuus* means a free-born man, often interpreted as a noble man.

117. Cicero, *Off.*, II.xii.43.

118. Ibid., III.iii.11, III.xix.77.

119. Ibid., I.xxx.108.

120. Ibid., I.xli.148.

121. Cicero, *In Verrem*, I.32, IV.116, VII.15. Burke, *A Grammar of Motives*, 65 points out that irony easily shifts from rhetoric to poetic because it shares a peculiar interweaving form of style and thought of figures which requires an audience to move through structured patterns of inference in interpreting what the speaker says.

122. See both Cicero, *Pro Caecina*, VII.32, "I, inexperience in the law, unskilled in the business of litigation...wish to be your pupil in this matter" (*ego homo imperitus iuris, ignarus negotiorum ac litium.... te uti in hac re magistro volo*) and Cicero, *Verr.*, V.159, "my eloquence, which is not significant" (*mea eloguentia, quae nulla est*). Translation is mine.

123. Cicero, *Academicae quaestiones*, II.16.

124. Plato, *Apol.*, 38a; *Resp.*, I.337a; *Symp.*, 216e.

insights of these two, Cicero is more fully aware of an inevitable link between the irony of speech and the irony of manner exemplified by Socrates since for Cicero, Socrates, the εἴρων whom the Greeks called such, was a *dissimulator* who conducted himself in the manner of *urbana dissimulatio* which is worthy of *homo ingenuus* (a man of nobility).

V. QUINTILIAN (C. 35–95 CE)

Of all the ancients, Quintilian produced the most thorough work on irony. He goes further than Cicero, paying attention more to the literary dimension of irony as a specific figure of speech. Quintilian polishes several aspects of irony discussed by his predecessors, especially Cicero, and amplifies them to more full expression.

As we previously examined, both Aristotle and Cicero characterized irony in association with jest or wit.[126] In his textbook on rhetoric, *Institutio oratoria*, Quintilian also mentions *ironia* when speaking of wit and jests: "What is irony (*ironia*)? Is not this even a kind of joke (*iocus*) which is in the weightiest form?"[127] Quintilian conveys that the whole principle of witty speech consists in expressing things in a way other than the direct and factual one.[128] Yet, he carefully warns that the user of irony as a type of wit must avoid the ultimate ambiguity (*ambiguitas*)[129] as well as incomprehensibility, which the Greeks call σκότισον (darken)[130] because irony, to some extent, carries with it an intended obscurity for a specific rhetorical effect. Therefore, Quintilian means *ironia* to be a controlled, as well as an intelligible, rhetorical device carefully thought out by the ironist.

---

125. Vlastos, "Socratic Irony," 84–85 argues that Socrates himself lifted εἰρωνεία out of the gutter of deceit and made it an acceptable mode of life.

126. Aristotle, *Rhet.*, III.xviii.7; Cicero, *De or.*, II.liv.218.

127. Quintilian, *Inst.*, 6.3.68, "quid ironia? nonne etiam quae severissime fit ioci paene genus est?" Translation is mine.

128. Ibid., 6.3.89.

129. Ibid., 8.2.16. In the same vein, Dane, *Mythology of Irony*, 66 says that "irony is the authoritative solution to the ambiguous text."

130. Quintilian, *Inst.*, 8.2.18, "some even labor for this vice; nor is it a new vice, for I find already in Titus Livy that there was once an instructor who commended his pupils to obscure what they were saying, using the Greek word *skotison*" (in hoc malum a quibusdam etiam laboratur: neque id novum vitium est, cum iam apud Titum Livium inveniam fuisse praeceptorem aliquem qui discipulos obscurare quae dicerent iuberet, Graeco verbo utens σκότισον). Translation is mine. Σκότισον is the first aorist imperative second person singular (cf. λύσον). Its stem is σκότις and its aorist indicative is ἐσκότισα.

Quintilian prefers the term *ironia*, replacing the Greek εἰρωνεία, and employs it with greater frequency[131] than *dissimulatio*. In *Institutio oratoria*, we can find only one explicit occasion where *dissimulatio* is singly used as a designation for irony.[132] Based on these textual evidences, it seems that in the time of Quintilian, *ironia* became the preferred term for the Greek εἰρωνεία.

Quintilian's discussion of irony is primarily delivered as a part of his well referenced theorization of tropes (*tropi*) and figures (*schemata*). Quintilian especially dedicates book nine (*liber nonus*) of *Institutio oratoria* for the distinction between tropes and figures, which was not clearly made in earlier theory but by the time of Quintilian was well-established. If tropes are unnatural uses of words, figures are unnatural configurations of words or turns of thought. In his own words, a trope is language transferred from its natural and principal meaning to another for the sake of elegance in refined speech.[133] A figure, on the one hand, is a configuration of certain words distinct from the common and chiefly obvious form.[134] In the same book nine of *Institutio oratoria*, Quintilian not only devotes the section 9.2.44-51 to a focused treatment of irony as a figure, but also attempts on several occasions to give it a definition. According to him, irony is generally "saying one thing and meaning the opposite,"[135] a definition that is still referred to today. In other places, essentially the same concept of irony is reiterated with a slight variance, as saying something different from what it means (*aliud dicit ac sentit*) or indicating one thing by alluding to another (*per aliam rem alia indicetur*).[136]

Although Quintilian considers εἰρωνεία primarily as a figure of thought[137] which is not very different in its generic character from a trope, for him, *ironia* is uniquely both a trope (*tropos*) and a figure (*schema* or *figura*) not like other tropes such as metaphor, metonymy, antonomasia, metalepsis, synecdoche, catachresis, allegory or hyperbole.[138] Irony is a trope because it says something different

---

131. Ibid., 6.3.68, 91; 8.6.54–56; 9.1.3, 7; 9.2.44–53; 9.2.65, 97.

132. Ibid., 9.2.44.

133. Ibid., 9.1.4, "tropos sermo a natruali et principali significatione tralatus ad aliam ornandae orationis gratia."

134. Ibid., 9.1.4–5, "figura conformatio quaedam orationis remota a compmuni et primum se offerente ratione."

135. Ibid., 9.2.44, "contrarium ei quod dicitur intelligendum est." Ibid., 6.2.15 says, "Irony, which asks to be understood in a sense other than that of the actual words" (εἰρωνεία *quae diversum ei quod dicit intellectum petit*). Translation is mine.

136. Ibid., 9.2.45; 9.2.97.

137. Ibid., 9.1.3, "Irony is found both among figures of thought and among tropes" (*ironia tam inter figuras sententiae quam inter tropos reperiatur*). Translation is mine.

from what it means through the technique of substituting words for words, and it is also a figure because it intends the whole meaning in a configuration of language that is neither expected nor ordinary. Thus, whereas a trope reveals the contrast existing between words and meaning, a figure can cover whole passages and the entire shape of the subject matter.[139] As seen together, by examining irony in the distinction between a trope and a figure, Quintilian not only provides more literary dimension to irony but also expands the scope of irony as had never been attempted before.

In addition to describing irony in literary terms, Quintilian treats the question of how irony is perceived, that is, how the interaction of the text, speaker, and audience are all essential to interpreting irony. He notes that there exists a close relation between irony and life which exemplified in the life of Socrates: " . . . a man's whole life (*vita universa*) may appear to hold irony (*ironia*) as was the case with Socrates. For he was called an ironist (εἴρων) because he assumed the role of an ignorant man in marvel at the wisdom of others."[140] For both Cicero and Quintilian, but more so for the latter, Socrates occupies the exemplary status as the epitome of the εἴρων. As we previously observed through the reports of Plato, Socrates' life as εἴρων elicited opposition from the Athenians. According to Quintilian, the ironic trope can be readily understood by all. However, the audience can misconstrue the figure, especially when the figure applies to irony as a mode of life. In this regard, as Plato reports, the fellow Athenians of Socrates provide a classic example of those who failed to understand irony as a figure (*schema*) portraying the life of the ironist.[141] Therefore *ironia*, traditionally known to Quintilian in its close association with Socrates, a great orator[142] and a morally superior philosopher,[143] comes to be both a mark of literary quality and moral quality as well. Likewise, we suspect an inseparable relation between irony and an entire moral being.[144]

---

138. Ibid., 9.1.4–5.
139. Ibid., 9.2.46.
140. Ibid., 9.2.46, " . . . cum etiam vita universa ironiam habere videatur, quails est visa Socratis nam ideo dictus εἴρων, agens impertium et admiratorem aliorum tamquam sapientium." Translation is mine.
141. Dane, *Mythology of Irony*, 51 notes that "the irony of an entire life" is a dangerous challenge to those forced to judge it.
142. Quintilian, *Inst.*, 1.11.17; 5.11.3; 10.1.83
143. Ibid., 8.4.23; 10.1.35
144. Ibid., *Prooemium* 9, "We educate the perfect orator, who cannot be except in the person of a good man. Therefore, we demand of him not only outstanding ability of speech, but all the virtues of character as well" (*oratorem autem instituimus illum perfectum, qui esse nisi vir bonus non potest, ideoque non dicendi modo eximiam in eo facultatem sed omnis animi virtutes exigimus*). Translation is mine.

At last, passing through the generations of Cicero and Quintilian, the two great Roman rhetoricians, it appears that a long-lived derision of irony as "deception" or "pretended modesty" characterized thus in Aristotle's *Ethica nichomachea*,[145] disappears, or at least is significantly minimized. This phenomenon is primarily indebted to Quintilian's view of *ironia* as the literary-rhetorical device operative on the ironist's sophistication and decent life.

Irony in the Middle Ages and the Renaissance

In large part, the discussion of irony during the Middle Ages and the Renaissance[146] was a recapitulation of the theories established in classical antiquity.[147] *Ironia* for this period is "well circumscribed in meaning."[148] The concept of *ironia* retained its connection to Socrates to some degree during the Middle Ages but more vigorously at the time of Renaissance,[149] for this age upheld Socrates as an exemplar of moral and philosophical virtue.[150] Also, the rhetorical perspectives of both Cicero and Quintilian on irony reigned for many years due to the way they were revered during the Middle Ages and the Renaissance.[151]

The medieval perspective on *ironia* was exclusively confined to categories of the figure or trope.[152] In this period, the rhetorical irony as a figure of speech was most favored.[153] The derogatory, pejorative senses of *ironia* derived from classical Greek εἰρωνεία were principally forgotten.[154] The representative

---

145. Aristotle, *Eth. nic.*, II.vii.9–II.vii.13.

146. For the study of irony, Dilwyn Knox, *Ironia*, 1 defines the terms Middle Ages and Renaissance "as no more than convenient means of denoting the periods 600–1350/1400 and 1350/1400–1600 respectively."

147. Elleström, *Divine Madness*, 17.

148. Knox, *Ironia*, 1. Further, as the only significant exception to the well-defined notion of *ironia* in the Middle Ages, Knox, ibid., 140–41 suggests Aristotle's definition of εἰρωνεία is self-deprecation. He adds that "although Aristotle's term was transliterated as *yronia*, *ironia* or in some similar manner, it was only very rarely confused with *ironia* as a figure or trope and the two meanings were only mentioned together to be distinguished."

149. Ibid., 97–101 writes that classical and Renaissance authors often associated *ironia* with Socrates in contrast to the decline of *ironia socratica* (Socratic irony) during the Latin Middle Ages.

150. Dane, *Mythology of Irony*, 1.

151. D. Knox, *Ironia*, 2, 98–100.

152. As an early source of the Middle Ages, the venerable Bede (*Beda Venerabilis*, c. 672–735 CE), a medieval Benedictine monk known for his work, *Historia ecclesiastica gentis Anglorum*, defines *ironia* as "a trope showing what it intends through its opposite (*ironia est tropus per contrarium quod conatur ostendens*)" in *Corpus Christianorum Series Latina*. CXXIIIA (Turnhout: Brepols, 1954), 162

153. D. Knox, *Ironia*, 38, 141.

intellect of the early medieval age, Isidore (c. 560–636 CE), Archbishop of Seville, considered irony both a trope and a figure as Quintilian previously suggested, and places *ironia*[155] as a subcategory of *allegoria*,[156] whose Greek root, ἀλληγορία (its verb ἀλληγορέω) is a combination between ἄλλος (another; ὁ ἄλλος the other) and ἀγορεύειν (to say, mention, proclaim). This connection between irony and allegory is not new. Quintilian also listed both *ironia* and *allegoria* (also translated in Latin as *inversio*)[157] among the tropes which are the artistic alteration of a word or phrase from its proper meaning to another.[158] Quintilian considers *inveriso*, which brings about a different intention of the speaker from what he actually says, to be an element of irony.[159]

One important difference between the earlier writers and those of the medieval age is the latter's particular *weltanschauung*. Edmond Reiss considers that irony may be the most meaningful term for describing the nature of medieval literature and that irony encapsulates the Middle Ages' perception of reality.[160] Furthermore, according to him medieval irony is a by-product of the Christian worldview of the Middle Ages, which is inherent to the Christian context itself.[161] Medieval irony carries theological characteristics marked by faith, hope, and reconciliation, referring to the relationship between three major realities: God, man, and nature. It seems that during the Middle Ages and the Renaissance, the ethical bearings and the rhetorical meanings of irony, expounded by the Greeks and the Romans respectively, embrace another dimension of irony: its religious aspect. Irony before and after the Middle Ages often pertains to negative and uncertain ideas, highlighting *discordia* (discord) and playing with *ambiguum* (ambiguity). Medieval irony, however, assumes the existence of norms governed by the ubiquitous God who has the power of bringing in the opposite. Just as God puts the elements of contradiction into harmony, the medieval artists and writers with ironic tastes enjoy imitating God

---

154. Ibid., 139–140. Knox notes that he found the only exception in the work of Liutprandus (c. 920–972 CE, a bishop of Cremona) interpreting "εἰρωνικοῶς" as "dissemblingly."

155. Isidore, *Etymologiae*, I.xxvii.28 attests to the earlier use of the common medieval spellings *yronia* and *hyronia* which Renaissance authors gradually disregarded.

156. Ibid., I.xxxvii.22–23, II.xxi.4. Yet, Angus Fletcher, *Allegory: the Theory of a Symbolic Mode* (Ithaca: Cornell University Press, 1964), 229–30 notes that the typical understanding of medieval rhetoricians, which reduced irony to its intimate association with allegory, has been denounced by modern scholars as an oversimplification.

157. Quintilian, *Inst.*, 8.6.44, 54.

158. Ibid., 8.6.1.

159. Ibid., 8.6.54.

160. Edmond Reiss, "Medieval Irony," *JHI* 42 (1981): 221.

161. Ibid., 211.

by juxtaposing, contrasting, synthesizing and interconnecting the opposites, which are the raw materials of irony.[162]

If the Middle Ages show rather less interest in Socrates as an ironic being, the Renaissance rediscovered Socrates as a central figure in the discussion of irony. Renaissance authors expanded the medieval notion of *ironia*, the figure or trope, by introducing *ironia socratica* (Socratic irony). Drawn from texts like Cicero's *De oratore* and Quintilian's *Institutio oratoria*, Renaissance authors understood irony as a sort of enigmatic humor and wit in relation to Socrates.[163] However, not everybody held it in high esteem because some claimed it to be boastful and mocking and not at all modest. Therefore, Desiderius Erasmus of Rotterdam (c. 1466–1536 CE), a Dutch theologian, humanist, and classicist who wrote in a "pure" Latin style, warned preachers to use *ironia* as a figure (or trope) sparingly or not to use it at all.[164]

The Concept of Irony in the Modern Age

During modern times, the interest in and study of irony have experienced a radical growth and expansion. David Kaufer states that "in the eighteenth century, the concept of irony was transfigured almost beyond recognition."[165] In fact, by the end of the eighteenth century, irony became a grand Hegelian concept connected to the evolutionary view of history and dialecticism, and most distinctively in relation to Romanticism. While from Roman times through the Middle Ages down to the middle of the eighteenth century irony was generally known as a rhetorical trope, during the late eighteenth and early nineteenth centuries in Germany, the concept of irony gained new and global meaning under the influence of Romantic thinkers.

The discussion of irony in the eighteenth century must begin with the work of a classicist and critic of irony, John Connop Thirlwall. He marked the modern age of irony by ushering in a new aspect not highlighted before. In a critical work on Sophoclean irony (1833),[166] he brought noteworthy

---

162. The best known medieval writers who employed irony in their works are Valla, Erasmus, Ariosto, Machiavelli, Boethius, Chrétien, Gottfried, Dante, Boccacio, Chaucer, Nicolaus de Bibera, and Sansovino. Sometimes *ironia* was noted in quite unexpected sources such as the Vulgate.

163. D. Knox, *Ironia*, 141.

164. Erasmus, *Ecclesiastes* V, 995 advises preachers to use *ironia* sensibly. We can find an earlier trace of the less receptive attitude toward irony in the thirteenth century in St. Thomas Aquinas's description of irony as a "vice" which "consists in belittling oneself." See Thomas Aquinas, "Question CXIII: Of Irony," in *Summa Theologica* (2d ed., trans. Fathers of the English Dominican Province; London: Burns Oates & Washbourne, 1935), 114.

165. Kaufer, "Irony and Rhetorical Strategy," 91.

attention to the understanding of irony as more than a verbal and behavioral mode in its adherence to comedy and to Socrates. Instead, Thirlwall paid more attention to the ironic event. As a result, he broadened the horizons of irony to incorporate a wider range of literary genres by including tragedy. Also, Garnett G. Sedgewick, who benefited from the work of Thirlwall, focused attention on the use of irony in tragedy by pointing out that irony has a clearer edge in tragedy than in comedy.[167]

In his study on "Sophoclean irony," Thirlwall formulated three labels for irony—"Sophoclean," "tragic," and "dramatic,"—which are received as synonyms. Historically, this seems to be the first application of these terms to irony.[168] This is why he is appropriately called the father of "tragic" as well as of "dramatic" irony. Furthermore, Thirlwall's contribution has led scholars to pay attention to the work of individual authors and to each author's particular use of irony as a literary technique. Due to Thirlwall's distinctive emphasis on Sophoclean drama, the literary critics of irony began to compare Sophocles' own ironic style to that of other tragedians such as Aeschylus and Euripides.[169]

As one moves farther into the nineteenth century, the definition of irony becomes murkier, corresponding to the expansion and experimentation with irony made especially by critics of a German Romantic background. Romanticism is the artistic, literary, and intellectual movement originating in Germany and England in the 1770s, which, by the 1820s, had swept throughout Europe. Romanticism refers to groups of people like artists, poets, writers, philosophers, politicians and social thinkers, as well as trends of the late eighteenth and early nineteenth centuries in Western Europe. This movement stressed strong emotion as a source of aesthetic experience, particularly the experience of wonder at the sublimity of undomesticated nature. It was a reaction against aristocratic, social, and political norms of the Enlightenment as well as against the scientific rationalization of art, literature, and nature. Accordingly, Sedgewick summarizes the transformation of irony by Romantics

---

166. John Connop Thirlwall, "On the Irony of Sophocles" (Philological Museum 2; repr., Geneva, New York: Hobart & William Smith Colleges, 1973), 483–537.

167. Sedgewick, *Of Irony*, 27.

168. Ibid., 22.

169. See Elder Olson, *Tragedy and the Theory of Drama* (Detroit: Wayne State University Press, 1961); States, *Irony and Drama*; Philip H. Vellacott, *Ironic Drama: A Study of Euripides' Method and Meaning* (New York: Cambridge University Press, 1975). The appreciation of irony based on the individual author's work is not limited to tragedy but also to comedy. Additionally, the most sought after authors for modern critics of irony encompass a wide range of writers including Shakespeare, Molière, Shaw, Goethe, Ibsen, Swift, Fielding and Paul de Man.

by saying that irony was not simply an artificial device of an author-speaker, but a "spiritual freedom viewing contradictions in the spectacle of life."[170]

Under the influence of Romanticism, the concept of irony made the remarkable jump from a literary device employed by an author to the way of life[171] or consciousness of both the world and men.[172] The efforts of classical authors to define irony in relation to comedy and Socrates are still taken as the authoritative foundation. Yet, attempts of the modern literary critics to define irony broadly in relation to life and world have resulted in what Haakon Chevalier characterized as "ages of irony"[173] and what W. C. Booth diagnosed as the "imperialistic expansion of irony."[174] Booth laments over the uncontrolled proliferation of irony in our time which has gone beyond repair:

> My first temptation was to conduct a requiem, or perhaps more accurately, a simple funeral, lamenting the disappearance into meaninglessness of a once-useful concept. Of course the word "requiem" would express a forlorn hope that there might be a resurrection after all, that we might, by taking thought, understand both why irony has proved to be such an imperialistic term and how we might use it, and talk about it, without making fools of ourselves.[175]

Before the eighteenth century, as we have seen in Quintilian's theory of rhetoric, irony was one rhetorical device among many with the focus on its explicit verbal form. It was readily understood as one of the rhetorical tropes. Yet, by the end of eighteenth century, it had expanded to become Karl Solger's principle of aestheticism—irony as the very principle of art—and a chief Hegelian concept for the dialectic evolution of history. While for Karl Solger (1780–1819), who is known as a theorist of Romanticism and irony, irony is

---

170. Sedgewick, *Of Irony*, 18.

171. Muecke, *Compass*, 235. Also, Thomson, *Irony*, 1, 14, views "irony as a criticism of life, hard to define as poetry."

172. Claudette Kemper, "Irony Anew, with Occasional Reference to Byron and Browning," *SEL*, 1500–1900, 7 (1967): 705 says irony as "the *schema*, attitude, or world view continues to be neglected in studies of literature in English." Further, Alan Wilde, *Horizons of Assent: Modernism, Postmodernism, and the Ironic Imagination* (Baltimore: Johns Hopkins University Press, 1981), 2 explains irony as a modern way of thinking: a "mode of consciousness, a perceptual response to a world without unity or cohesion."

173. Haakon Chevalier, *The Ironic Temper: Anatole France and His Time* (New York: Oxford University Press, 1932), 10.

174. Booth, *Rhetoric*, 140.

175. Booth, "The Empire of Irony," 723.

purely an aesthetic concept,[176] for German idealist Georg Hegel (1770–1831) and especially, Danish critic and philosopher Søren Kierkegaard (1813–1855), it is understood as a moral concept.[177] It is known that there are complex relations between the philosophies of Hegel and Kierkegaard,[178] and when it comes to irony some twin-like similarities exit. Hegel bestows a unique philosophical stamp on the idea of irony. For him, the characteristic tension of irony is the center of all phenomena.[179] While Hegel perceives irony as a key ingredient of life and cosmos, Kierkegaard takes it as a synonym for Romanticism, and even as an essential attribute of God.[180] In 1841, Kierkegaard presented his doctoral dissertation on irony to the University of Copenhagen. In his dissertation, *The Concept of Irony with Continual Reference to Socrates*, he provided a profound, scholarly, but mystical evaluation of irony. The dissertation depicts the inseparable relation between German Romanticism and irony, which becomes evident in his own remark, "throughout the whole discussion I use the term 'irony' and 'ironist'; I could just as well as 'romanticism' and 'romanticist.' "[181]

Booth notes that thinkers in the modern period promote the idea of the ironic nature of the cosmos and notices that there is "a striking parallel between traditional God-language and modern irony-language."[182] Likewise, Muecke explains that a noticeable tendency of modern critics of irony is to treat irony as something like a black hole. Muecke considers that such an attitude has its root in the German Romantic ironists, who invested irony with ultimate freedom, yet destructive power. He says that

---

176. Søren Kierkegaard, *The Concept of Irony with Constant Reference to Socrates* (trans. Lee M. Capel; Bloomington: Indiana University Press, 1965), 331 describes Solger as the "spokesman for romanticism and romantic irony." Also, Dane, *Mythology of Irony*, 75 calls Solger the "aesthetician of the romantic school."

177. Kierkegaard is considered to be the founder of the modern concept of irony. Dane, *Mythology of Irony*, 8 notes that Kierkegaard's study on irony, *The Concept of Irony with Constant Reference to Socrates*, has served as a starting point for many twentieth century studies of irony.

178. The standard view on the subject is that Kierkegaard criticized Hegel's philosophy with contempt. However, a recent study, Jon Stewart, *Kierkegaard's Relations to Hegel Reconsidered* (New York: Cambridge University Press, 2003), shows that Kierkegaard's criticism was not of Hegel but of a number of contemporary Danish Hegelians.

179. Hegel, *Hegel's Lectures on the History of Philosophy*, trans. E. S. Haldane (New York: The Humanities Press, 1955), 400.

180. Muecke, *Compass*, 246 critically attributes Kierkegaard's subordination of irony to the ethical and the religious to Kierkegaard's "commitment as a Christian to a closed-world ideology."

181. Kierkegaard, *The Concept of Irony with Continual Reference to Socrates*, 275.

182. Booth, "The Empire of Irony," 737.

> The German Romantic ironists were on occasion inclined to exult in the freedom that irony gave them to soar above the earth, that "dim spot that mortals call the world." But some later explorers and exploiters of this free space were to find out that "above" and "below" became less and less meaningful and they began to wonder whether the infinite heavens were not after all only the bottomless pit, and whether the archetypal ironist were not the Devil instead of God . . . but whether irony, taken far enough, necessarily ends in nihilism and world-destruction is a matter for argument.[183]

Irony of the twentieth century emerged as "romantic irony" or "new critical irony" under the continuing influence of Romanticism and a new literary trend, "New Criticism."[184] New Criticism was an important trend in English and American literary criticism of the mid-twentieth century, from the 1920s to the early 1960s.[185] New Critics took "ambiguity," which is also called "overdetermination,"[186] as an important concept and emphasized the multiple meanings concurrently present in language. Methodologically, New Criticism focused on explication or "close reading"[187] of the work itself and rejected historicism's attention to extra-textual sources such as biography and sociological evidence. Irony in this generation became the distinguishing norm of most literature,[188] a critical mark of all good literature and a way of life.[189] New Critics like Cleanth Brooks asserted that all good literature must have irony[190] and J. A. K. Thomson suggested treating irony as one treats poetry.[191]

It is reasonable to say that twentieth century romantic irony is extremely versatile and existentialistic. Romantic irony is something like the self-conscious attitude of the artist towards his artistic work. It features the ironist's creative subjectivity as comparable to meditation. For this reason, Kierkegaard

---

183. Muecke, *Compass*, 229–30.

184. The movement, New Criticism, received its name from the publication of John Crowe Ransom's book *The New Criticism* (Norfolk: New Directions, 1941).

185. See M. H. Abrams, *A Glossary of Literary Terms*, 4th ed. 4th ed. (New York: Holt, Rinehart & Winston, 1991), 246–48.

186. I. A. Richards, *The Philosophy of Rhetoric* (New York: Oxford University Press, 1936), 39 borrows Sigmund Freud's term, "overdetermination," sometimes translated as "ambiguities," to refer to the multiple meanings which he believed were always simultaneously present in language.

187. Abrams, *A Glossary of Literary Terms*, 247.

188. Dane, *Mythology of Irony*, 121.

189. Booth, *Rhetoric*, 176.

190. Cleanth Brooks, "Irony and 'Ironic' Poetry," *College English* 9 (1948): 231–37.

191. Thomson, *Irony*, 2.

characterizes the activity of irony as "egoistical."[192] When Booth speaks about the "imperialistic expansion of irony," an appropriate characterization of the modern discussion of irony, he means that modern criticism of irony not only has embraced "disagreements multiplied beyond a given point"[193] but also has fed on the chaotic results of this multiplication almost to "the point of speculative suicide"[194] which ends in ironic corrosion dissolving all meanings into the one supreme meaning: "no meaning!"[195] This seems to be an inevitable outcome of the influence of Hegel, specifically his characterization of irony in terms of "subjectivity" (*subjektivität*),[196] and "infinite absolute negativity" (*unendliche absolute negativität*).[197] It is a fair assessment to make that the study of irony espoused by the romanticists is an entirely different entity from earlier discussions on the subject because they juggle with irony until the word loses its meaning and turn it into something unrecognizable. This radically different nature of modern irony is characterized by Alan R. Thompson as an escape

---

192. Kierkegaard, *The Concept of Irony with Continual Reference to Socrates*, 431.

193. Booth, *Rhetoric*, 133.

194. Ibid. Booth notes that "modern criticism has multiplied contradictions, and modern theory has been led to dwell upon the chaotic results almost to the point of speculative suicide. Disagreements multiplied beyond a given point cannot help suggesting that there is no art of interpretation—only a game of competing improvisations. The critic with the most persuasive style wins, because there are after all no rules imposed by 'the work itself,' and there is no referee." Further, in "The Empire of Irony," 735, Booth quotes Kenneth Burke's saying that "whatever I *think* I say turns out to mean something else, because 'I' am really an indeterminate 'we,' . . . every human statement is, for Burke, necessarily 'ironic,' when viewed from any rival, incongruous perspective." Burke (1897–1993) is a major American theorist and philosopher whose primary interests are rhetoric and aesthetics.

195. Booth, *Rhetoric*, 93.

196. Kierkegaard, *The Concept of Irony with Continual Reference to Socrates*, 242, 264 consider irony to be a "qualification of subjectivity" and comments that Hegel is the master who theorizes subjectivity of irony. He writes that "whereas the first form of irony was not combated but was pacified by subjectivity as it obtained its rights, the second form of irony was combated and destroyed, for inasmuch as subjective was unauthorized it could obtain its rights only by being annulled." Muecke, *Compass*, 242 notes that "Kierkegaard saw Romantic Irony as a dissolution of objectivity in the interest of a preservation of subjectivity, a process which involves in the end the reduction of all reality to the bare self-consciousness of the completely bored ironist." Further, Muecke expresses his conviction that Kierkegaard has misrepresented Romantic irony as essentially negative and destructive which is far different from Romantic irony in Friedrich Schlegel's perspective.

197. Kierkegaard, *The Concept of Irony with Continual Reference to Socrates,* 261 and note 128 of page 486. In fact, both phrases are borrowed by Kierkegaard from the lectures of Hegel on aesthetics.

from responsibility.[198] David Worcester compares it to a drug habit, saying "irony offers an escape from mental pain as morphine."[199]

The radical expansion of irony since Romanticism shows itself not only in disagreement over the definition of irony but also over basic categories and the respective concept for each category.[200] Even the varied use of nomenclature employed by critics to classify irony attests to the abnormally overgrown concept of irony and the genuine difficulty inherent in identifying it. For example, verbal irony is variously referred to as irony of speech, rhetorical irony, dialectic irony[201] or linguistic irony.[202] Character irony is termed Socratic irony,[203] irony of character[204] or irony of manner (that is, behavioral irony).[205] Dramatic irony is labeled situational irony, Sophoclean irony,[206] tragic irony,[207] practical irony,[208] irony of fate (irony of events),[209] irony of simple incongruity,

---

198. Thompson, *The Dry Mock*, 256. In a similar fashion, Muecke, *Compass*, 236 describes "irony as a means of avoiding decisions in situations in which a decision is either impossible or clearly unwise is, though self-protective, usually heuristic as well."

199. Worcester, *Satire*, 141–42.

200. For example, the following are various definitions made by several key critics with regard to dramatic irony or situational irony. While Thomson, *Irony*, 35 and Thompson, *The Dry Mock*, 29 describe dramatic irony in much the same terms used for verbal irony, Sedgewick, *Of Irony*, 49 and Muecke, *Compass*, 61–63, 92 explain it as the sense of contradiction felt by spectators of a drama who see the character acting in ignorance of his condition. Furthermore, Paul D. Duke, *Irony in the Fourth Gospel* (Atlanta: John Knox, 1985), 26 and Dorothy Jean Weaver, "Power and Powerlessness: Matthew's Use of Irony in the Portrayal of Political Leaders," *SBL* 31 (1992): 454–66 distinguish dramatic irony from situational irony, although Richard G. Moulton, *The Moral System of Shakespeare* (London: The Macmillan Company, 1903), 209–10 and Sedgewick, *Of Irony*, 48–49 define them as one and the same. It seems that under the influence of Thirlwall, most of these scholars, especially Sedgewick, chiefly consider dramatic irony as an irony that occurs on the stage. Sedgewick, ibid., 49 says that "my belief, or perhaps my delusion, is that these conceptions (regarding dramatic irony) are extraordinarily fruitful in the study of drama—fruitful in ways that have been neglected. And the more distinguished the drama is, the more fruitful the idea of dramatic irony becomes." However, this is a rather narrow understanding because it has been proven that other genres of literature also contain this type of irony. In this regard, Dane, *Mythology of Irony*, 121 correctly says that dramatic irony can mean not only "an irony pertaining to drama" but also "a dramatic form of irony."

201. Thirlwall, "On the Irony of Sophocles," 484.

202. Ronald Tanaka, "The Concept of Irony: Theory and Practice," *JLS* 2 (1973): 46.

203. Vlastos, "Socratic Irony," 79–97. Especially in page 86, Vlastos calls "Socratic irony" a "complex irony." According to him. in "complex" irony what is said both is and is not what is meant in contrast to "simple" irony in which what is said is simply not what is meant.

204. Thompson, *The Dry Mock*, 7–8.

205. Ibid.

206. Thirlwall, "On the Irony of Sophocles," 383, 494.

207. Ibid., 483, 493–94, 536–37.

irony of self-betrayal or irony of dilemma.²¹⁰ In addition to these, more classifications have sprung from the pens of various scholars.²¹¹ The fact that the forms and definitions of irony vary widely indicates a noticeable weakness in current scholarship. This present condition calls for a normative work, to bring together the variety of perspectives which have resulted from the critics' synchronic-individualistic reception of irony.²¹² This is an ongoing need within the study of irony.

It seems clear that a distinguishing characteristic defining the history of the concept of irony in modern times is closely related to the shifts and trends of the

---

208. Ibid., 485–87.

209. Thompson, *The Dry Mock*, 29–30 and Muecke, *Compass*, 44, 102–4. Yet, Muecke tries to subtly differentiate between dramatic irony and irony of events based on their effects. On page 105, he writes that "the difference between the effect of Dramatic Irony and the effect of Irony of Events resembles the difference between suspense and surprise."

210. Muecke, ibid., 99–113 places irony of simple incongruity, irony of events, dramatic irony, irony of self-betrayal, and irony of dilemma under the same category as irony that occur in "ironic situations."

211. Glenn S. Holland, *Divine Irony* (London: Associated University Presses, 2000),54 speaks of Augustan irony, Muecke, *Compass*, 20 of simple and double irony, and Kemper, "Irony Anew," 705 of pedantic irony as practiced by Jesus and Socrates. According to Kemper's observation, pedantic irony stands in contrast to cosmic irony because in pedantic irony, a person having knowledge controls the known and manipulates the unknown, but in cosmic irony, the gods or blind natural law are in control, not man. Furthermore, Brooks, "Irony and 'Ironic' Poetry," 233 notices comic, playful and gentle irony in contrast to Muecke, *Compass*, 51 who speaks of bitter, heavy irony. Thomas Mann, "The Art of the Novel," in *The Creative Vision* (eds. Haskell M. Block and Herman Salinger; New York: Grove, 1960), 88 speaks about epic irony, Muecke, *Compass*, 159–77 about Proto-Romantic and Romantic irony, and Worcester, *Satire*, 76 notes Post-Romantic (Chaucerian) irony or irony of fate. In addition to these, the list goes on to include general, universal, cosmic and modern irony (New Critical irony), self-irony, impersonal, self-disparaging, ingénue and dramatized irony which are found in Muecke, *Compass*, 119–51, private irony in Kaufer, "Irony and Rhetorical Strategy," 104, and *Ironie d'épreuve* as a sort of verbal irony in Henri Clavier, "La méthode ironique dans l'enseignment de Jésus," *ETR* 5 (1930): 87. Hoggatt, *Irony in Mark's Gospel*, 150 reveals another name for *Ironie d'épreuve* peirastic irony. Its origin is from the Greek verb, "πειράζειν"(to make proof of or to attempt to do), and is intended to test the other's response. It may in fact declare the opposite of the speaker's actual intention. An excellent example of peirastic irony is found in Gen 19:2-3, in which the angels of the Lord test the seriousness of Lot's offer of hospitality by declaring the opposite of their true intentions. There are more ironies which have been identified such as irony of chance, sentimental irony, mediate irony, disjunctive irony, suspensive irony, musical irony, pictorial irony, architectural irony, culinary irony and ironic mimicry. See Linda Phyllis Austern, "Sweet Meats with Sour Sauce: The Genesis of Musical Irony in English Drama after 1600," *Journal of Musicology* 4 (1985–1986): 472–90.

212. Wilde, *Horizons of Assent*, 2 comments that "irony is not a word with a history, but a modern way of thinking: a 'mode of consciousness, a perceptual response to a world without unity or cohesion," and Dane, *Mythology of Irony*, 7, 33–40 criticize the ahistorical use of the definition and interpretation of irony. Also see David J. Amante, "The Theory of Ironic Speech Acts," *Poetics Today* 2, 2 (1981): 80.

intellectual history of Western Europe. Thus the modern conceptual history of irony has resulted in a paradox: gaining its significant expansion on one hand, yet losing its substance on the other as the consequences of its transfiguration.

Summary

Irony is a complex topic of study. Far before it was given a technical name, εἰρωνεία, irony was consistently a part of human intellectual culture. Though irony is not confined to any specific culture, the Greeks are typically thought of as the group with whom to begin when seeking to understand and define irony. The ancient Greeks habitually employed irony in their Comedy and passed down to us the primary models of ironic speech, event, and character mainly performed in the theater. Yet, specific reflection on irony is quite limited since we observed that the ancients received it quite naturally without forming systematic conceptualizations. It is not an overstatement that the winning of the Dionysia festival[213] depended on how a dramatist creatively employed irony through the stock characters' familiar interactions following the pattern of *persona* designed to elicit laughter from the audience-reader. In their discussions, early critics of irony heavily depend on the observation of the characteristics of an ironic figure, the εἴρων, whose image is established in his verbal and behavioral patterns that contrast with his dramatic counterpart, the ἀλαζών. The chief characteristic of the εἴρων depicted in comedy was deception or mockery, which was readily understood as the intent of εἰρωνεία. Though the εἴρων was a protagonist, he was not necessarily the audience's favorite. His reputation made him too deceptively clever for the audience to be enchanted by him without warning bells sounding in their minds. It is almost as if a sticker saying "Be careful!" were glued on the forehead of the εἴρων.

Aristophanes comes forward as the earliest important critic of irony. His work exemplifies the complexity of irony. In his portrayal of the εἴρων in his comedy *Nubes*, we observe some flexibility, signaling the fluid concept of irony in earlier times. Perhaps his purpose to deride Socrates as a hateful εἴρων whose εἰρωνεία is perceived as the prime example of the Sophists causes him to play with the conventional relationship between the εἴρων and the ἀλαζών.

---

213. Christiane Sourvinou-Inwood, *Athenian Myths & Festivals* (New York: Oxford University Press, 2011), 21–22, explains that the Dionysia is one of the main religious festivals after Panathenaia held in the city Dionysia. This was an advent festival, a common type of Greek festival celebrating the deity's arrival. The Athenians re-enacted their reception of the god with honor after they had spurned him and aroused his anger. The dramatic and dithyrambic competitions were ritually connected with the reception of Dionysos. Among notable winners of the City Dionysia are the illustrious trilogists, Aeschylus, Sophocles, and Euripides, and a comic dramatist, Aristophanes.

Though he paints Socrates in the mask of the ἀλαζών, he explicitly links εἰρωνεία to the person of Socrates. Due to his effort, εἰρωνεία and Socrates become a pair that generates a long and complex conceptual history of irony. However, Aristophanes' criticism of εἰρωνεία is not without problems because his negative perception of his contemporary philosopher, Socrates, prevented him from producing an impartial view on irony.

Unpopular implications attached to irony in relation to the Greek Old Comedy and its alleged link to sophistry cited by Aristophanes lasted throughout the following generations. However, as time moved away from the controversial figure of Socrates and his contemporaries, fewer writers viewed irony through this tainted lens. Plato, the architect of Socratic irony,[214] describes Socrates as an ironic being who speaks and acts ironically. In the *Apologia*, he attests to the historicity of the Aristophanic accusation made against Socrates. Significantly, in his other imaginative narrative, *Symposium,* Plato indirectly attempts to save Socrates from being perceived negatively by ironically caricaturing him as the Silenus whose admirable treasures are hidden within, despite his unworthy appearance.

The ancient Greeks understood irony to be inextricably connected to ethics. We notice such an attitude in Aristophanes and Plato. Above all, it is Aristotle who explicates irony in its ethical value in terms of speaking and acting truthfully. In the *Ethica nichomachea*, he constructs a diametrically opposite paradigm between the εἰρωνεία, minimizing the truth, and the ἀλαζονεία, blowing up the truth. These are the two extreme poles diverging from "the mean," where the truth lies. According to Aristotle, neither extreme is virtuous nor the behavioral mode of the truthful man. However, he does elevates εἰρωνεία as ethically more tolerable than the ἀλαζονεία by speaking of εἰρωνεία with noticeable sensitivity and at the same time with interesting ambiguity in contrast to his harsh and clear-cut dealing with the ἀλαζονεία.

Bringing about a unique difference with the Greeks, the practical Romans[215] began to be concerned with the literary-rhetorical aspect of irony. Both Cicero and Quintilian carve out a new mask for irony that replaces the old one fixed by the Greeks. For Cicero, irony is a trait of the freeborn. It is no

---

214. Dane, *Mythology of Irony*, 21, notes that the association of irony with Socrates may originate with Plato, but its presence is chiefly a product of the later rhetorical tradition.

215. Horace (65–8 BCE), *Ars poetica*, 320–325 describes the Romans' practicality in contrast to the Greeks' artistry: "the Muse gave talent to the Greeks, she gave speech in artistic phrase to the Greeks; they longed for nothing but glory. Through lengthy reckonings, the Roman boys learn how to divide a copper coin (*as*) into a hundred parts" (*Grais ingenium, Grais dedit ore rotundo Musa loqui, praeter laudem nullius avaris. Romani pueri longis rationibus assem discunt in partis centum diducere*). Translation is mine.

longer an object of derision but a sign of urbanity, *urbana dissimulatio*. Overall, Cicero paints irony positively, with light brush strokes, as a "type of humor," using terms like *lepos* (wit), *facetus* (elegance), *humanitas* (refinement), *dulcis* (sweet, pleasant), *festivus* (merry), *elegans* (elegant), and *urbanus* (gentlemanly, polished).[216] Not far from Cicero's tradition, Quintilian, the most influential rhetorician of all time, evaluates irony as a unique figure of speech, which can be both trope and scheme. In Quintilian's work, *Institutio oratoria*, we find the most extensive discussion of irony as a rhetorical device employed by the orator. Through the Romans' critical discussions of irony, its horizon became widened from being defined in a limited verbal sense to being embraced as a mode of thought and perhaps a mode of life on a deeper level. As a result, Socrates was also reevaluated as the achiever of both moral quality and rhetorical skill corresponding to the idea that irony is an outlook of life that is commensurate with an ironic life-style.

Medieval and Renaissance ideas on *ironia* were multifaceted. However, throughout the middle ages and the Renaissance, irony retains its general definition as one of the rhetorical tropes, yet is best known in its particular connection to allegory. In the middle ages, irony is by no means repugnant, but rather expressive of spiritual sensitivity in general, or the Christian faith in particular, articulating the reconciled relationship between God and man bound by eternity. While a sense of pessimism about man's potential and the paradoxical universe tweaks the ironic consciousness of the modern mind, a humble recognition of man's place in creation dominates medieval irony. The seed of Hegel's nihilistic concept of irony, "absolute negativity," is hardly found in medieval irony since the spirit of the medieval age has its foundation in the faith that eternity is beyond irony. It resounds with the medieval understanding of *historia* (history) that all human endeavors fall into the bosom of the eschatological ultimate. The mystic idea of God expressed by the German cardinal Nicholas of Cusa (1401–1464 CE) in his theological formula, *coincidentia oppositorum* ("coincidence of opposites" or "unity of opposites")[217] that God holds all things, though different, in his infinity is an excellent representation of the medieval ironic view. In short, medieval irony is founded on the notion of the ultimate compatibilities of realities.

While the term *irony* was common from classical antiquity to the Renaissance, and its ubiquitous definition was saying the opposite to the

---

216. Cicero, *De or.*, II.ixvii.269–70; *Off.*, I.xxix.104–108. See also Quintilian, *Inst.*, VI.iii.17–21.

217. Nicholas, *De docta ignorantia* III.1. Nicholas was known for his mystical writings on Christianity which emphasize the possibility of knowing God with the divine-human mind.

intended meaning, the efforts of the modern critics to improve the concept of irony are unwittingly ironic because their efforts make the situation compound and murky. As a consequence, modern criticism of irony attests to the kaleidoscopic existence of irony in the broadest possible way. In modern times, irony has become the principal criterion for determining first-rate art and broadly embracing speech, literature, painting, music and even fashion. In this understanding, irony possesses the capacity to move with the flow of Western European intellectual history. We observe a transformation of irony in modern times. Irony is not limited anymore to its literary-rhetorical quality, but is now comfortably used as a device through which to view life and world. The scope of irony has been dramatically broadened, encompassing various kinds of ironic phenomena that were not considered distinctive forms of irony before. Therefore, speaking of the transfiguration of irony in the modern age, particularly since the nineteenth century, it is fair to say that even though irony gained its distinctively critical voice through the transformation invested in it by the modern critics under the influence of Romanticism, it became widely dissected, almost to the point of losing its essence.

Toward a Working Definition of Irony

Notwithstanding the increasing attention devoted to irony since the eighteenth century, the study of irony remains in a state of flux. In this regard, Douglas C. Muecke' attempt seems reasonable when he suggests listing examples of irony rather than defining it precisely.[218] However, establishing a working definition of irony for the project at hand seems necessary. Considering both the simplest, yet the most fundamental, definition of irony—the use of words to reveal something other than their literal meaning—and irony's complex literary dimension, this book proposes the following working definition: irony is a persuasive, indirect, and economical revelation, pointing to a reality different from that which appears on the plane of word, event, or character.

First, irony is a persuasive rhetorical device proven and sought after by the skillful speaker-author. Irony is not a tool for a dull mind but rather for a keen mind. Second, irony yields by no means an ordinary literal interaction because it represents the author's ingenuity and indirection[219] within the narrative. It is indirect because it is designed by an ironist with the intention of rejecting a falsely assumed belief presented on the surface level. Traditionally, Cicero

---

218. Muecke, *Compass*, 19.

219. Some scholars use the term "pretense" instead of "indirection." See Herbert H. Clark and Richard J. Gerrig, "On the Pretense Theory of Irony," *JEP: General* 113 (1984): 121–22.

defined irony as a fine device for indirection, reflected in his formula, *aliud dicere ac sentias* (saying one thing and meaning another).[220] Horace compares irony's forceful indirectness to *cos* (a whetstone) that sharpens the knife, but of itself cannot cut (*acutum reddere quae ferrum valet, exsors ipsa secandi*).[221] The idea is that if irony is directly spelled out, it ceases to be irony.[222] Third, irony is an economical tool of communication which is more effective than straight talk. [223] Richard A. Lanham says that the more sophisticated the irony, the more that is implied, the less stated.[224] Therefore, irony communicates more in less space by using the form and condition of reduction.[225] Finally and most importantly, irony is an act of revelation pointing to the substance or meaning of word, event, or character in communication. The Matthean passion narrative's irony exhibits all these characteristics when it illuminates the meaning and significance of the death of Jesus.

Constitution of Irony: Formal Elements of Irony

Once a working definition of irony is in place, identifying the formal elements of irony is achievable. The book proposes several key elements of irony including (i) the ironist; (ii) a reader of irony; (iii) the collaborative communication between the ironist and his reader; (iv) a double-layered story phenomenon;[226] (v) a fundamental conflict (ὁ ἀγών), opposition, disparity or incomparability between the two levels of story;[227] (vi) an element of "innocence,"[228] manifested in two ways as blind self-confidence on the part of the victim of irony or pretension by the ironist; and (vii) the literary outcome of irony which is equal to a revelation or an awakening experience in the mind

---

220. Cicero, *De or.*, II.lxvii.269.

221. Horace, *Ars*, 303. Modern scholars such as Maurice Natanson, "The Arts of Indirection" in *Rhetoric, Philosophy and Literature* (ed. Don M. Burks; West Lafayette: Purdue University Press, 1978), 39–40, Spencer, "The Wise Fool," 349–60 and Holland, *Divine Irony*, 156 all highlight the indirect nature of irony as its top quality.

222. Tindale and Gough, "The Use of Irony," 6.

223. Gail R. O'Day, *Revelation in the Fourth Gospel* (Philadelphia: Fortress Press), 31 notices the economical nature of irony as a means of communication.

224. Richard A. Lanham, *A Handlist of Rhetorical Terms: A Guide of Students of English Literature* (Berkeley: University of California Press, 1968), 61.

225. Booth, "The Empire of Irony," 729; Tindale and Gough, "The Use of Irony," 13.

226. Muecke, *Compass*, 20.

227. Sedgewick, *Of Irony*, 26 uses the phrase, the "clash between appearance and reality in events or language" in his explanation of dramatic irony. Also, Brueggemann, *Solomon*, xii explains irony as a literary strategy for exposing contradictions which normal perception can miss.

228. Muecke, *Compass*, 20.

of the reader. These requirements constitute irony and are necessary for the interpretation of irony.

THE IRONIST

The ironist shapes irony for communication. The irony of a narrative arises through the ironist's intentional molding of that narrative.[229] The ironist in literature is typically perceived as either the implied author, who arranges material meaningfully with an ironic intention, or a character within the narrative, who can be labeled the εἴρων. In cases where the ironist is not a character in the story but rather the omniscient, undramatized, detached, third person, implied author, his presence is felt through the narrator's voice, as he provides information and presents the story through plot and characterization.[230]

The ironist's intention is to form a rhetorical net which draws the reader into his unique communication conspiracy, that is, irony. The ironist intends his language and the plot of the story, both of which are indispensible for the reading of irony, to be detected by his intended reader. Accordingly, he tills the ground, the story, and plants "cues"[231] along the furrows of the plot pointing to his ironic intention. This is why David J. Amante considers that the ironist undertakes by far the most unique role since he must be intentional about his irony and be capable of giving signals to his ironic meanings.[232] The common signals pointing to the existence of irony depend on the type of irony. Some intelligible linguistic and contextual clues of irony are: use of some form of the word *irony*, the use of hyperbole, understatement, incoherence, or discontinuity, a lack of correspondence with reality.[233] The clues of irony also include repetition, the conflict between propositions regarding words, situations and characters and betrayal against exhibited knowledge and beliefs of the implied author.

The goal of the ironist is to communicate *meaning*—the content of *reality* that matters. The ironist would use an overt statement to make his point

---

229. The existence of the ironist and his intentional creation of irony correspond to Booth's theory of "Stable Irony," which this book adopts as a methodology along with the stance of narrative criticism. See the discussion in chapter 1.

230. Kaufer, "Irony and Rhetorical Strategy," 90 mentions that irony is a technique of indicating, through character or plot development, an intention or attitude opposite to that which is clearly stated.

231. Amante, "Ironic Speech Acts," 83 asserts that "it is mandatory that some clue to irony be provided by the ironist."

232. Ibid., 83.

233. Booth, *Rhetoric*, 49–73; Hagen, "Verbal Irony," 11

and reject the reader's literal judgment.[234] He delights in devising a relatively new, less trodden path through which to convey his meaning. In this regard, the ironist must be quite literarily competent because if irony has to be disenchanted by being spelled out, then its effect is diminished and if it is too elusive, then the reader will easily overlook it. Given the fact that irony is a genus of subtlety, designed to produce shock, the ironist can be neither too transparent nor too elusive.

David Kaufer theorizes that an important function of the ironist is to "bifurcate his audience."[235] According to Kaufer, the ironist possesses the ability to associate himself with or distance himself from his audience. In order to achieve a cooperative relationship with his intended reader the ironist employs a tactic known as "foregrounding norms."[236] Throughout the narrative, the ironist purposefully repeats the norms of the story by using complementary signifiers, images, and literary cues that effectively glue episodes together under the ironic rubric of the story he intends to create. The ironist's act of "foregrounding norms"[237] or of "creating the bond of agreement"[238] constructs the yellow brick road leading Dorothy—a committed reader of irony—back home. This allows the reader to interpret irony. The norms that the ironist instills in the narrative make the reader's interpretative task achievable.

The ironist, however, occupies a spiritually high seat, keeping an "aesthetic distance"[239] or "detached sympathy"[240] from his characters and hiding his emotional involvement. His control over the story with a bird's-eye view resembles the divine attribute of omniscience. In this regard, John C. Thirlwall perceives a theological cast to irony. He sees that irony, like everything else in dramatic poetry, grows out of the religious or philosophic sentiments of the

---

234. Duke, *Irony in the Fourth Gospel*, 34.

235. Kaufer, "Irony and Rhetorical Strategy," 98.

236. David S. Kaufer and Christine M. Neuwirth, "Foregrounding Norms and Ironic Communication," *QJS* 68 (1982): 28–36. Tindale and Gough, "The Use of Irony," 4 calls Kaufer's "norms" "background norms."

237. Booth, *Rhetoric*, 33–34 suggests a similar idea when he identifies the presence of unstated assumptions that the ironist and his reader share. His theory of stable irony is based on the notion of authorial clues (i.e. norms or perspectives) that enable the ironic communication between the two parties. In response to this, Kaufer, "Irony and rhetorical strategy," 93 evaluates Booth's stable irony as an attempt to restore some of the ironist's lost significance.

238. Tindale and Gough, "The Use of Irony," 10 write that "the success of the ironic argument will depend very much upon the skill of the writer as an ironist, on his ability to relate his ideas to his reader through the initial bond of agreement."

239. Thompson, *The Dry Mock*, 22.

240. Sedgewick, *Of Irony*, 251.

poet.²⁴¹ The ironist is like the divine-human, exercising wide, sweeping vision and complete control.²⁴² Douglas C. Muecke supports this view by saying that God, as the ultimate "outsider," provides an analogy for the ironist because God is the ironist *par excellence*.²⁴³ He is omniscient, infinite, transcendent, absolute and free. The ironist is close to the divine point of view not only because he approaches the matter with a divine attitude and confidence but also because he is concerned with elevated objectives, both of which operate on superior ground. He is free, secure, and detached. His freedom is expressed by his mobility, his security is ascertained by his lofty understanding, and his detachment is testified to by his ability to laugh. His freedom is the sign of mental agility,²⁴⁴ his security of spiritual superiority, and his ability to laugh of invulnerability.

AN IRONICALLY COMPETENT READER

Irony does not take place without an audience. Two types of audiences are available depending on the identity of an ironist. In a narrow sense, if the ironist is a character within the story, the εἴρων, his partner will be an ironic ally within the story whose perception is keen enough to understand the words and actions of the εἴρων. In a broad sense, if the ironist is the implied author whose voice narrates the story, his intended counterpart will be an ironically capable, implied reader.

When we focus our discussion on irony employed by an implied author, the ideal reader is expected to be one who is competent, conscious, and perceptive. He adheres to the textual information in order to find the reality of the story which the characters in the narrative are blind to.²⁴⁵ In the same vein, Jerry C. Hoggatt describes the role of the reader as the jury who is summoned by the ironist to pass the verdict on the issue under discussion.²⁴⁶ Therefore, the ironically capable reader is expected to demonstrate well informed judgment as a result of establishing a confederacy with the ironist. Establishing a confederacy with the ironist also means that the reader is sympathetic towards the rhetorical strategy of the irony through which the intended revelation is disclosed. In the

---

241. Thirlwall, "On the Irony of Sophocles," 489–90, 535–37.
242. Holland, *Divine Irony*, 54 speaks of "godly control" of the ironist.
243. Muecke, *Compass*, 228.
244. Ibid., 247, writes that "the ironist's virtue is mental alertness and agility. His business is to make life unbearable for troglodytes, to keep an open house for ideas, and to go on asking questions."
245. Seymour Chatman, *Story and Discourse: Narrative Structure in Fiction and Film* (Ithaca: Cornell University Press, 1978), 229.
246. Hoggatt, *Irony in Mark's Gospel*, 119.

end, what the ironically capable reader accomplishes is a "sympathetic reading of the writer's ironic intent."[247]

One difficult question to answer is whether every real reader can be an ideal reader at his first attempt to read irony. Since irony meets the eye of the reader at a high altitude rather than low ground, the reader with an attentive mind needs to climb up the ladder of information provided by the ironist within the bounds of the narrative. Unfortunately, there always is the danger of either an under-reading or over-reading of irony due to reading errors. Since a successful reading of irony is susceptible to some varying human conditions such as the background and experience of a reader,[248] it is reasonable to say that the impact of irony increases for a perceptive, skilled, and experienced reader as opposed to a dull-witted, naïve and inexperienced reader.

A number of scholars of irony speak in an accord that the success of ironic communication primarily depends on a literarily skilled and experienced reader. Although Christopher W. Tindale and James Gough consider the success of ironic communication very much dependent on the skill of the writer as an ironist, and more specifically on his ability to relate his ideas to his reader through the initial bond of agreement,[249] they also point out the significance of the aptitude of the reader.[250] Likewise, William F. Thrall and Addison Hibbard assert that the ability to recognize irony is one of the surest tests of intelligence and sophistication on the part of the reader.[251] R. Alan Culpepper considers the success of ironic communication dependent on the reader's "repeated readings of a narrative" because "even the most perceptive reader is never sure he or she received all the signals the text is sending."[252] As the narrative unfolds, the reader of irony is obliged to process the story on a deeper level by reminiscing on the information given, connecting the dots and correcting his understanding with each disclosure that occurs in the narrative. Eventually, these activities will enable him to accomplish meaningful progress towards the goal: interpreting irony.[253]

---

247. Tindale and Gough, "The Use of Irony," 6.

248. Booth, *Rhetoric*, 15 mentions Hume's lists of "external hindrances" and "internal disorders" that disable the proper interpretation of irony. In 222–227, he explicates "five crippling handicaps" of the reader: ignorance, inability to pay attention (i.e. being blind-sighted), prejudice (i.e. dogmatic), lack of practice (i.e. inexperienced), and emotional inadequacy (i.e. obstinacy).

249. Tindale and Gough, "The Use of Irony," 5.

250. Ibid., 10.

251. William F. Thrall and Addison Hibbard, *A Handbook to Literature* (rev. C. H. Holman; New York: Odyssey, 1960), 248.

252. R. Alan Culpepper, *Anatomy of the Fourth Gospel: A Study in Literary Design* (Philadelphia: Fortress Press, 1983), 151.

Detecting and reconstructing irony presupposes commitment and like-mindedness on the part of the reader, which is not only an attestation to a bond that he shares with the ironist but is also an inevitable product of that relationship. Through becoming a conspirator with the ironist by accepting his values and beliefs,[254] the reader attempts to reconstruct irony, which requires willingness and intellectual modesty. Humility is an obvious trait demanded of the reader of irony due to the self-imposed limit of stable irony: the control of the ironist. It is analogous to "building a new house in a new location"[255] by relying on somebody's blueprint. Paul D. Duke explains what this means.

> In using irony an author invites the reader to reject an ostensible structure of meaning. The meaning to be rejected is often far more than the literal meaning of a particular sentence or expression, but rather a whole structured "world" of meanings or values which the author spurns . . . the perceptive reader, however, will abandon this house of meaning, mentally demolishing it, and from its rubble leap to the new structure on a higher site where the author and all sound readers dwell together. From this new house of meaning the author and perceptive reader can view the rejected structure and its uniformed inhabitants at pleasurable distance.[256]

In conclusion, the successful reconstruction of irony is contingent on an agreement that the ironist and his intended reader share. Therefore, the reader's evaluation of whether some specific words, events or character depictions are ironic must be in keeping with the whole presentation of the story and the evaluative points of view of the ironist that the reader adopts as norms. The reader's submission to the ironist's perspective is the sign of his compliance to be led, instructed and enlightened.

The Implicit, Interpretative Community and the Victim of Irony

To use irony as a rhetorical device is to practice the art of persuasion. For this reason, the corroboration between the ironist and his reader is imperative. When this corroboration proves to be successful, the relationship between

---

253. Booth, *Rhetoric*, 33–39 employs the phrase, "reconstruction of irony," in place of "interpretation," "understanding," "decipherment," or "translation" of irony. According to Booth, the successful reconstruction of stable irony depends on an agreement that the ironist and his intended reader share.

254. Holland, *Divine Irony*, 51–52.

255. Booth, *Rhetoric*, 11.

256. Duke, *Irony in the Fourth Gospel*, 34.

the ironist and his intended reader is marked by association and sympathy but an unsuccessful corroboration results in antipathy and aloofness.[257] As we examined earlier, in Kaufer's theory of "bifurcation,"[258] irony can cause a double audience as Henry W. Fowler describes this phenomenon in the following:

> Irony is a form of utterance that postulates a double audience, consisting of one party that hearing shall hear and shall not understand, and another party that, when more is meant than meets the ear, is aware both of that more and of the outsiders' incomprehension.[259]

A few critics of irony attest to the social-rhetorical function of irony, which generates a unique community of interpretation. Jerry C. Hoggatt[260] and Gail R. O'Day[261] assert that irony establishes a sense of community, and Chaim Pereleman speaks of "agreement" which unites the two parties: the ironist and his reader.[262] Their concepts of interpretive community correspond to Wayne C. Booth's "kindred spirits,"[263] David Kaufer's "close-knit group,"[264] Kenneth Burke's "fundamental kinship,"[265] Herbert H. Clark and Richard J. Gerrig's "inner circle,"[266] and finally Glenn S. Holland's "our kind of person" who possesses the shared sympathetic view.[267] Although Booth notices the paradoxical nature of irony which is simultaneously inclusive and exclusive, in his discussion of stable irony he gives weight to the inclusiveness of irony because of his conviction that "every irony inevitably builds a community of

---

257. Kaufer, "Irony and Rhetorical Strategy," 94.

258. Ibid., 98.

259. Henry W. Fowler, *A Dictionary of Modern English Usage* (New York: Oxford University Press, 1959), 295–96.

260. In his study of irony in Mark's Gospel, Hoggatt, *Irony in Mark's Gospel*, 4 believes that irony serves the community of saints. Compare with the discussion of Booth, *Rhetoric*, 27–29.

261. O'Day, *Fourth Gospel*, 31 notes that irony "reveals by asking the reader to make judgments and decisions about the relative value of stated and intended meanings, drawing the reader into its vision of truth, so that when the reader finally understands, he or she becomes a member of the community that shares that vision, constituted by those who also followed the author's lead."

262. Chaim Perelman, *The New Rhetoric: A Treatise of Argumentation* (trans. John Wilkinson and Purcell Weaver; Notre Dame: University of Notre Dame Press, 1969), 208.

263. Booth, *Rhetoric*, 28.

264. Kaufer, "Irony and Rhetorical Strategy," 100 notes that irony pursues group cohesion.

265. Burke, *A Grammar of Motives*, 514.

266. Clark and Gerrig, "On the Pretense Theory of Irony," 122. Also see John J. Enck and Elizabeth T. Foster, eds., *The Comic in Theory and Practice* (New York: Appleton-Century-Crofts, 1960), 4.

267. Holland, *Divine Irony*, 49–50.

believers even as it excludes."²⁶⁸ On the same note, David Kaufer says that ironies are "intended to be transparent to an understander" in order to make the reader commit himself to evaluative judgments which irony requires.²⁶⁹ Although irony is meant to be transparent to its beholder, deciphering irony is certainly not a cup of tea for everyone, particularly the first time reader. Its content is only presented through a dim glass, in that it must be discerned with patience and attention. By nature, a rhetorical posture of irony charms the reader into the interactive relationship with it, and thereby also with the ironist.

Due to the covert and indirect nature of irony,²⁷⁰ it has often been questioned whether the ironist is employing a form of elitism.²⁷¹ To some degree, this type of question seems justifiable because the ironist sustains a privileged status. He is godlike in his superior knowledge and ability to engineer not only the story's world but also the reader's way of thinking. He possesses facts and understandings which characters of the narrative could not obtain or have access to. In this regard, his image becomes that of more than just an ordinary writer. Likewise, irony is often considered to be something designed to deceive some readers while granting a sense of pride to others.²⁷² Certainly, irony is not for the fool, who takes words, situations, or characters at face value, especially when literary signals invite him to reconsider the object of irony. Nevertheless, the reader of irony need not be viewed as an elitist, because no reader is exempt from common handicaps such as undue exertion of himself over the text or shortsightedness.²⁷³ However, an ironically capable reader, the

---

268. Booth, *Rhetoric*, 28.

269. David Kaufer, "Ironic Evaluations," *Communications Monographs* 48 (1981): 25–26.

270. Tanaka, "The Concept of Irony," 49 speaks of the possibility of confusion in the interpretation of irony since everything depends on the hearer's recognition of some ambiguous inference by which the ironic speaker's intentions are recognized.

271. Kierkegaard, *The Concept of Irony with Continual Reference to Socrates*, 248 criticizes irony of elitism, "the ironic figure of speech has still another property that characterizes all irony, a certain superiority deriving from its not wanting to be understood immediately, even though it wants to be understood, with the result that this figure looks down, as it were, on plain and simple talk that everyone can promptly understand; it travels around, so to speak, in an exclusive incognito and looks down pitying from this high position on ordinary, prosaic talk. In everyday affairs, the ironic figure of speech appears especially in the higher circles as a prerogative belonging to the same category as the *bon ton* [good form] that requires smiling at innocence and looking upon virtue as narrow-mindedness, although one still believes in it up to a point." Further, Holland, *Divine Irony*, 157–59 writes that "irony is elitist, that is, it is usually understood as something that sets apart an elite . . . from the masses . . . this elitism accounts in part for irony's reputation since the time of Cicero as a gentlemanly form of discourse."

272. Booth, "The Pleasures and Pitfalls of Irony: or, Why Don't You Say What You Mean?" in *Rhetoric, Philosophy, and Literature: An Exploration* (ed. Don M. Burks; West Lafayette, Ind.: Purdue University Press, 1978), 2.

counterpart of the ironist, is characterized as open-minded and perceptive to a new and superior idea. He is willing to give up his perspective and dogma and is ready to accept the ironist's "norms for communication."[274] This type of reader seeks to relocate himself to a higher plane of ideas and values[275] by adopting the values of the ironist[276] and by taking pleasure in sharing the ironist's bird's-eye view. In the end, the reader takes a leap of intuition which enables him to pass judgment on characters in the story from his elevated, advantageous position. Technically, such an ironically capable reader is called the "confederate of the ironist"[277] in their "reflexive relationship."[278] In his "reflexive relationship" with the ironist, the confederate of the ironist assumes a position of intellectual humility and adopts the normative point of view of the ironist expressed in the world of narrative. By this process of sharing values and following a particular reading of the text, a projected relationship, that is, the implicit confederacy, can be established. In this way, and only this way, irony brings about an "impact"[279] of grand proportions on the reader's outlook on life.

Since irony is paradoxically both inclusive and exclusive, he who does not form an interpretive confederacy with the ironist becomes the "victim" of the ironist either as the character within the story or as the reader.[280] The distinctive characteristic of the victim of irony is his overgrown confidence in his own knowledge or qualification, which eventually leads him into the trap of irony. Typical victims of irony fit into one of the following categories: those to whom one speaks ironically, those of whom one speaks ironically, those unable to

273. Dane, "The Defense of the Incompetent Reader," *Comparative Literature* 38 (1986): 53–72 underlines many attempts to define literary competence, especially Chomsky's effort, in contrast to the defense of literary incompetence. He compares the given technical standards of literary competence with the overall lack of interest in defining and assisting literary incompetence. On page 63, he says that "the victims of irony are not incompetent in Chomskyan terms . . . A victim must be able to understand the literal level of irony. Furthermore, there need not be a wide gulf separating sophisticated readers of irony from victims . . . A reader with the literary competence sufficient to make him a victim of irony can at least have the *ironic* message (which is in itself no more complex than the literal message) explained to him. In other words, he need not be a sophisticated reader in order to understand what these supposedly sophisticated messages are."

274. Kaufer, "Ironic Evaluations," 36–37.

275. Mark Allan Powell, *What is Narrative Criticism?* (Minneapolis: Fortress Press, 1990), 30; Weaver, "Power and Powerlessness," 466.

276. Booth, *Rhetoric*, 171; Dane, "The Incompetent Reader," 69.

277. Kaufer, "Irony and Rhetorical Strategy," 100; Tindale and Gough, "The Use of Irony," 2.

278. Tindale and Gough, ibid., 6.

279. Hagen, "Verbal Irony," 13.

280. Clark and Gerrig, "On the Pretense Theory of Irony," 122. Also, Amante, "Ironic Speech Acts," 80–81 calls a victim of irony a "target for the irony."

perceive that they have been ironically addressed, those unable to recognize irony directed towards others, those who fail to notice that they are victims of circumstances or intrigue, and those unable to understand that their own words betray them. At times, victims of irony are naïve enough to expect that the ironist will be upfront about his intention, or they may simply resist the idea of adopting the view of the ironist.[281] At other times, the victims will be characters within the narrative who are plainly unaware of how the narration is ironically victimizing them. It is important to acknowledge once more that the primary intent of irony is not to exclude but rather to include by forming an agreement despite of the secretive nature of irony. Therefore, Booth rightly observes that "the bringing together of author and reader is the single most valued function of irony in literature."[282]

A DUALISTIC STORY-WORLD AND ITS CONTRAST

In the story world, irony operates through a double-layered (or two-story) phenomenon.[283] The ironist presents the two worlds of the story, *what is apparent* (the world of appearances) and *what is hidden* (reality), in dynamic juxtaposition by implying that there is more than what it seems on the surface. This is done because the rhetorical interplay between the text and subtext of irony generates a phenomenon of layered meaning. Since irony is principally designed for the communication not of what is said, but of what remains unsaid,[284] it is found where there is a discrepancy between what appears to be happening on the level of the plain text and what is actually happening on the level of the veiled subtext. The interpretation of irony occurs when the opposite of every expectation or assumption comes true and, as result, conflict is felt.[285] In fact, the greater the contrast of appearance and reality, the more the striking irony is revealed.

Irony lays bare a different realm of values. Although not every contradiction produces irony such as the case of paradox, irony arises through the conflict between the two different perspectives that are expressed in a discrete story-world.[286] The ironist intentionally puts these two disparate worlds together in a fundamental contrast causing the conflict. Each discrete story belongs in a respective conceptual world, with the two worlds in opposition

---

281. Hoggatt, *Irony in Mark's Gospel*, 156 speaks of an "unyielding reader."
282. Booth, *Rhetoric*, 204–5, 217.
283. Muecke, *Compass*, 19. Also, Thompson, *The Dry Mock*, 10 calls it the two levels of story.
284. Holland, *Divine Irony*, 46.
285. Arthur Applebee et al., *Literature and Language: English and World Literature* (Evanston: McDougal, Little & Co., 1992), 652.

in terms of their irreconcilable realities. Each world propagandizes a respective value which requires the reader's discernment, a so-called value judgment. The relationship between these two worlds is not complementary but rather contrasting, conflicting, and hierarchical. Each world espouses a distinctive worldview that affects the very configuration and presentation of the story, including the components of the events and the inner make-up of the characters. Therefore, it is important for the reader to bridge the two worlds in opposition and to understand the respective values proposed by each world.

Greek dramas illustrate in the story world how each discrete value, worldview or perspective is represented through the opposed characters, known as the εἴρων and ἀλαζών. For example, in comedy, the εἴρων, the understater, triumphs over the ἀλαζών, the self-deceiving impostor, by deliberately presenting himself as less than what he actually is.[287] Historically, the Platonic Socrates embodied this triumphant figure, the εἴρων, who exposes the ἀλαζών as foolish and blind by speaking and acting on the hidden reality. In contrast to the εἴρων, the ignorance of the ἀλαζών causes him to speak and act in ways which are to be rejected from the point of view of higher reality. Unfortunately, the ἀλαζών serves as the champion and custodian of every idea denounced by the εἴρων and the condition of the ἀλαζών gets worse when he firmly believes that the norm to which he is clinging is impregnable. The ἀλαζών's self-sufficiency begets a dramatic conflict (ἀγών or ἀγωνία) with the εἴρων, that almost always finds its resolution in the victory of the εἴρων. Since the values upheld by the ἀλαζών are inferior to those of the εἴρων, the conflict inherent to their incompatibility elicits a sense of absurdity and pain which often accompanies laughter.

Students of irony in modern times employ various descriptions for this typical two-story phenomenon of irony: an appearance vs. a reality;[288] expectation vs. event;[289] how things seem to be vs. how they really are;[290] the lower, rejected, literal meaning vs. the superior, new, transcendent meaning;[291]

---

286. Irony originates in a conflict. Sedgewick, *Of Irony*, 38 notes that "irony in its general sense precedes and underlies the spectacle of conflict." Also see, Holland, *Divine Irony*, 157; James G. Williams, "Irony and Lament: Clues to Prophetic Consciousness," *Semeia* 8 (1977): 52.

287. Abrams, *A Glossary of Literary Terms*, 200–201.

288. Chevalier, *The Ironic Temper*, 42. Sedgewick, *Of Irony*, 13 describes Socratic irony saying, "It is a war upon appearance waged by a man who knows reality."

289. Thompson, *The Dry Mock*, 10.

290. Holland, *Divine Irony*, 157.

291. Duke, *Irony in the Fourth Gospel*, 34, 37, explains that in using irony an author invites the reader to reject an ostensible structure of meaning.

surface meaning vs. below the surface meaning;[292] and literal vs. non-literal meanings of irony.[293] Besides these, more descriptions of the dualistic story phenomenon of irony are used.[294] Other terms can stand in place of contrast such as disequilibrium, discrepancy,[295] contradiction,[296] incongruity,[297] incompatibility,[298] dissonance, tension, opposition,[299] or confrontation between incompatible elements invalidating each other.[300]

Irony is a useful tool to challenge an unquestioned dogma and status quo. It operates on the plane of contrast and conflict. Irony defies appearance and produces an outside perspective which offers new insights lying close to the heart of reality. Given the fact that irony inherently presents itself in a double-layered story world, the reader must adopt the means of negation,[301] and subtraction,[302] and make an interpretative leap[303] to avoid the ostensible

---

292. Holland, *Divine Irony*, 37–38.

293. Kaufer, "Irony and Rhetorical Strategy," 97.

294. Donald H. Juel, *Messiah and Temple: The Trial of Jesus in the Gospel of Mark* (SBLDS no. 31; Missoula: Scholar's Press, 1977), 73 describes it as mystery for the character vs. revelation to the reader, Duke, *Irony in the Fourth Gospel*, 34 as the shadowy (ostensible-apparent) world vs. the real (ideal) world, Powell, *Narrative Criticism*, 31 as the shadow vs. the reality, Dane, "The Incompetent Reader," 64 as the ironic reading (the highest reading) which is that of the consensus vs. the literal reading which is that of the victim, and both Muecke, *Compass*, 19 and Weaver, "Power and Powerlessness," 466 as the lower ground (the lower level of the story) vs. the high ground (the upper level of the story). Furthermore, see the discussion of vehicle and tenor, Richards, *The Philosophy of Rhetoric*, 96–97, 104–05. These concepts are applicable to irony. Hoggatt applies James E. Miller's paradigm of "text and subtext" in his study of the Markan irony. It is apparent in the title, *Irony in Mark's Gospel: Text and Subtext*. On page 1, Hoggatt specifies that "the subtitle of this book—'Text and subtext'—is taken from a discussion of the relationship of language and thought in James Miller's 'rhetoric of imagination,' *Word, Self, Reality* . . . Miller's distinction between text and subtext lies at the core of this rhetoric of irony. Irony occurs when the elements of the story-line provoke the reader to see beneath the surface of the text to deeper significances." Further, Hoggatt, ibid., 61 employs another set of descriptive words, the secondary vs. the primary meaning of double entendre. If the two levels of meaning are not necessarily opposed to each other, the reader is called to recognize both levels of meaning. However, certainly the primary meaning always supersedes the secondary meaning of the text in its quality and significance.

295. Thompson, *The Dry Mock*, 10.

296. Muecke, *Compass*, 20.

297. Joseph T. Shipley, *Dictionary of World Literature, Criticism, Forms, Technique* (New York: Philosophical Library, 1943), 331.

298. Williams, "Irony and Lament," 51.

299. Muecke, *Compass*, 20.

300. Ibid., 29.

301. The operation of negation distinguishes irony from other figures. See Booth, *Rhetoric*, 18–19, 22–23, 25, 27.

302. Ibid., 27.

meaning of the story. The reader cannot simultaneously embrace both the appearance and the reality of irony. He accepts one and rejects the other since in the world of irony one is meant to be superior to the other.

An Element of Innocence

The idea of "innocence" as an ingredient of irony largely depends on D. C. Muecke's contribution. Irony makes either the ironist or the victim exhibit innocence in distinctive ways. The innocence of the former means literary dexterity as well as control in contrast to the latter's ignorance and impotence. Muecke opines that

> There is in irony an element of "innocence"; either a victim is confidently unaware of the very possibility of there being an upper level or point of view that invalidates his own, or an ironist pretends not to be aware of it.[304]

We previously examined two potential types of victims: the character within the story and the imperceptive reader outside the story. In general, the victim of irony is the character in the story (sometimes certain character groups), who functions as the ἀλαζών, on the far end of the scale from his counterpart, the εἴρων. The reader can become the victim of irony by forming an agreement with the ἀλαζών rather than with the εἴρων. His adherence to the ideas repudiated by the ironist makes him estranged from the ironist and therefore, this condition leads him to failure as an implied reader of irony.

The typical victim exhibits innocence, not comprehending the ironic saying, the ironic situation or his own role as the victim of irony. The term innocence as a constitutive element of irony refers not to the victim's ethical disposition but to his naïvete regarding the dual-layered reality of the story. For that reason, expressions such as "blind confidence" or "ignorance" seem more fitting than innocence. If the guilt of the innocent ἀλαζών is his "confident unawareness or impercipience,"[305] the guilt of the innocent reader implies his stubbornness or inexperience. That innocence is "being guilty" is oxymoronic, yet characteristically possible in the arena of irony.

In the story world, the ἀλαζών assumes that he is surely right in his speaking and acting. Clinging to the lower level of the story, he assures himself,

---

303. Duke, *Irony in the Fourth Gospel*, 15, 34, 37. Likewise, Weaver, "Power and Powerlessness," 454, describes it as "an act of mental gymnastics."
304. Muecke, *Compass*, 20.
305. Ibid., 30.

"it is the way things should be." Yet, his strong conviction regarding his stability reversely testifies to his role as a victim. He does not have the ability to understand the bigger picture of reality beyond the world of appearances in which he finds himself at home. The sense of security of the ἀλαζών often corresponds to the idea that he is a man of ὕβρις (insolence). He is intellectually blind and spiritually arrogant.[306] He is not capable of suspecting that things may not be as he supposes or expects them to be because he does not have a single bit of doubt that he is mistaken. Therefore, the ὕβρις of the ἀλαζών is intolerable as Muecke says, "Simple ignorance is safe from irony, but ignorance compounded with the least degree of confidence counts as intellectual hubris and is a punishable offence."[307]

The other kind of innocence exhibited by the ironist, technically the εἴρων, is a totally different concept. It is not the kind of self-inflicted blindness carried by the ἀλαζών, but rather a low-keyed dissimulation (*dissimulatio, simulatio*)[308] or pretense (προσποίησις)[309] that the ironist takes up as his chosen mode. While ancient Greeks once thought that the ironist's disguise was contemptible, a tool of willful deception, commentators since Aristotle have seen irony in speaking and acting as a sign of sophistication for the learned freeborn. This very notion is well entertained in Cicero's definition of irony as *urbana dissimulatio*. The innocence of the ironist is considered the ironist's unique tactic and ability to filter out those who are compatible with himself and simultaneously disclose the impropriety of those who are not with him.[310] In other words, the ironist's innocence creates a covert-stable irony and thereby, it produces the bifurcated reader: the insider and the outsider. Therefore, to perceive the ironist's innocence is commensurate to interpreting irony.

The study of "how irony works" is a quite intriguing enterprise. Even though not all opposing elements create irony, the most revealing irony is presented when the intensity caused by disparity between the opposite perspectives corresponds to the relationship between unawareness of the victim and the innocence of the ironist. Therefore, the degree of subtlety of the

---

306. Ibid., 38 describes the victims of irony as "too confident of their wisdom and too ignorant of their ignorance."

307. Ibid., 30.

308. Ibid., 20 notes one exception to this that "in sarcasm or in very overt irony the ironist does not pretend to be unaware of his real meaning and his victim is immediately aware of it."

309. Sedgewick, *Of Irony*, 5.

310. The compatible reader of the ironist can be described as one who is able to perform the "intellectual dance," teaming with the ironist. Booth, "The Empire of Irony," 729, describes the "intellectual dance" as the reader's mental process for understanding, which yields a tight bond with the ironist.

silent ironist hidden behind the innocent *persona* is telltale of the degree of misperception that the victim can presume. Rarely, the pretense of the ironist can be made transparent or overt in statements like "it is ironical that" or "I am saying ironically." In the case in which the ironist gives up his innocence, Booth's stable irony, which requires that the ironist conceals his intent, is absent. When the ironist is blatantly honest about his intention by setting aside the secretiveness to which irony is entitled,[311] he not only sacrifices the pulling power of irony to attract the reader but also reduces the reader's pleasure in reaching an understanding of the veiled reality through his own intellectual navigation.

THE REWARD OF IRONY

The successful reading of irony benefits the implied reader of irony with appropriate rewards. Irony is something like a treasure hunt that requires the reader to decipher an intricate map riddled with clues and inferences, and grants him a hidden treasure, that is, *pleasure*,[312] in return.

Irony by its nature is intellectual, economic, and reflexive. It leaves a spiritual etching on the mind of an attentive, yielding observer. Garnett G. Sedgewick writes that "Its force derives from one of the keenest and oldest and least transient pleasures of the reflexive human mind—the pleasure in contrasting appearance with reality."[313] Since irony is an invitation to mutual interaction between the ironist and the reader toward the goal of communication, membership and pleasure are secured when irony is properly perceived. Irony is characteristically "pleasant"[314] for both the ironist himself and his reader. As we examined earlier in an overview of the conceptual history of irony, Cicero noticed that irony is different from literal speech where the speaker's thoughts are in strict harmony with the thing said.[315] He is the first one who pays attention to the intrinsic pleasure that is felt by the ironist because saying one thing and meaning another is inherently gratifying for the speaker. Likewise, the reader experiences pleasure by achieving proper competence as a partner of the ironist. The competent reader of irony experiences a very compact process: (i) suspicion of irony, (ii) the moment of shock, then (iii) the

---

311. Regarding the secretiveness of irony, see Tindale and Gough, "The Use of Irony," 12 and Sonia S'hiri, "Literary Discourse and Irony: Secret Communion and the Pact of Reciprocity," *EWPL* no. 2 (1991): 126–42.

312. Booth, *Rhetoric*, 13 depicts it as an emotional effect of irony.

313. Sedgewick, *Of Irony*, 5.

314. Booth, "The Empire of Irony," 727, 729.

315. Cicero, *De or.*, II.LXXI.289.

"aha-moment," the enlightenment which is not an instant gratification but an enduring effect modifying the reader's perspective.

The pleasure that irony begets is somewhat close to humor.[316] Irony often includes a comic element because it creates an absurd, laughable situation in which true relation to reality is discovered in an embarrassing incongruity. Thus, laughter and understanding are often appropriate responses to irony. However, the essential quality of ironic laughter is neither carefree nor frivolous, because irony is an outcome of painful discord and conflict. Thus, G. S. Holland defined irony as the mixture of pleasure and pain.[317] Also, A. R. Thompson observes that if pure comedy is the effect of a sudden contrast which gratifies our feelings without hurting them, irony results from a comic situation when we are also pained.[318] In this sense, "dry mock" is a quite suitable name for irony,[319] since the laughter caused by irony withers on the lips of the reader.[320]

Though the corrective and didactic function of irony is suitable for the comic in its exposure of the chronic absurdity of the victim, it is in fact not a device of dismissible amusement. Irony does not aim at short-lived teasing as comedy does. It is rather serious in forcing the reader to choose the high cause of reality worthy of consideration. In the end, irony benefits the reader with a perspective that is only reached by crossing the ironic bridge lying between the two significantly different worlds of idea and quality.

---

316. We observed the historical treatment of irony as a sort of wit by ancient critics, particularly Cicero and Quintilian, in "Concept of Irony among the Early Authors" earlier in this chapter.

317. Holland, *Divine Irony*, 52.

318. Thompson, *The Dry Mock*, 19.

319. Worcester, *Satire*, 78 calls irony "dry mock," adopting the practice of a sixteenth century writer.

320. Thompson, *The Dry Mock*, 15.

3

Conventional Ironies

Irony is characteristically protean (*proteusartig*).[1] During the lengthy and intricate history of the study of irony, scholars have recognized various forms of irony. With this in mind, the book proposes to narrow the scope for the reading of Matthean passion narrative's irony to the three traditionally recognized forms of irony: verbal, dramatic, and character irony. We will categorize them as "conventional irony."

Well before irony had acquired its technical terminology, these three types of irony were recognized by their frequent occurrences. Also, each conventional irony has made a distinctive progress of its own amid the flow of the comprehensive history of irony. Chapter 3 will provide the definition of conventional irony as it pertains to each form. Next, it will describe each form of conventional irony by observing them within ancient classical literature and the Christian Scriptures in order to assist the reader to build firsthand experience with conventional irony. The selected Greek and Latin dramas are *Nubes* by Aristophanes (c. 446–388 BCE), *Oedipus Rex* by Sophocles (c. 495–406 BCE), *Bacchae* by Euripides (c. 480–406 BCE), and *Metamorphoses* by Apuleius (c. 123–180 CE). These writings will be examined because they provide fundamental examples of actual occurrence of irony, especially the long-established classical examples of conventional irony within literature. These sources are selected to strengthen the reader's understanding of irony and make him able to detect conventional irony, deepen familiarity with definitions, characteristics, and functions of irony, and finally to properly decipher conventional irony within a given literary context. There is no intention of offering a full comparative study.

Conventional irony requires a competent reader to read between the lines since irony is catching "the hidden," or unspoken dimensions of the text, behind "the apparent." In his book, *Metamorphoses*, the ancient ironist Lucius Apuleius

---

1. Otto Ribbeck, "Über den Begriff des eirōn," *Rheinisches Museum* 31 (1876): 400.

advises his intended reader with the statement, "You reader, pay attention! You shall delight" (*lector intende, laetaberis*).[2] When the reader retains *intentio* (concentration) proper to the interpretation of irony, he can effectively perceive the existence of irony. Sometimes, the reader may detect combinations of irony, such as an instance of verbal irony with dramatic irony, a moment of dramatic irony in an example of character irony, an occurrence of character irony with a case of verbal irony, or in some cases, all in one. On these occasions the reader may experience a difficulty in distinguishing each irony in a strict sense.

Verbal Irony

Verbal irony is the most ancient, the most frequently employed, and the simplest form of irony. Though verbal irony is the simplest form, it does not mean that its implication is simple. To grasp its full nuance, it is necessary for the reader to follow the plot of the story closely by paying attention (*intentio*) to the whole context, since no irony is non-contextual.

Verbal irony arises from the nuanced interaction of written words, speech or placement of words such as word-play.[3] Originally this one concept, "an ironic mode of speech," dominated the entire discussion of irony.[4] This corresponds to the fact that the alleged root of εἰρωνεία (a technical term for irony) is derived from the Greek verb, εἴρω (to speak, say). One can easily observe the preeminence of verbal irony in the listings of definitions given by English dictionaries. Most of them place the concept of irony pertaining to words and speech as the primary definition of irony and the concept of irony pertaining to events and situations as the secondary. For example, both the *Oxford English Dictionary* and the *American Heritage Dictionary* define irony in an identical way as follows.

> 1. A figure of speech in which the intended meaning is the opposite of that expressed by the words used; usually taking the form of sarcasm or ridicule in which laudatory expressions are used to imply condemnation or contempt. 2. A condition of affairs or events of a

---

2. Apuleius, *Metamorphoses*, I.1. Translation is mine.

3. Edwin M. Good, *Irony in the Old Testament* (Philadelphia: Westminster, 1965), 81–114. Also, James G. Williams, "Irony and Lament: Clues to Prophetic Consciousness," *Semeia* 8 (1977): 63 talks about the kind of word-play used by ancient Israelite narrators which juxtaposes the same or similar words in such a way as to produce irony, so-called, *paronomasia*.

4. John Connop Thirlwall, "On the Irony of Sophocles" (Philological Museum 2; repr., Geneva/New York: Hobart & William Smith Colleges, 1973), 483 calls verbal irony as the "most familiar species of irony."

character opposite to what was, or might naturally be, expected; a contradictory outcome of events as if in mockery of the promise and fitness of things.[5]

1. The use of words to convey the opposite of their literal meaning.
2. Incongruity between what might be expected and what actually occurs.[6]

In a story world, verbal irony pertains to speech or words which the ironist places into the mouths of characters within a narrative with the purpose of bringing about the ironic reversal of the meaning of speech or words. It creates a gap or incongruity between "what is said" and "what is meant" as a result of that the ironist stylistically chooses and arranges words in an ironic manner in order to point to certain connotations or senses for the reader.

As previously examined in chapter 2, verbal irony was traditionally categorized as one of the tropes. It is tongue-in-cheek and requires an intelligent and attentive reading of things beyond the surface of what has been said. Though the ironist says one thing but implies another,[7] or more specifically, signifies the opposite of what he says,[8] the verbal deliberation of the ironist must be disclosed to his intended reader through the given textual clues imbedded in the story's plot.

In speech, the tone and verbal gestures of the ironist can indicate that he wants to communicate something sharply different from the ostensible meaning of his statement.[9] The ironic speaker knows how to manipulate an ironic tone that can signify a contrast between what he simply says and what he really means. For example, the conversation between Mozart and his opponent,

---

5. J. A. Simpson and E. S. C. Weiner, eds., *The Oxford English Dictionary* VIII, 2nd ed. (Oxford: Clarendon, 1989).

6. *The American Heritage Dictionary*, 3nd ed. (New York: Dell, 1994), 443.

7. We previously established that Cicero, *De oratore* II.lxvii.269 gives the most essential definition of irony, "saying one thing and meaning another" (*aliud dicere ac sentias*). This definition is fundamentally applicable to all of conventional ironies.

8. Alan R. Thompson, *The Dry Mock: A Study of Irony in Drama* (Berkeley: University of California Press, 1948), 4.

9. In conversation, a speaker's attitude and evaluation toward what he is talking about partly become visible through his choice of tone of voice and attending verbal gestures. See Christopher W. Tindale and James Gough, "The Use of Irony in Argumentation," *Philosophy & Rhetoric* 20 (1987): 9, 11; Christopher R. Reaske, *Mirrors: An Introduction to Literature*, 3nd ed. (New York: Harper and Row, 1988), 197; Arthur Applebee et al., *Literature and Language: English and World Literature* (Evanston, IL: McDougal, Little & Co., 1992), 901.

Salieri, in the movie *Amadeus* (1984) serves as a good example of verbal irony delivered through a particular tone of voice and gesture. Salieri, the court composer of Emperor Joseph II, is festering with enflamed hatred and jealousy toward Mozart and most of all, toward Mozart's musical genius which he believes is the manifestation of God's unjust favoritism on Mozart. Salieri becomes obsessed with the idea of destroying Mozart in order to scorn God and his prodigy. While Salieri disguises himself with a mask of friendship toward Mozart, behind his back Salieri impedes every step of Mozart's advancement. During the time of staging the "Marriage of Figaro," Salieri reports to the national opera director, Herr Rosenberg, that Mozart employs ballet in Figaro's wedding, which goes against the emperor's edict banning ballet in his operas. Rosenberg rips out the part of the ballet scene from the score and commands Mozart to rewrite the music. Indignant Mozart, not knowing who in fact stirred up the incident against him, visits his own enemy, Salieri. The following conversation between Mozart and Salieri showcases the effective delivery of verbal irony through the tone and gestures of the character who is employing irony and the pleasure of the audience when verbal irony is clearly insinuated. As you read below, Salieri is greatly disappointed that the score was actually not burned but saved. In his seeming gratitude expressed in his statement, "Thank God," the audience senses the opposite emotion.

> Mozart: Please, please. I've no one else to turn to.
> Salieri: What is it?
> Mozart: It's unbelievable. The director has actually torn up a huge section of my music. They say I have to rewrite the opera. But, it's perfect as it is. I can't rewrite what's perfect. Please, can't you talk to him? Please.
> Salieri: Why bother with Rosenberg? He is obviously no friend of yours.
> Mozart: I could kill him. I mean really, kill him. I actually threw the entire score in the fire; He made me so angry.
> Salieri: You burned the score?
> Mozart: Oh, no. My wife took it out in time, heh.
> Salieri: Thank God.

Hearing Salieri's tone of voice and observing his body language in the actual movie will give a better indication of the verbal irony present in his statement. However, in written text, the ironist, unable to rely on the inflection of a voice, employs words spoken by characters to establish a distinctive literary tone that will convey his ironic attitude toward the matter at hand and therefore demand "reading between the lines."[10]

The account of "Cupid and Psyche" in *Metamorphoses* by Lucius Apuleius also provides good examples of verbal irony.[11] The story goes that a certain king and queen have three daughters of remarkable beauty, but the beauty of the youngest, Psyche, is so extraordinary that the sheer poverty of human language cannot describe it properly.[12] Consequently, her beauty provokes the jealousy of Venus because men turned their devotion to this young girl by deserting her altars. Venus arranges revenge against Psyche with her son, Cupid, and commissions him to drop bitter water drawn from one of the two fountains in Venus' garden on Psyche. However, approaching Psyche in her sleep, Cupid becomes mesmerized by her beauty, and by mistake wounds himself with his own arrow. Psyche, henceforth frowned upon by Venus, suffers forlorn solitude despite of all her incomparable charms. Kings, nobles, and young men all eagerly cast their eyes upon her, but nobody presents himself to demand her in marriage. Meanwhile, her sisters get married. Her parents, suspecting divine hostility (*caelestibus odiis et irae superum metuens*), consult the ancient oracle of the Milesian god but get a gloomy response that they should desert Psyche on a lofty mountain crag for her destined cruel, wild and reptilian monster husband (*saevum atque ferum vipereumque malum*).[13]

Yet, what really happens on the upper level of the story is that Cupid, falling in love with Psyche, prepares a nuptial for himself and extravagantly arranges all the situations to make it happen. Psyche, despairing and saddened by her misfortune, is led into her abode prepared by the god himself and eventually begins to enjoy all the heavenly luxuries and comforts ready for her. The circumstances are quite engaging and mysterious. She has not only vocal attendants without form but also an unknown husband who comes only in the hours of darkness and flees before the dawn. In time, Psyche becomes pregnant. Being inflamed by his ardent affection toward Psyche, Cupid often assures her with his words of love and passion, all the while charging her to make no attempt to see or reveal him.

---

10. Applebee, ibid., 901.

11. Apuleius' *Metamorphoses* is the lengthy fictional narrative, later called "The Golden Ass." The story is narrated by Lucius, who, because of his curiosity of magic, is turned into an ass. After his ordeal with various men he is finally restored to his old self by the help of the goddess Isis. The account of "Cupid and Psyche" is found in *Metam.*, IV.28–V.31.

12. Ibid., IV.28.

13. Ibid., VI.32–33.

After a honeymoon of some time, Psyche begins longing to reunite with her family, imploring Cupid to show her favor. Finally, under the firm stipulation that she must guard the secret, otherwise she will lose all her bliss, Cupid permits Psyche to invite her sisters to their extraordinary home filled with celestial delights and wonders. As soon as her sisters lay their eyes on Psyche's unimaginable privileges and happiness, an irrepressible jealousy begins to consume them. Thus, the sisters begin to grumble over their ordinary lives and brood evil thoughts to harm Psyche. They become bold and sly, and decide to give her ill advice. In this context we meet the following verbal irony in which the sisters, being ignorant of the reality beyond their perception, speak the truth, which is what is exactly intended to be declared by the ironist:

> Psyche, you are not the little girl you used to be, but you are now yourself a mother. Think what a good thing for us you are carrying in your purse! With what delight you will make our entire house happy! O how the joy of that golden baby will bless us! If he resembles his parents, as he ought to, in beauty, he will be absolutely born a Cupid.[14]

Psyche's sisters are spiritually double blind-folded because they have not only a devious intention[15] but also false information regarding Psyche's husband. They think him to be a monster, based on the oracle that their parents had once received. In contrast to the ignorance of the sisters, the reader, knowing the context of the story, understands that such a twist of information regarding who is the real husband of Psyche adds flavor and dramatic suspense to the story. Therefore, the irony observed in this love affair between Psyche and Cupid is complex in form including both situational and verbal. The irony created by Cupid himself is situational because Cupid, being commissioned by his mother, Venus, to carry out vengeance against Psyche, falls as the very victim of his own arrow and therefore, frustrates his mother's will. Also, the irony which wraps the ill-willed words of Psyche's sisters is verbal because the sisters hit upon reality by unknowingly suggesting that Psyche is indeed expecting the child of Cupid himself, who is identified as a god of love[16] and whose beauty

---

14. Ibid., V.14, "Psyche, non ita ut pridem parvula, et ipsa iam mater es. Quantum, putas, boni nobis in ista geris perula! Quantis gaudiis totam domum nostrum hilarabis! O nos beatas, quas infantis aurei nutrimenta laetabunt! Qui si parentum, ut oportet, pulchritudini responderit, prorsus Cupido nascetur." Translation is mine.

15. Ibid., V.9 and 15 speak of their envy (*gliscentis invidiae*) and pretended affection (*affectione simulata*).

16. Ibid., V.23, "Thus, being ignorant of it, Psyche of her own accord fell in love with Love" (*sic ignara Psyche sponte in Amoris incidit amorem*). Translation is mine.

is beyond expression.[17] Further, Apuleius, the ironist himself, speaks overtly a verbal irony when he depicts the inferior quality of Psyche's sisters by speaking "those worthy sisters" (*sorores egregiae*),[18] which clearly implies the opposite. Given the fact that the ancient drama is orally performed, it is amusing to have a mental picture of Apuleius saying this with a smirk on his face while looking at his audience.

As all ironies do, verbal irony implies an ironist, someone consciously employing a technique behind the scene because this type of irony is closely bound to the ironist's specific tactic and strategic control over words. In the story world, the verbal irony of the εἴρων represents the norms and values of the implied author-ironist of the story, through the way in which the ironist entrusts ironic words in his protagonist's mouth. Dorothy Jean Weaver explains this in saying that "verbal ironies are those in which the ironist communicates the irony in his/her own voice or in the voice of an 'innocent' character within the narrative itself."[19]

On some occasions, however, this master ironist also permits the ἀλαζών to speak ironically in his ignorance and self-unawareness so that the very speaker falls into the trap of his own verbal irony. In such a cases, the effect of verbal irony is a self-mocking of the ἀλαζών. For example, in the parable of the Pharisee and the tax collector in Luke 18:9-14, Jesus speaks against the self-righteous.[20] The parable goes that a Pharisee and a tax collector go up to the temple to pray and exhibit starkly contrasting attitudes in their supplication. The former brags that he is spiritually superior to the so-called *sinners* (18:11),[21] while the latter identifies himself as a *sinner* by imploring the mercy of God (18:13).[22] The words of the Pharisee, "God, I give thanks to you that I am not like other men" (8:12), bring about an ironic reversal from self-glorification to self-mockery as Jesus openly explains that the one who is justified (δεδικαιωμένος, 8:14) in God's sight is the tax collector and not the Pharisee. Therefore, the words of the Pharisee, ignorantly claiming self-knowledge of his excellence, testify to his wretchedness and spiritual

---

17. Ibid., V.22 gives an elaborate description of the beauty of Cupid.

18. Ibid., V.9.

19. Dorothy Jean Weaver, "Power and Powerlessness: Matthew's Use of Irony in the Portrayal of Political Leaders," *SBL* 31 (1992): 455.

20. Luke 18:9, "Who think in themselves that they are righteous and have a contempt for everybody else" (τοὺς πεποιθόντας ἐφ' ἑαυτοῖς ὅτι εἰσὶν δίκαιοι καὶ ἐξουθενοῦντας τοὺς λοιποὺς).

21. Luke 18:11, "Robbers, unjust, adulterers or even like this tax collector" (ἅρπαγες, ἄδικοι, μοιχοί, ἢ καὶ ὡς οὗτος ὁ τελώνης).

22. Luke 18:13, "God, be merciful to me a sinner" (Ὁ θεός, ἱλάσθητί μοι τῷ ἁμαρτωλῷ).

estrangement from God. His faulty and limited awareness of the self, accompanying his arrogant self-praise, is a toxic combination of characteristics which not only deters the grace of God but also makes him scarcely open his mouth without victimizing himself.

A well-known conversation between David and Nathan, the prophet, exemplifies another case of the ἀλαζών's self-criticism. The verbal irony of 2 Samuel 12:1-6 exposes David as ἀλαζών. God has sent Nathan to David, who had sinned against God by committing adultery with Bathsheba and killing her husband, Uriah. Instead of chiding him directly, Nathan tells David a story of a poor man with one little ewe lamb. The poor man cherishes that lamb as if it were a daughter to him (כְּבַת לוֹ־וַתְּהִי, 12:3). However, the rich man snatches it away, kills it, and serves his guest with it. On hearing this, David becomes enraged and says to Nathan, "As the Lord lives, the man who has done this shall surely die!" (12:5b). There is a strikingly obvious inconsistency between David's damning ignorance of the serious nature of his own injustice against Uriah, his faithful servant (2 Sam. 11:7-13), and his rage and judgment of the rich man's misdeed in Nathan's story. Nathan's choice of language in his portrayal of the story is self-descriptive enough to reflect David's deed: the poor man in love with his little ewe lamb stands for Uriah, the little lamb in the bosom of the poor man represents Bathsheba, and the rich man full of greed and violence stands for David. However, the voluntary confession of sin that Nathan's story could have elicited from David does not occur. Rather, David utters an irony which indirectly identifies him as the criminal deserving death (12:5b). David's moral and spiritual blindness seem to be beyond remedy when he confidently speaks that he will make the rich man pay his due commensurate to his crime, without noticing that his crime is greater than the rich man's wrongdoing. If a fair payment appropriate for the rich man, who stole a little ewe lamb, is his own death, what punishment would be reasonable for David, who not only coveted his neighbor's wife but also committed the actual murder of that innocent man? In this way, the saying of David in 2 Samuel 12:5 exemplifies a powerful self-condemnation delivered through the ironic sayings of the ἀλαζών in his absurdity and condemning ignorance.

There has been confusion acknowledged by the critics in distinguishing verbal irony from other figures of speech, and particularly sarcasm.[23] Here, we will briefly examine fundamental differences between verbal irony and sarcasm so that the terms are understood distinctly and that any confusion the

---

23. Thompson, *The Dry Mock*, 5 calls verbal irony with a heavy tint of sarcasm, the "dry mock," which he used for his book title. He writes of verbal irony that it is "almost always offensive." Another scholar, R. Reed Lessing, *Jonah* (St. Louis: Concordia Publishing House, 2007), 23 relates irony to satire.

proper interpretation of verbal irony may be avoided. Although verbal irony and sarcasm are not the same, sarcasm is quite often mistaken for verbal irony because the two concepts have become so intertwined.[24] Basically, in both cases, what the author says and what he means by it are in opposition. There seems to be a division among the literary critics as to which one of these two is the generically broad category. While Cleanth C. Brooks notes sarcasm as the most direct and blatant form of irony,[25] David J. Amante views it as the minimal form of irony.[26] Further, Jerry C. Hoggatt considers verbal irony a bigger concept than sarcasm which is a subgenre of verbal irony. He notes four forms of verbal irony—deliberate ambiguity, sarcasm, hyperbole, and meiosis—that are uttered with the speaker's full consciousness.[27] Conversely, D. C. Muecke places irony under the umbrella of sarcasm.[28]

Perhaps, the following observations might be helpful. First, sarcasm is often viewed as a suitable tone for the ironist,[29] because even though the ironist of the narrative avoids a personal tone, he may retain a sarcastic edge in his voice. That is partially why verbal irony is frequently misjudged as sarcasm. Albert N. Katz, however, believes that the major distinction between them is that ridicule is an important element in sarcasm, but not in verbal irony.[30] For this reason, David Holdcroft evaluates sarcasm as a more low-brow version of irony.[31] Second, D. C. Muecke suggests that whereas the ironist pretends to be innocent in his intent, the author of sarcasm does not pretend to be unaware of his real meaning and does not anticipate his reader to be either.[32] If victimization is a goal of sarcasm by letting the reader be caught in a net of the author's craft, verbal irony rather intends "meaningful communication"[33] and establishing "confederacy."[34] Some verbal irony is sarcastic, but if it ends there, it turns out to be failed,

---

24. William F. Thrall and Addison Hibbard, *A Handbook to Literature* (rev. C. H. Holman; New York: Odyssey, 1960), 248.

25. Cleanth Brooks, "Irony as a Principle of Structure," in *Literary Opinion in America*, ed. M. D. Zabel (New York: Harper & Brothers, 1951), 730.

26. David J. Amante, "The Theory of Ironic Speech Acts," *Poetics Today* 2, 2 (1981): 80.

27. Jerry C. Hoggatt, *Irony in Mark's Gospel: Text and Subtext* (New York: Cambridge University Press, 1992), 85.

28. Douglas C. Muecke, *The Compass of Irony* (London: Methuen, 1969), 54–55.

29. Muecke, ibid., 64; David Kaufer, "Ironic Evaluations," *Communications Monographs* 48 (1981): 25; M. H. Abrams, *A Glossary of Literary Terms*, 4th ed. (New York: Holt, Rinehart & Winston, 1991), 99.

30. Albert N. Katz, "The Uses and Processing of Irony and Sarcasm," *Metaphor and Symbol* 15 (2000): 1–4.

31. David Holdcroft, "Irony as a Trope, and Irony as Discourse," *Poetics Today* 4 (1983): 495.

32. Muecke, *Compass*, 20.

33. Amante, "Ironic Speech Acts," 78.

ineffective irony. Third, sarcasm is more vocally oriented than verbal irony. When it is spoken, sarcasm is emotionally bitter, crude, and cutting speech in contrast to the cool,[35] dispassionate, and calculated "indirection" of irony.[36] Despite these defining differences between a verbal irony and sarcasm, in many cases sarcasm written in texts is hard to distinguish it from a verbal irony.

Dramatic Irony

Dramatic irony, which has been given various names,[37] pertains to a deliberately ironic event or situation within the narrative. This concept applies not to statements but to events, situations and the broad structure of the story, which is the plot.[38] Broadly speaking, dramatic irony is considered a plot device.[39] This type of irony illumines the duality of the difference between what appears to be happening and what is actually happening.

Dramatic irony was long underemphasized in comparison with verbal irony until the nineteenth century when John Connop Thirlwall ushered in the concept of dramatic irony with his study on the Sopoclean tragedy.[40] In

---

34. David Kaufer, "Irony and Rhetorical Strategy," *Philosophy & Rhetoric* 10 (1977): 100; Tindale and Gough, "The Use of Irony," 2. For more discussion on the interpretive community existing between the ironist and the ironically capable reader, consult "The Implicit, Interpretative Community and the Victim of Irony" of Chapter Two.

35. Thrall and Hibbard, *A Handbook to Literature*, 248 uses the term, "coolness" to describe the mental and spiritual status of the ironist. This concept has some other synonyms such as "detachment" or "indirection." Muecke, *Compass*, 93–94, 114, 216–17, explains detachment as the behavioral mode of the ironist. Especially, in page 94, he writes that a satirist "may be motivated by indignation, disgust, or contempt; but as an ironist he will conceal his real feelings under a show of dispassionate logic, gravity, or urbanity, or even go beyond neutrality to express the opposite of what he really feels by pretending sympathy, earnestness, or enthusiasm."

36. Thrall and Hibbard, *A Handbook to Literature*, 248 coins the term, "unemotional detachment," on the part of the ironist, and further writes that "it (irony) is usually lighter, less harsh in its wording though in effect probably more cutting because of its indirectness. It bears, too, a close relationship to innuendo."

37. Such as situational, sophoclean, tragic or practical irony, irony of fate or irony of events. We observed various names given to dramatic irony in the section, "The Concept of Irony in the Modern Age" of Chapter 2.

38. Aristotle, *Poetica*, VI considers plot, the so-called "arrangements of the incidents," as the most important feature of tragedy.

39. Joseph T. Shipley, *Dictionary of World Literature, Criticism, Forms, Technique* (New York: Philosophical Library, 1943), 331 defines dramatic irony "as a device whereby . . . incongruity is introduced in the very structure of the plot, by having the spectators aware of elements in the situations of which one or more the character involved are ignorant."

40. Garnett G. Sedgewick, *Of Irony: Especially in the Drama* (Toronto: University of Toronto Press, 1935), 22 explains that prior to Thirlwall's essay, there is no recorded use of the term, dramatic (that is,

the beginning of his article, Thirlwall clearly states that irony is a tragic poet's attribute.[41] Although the concept of dramatic irony only came to scholarly attention in 1833, the publication year of Thirlwall's essay, "On the Irony of Sophocles," and the term was not universally acceptable even as late as 1907,[42] this type of irony has been employed since ancient times.

Thirlwall paid attention to the ironic event in tragedy. By doing so, he broadened the horizon of irony to incorporate a wider range of literature. Tragic irony as a synonym for dramatic irony refers not only an irony pertaining to dramatic tragedy but also an irony that has tragic overtones. The book prefers to use the term, "dramatic irony," to "tragic irony" despite the following shortcomings. First, dramatic irony can give the impression that this type of irony mainly belongs to the theater. Garnett G. Sedgewick represents this view saying, "Dramatic irony, in brief, is the sense of contradiction felt by spectators of a drama who see a character acting in ignorance of his condition."[43] Also, Muecke expresses an identical view that "dramatic irony is pre-eminently the irony of the theater, being implicit in the very nature of a play."[44] Even though dramatic irony originally referred to the irony of events as exhibited in a play,[45] it is not found only in drama, but also broadly includes any dramatic form of irony which attends to an ironic situation.[46] Second, the concept of dramatic irony is the child of Thirlwall's monumental study of the Sophoclean tragedies. Therefore, Thirlwall's dramatic irony primarily concerns Sophocles' use of irony as the author's technique to highlight the tragic elements of his writings. It is known that Sophoclean irony works in such a way that his tragic character sees the yellow caution signs proclaiming personal calamity ahead, but does what he is about to do anyway. However, dramatic irony is actually found not only in tragedy but also in comedy. The effects brought forward in each case, however, may be different. If the dramatic irony used in tragedy points to the significance of the situation and stirs up the reader's sense of ἔλεος (pity) and φόβος (fear),[47] the irony of events used in comedy makes

Sophoclean or tragic) irony as applied to irony. See "The Concept of Irony in the Modern Age" of Chapter One for the discussion on Thirlwall and his contribution to the study of irony in modern times.

41. Thirlwall, "On the Irony of Sophocles," 483.
42. Sedgewick, *Of Irony*, 23.
43. Ibid., 49.
44. Muecke, *Compass*, 105.
45. Thompson, *The Dry Mock*, 29–30.
46. Joseph A. Dane, *The Critical Mythology of Irony* (Athens: University of Georgia Press, 1991), 121; Applebee, *Literature and Language*, 161.
47. According to Aristotle, *Poet.*, IX, XIV, these senses will guide the reader to experience the spiritual "κάθαρσις" (purification).

the outcome incongruous to the expectation in a painfully comic way. When we give consideration to all these facts, dramatic irony is not limited to one genre of literature. Rather, dramatic irony is a bigger concept than tragic irony and pertains to the ironic event or situation that brings about the reversal of meaning in the story world.

Sophocles' *Oedipus Rex* is esteemed, perhaps more than any other writing of antiquity, as a fine specimen of dramatic irony.[48] In this tragic play, Oedipus, the king of Thebes, assumes the role of a fated hero who unknowingly kills his own father, Laius. The entire story hinges on the secret of Oedipus of which he himself is ignorant.[49] When he was an infant, Oedipus was deserted by his parents, Laius and Jocasta, as they attempted to thwart the hideous oracle that their son would be a great threat against the kingship as well as their marriage. Yet, Oedipus was rescued by a shepherd and raised in the court of King Polybus of Corinth. Later, the adult Oedipus hears of the rumor that Polybus and his wife, Merope are not his actual parents, and leaves Corinth. On the road to Thebes, being unaware of his past, Oedipus fatefully meets his biological father, Laius, argues over which wagon has the right-of-way, and being driven by his unchecked pride, slays his own father. Meanwhile, the kingdom of Thebes was under the curse of the riddle of the Sphinx. Before his entry to the city, Oedipus solves that riddle and sets the kingdom free from malice. As a liberator, Oedipus is welcomed by the Thebans and given the throne of Thebes, which was the throne of his father, Laius, as well as the widowed queen, Jocasta, the biological mother of Oedipus. In the meantime, a plague came over the city. Smitten hard by the plague the Thebans make cry out to their new king, Oedipus to find the murderer of Laius because Apollo's oracle explains that the cause of the plague has to do with the murder of Laius, the former king of Thebes, and the cure lies in bringing his murderer to justice. As Oedipus undertakes his investigation, the blind, aged prophet, Tiresias entreats him to quit the search. Yet, Oedipus, being obstinate, accuses Tiresias of murdering Laius and conspiring with Creon, his mother's brother to overthrow Oedipus.

---

48. Thirlwall, "On the Irony of Sophocles," 494, 536. Holland, *Divine Irony* (London: Associated University Presses, 2000), 69 reiterates Thirlwall's view.

49. Interestingly, Sophocles supplies an ironic cue in the very name of "Oedipus," telling this figure to be the generator of irony surrounding his life. Peter L. Rudnytsky, *Freud and Oedipus* (New York: Columbia University Press, 1987), 266 notes that the Greek meaning of *Oedipus* can be *know-foot* based on the analysis that the first syllable of Oedipus' name, *oido*, means "I know" and the second syllable, *pous*, means "foot." Therefore, the ironic point of his name becomes evident because Oedipus was completely *unknowing* of his own destiny, thus, he fell hard in his futile actions such as the search for Laius' murderer and the emphatic denial of his fallibility.

Thus, the search continues, and Oedipus inevitably comes closer to the tragic truth, ultimately learning that he has committed patricide and violated natural law by being the husband of his own mother, Jocasta. Laius and Jocasta once received an old prophecy that her son should kill his father and have children with his mother. To prevent its fulfillment, the queen had deserted their infant son, Oedipus, in the mountains. However, as we have seen, despite all these efforts to bend their portentous fate, Oedipus, being ignorant of his past, came across his father and killed him. It is utterly tragic that Oedipus is at the center of all these incidents of horror, cannot be exempt from culpability regardless of his innocent ignorance, and comes to the realization that the ancient prophecy has been fulfilled in each dreadful detail. He turns out to be the victim of his own fate and finitude. Correspondingly, the story ends with the characters' acceptance of their dooms. Jocasta, in her honor, hangs herself and Oedipus stabs out his eyes to be blind. In all of these events, the reader is *knowing* in contrast to Oedipus' *unknowing*, because the reader takes advantage of the superior knowledge of the old prophecy on which the entire story hinges.

In the context of the story, dramatic irony does imply an ironist responsible for the narrative. The ironist, as master of the situation, deliberately conceals an ironic event or more precisely the meaning of the event, from the characters of the narrative while disclosing it to the reader. He intends the reader's knowledge of events wrought by the interactions of the characters to surpass that of the characters. Therefore, dramatic irony emerges from the contrast between the perception of a situation by the character who has a limited understanding of the real state of affairs and the reader who is fully aware of what is really happening. The reader of dramatic irony not only has a much larger reservoir of information for the proper understanding of the nature of the events but also has the privilege of observing the events from a different vantage point than the characters. The reader is called upon for "reminiscence and anticipation"[50] based on his repertoire of knowledge in the process of establishing a distinctive subtext of his own.[51]

The biblical story of Ehud's killing of Eglon, King of Moab, in Judges 3:12-25 serves as an example of dramatic irony that illustrates the reader's privileged status of knowledge and the way that his "reminiscence and anticipation" cooperate in interpreting the irony. Furthermore, the dramatic irony of this story highlights the reader's superior knowledge and Eglon's ignorance as the victim. Judges 3:12-15 draws the reader's attention to the

---

50. Sedgewick, *Of Irony*, 44, considers these two elements as common functions of a great dramatic irony, at least in tragedy.

51. Hoggatt, *Irony in Mark's Gospel*, 2.

ultimate, divine control over the situation as the norm. It was God who placed Israel under the sway of Eglon for eighteen years because Israel was evil in the sight of the Lord (Judg. 3:12, 14). Also, it is the same Lord who, hearing Israel's cry for help, raised up for them a deliverer, a left-handed man Ehud, the son of Gera, the Benjaminite (Judg. 3:15). Commissioned by God, Ehud prepares himself with a double-edged sword to carry out the assassination of Eglon. As usual, Ehud presents the tribute of Israel to Eglon, in a gesture to make Eglon *un-gird*, while he himself is *girded* (וַיַּחְגֹּר, Judg. 3:16) with a deadly weapon with a specific purpose in mind. Ehud's "secret message" (סֵתֶר־דָּבָר, Judg. 3:19) for the king adds a thrill to the picture because it entices Eglon's voluntary isolation with Ehud so that Ehud can bring out the ironic reality of the "secret message." As soon as Eglon sends out his attendants, a second time Ehud says more specifically that he has "a message from God" (דְּבַר־אֱלֹהִים, Judg. 3:20) for him, which intrigues Eglon, making him want to hear even more. In this way, Ehud methodically approaches Eglon as a hunter patiently but systematically zooming in on his prey.

Dramatic irony is often coupled with good suspense. The reader who is fully aware of Ehud's undertaking of the divine commission consciously *recollects* the information and *anticipates* its completion. Therefore, when Ehud says to Elgon that he has a secret word from God, the reader can concur that it is all true but in a substantially different way than on the surface of the story. On hearing the statement of Ehud, "Oh! King, I have a message from God for you" (Judg. 3:20), the reader experiences suspense because he anticipates otherwise than does Eglon in the story world. Robert Alter explains that "Ehud's statement is a rather obvious but nevertheless effective piece of dramatic irony"[52] because the statement points to an ironic event in which "what appears to happen" will clearly betray "what is going to happen." What Ehud has for Eglon is actually from God on the ostensible level, but not a *word* (דָּבָר), which glides into his ear but a *thing* (דָּבָר),[53] a *sword* (חֶרֶב), with which Ehud pierces Eglon's belly. Another level of complexity in this dramatic irony is revealed in the word of Ehud that he has a "secret (סֵתֶר)" word for the king. Again, it is strikingly true when the reader recollects how Ehud hid the sword "on his right thigh under his clothes" (מִתַּחַת לְמַדָּיו עַל יֶרֶךְ יְמִינוֹ, Judg. 3:16) and further that Eglon chose to be left alone with Ehud so that the *word* (חֶרֶב) of God, in its true nature, the sword from God, will fulfill its purpose in secrecy.

---

52. Robert Alter, *The Art of Biblical Narrative* (New York: Basic Books, 1981), 40.

53. The Hebrew term, דָּבָר, can cover wide range of meanings such as speech, word, message, matter or thing. See *A Hebrew and English Lexicon of the Old Testament*, ed. Francis Brown et al., trans. Edward Robinson (London: Oxford University Press, 1955), 183.

As we observe in this story of Ehud and Eglon, the privileged status of the reader in knowing more than the characters allows to his participation in the upper level of the double-layered stories. The fundamental clash between the two levels of the story exposes a certain character or group as blind to the reality which the upper level of the story portrays. Therefore, the reversal of fortune of the characters, what Aristotle terms περιπέτεια (*peripeteia*)[54] is key, since dramatic irony requires a reader of superior knowledge regarding the precise nature of the situation in contrast to the characters' blindness concerning an event in which they are involved.

Another classic tragedy worth mentioning in connection to dramatic irony is Euripides' *Bacchae*.[55] The most dramatic scene of the *Bacchae* begins when frenzied Agave enters, carrying the head of her slain son, Pentheus, the grandson of Cadmus the king of Thebes. This provides an excellent example of dramatic irony that underlines the character's utter ignorance of reality and its tragic result. This story is horrific in that the mother, who beheaded her son as if he were a wild beast and carried his blood-soaked head in her arms, slowly comes to a realization of her own unspeakably brutal crime.[56] Being lost in her Bacchic madness, Agave meets her father Cadmus and engages in a conversation that unfolds the dramatic irony of the tragic event of which she is unaware. Gazing at Agave's bloodstained hands, Cadmus perceives an affliction coming upon his household, while in her ecstasy, Agave boasts of her valor and prize, and puzzles about her father's lament. In the following conversation, Cadmus functions as the projection of the ironist. His staccato questions shake Agave in her frenzy to get to the point which matters most.

> Cadmus: To what house camest thou with bridal-hymns?
> Agave: Echion's—of the Dragon—seed, men say.
> Cadmus: Thou barest—in thine halls, to thy lord—whom?
> Agave: Pentheus—born of my union with his sire.
> Cadmus: Whose head—*whose* ?—art thou bearing in thine arms?
> Agave: A lion's—so said they which hunted it.[57]

---

54. According to Aristotle's *Poet.*, XI, the *peripeteia* means the reversal of the situation in the plot of a tragedy, in other words, the change of fortune for the hero. An event occurs contrary to the audience's initial expectations and is therefore surprising. Nonetheless, it appears as an inevitable outcome of the previous actions.

55. Euripides wrote this tragedy, *Bacchae*, in Athens before 405 BCE. This play is known as the most difficult of all the Greek tragedies to interpret despite its literary quality. In *Bacch.*, Euripides attends to the question of the wild and orgiastic worship of the god, Dionysus, the son of Zeus and Semele, daughter of the Theban king, Cadmus.

56. Euripides, ibid., 3:1024–1152.

Agave's nocuous innocence marked by her ignorance of the situation is manifested in her own statements. Euripides exploits Agave's *alazonic* innocence as the scene unfolds. As the suspense, corresponding to the gravity of this tragedy, grows, Euripides rushes Agave's realization, not even allowing her to have a moment for gasping. He lets Agave brag about her game in wanton insolence (ὕβρις), then immediately takes a drastic turn and places her under the light of painful awakening, "No! Wretched! Wretched! Pentheus' head I hold!" (οὐκ ἀλλὰ Πενθέως ἡ τάλαιν ἔχω κάρα).[58]

Since dramatic irony arises in the situation of contradiction, it is sometimes confused with the paradox of impossible situation or position. Having in mind that not every contradiction creates irony equips the reader to critically filter out dramatic irony from among many quasi-ironic situations. The essential difference between dramatic irony and paradox lies in their evaluation of the worlds in juxtaposition. If the former creates a hierarchical order of views in which one is superior to the other in its quality, the latter yields a puzzle or dilemma in which value judgment becomes vague because its premises, though they seem to be contradictory, do not really imply contradiction.[59] If the situation presented by dramatic irony is bound to the matter of "true and false" or "superior and inferior," that of a paradox is not so. The situation of "Buridan's ass"[60] best exemplifies a paradoxical situation which should not be confused with dramatic irony. An ass placed exactly in the middle of two stacks of hay of equal size and quality is unable to engage in moving toward either side because the alternative choice is equally attractive, desirable and accessible. This paradoxical situation causes the ass a dilemma of fortune that he must starve until he reaches a decision. For this case to be an ironic situation, the observer should be able to make a value judgment of either/or based on some external criteria that points to the discrepancy of quality between the two objects of interest.

---

57. Ibid., 3:1273–1278 (Way, LCL).
58. Ibid., 3:1284 (Way, LCL).
59. Matt. 13:13 and Mark 8:18 serve as examples for this. They show Jesus' use of paradox in his teaching, "they have ears but hear not," and "they have eyes but see not."
60. Jack Zupko, *Jean Buridan: Portrait of a Fourteenth-Century Arts Master* (Notre Dame: University of Notre Dame Press, 2003), 258 explains that this paradox is named after the fourteenth century French philosopher Jean Buridan. The classical example of Buridan's ass goes back to Aristotle, *De Caelo*, 295b, 31–34 in which he depicts a man in a dilemma, placed equal distances from food and drink. The man remains unmoved because he is as hungry as he is thirsty.

Character Irony

One of the typical functions of irony is to reveal character.[61] The traditional perception of character irony chiefly relies on old comedy, specifically the paradigm of εἴρων–ἀλαζών. Later it became inseparable from Socrates,[62] the epicenter of εἰρωνεία (irony), who takes on the behavioral mode of the εἴρων to devalue what others value. By employing irony, Socrates characterizes his wrongheaded opponent, the ἀλαζών, as a man of superficiality.

Historically, character irony has been discussed less by the critics, in spite of its antiquity and authenticity. Muecke says that the two kinds of irony most familiar to English-speaking people are verbal and situational ironies.[63] The reason for the unpopularity of character irony in scholarly discussions can be inferred through a consideration of its origin. Although the ancient εἴρων–ἀλαζών paradigm has its roots deep in old comedy, the history of εἰρωνεία shows that it only began to gain significant attention through its connection with Socrates. Yet, the tool with which Socrates disclosed the ignorant self-absorbance of the ἀλαζών was his famous pedagogic methodology, ἔλεγχος (transliterated as *elenchus*), the so-called "Socratic debate" or "dialectic method of inquiry"[64] which is closely related to verbal irony.[65]

Among the qualified critics of irony, Alan R. Thompson has emphasized that character irony is its own discrete form. He defines character irony as irony of character or of manner, in which a person's true character is shown to be in painfully comic contrast to his overt appearance or manner.[66] Yet, Thompson's

---

61. Sedgewick, *Of Irony*, 50; Alter, *The Art of Biblical Narrative*, 37.

62. See Gregory Vlastos, "Socratic Irony," *CQ* 37 (1987): 79–97; Hugh H. Benson, ed., *Essays on the Philosophy of Socrates* (New York: Oxford University Press, 1992), 66–86; Alexander Nehamas, *The Art of Living: Socratic Reflections from Plato to Foucault* (Berkeley: University of California Press, 1998), 46–101; Diskin Clay, *Platonic Questions: Dialogues with the Silent Philosopher* (University Park: Pennsylvania State University Press, 2000), 93–101; Holland, *Divine Irony*, 90–101.

63. Muecke, *Compass*, 42.

64. The *elenchus* is the technique Socrates uses to investigate the nature or the definition of ethical concepts. Its general rule is that Socrates' partner must answer every question according to his own beliefs. Socrates undertakes a disavowal of knowledge to begin his critical question that starts from his partner's initial statements. Meanwhile, he seeks clarification of that claim and eventually gets to the point of eliciting his partner's consent which will turn out to be inconsistent with the initial claim. In this way, Socrates exposes and challenges his partner's mental confinement or absurdity. See Gregory Vlastos, "The Socratic Elenchus," in *Oxford Studies in Ancient Philosophy*, ed. Julia Annas (Oxford: Clarendon, 1983), 1:27–58.

65. Northrop Frye, *The Great Code: The Bible and Literature* (New York: Harcourt, 1982), 8, writes that "his [Socrates] celebrated 'irony' was a momentous step in transforming the use of language: it implied renouncing the personal possession of wisdom in favor of an ability to observe it."

definition of character irony is rather too narrow because he shows a tendency to define every irony according to the form of its comic element.[67] This book does not agree with Thompson's view because his emphasis on the comic element as the key feature of irony unfortunately excludes other examples of character irony that may not necessarily convey the comic trait. It is not a definite attribute of character irony to elicit laughter. Rather, it can expose the drastic contrast and reversal between the two essentially opposite characters: the temporarily powerful nature of ἀλαζών vs. the ultimately superior nature of the underdog εἴρων. Therefore, character irony more broadly pertains to a character and his way of life that results in the reversal of how status is assigned or perceived.

In the story world, character irony deals with the deliberately ironic relationship of the characters. Its basic model arises from the sharp contrast between two diametrically opposite characters, εἴρων and ἀλαζών, and operates through a sharp conflict in their values. While the former stands for a protagonist who promotes and acts upon the normative values which the story defends, the latter serves as an antagonistic and shadowy figure who acts against the values upheld by the story. The clash of values demonstrated by these two characters is persistent and irreconcilable. The reader finds pleasure in that character irony reveals the incompatible natures of the ἀλαζών and the εἴρων which causes a dramatic clash and calls for the resolution of the conflict. The conventional image of the ἀλαζών is that of a victim. He talks and acts continuously in ignorance of his condition and in wrong self-conviction. Therefore, the role of the ἀλαζών as a victim is significant in that he functions as a foil to disclose the εἴρων, the ultimate victor. This reminds us of Cicero's interpretation that the εἴρων and the ἀλαζών are correlative terms and that neither is intelligible apart from the other.[68]

The Matthean use of irony in its portrayal of the political and religious leaders supplies excellent examples of the ironic function of the traditional

---

66. Thompson, *The Dry Mock*, 7–8. Also, David Worcester, *The Art of Satire* (Cambridge: Harvard University Press, 1940), 90, defines character irony with the term "irony of manner."

67. Other scholars, who emphasize the comic element as the key feature of irony, are Jakob Jónsson, *Humor and Irony in the New Testament Illuminated by Parallels in Talmud and Midrash* (Reykjavik: Bókaútgáfa Menningarsjóts, 1965); Kenneth Burke, *A Grammar of Motives*, 2nd ed. (1955, repr.; Berkeley: University of California Press, 1969); and Candace D. Lang, *Irony/Humor: Critical Paradigms* (Baltimore: Johns Hopkins University Press, 1988). Burke considers irony as a constitutive element of motive and a synonym for comedy. In opposition, scholar J. C. Hoggatt criticizes Jónsson's obsessive attention to the humor of Jesus' sayings, which entirely misses the obvious ironies within Jesus' story. See Hoggatt, *Irony in Mark's Gospel*, 2–3.

68. Cicero, *De officiis*, I.30.

εἴρων–ἀλαζών paradigm. Dorothy Jean Weaver suggests that irony is used by the Matthean author to depict the character contrast between Jesus and key political leaders specifically in relation to their exercise of authority and power.[69] Weaver was not specific in labeling what type of irony the implied author of Matthew employs but rather she concentrates on irony revealing the characters' personalities. Irony reveals the power*fulness* of Jesus who appears as power*less* by undermining the seemingly powerful pretenders—Herod the king (ch. 2), Herod the tetrarch (ch. 14), and Pilate the governor (ch. 27).[70]

In the same way which the Matthean implied author depicts the political leaders in an ironic contrast to Jesus, he also casts the Jewish religious readers, the chief opponents of Jesus, ironically. Through this ironic contrast between the protagonist and his antagonists the author intends to produce the reversal of fortune of these characters at the story's climax—Jesus' passion—where the conflict finally finds its resolution. To achieve this, the implied author supplies his reader with the indispensible information regarding "who they actually are": Jesus as the son of God (1:1, 18, 20)[71] and the religious leaders as "children of hell" (23:15) whose evilness is their trademark.[72] This inside information enables the reader to accurately evaluate the situation in conflict and to perceive the real nature of all the accusations heaped up against Jesus. For instance, consider allegations made against Jesus as a blasphemer (9:1-8) by the religious leaders. In chapter 9, the religious leaders condemn Jesus for claiming authority to forgive sinners and charge him with blasphemy because they take Jesus' act of forgiving as a claim to be God himself. In truth, Jesus has the authority to forgive as he speaks publicly, "The Son of Man has the authority on earth to forgive sins"

69. Weaver, "Power and Powerlessness," 454–66.

70. Weaver, ibid., 466 concludes that "Matthew invites his readers to join him on the higher ground from which he and they together can view the impotence of all human power in the political arena vis-à-vis the genuine potency of divine initiative." Also Warren Carter, *Matthew and Empire: Initial Explorations* (Harrisburg: Trinity Press International, 2001), 57–74, expresses a similar view. According to Weaver the political leaders of the day—Herod the king, Herod the tetrarch, and Pilate the governor—exhibit unfitting traits while Jesus is ironically portrayed in his regal nature through a variety of implicit and explicit indicators. Weaver characterizes the political leaders as "terrified," "deceiving," and "passive" for Herod the king, "deeply superstitious and fearful" for Herod the tetrarch, and "vulnerable," "indecisive," and "impotent" for Pilate.

71. Further passages that identify Jesus as the Son of God are Matt. 2:15; 3:17; 4:3, 6; 7:21; 8:29; 10:32-33; 11:25-27; 12:50; 14:33; 15:13; 16:16-17; 17:5; 18:10, 14, 19, 35; 20:23; 24:36; 26:29, 39, 42, 53, 63; 27:40, 43, 54; 28:19.

72. Jack Dean Kingsbury, "The Developing Conflict between Jesus and the Jewish Leaders in Matthew's Gospel," *CBQ* 49 (1987): 57–73 notes that in the Gospel of Matthew, the Pharisees as well as other religious leaders appear to serve as a personification of evil, which the book regards as the chief ἀλαζών.

(9:6). Also, it is God himself who calls his son (3:17; 17:5) to be the savior of his people (1:21; 20:28; 26:28). Therefore, it is not Jesus, but his very accusers who assume the role of blasphemers when they misidentify Jesus as such.

Walter Brueggemann offers another Matthean example of character irony operating between Jesus and King Solomon, which exposes the former's superior origin and identity in contrast to the latter's less-than-perfect status and quality. Brueggemann interprets the theological significance of Solomon in the whole canonical context of the Scriptures. According to him, Solomon is a figure whose identity and condition can be hardly construed without an ironic interpretation because even though the Solomonic narrative in the Old Testament presents Solomon a constructed model of royal power, "the thickness of the literature" tells otherwise.[73] Therefore it is pivotal to understand the interface of theological intentionality and ironic articulation to interpret the character of Solomon.

Brueggemann suggests that the author of Matthew intentionally contrasts Jesus and Solomon in order to reveal Solomon's lowliness but to reveal the opposite for Jesus.[74] Matthean author does so indirectly by employing character irony. Brueggemann suggests that when Solomon is compared to the Matthean Jesus, who also belongs to the Davidic lineage, Solomon's true status and condition as an individual king is best disclosed. Several criteria drawn from the Gospel confirm this view. First, the Matthean genealogy of Jesus contains an odd description when it comes to Solomon: rather than calling his mother by her personal name, Bathsheba, she is called, "the wife of Uriah" (1:17) in contrast to the other three women whose names (Tamar, 1:3; Rahab and Ruth, 1:5) Matthew specifies in relation to the Davidic lineage. The author employs irony here, not wanting to be too explicit about the scandalous origin of Solomon, and at the same time not wanting to be silent about it. To do that the author plays with the irony which seems to be inherent in the origin of the character, Solomon. The Matthean introduction of Solomon in Jesus' genealogy presents the ironic contrast: the problematic origin of Solomon as a king on the surface level and concurrently, the constant divine operation through the Davidic genealogy on the higher level of the story despite the failure on the mundane level. Through this dualistic paradigm that the character irony brings, the author intends his reader to perceive the ironic portrait of Solomon as the foil for the truly ideal King of Israel, Jesus. Second, when Jesus teaches his disciples not to be anxious about earthy possessions (6:24-34), he singles out

---

73. Walter Brueggemann, *Solomon: Israel's Ironic Icon of Human Achievement* (Columbia: University of South Carolina Press, 2005), xii.

74. Ibid., 245–53.

Solomon as "a cipher for failed wealth and for futile, empty self-securing."[75] Given the fact that the Deuteronomic portraits of Solomon glorify him in his unusual acquisitions of wealth and glory,[76] Jesus' interpretation of Solomon as an example of lowliness must have been shockingly ironic to his firsthand Jewish audience such as his disciples. Regardless that whether Jesus' view on Solomon was historical or not, the Matthean author methodologically reveals Jesus Christ as the king "who is greater than Solomon" (12:42) and in order to do this, he skillfully employs character irony.

---

75. Brueggemann, *Solomon*, 246.
76. Deut. 17:16–17; 1 Kgs. 3–11.

4

Irony of the Matthean Passion Narrative

The Matthean passion narrative is a distinct literary unit and the *telos* of the entire narrative because the literary-rhetorical dimension of the Gospel points to its culmination in the Matthean passion narrative (26:1—27:66). The major event, the death of Jesus, serves as an integral part of the Gospel. Narrative criticism requires that this unit be expounded upon in close connection to the progression and emphases of other parts of the story. For instance, in the Matthean birth narrative an angel (1:20) discloses the meaning of the name of Jesus and notes that he will save his people from their sin (1:21). This revelation is a principal *kerygma* that will function as a driving force of Jesus' life and death like an automobile engine generating power. He will accomplish this divinely-willed salvation by giving his life as a ransom for many (20:28), more specifically through shedding his innocent blood (27:4, 19, 24) of the covenant (26:28). This central theme of the Matthean passion narrative is presented through the lens of irony.

The first half of chapter 4 will delineate the Matthean passion narrative (26:1—27:66) from the stance of the literary-rhetorical indicators of the text and include a brief examination of the Matthean scholarship trying to limit the Matthean passion narrative. The foremost goal of limiting the Matthean passion narrative is to circumscribe the immediate context for the Matthean passion narrative's conventional ironies. The second half of chapter 4 will focus on the Matthean passion narrative's use of irony, specifically on how irony contributes to the theological significance of Jesus' death. Both these dimensions of the investigation of the Matthean passion narrative will highlight several aspects of the First Gospel's passion story: first, the Matthean passion narrative interacts frequently with other parts of the Gospel, second, the Matthean passion narrative is purposefully crafted by the implied author-ironist, and third, the interpretation of the Matthean passion narrative's conventional ironies requires the kind of comprehensive and holistic reading of the story which narrative criticism can offer.

Limits of the Matthean Passion Narrative (26:1—27:66)

The Gospel of Matthew is a story about Jesus' life, death and resurrection. Although there are debates over the original use of Matthew as an ancient *bios*,[1] a catechism,[2] a lectionary,[3] an administrative manual or an apologetic-polemical treatise,[4] Jack Dean Kingsbury and Mark Alan Powell, both proponents of narrative criticism, suggest that Matthew is primarily a story of Jesus.[5] Kingsbury finds three storylines in Matthew: the story of Jesus, of the Jewish religious leaders who opposed Jesus.[6] The story of Jesus is inseparable from the stories of the disciples and of his opponents.

The Gospel of Matthew is a narrative dealing the life and mission of Jesus. Technically, a story is narrated sequence of events in their temporal and causal connections,[7] namely, the *what* of the narrative.[8] The story of Jesus consists of various events, arranged in roughly chronological order from his birth to death. Such events have been described as "kernels and satellites."[9] These

---

1. P. L. Shuler, *A Genre for the Gospels: the Biographical Character of Matthew* (Philadelphia: Fortress Press, 1982), 92–109.

2. Ernst von Dobschütz, "Matthew as Rabbi and Catechists," in *The Interpretation of Matthew*, ed. Graham N. Stanton, 2nd ed. (Edinburgh: T&T Clark, 1995), 1–27; John H. Hayes and Carl R. Holladay, *Biblical Exegesis: A Beginner's Handbook* (London: Westminster John Knox, 1987), 79.

3. M. D. Goulder, *Midrash and Lection in Matthew* (London: SPCK, 1974), 70–94.

4. B. W. Bacon, "The Five Books of Matthew against the Jews," *The Expositor* 15 (1918): 56–66.

5. Jack Dean Kingsbury, *Matthew as Story* (Philadelphia: Fortress Press, 1988), 1–44. Mark Allan Powell, "Toward a Narrative-Critical Understanding of Matthew," *Int* 46 (1992): 341. Also, in his attempt to investigate Christian origins and the New Testament without divorcing theology from history, Nicholas Thomas Wright suggests that the New Testament must be read as stories, and the Story, within the appropriate context with sensitivity to its different levels of meaning. See Wright, *The New Testament and the People of God* (Minneapolis: Fortress Press, 1992), 6.

6. Kingsbury, "The Developing Conflict between Jesus and the Jewish Leaders in Matthew's Gospel: A Literary-Critical Study," *CBQ* 49 (1987): 57–73.

7. Gerard Genette, *Narrative Discourse: An Essay in Method* (Ithaca, New York: Cornell University Press, 1980), 33–85 highlights temporal relations of events within a story. Both Edward Morgan Forster, *Aspects of the Novel* (New York: Harcourt, 1927), 86 and Powell, *What is Narrative Criticism?* (Minneapolis: Fortress Press, 1990), 42 discuss the principle of causality as a definitive characteristic of the plot of a story.

8. Seymour Chatman, *Story and Discourse: Narrative Structure in Fiction and Film* (Ithaca: Cornell University Press, 1978), 9.

9. The story of Jesus as a whole consists of the major and the minor blocks of the story, which S. Chatman respectively calls "kernels" and "satellites." See Chatman, ibid., 53–56. Frank J. Matera, "The

events are linked to each other under an overarching theme rather than from a strictly cause and effect relationship. Characteristically, a story is a teaching and learning tool attempting to communicate with and impact the reader. In this regard, the voice of the narrator or the mode of presentation, that is, the *how* of the narrative[10] is also an indispensible element for interpretation. This work considers the *what* and the *how* of the Matthean passion narrative, and assumes that the implied author of the Matthean passion narrative and his voice projected by the story wrought a meaningful story of Jesus. This story culminates in Jesus' death which is shown by a consistent perspective and corresponding plot which the author intended the reader to find in the deep innards of the story.

Since the relationship between the kernels and satellites of the Matthean passion narrative implies a logical hierarchy, the issue of the design of the implied author, known as plot, comes to the fore. The plot is the implied author's plan for the narrative to advance the story with continuity between episodes while maintaining rhetorical patterns and overarching logic of the story.[11] Taken as a whole, the plot of the Matthean passion narrative not only reflects this unit as a distinctive literary unit but also testifies to its logical connection to other parts of Matthew.[12] The temporal and causal sequence of the Matthean passion narrative is by no means a random occurrence, but rather a carefully thought-out creation of the implied author.

The plot of a story reflects the temporal and causal connection of the events and this makes addressing the implied author's point of view unavoidable. The arrangement of events has an inevitable link to the central narrative logic, that is, the authorial point of view. In short, the point of view refers to "the norms,

---

Plot of Matthew's Gospel," *CBQ* 49 (1987): 240 further elaborates the theory saying that though both kernels and satellites refer to events that construct the story, not all events are equal in their significance. A kernel which is also called "macrostructure," by H. J. Bernard Combrink, "The Macrostructure of the Gospel of Matthew," *Neot* 16 (1982): 1–20, is a major event or crux according to Matera, "The Plot of Matthew's Gospel," 243. If kernels are the major arteries of the story, supplying oxygen and nutrition essential to life, then satellites, the groups of minor events, are the regional veins around them, assisting or making more complex the function of the arteries to which they are connected. Chatman, *Story and Discourse*, 53 defines the kernel as hermeneutically significant because it advances the plot of a story by raising and answering questions. Therefore, missing or misinterpreting kernel(s) of a story means incomplete understanding of the narrative in contrast to the omission of a satellite which will impoverish the narrative aesthetically, without affecting the logic of the story.

10. Chatman, ibid., 31–34, defines "discourse" as the *how* of the narrative or the mode of presentation.

11. Warren Carter, "Kernels and Narrative Blocks: The Structure of Matthew's Gospel," *CBQ* 54 (1992): 466 explains that plot is skillfully arranging a story episodically.

12. Aristotle, *Poetica*, sections 7–10 underlines unity as a key characteristic of a plot.

values, and general worldview that the implied author establishes as operative for the story."[13] The point of view and the plot of a story interact closely. Though Frank Matera identifies the foremost feature of a plot as "an organizing principle" which confers logic and meaning to disparate events,[14] Kevin Smyth explains that a plot itself is an outcome or manifestation of the ruling idea which causes and governs the formation of a story.[15] In my view, both Matera's "organizing principle" and Smyth's "ruling idea" mean the same thing: the implied author's point of view gives a story both organization and meaning. In other words, understanding the point of view that governs the story is the best way for the reader to gain a bird's eye view of the story's integral plot which will eventually allow the reader to recognize kernels key to its interpretation. Reading a story is a creative act in the sense that the reader engages the story-world and experiences being the implied reader envisioned by the text, but not in the sense that he may replace the implied author's evaluative point of view. Therefore, as an analogy, the plot and the point of view are like a pair of horses pulling a chariot, that being the story, driven by the implied author.

The Gospels suggest their implied authors' points of view align with God's perspective,[16] which is true and normative for their works.[17] Likewise, the implied author of Matthew is faithful to the particular perspective which he adopts from God. Accordingly, in his effort to maintain God's point of view, the Gospel's implied author selects events necessary for an informative story, decides their relevance, and arranges them in a congenial manner in order to keep their thematic connection as coherent as possible.

The Gospel of Matthew presents the divinely-willed salvation in Jesus (1:21; 20:28; 26:39, 54) as the key perspective of the implied author through which he meaningfully organizes the events of the story. In essence, the story of Matthew is the story of Jesus the Jewish Messiah, as the genealogy indicates (1:1). The Matthean genealogy of Jesus reveals that God is in control and purposefully measures human history. It is the message of Jesus' genealogy in Matthew that though history seems to flow aimlessly, it is God who is sovereign over it and intends to redeem it through his chosen agent, his Son. The implied author's simplification of the genealogy underlines the unique

---

13. Powell, Narrative Criticism, 24.
14. Matera, "The Plot of Matthew's Gospel," 24.
15. Kevin Smyth, "The Structural Principle of Matthew's Gospel," *IBS* 41 (1982): 207.
16. W. Carter, *Matthew: Storyteller, Interpreter, Evangelist* (Peabody: Hendrickson, 1996), 146–47 notes that "the story of Jesus is told from God's perspective."
17. Kingsbury, "The Figure of Jesus in Matthew's Story: A Literary-Critical Probe," *JSNT* 21 (1984) 4–7.

Father-Son relationship between God and Jesus which is itself a constant theme of Matthew.[18] Jesus' filial relationship to God is significant for the development of the story because such a relationship explains the Son's authority in revealing and doing his heavenly Father's will which is none other than saving men (1:21). In other words, the person and mission of Jesus are the manifestation of this divine saving will about which the Gospel's author is explicit from the very inception of the Gospel.

The narrative segment of 1:1—4:11 describes God as the director of salvation history.[19] The most important kernel for the whole Gospel is found in 1:18-25 and it answers two questions: first, "who is Jesus ?": the issue of the identity of Jesus, and second, "why has he come?": the basis of his ministry in relation to the divine will. This first kernel of the Gospel, 1:18-25, functions as the bedrock on which the entire story of Jesus is founded. It characterizes the whole story of Matthew as God's involvement in human history with the specific goal of salvation for mankind which begins with the Jewish people. Once again the crux of the idea of the Gospel is that Jesus, the Christ Savior came among his people to save them from their sins (1:21) according to the divine master plan .God bestows the name, *Jesus* on his Son and with it God's saving will toward men is reflected[20] since the person of Jesus represents the presence of Emmanuel (1:23, 28:20). Jack D. Kingsbury emphasizes the significance of the name of Jesus for the saving story of Matthew. He expounds:

> "Jesus" is the personal name of the protagonist of Matthew's story. Although Joseph is the one who gives Jesus his name (1:25), he does so on instructions from the angel of the Lord (1:20). Ultimately, therefore, God himself is the source of Jesus' name. As to meaning, "Jesus" denotes that "God [is] salvation," and the angel touches on this as he tells Joseph that Jesus "will *save* his people from their sins" (1:21). Accordingly, the force of the name "Jesus" is that in the one thus called, God is active to save. Hence, of all the traits Matthew ascribes to Jesus in the course of his story, the one most fundamental is that he is "saving."[21]

In essence, a red thread weaving through reoccurring thematic dots of Matthew begins from 1:21. As previously mentioned, this key verse functions as the

---

18. Matt. 1:18, 20, 23; 3:17; 16:17; 17:5, etc.
19. In this light, Carter, *Matthew*, 160 explains that the author presents God as the initiator of the plot.
20. Matt. 1:21; 2:6; 3:15; 4:16, 19; 20:28; 26:39.
21. Kingsbury, *Matthew as Story*, 45.

epicenter of the story of Jesus' life and death for the First Gospel. Meanwhile, a crucial question in relation to Jesus and his name lingers unanswered in the mind of the reader. The question is not about "*who* Jesus is," given that this is answered in the Gospel's first chapter, but about "*how* Jesus will save his people."

The Gospel of Matthew presents the two stages of Jesus' life in 4:17 and 16:21 with a distinctive temporal phrase, "from that time Jesus began to." The former of these two passages indicates the inception of Jesus' public ministry with an eschatological proclamation of the kingdom of heaven and the latter passage marks the intensification of the conflict between Jesus as protagonist and his opponents, and its resolution in his death on the cross. In the opening of the second stage of Jesus' public ministry, Peter's confession of Jesus (16:16) finally establishes a proper time for Jesus to begin to predict the reality of his death openly (16:21) which is in fact Jesus' way of forecasting how he will achieve his saving ministry (1:21). This theme grows steadily as Jesus' ministry goes through the phases of conflict brought to Jesus by his various opponents such as Satan, the religious leaders, and even his disciples. As the crisis caused by conflict between Jesus and his opponents intensifies, the reader's expectation of how divine salvation will be accomplished through Jesus gets stronger. It is the author's intent that the reader finds the answer in the Matthean passion narrative, where Jesus' cross, a most unlikely place for victory, serves as the termination to the conflict and the ironic disclosure of how.

As early as Matthew chapter 2 Jesus is identified as the Christ Savior (1:1, 17-18, 21) and as the King of the Jews (2:2). Yet oddly enough, the King of the Jews is recognized and worshipped for the first time by the Gentiles (2:8), the magi from the East (2:1-2), and not by the Jews. Also, the life of the infant Jesus is described as being in danger because of the threat of King Herod (2:1-3). This same chapter depicts a wider unwelcoming attitude on the part of Jerusalem represented by her religious leaders (2:3; 8:10; 15:24; 23:37). All Jerusalem (πᾶσα Ἱεροσόλυμα, 2:3), the city of the God of Israel (5:35; 21:1-9), together with Herod the king is "disturbed at" (ἐταράχθη, 2:3) the arrival of her loyal (Davidic) Messiah (1:1, 17; 2:2). It is the beginning of the seeds of conflict which moves the story of Jesus forward to its resolution in his death. While the kernel 1:18-25 strategically discloses Jesus' identity and raises the most significant question essential to the understanding of the life and mission of Jesus (How will Jesus save his people from their sins?), the report of an initial conflict between Jesus and his people at the time of his birth makes an early connection to the Matthean passion narrative where a wrinkle in their relationship is destined to be ironed out.

The First Gospel progressively has insinuated the idea that righteous blood has redemptive effect from the early chapters on (2:16-18; 14:1-10; 23:29-39) and that therefore, Jesus' shedding of his innocent blood (26:28; 27:4, 19, 24) is the only way to achieve the "forgiveness of sins" which is the key theme of this Gospel. It is in the Matthean passion narrative where at last the most essential pieces of information necessary to unlock the meaning of the death of Jesus converge and synergize toward a common goal: Jesus the Christ (*who*; 1:1) carries out the divine-willed salvation (*what*; 1:21) by shedding his innocent blood on the cross (*how*; 20:28; 26:28; 27:4, 19, 24). First, the name of *Jesus*, "he will save his people from their sins," constantly reappears throughout the Gospel and more intensely so in the Matthean passion narrative [22] as if the implied author intends to remind his reader that the essence of Jesus' entire ministry is *saving the people*. Correspondingly Jesus exhibits his perfect devotion as the Son who carries out the very will of his Father (3:17; 12:18; 17:5). Second, the implied author intentionally uses the adverb "then (τότε)" in strategic places in chapter 26 (vv. 3, 14, 16, 50, 56) to reinforce the idea that what drives Jesus' passion to its fulfillment is "divine necessity" [23] ("the will of God"; τὸ θέλημα τοῦ θεοῦ, 26:39) and that God himself intended the death of his Son (3:17; 17:5) as the modus of divine salvation. Third, as the Matthean passion narrative progresses, its various scenes—the disciples' denial and flight (26:31-35, 56, 69-75), the arrest (26:47-56) of Jesus, the trials (before Caiaphas, 26:57-68; before Pilate, 27:11-26), the mockery of the soldiers (27:27-31), the crucifixion and death of Jesus (27:32-56), and the burial of Jesus (27:57-66)—all testify that Jesus himself singly carries out this divinely-willed task of salvation. That the idea that the Son of God must die to save men is foreign to men is shown by the fact that the chief disciple, Peter rebukes the idea passionately (16:15-23). The divine saving plan does not require human counsel or consent for its actualization but instead it steadily runs its due course. As Jesus alone understands his Father's will (16:23b), he alone brings it to its consummation as demonstrated in the Matthean passion narrative.

Approaching it from different perspectives and criteria, some Matthean scholars place the limits of the Matthean passion narrative at different verses.[24] For example, Raymond E. Brown, in his comprehensive study regarding the

---

22. Matt. 26:1, 4, 6, 10, 17, 19, 26, 31, 34, 36, 49-51, 55, 57, 59, 63-64, 69, 71, 75; 27:1, 11, 16-17, 20, 22, 26-27, 37, 46, 50, 54-55, 57-58.

23. John P. Heil, *The Death and Resurrection of Jesus: A Narrative-Critical Reading of Matthew 26–28* (Minneapolis: Fortress Press, 1991), 33, treats the death of Jesus as the divine necessity.

24. Raymond E. Brown, *The Death of the Messiah: From Gethsemane to the Grave*, 2 vols. (New York: Doubleday, 1993), 1:38-39, notes that there are various theories as to how Matthew should be divided

death of Jesus in the four Gospels, considers the unit of the Matthean passion narrative to be 26:30—27:66.²⁵ Brown does not begin the Matthean passion narrative with 26:1-2 though he explains that "Matt. 26:1-2 is a parallel for Mark 14:1 and so starting the passion narrative there once again includes the Last Supper."²⁶ Instead, Brown views Jesus going with disciples to the Mount of Olives (26:30-35) after sharing the Last Supper, which was factually a Passover meal, as a transitional episode which ends in Jesus' burial (27:66).²⁷ This is based on Matthew's use of "then" (τότε, 26:31) indicating a break.²⁸ Now, Jesus is accompanying the disciples onto the actual site where he reaffirms the divine saving will (26:39) and is consequently arrested. However, Brown's model does not explain how the burial of Jesus (27:57-66) and its satellite event of the guarding of the tomb (27:62-65) relate to the beginning of the Matthean passion narrative (26:30-35): Jesus going with disciples to the Mount of Olives. It raises the question of why the scene of Jesus' crucifixion and death (27:32-56) does not conclude the Matthean passion narrative as the outcome of his obedience to the will of God to which the earnest prayers of Jesus at Gethsemane attest (26:39, 53-54). A similar question can be posted to Donald Senior's limit of the Matthean passion narrative (26:1—27:56). Senior provides a rather simple explanation that the passion of Jesus begins with a final formal introduction to the passion (26:1-5) and meets its end at the climatic death scene (27:45-56).²⁹ Senior leaves out the burial narrative (27:57-66) on the ground that through the addition of an adverb, "there" (ἐκεῖ, 27:55), Matthew reinforces the connection of the women present at the cross with the acclamation of the centurion (27:54) and that the Matthean burial narrative is oriented to the resurrection account. While Brown leaves out the proleptic preparation of Jesus' burial by a woman at Bethany and yet concludes the Matthean passion narrative with the burial scene of Jesus, Senior begins the passion story unit with Jesus' imminent death prediction and his burial anticipated through anointing of Jesus by a woman at Bethany (26:12), however, he ends it at the crucifixion scene and leaves out the actual burial of Jesus and its satellite event, the placement of the guards securing his tomb.

---

and particularly difficult is discerning where Matthew draws the line between the passion and the resurrection of Jesus.

25. Ibid., 1:38, 117–145; 2:1284–1313.
26. Ibid., 1:38.
27. Ibid., 1:39.
28. Ibid., 1:127.
29. Donald Senior, "Matthew's Special Material in the Passion Story: Implications for the Evangelist's Redactional Technique and Theological Perspective," *ETL* 63 (1987): 273, see footnote 4.

Unlike Brown and Senior's narrow limits of the Matthean passion narrative, some Matthean scholars broadly outline the unit by including all the elements of Jesus' passion such as persecution, conflicts, trials, death and resurrection (that is, vindication). This model emphasizes an inseparable link between Jesus' death, resurrection, and great commission all together as the recapitulation of the divine saving will and celebration of its fulfillment. Richard A. Edwards outlines the Matthean passion narrative as 26:1—28:20. He places 28:1-20 under the heading; "The Son's Obedience Vindicated," as a subdivision of 27:27—28:20: "The Son's Death and Vindication."[30] Jack Dean Kingsbury also defines the Matthean passion narrative as 16:21—28:20. According to Kingsbury, Matthew's Gospel is specifically a story of Jesus' life,[31] he who is the Son of God. He structures Matthew into three main parts in an attempt to integrate the entire story of Jesus within the Christological theme:[32] the person of Jesus the Messiah (1:1—4:16), the proclamation of Jesus the Messiah (4:17—16:20), and the suffering, death and resurrection of Jesus the Messiah (16:21—28:20).[33] Therefore, the Matthean passion narrative proper implied by Kingsbury sees Jesus' first passion and resurrection prediction in 16:21 as the beginning, yet also the climax of the revelation of Jesus the Messiah.

What is a commonly proposed view is that 26:1-5 provides a contextual transition by narrating Jesus' passion prediction (26:2) immediately following the lesson of Jesus on the final age and his exhortation for vigilance in chapter 25. As if the implied author is underlining the control and authority of Jesus over his death, the corresponding plot of Jesus' opponents to kill him (τότε, "then"; 26:3) fittingly comes after the last passion prediction of Jesus (26:2). The following proleptic anointing of Jesus for his burial by a woman at Bethany (26:6-13) is a kernel within the Matthean passion narrative that cannot be removed without damaging the logic and flow of the passion story of Jesus. It is not only inseparable to the later burial scene of Jesus (27:57-61) and therefore, defines the end limit of the Matthean passion narrative, but it is theologically reflective of the Matthean proclamation of the meaning of the death of Jesus. Jesus declares that the Bethany woman must be remembered wherever *this gospel* (τὸ εὐαγγέλιον τοῦτο, 26:13) is preached throughout the world (26:10-13) because Jesus deems the woman's act of anointing his head as a participation in and a preparation for the fulfillment of the divinely-willed

---

30. Richard A. Edwards, *Matthew's Story of Jesus* (Philadelphia: Fortress Press, 1985), 91–95.

31. Kingsbury, *Matthew: Structure, Christology, Kingdom* (Philadelphia: Fortress Press, 1975), x.

32. Ibid., 8 asserts that "Matthew did in fact intend that this formula should indicate the broadest divisions of the Gospel."

33. Ibid., 9, 161–67.

salvation which is about to occur in his imminent death (26:12). What Jesus implies by *this gospel* is none other than his innocent death—the saving will of God toward his people (1:21) crystallized in and achieved by his obedient Son (26:42).

A Narrative-Critical Reading of the Matthean Passion Narrative's Conventional Ironies

The Matthean passion narrative's conventional irony is present yet hidden.[34] This section will focus on the Matthean passion narrative's conventional irony as the rhetorical device of the implied author (the so-called divine ironist),[35] and their impact on the theological exposition of the death of Jesus is the major focus of this work. Therefore, in the last half of chapter 4, the book will methodologically zoom in on the textual instances of conventional irony which contain interwoven verbal, situational, and character irony central to the plot of the Matthean passion narrative.

A narrative-critical reading examines the structure of the Gospel of Matthew without reference to any particular source theory. As chapter 1 explains in detail, the reading of the Matthean passion narrative's conventional irony depends on the reader adopting the principles of narrative criticism. These include the coherence of the narrative as a whole story, the presence of the implied author and also his counterpart, the implied reader, the importance of the text, and the rhetorical-persuasive strategies of the narrative. In this case, it is irony as the rhetorical device of the implied author in relation to Booth's textual-bound "stable irony" which is of specific interest.[36] Narrative criticism is a mechanism explaining how the story of the Matthean passion narrative unfolds for its implied reader. The reader's adoption of the principles of narrative criticism is accepting the textual invitation to become its implied reader. The implied reader is supposed to focus on the flow of the narrative, thematic continuity between episodes and literary-rhetorical features like irony that preserve its continuity in order to persuade. The implied reader looks for rhetorical patterns[37] to identify the causal links that provide the narrative

---

34. Craig S. Keener, *A Commentary on the Gospel of Matthew* (Grand Rapids: Eerdmans, 1999), 607, comments that irony is latent in the Matthean passion narrative.

35. In this chapter these terms are interchangeably used to designate the one who intentionally envisioned and accordingly embedded ironies in the Matthean passion narrative. See chapter 1 for the information regarding the implied author of the Gospel as the divine ironist.

36. Chapter 1 explains that the book adopts the principles from narrative criticism and Booth's stable irony as the methodology for expounding the Matthean passion narrative's conventional irony and its theological implications on the death of Jesus.

with its particular logic and purpose[38] by paying attention to the story lines which depict the development of the most significant characters and their relational dynamics which create events. Relying on these observations, the implied reader of the Gospel of Matthew will recognize that the Gospel as a whole is interrelated. Building up the story of Jesus the divine ironist of Matthew influences his implied reader's reactions to what follows so that he may create the best possible context for receiving the Matthean passion narrative's rhetorical thrust, namely the ironic revelation of the meaning of Christ's death which is the *telos* of the Gospel's passion story of Jesus.

Employing the principles espoused by both narrative criticism and Booth's stable irony, we will examine the Matthean passion narrative's conventional ironies section by section: 26:1-56 (Jesus' burial anticipated through the anointing of Jesus by a woman at Bethany, and the arrest of Jesus at Gethsemane), 26:57—27:10 (the interrogation of Jesus before the Sanhedrin), 27:11-26 (the interrogation of Jesus before Pilate), 27:27-56 (the crucifixion), and 27:57-66 (the burial of Jesus). Instead of lining up cases of irony under each category of conventional irony, their occurrences according to the chapter of the Matthean passion narrative in which they are found will be studied in order to avoid dealing with the Gospel's passion story unit fragmentarily. Once again, it is worth reminding us here that not every case of conventional irony in the Matthean passion narrative belongs to only one category. In fact, the Matthean passion narrative's conventional irony is rather complexly woven in the fabric of the narrative and in the literary world projected by the story.[39] Its reader may detect combinations of irony, such as an instance of verbal irony with situational irony, a moment of situational irony in an example of character irony, an occurrence of character irony with a case of verbal irony, or in some cases, all in one.

According to Matthew, God's will is to gather and save his people who are like lost sheep without a shepherd (9:36; 10:6; 15:24). Jesus came to his people to reclaim them as their shepherd (ποιμήν, 18:12; 25:32f; 26:31), whose profound identity simultaneously encompasses Christ the Lord, the King of the Jews, the Son of God and the Son of Man. The Gospel's implied author steadily discloses through Jesus' direct and indirect indication of his suffering throughout the

---

37. H. J. B. Combrink, "The Structure of the Gospel of Matthew as Narrative," *TynBul* 34 (1983): 61–90.

38. Matera, "The Plot of Matthew's Gospel," 233–53.

39. Ronald Tanaka, "The Concept of Irony: Theory and Practice," *JLS* 2 (1973): 47 notes that "though it is easy, in principle, to distinguish event and linguistic irony, it is not so simple a matter in literary contexts."

Gospel[40] that God not only wills human salvation (1:21), but also the way in which it is achieved.[41] In a distinct fashion, the Matthean passion narrative portrays the "passion" of Jesus as the "cup" (τὸ ποτήριον, 26:39) in association with the will of God (τὸ θέλημα τοῦ θεοῦ, 26:42, 55-56) which only the Son of God can "drink." In other words, Jesus essentially accomplishes this saving will of God (τὸ θέλημα τοῦ θεοῦ as revealed in 1:21) through his obedience that leads to his death.

Prior to the Matthean passion narrative, Matthew demonstrates the substantial difference between the divine perspective and human perspective[42] which is an essential ingredient for irony. God will reveal his ways to infants (1:25) but his plan will be concealed from the wise and understanding (11:25). According to this Gospel, "infants" (νηπίοις) are those who depend on the revelation of the divine will disclosed by Jesus (11:27; 16:17), the sole carrier of the divine perspective in contrast to the "wise and understanding" (σοφῶν καὶ συνετῶν) who are unwarrantedly confident in their understanding of the will of God.[43] The implied author thus illustrates the "wise and understanding" as a distinctively negative character group, as. "hypocrites"[44] whose blind pride in their own knowledge and understanding becomes the target of Jesus' acute reprehension just as the ἀλαζών is the object of scorn and ridicule for the εἴρων.

From the beginning of the Matthean passion narrative, its ironist implies a double-layered story phenomenon surrounding the life and death of Jesus which projects two sharply contrasting perspectives. Actually, within the stories of the Gospel, it is hard to find a vignette that plays on and embodies this kind of gap between the heavenly perspective and the earthly perspective more than the story of Jesus' passion. The Matthean passion narrative's ironist emphasizes

---

40. Matt. 12:40; 16:21; 17:12, 22-23; 20:18-19; 21:38, 39; 23:34; 24:9; 26:2, 11-12.

41. Donald Guthrie, *New Testament Theology* (Leicester: Inter-Varsity, 1981), 55 explains that a theocentric approach to the New Testament is necessary because it enables us to see God in Christ reconciling the world to himself through his initiative.

42. Matt. 11:25-26; 13:11-15; 15:11-20.

43. See Matt. 9:3, 11117, 34; 12:318, 14145; 15:1111; 16:114; 19:4; 21:16, 42; 22:29131. Kingsbury, *Matthew as Story*, 15, 137, 145 considers "infants" in the section 11:2—16:20 to be the disciples of Jesus (11:25-27) who are enlightened in contrast to the wise in Israel who are darkened and without understanding. More specifically, Richard T. France, *Matthew: Evangelist & Teacher* (Illinois: InterVarsity, 1989), 286 considers the wise and understanding to be Israel's leaders who are in fact blind and without understanding. Also, Ulrich Luz, *Matthew 8–20* (ed. Helmut Koester; trans. James E. Crouch; Minneapolis: Fortress Press, 2001), 162–63 identifies the wise and understanding as the "entire religious aristocracy" in contrast to the νήπιοι with the "*am ha arez*."

44. Matt. 15:7; 22:18; 23:13, 15, 25, 27, 29; cf. 6:2, 5, 16.

Jesus' authority and control over his own passion,[45] though it seems on the ostensible level of the story that his opponents are in charge of it. As we already have discussed, although the implied author frequently employs an adverb, τότε (then) throughout the Gospel, he uses this adverb more frequently in chapter 26 (13 times)[46] than in any other chapter. His strategic use of an adverb τότε in chapter 26 effectively communicates that Jesus becomes conductor of his own requiem by willingly giving up himself for the divine cause (26:42, 53-54). For instance, Jesus had predicted his imminent betrayal and death (26:2) in relation to the Jewish feast, Passover (26:2, 17-19). Logically, if the Passover has nothing to do with Jesus' passion, then why would the implied author even bother to mention it four times (26:2, 17, 18, 19)? This question must be answered. Although the Matthean passion narrative is not specific in linking Jesus with the motif of the "lamb of God" who carries away the sins of the world as the Gospel of John does (John 1:29, 36), it is not hard to perceive the intent of the Matthean passion narrative's implied author to portray the preparation for the coming death of Jesus for the salvation of his people (1:21) in the light of the preparation for the Passover meal (26:17-19) which involves sacrificing an innocent lamb and shedding its redemptive blood. Therefore, Jesus' prediction that he would be delivered up on the Passover day to be crucified (26:2) is sufficient to link the image of the paschal lamb with Jesus and the significance of Jesus' death on the Passover day with what the Passover theologically implies to the people of God: God's salvation for his people (1:21; 20:28; 26:28). Therefore, the Passover motif serves as a vehicle delivering the meaning of the death of Jesus as the fulfillment of God's saving work attested in human history.[47]

Only then (τότε, 26:2) when Jesus made the prediction of his impending betrayal and death, did the chief priests and the elders of the people gather under the leadership of Caiaphas, the high priest, (26:3) and take counsel together to arrest Jesus and to kill him (26:4). In other words, even the murder plot against Jesus by the religious leaders is subject to Jesus' full control corresponding to his knowledge of the looming passion and death.[48] Therefore, it is observed that within a brief time of transition from 26:2 to 26:4, the ironist reveals

---

45. Anthony J. Saldarini, *Jesus and Passover* (New York: Paulist, 1984), 62, mentions that Matthew emphasizes Jesus' sovereign control over his death and the self-sacrifice implied in his actions.

46. Matt. 26:3, 14, 16, 31, 36, 38, 45, 50, 52, 56, 65, 67, 74.

47. Consider the theological implication of Matthew's genealogy of Jesus.

48. David B. Howell, *Matthew's Inclusive Story: A Study in the Narrative Rhetoric of the First Gospel* (Sheffield: Sheffield Academic, 1990), 154 comments that "the final section of the Gospel is introduced with a prediction of the imminent passion and crucifixion during the Passover feast (26:2) which gives the implied reader the impression that Jesus is in full control of his destiny."

the two story-worlds phenomenon essential for irony and its interpretation of the entire vista of Jesus' passion. As 26:2 shows on the upper level of the story, it is Jesus who willingly takes up the cross to achieve his Father's saving will (1:21; 3:15; 18:14; 26:28, 39, 54). Yet, what is happening on the lower level of the story: the opponents of Jesus plan to kill Jesus by stealth (δόλῳ, 26:4; cf. 12:14). There exists a fundamental contrast and inconsistency in this picture. While Jesus navigates his own passion with clairvoyance and undivided commitment, his opponents plot to seize Jesus by furtiveness, thus showing their ignorance of their seeming prey. This unveils an unbridgeable disequilibrium of perspectives between these two main parties in the story: while Jesus the protagonist represents the perspective of God, the religious leaders, the corporate antagonist, embody that of men. Different perspectives create a double-layered story and pull each character group in opposite directions endorsing their differing goals. This phenomenon cultivates irony and we are about to examine the examples of conventional irony in the Matthean passion narrative.

Chapter 26 and Instances of Conventional Irony

Situational Irony in the Case of the Disturbance ('Ο ΘΟΡΥΒΟΣ) among the People (26:1-5)

The first irony detected in the Matthean passion narrative is a situational irony in 26:5, "But they said, 'not during the feast (μὴ ἐν τῇ ἑορτῇ), lest there be a tumult (ὁ θόρυβος) among the people.' " This situational irony surrounding an assumed θόρυβος must be read in relation to the scene in which the stirred up crowds in one accord shout for the crucifixion of Jesus (27:22-23). Ignorant of what is actually happening that Jesus' passion is according to God's orchestration, "the chief priests and the elders of the people" (26:3, 47), being collectively antagonistic toward Jesus, begin to plot against him. They reach a decision to arrest and kill Jesus but to avoid the feast (τὸ πάσχα, 26:2) due to the potential tumult (ὁ θόρυβος, 26:5) that may occur among the people (ἐν τῷ λαῷ, 27:5).

Before discussing this irony in relation to tumult, let us look into the narrative's contrasting realities hidden behind the draped yet penetrable curtain of irony. First of all, there exists a sharp contrast in the quality of character between Jesus and his opponents. While the former, as the Christ Savior, the Son of God, the son of David and the Son of Man,[49] encompasses all the power

---

49. Matt. 1:1, 17, 21; 2:2, 4-6 3:17; 4: 3, 6; 9:6; 16:16; 17:5; 21:9, etc.

and might that one can imagine, his opponents, the Jewish religious leaders, are associates with the evil one (13:19, 38) who is the arch enemy of God (4:8-9). Further, Jesus cares for the people, yet his opponents fear them (21:26) and act to destroy them (23:15).[50] Secondly, another kind of contrast is examined in these two characters' words and actions. Jesus makes it clear that he will be betrayed and crucified by the hands of "the high priests and the elders of the people" (26:2, 3-5), precisely at the time of the Passover (τὸ πάσχα, 26:2). As 26:2 shows, Jesus possesses superior knowledge regarding his opponents' identities and the details of his passion involving both his betrayal and crucifixion (26:2b). Jesus' mention of the Passover as the immediate temporal context for his passion sheds a theological light on the nature of his mission which is about to be accomplished through his death on the cross.[51] Historically, the Passover is the

---

50. In light of 1 John 4:18, "There is no fear in love, but perfect love casts out fear; for fear has to do with punishment, and whoever fears has not reached perfection in love," (NRSV) it appears that the religious leaders' fear of the crowds is due to their lack of love and care toward the people which contrasts to the Matthean emphasis on Jesus' reoccurring message of "do not fear" to both the people and his disciples who exhibit weakness and are lost in doubt (14:27; 17:7; 28:5, 10). This explains the reason why the Matthean Jesus has compassion on the crowds, who are like sheep deprived of their shepherd (πρόβατα μὴ ἔχοντα ποιμένα, 9:36; 10:6; 15:24; 25:32-33) and emphatically proclaims to his opponents that he desires mercy not sacrifice (9:13; 12:7; 23:23). The implied author of Matthew underlies Jesus as the kingly shepherd for whom the distressed and helpless sheep are longing (2:6) and to whom they beg for mercy (9:27; 15:22; 17:15; 20:30-31). He will gather these lost sheep by willingly laying down his life for them (26:31). J. P. Heil, "Ezekiel 34 and the Narrative Strategy of the Shepherd and Sheep Metaphor in Matthew," *CBQ* 55 (1993): 698–708 examines the Matthean use of the metaphor of shepherd and sheep in relation to the tradition of the Jewish Scriptures (Mic. 5:1; 2 Sam. 5:2; Zech. 13:7). He especially focuses on Ezek. 34 as the key text providing the semantic field for the Matthean shepherd metaphor. He writes, 707, that "there is a subtle rhetorical progression in the references to Jesus as shepherd. Although it is implied throughout the shepherd metaphor that Jesus is *the* shepherd, the fact that he is not explicitly so designated until his prediction that God will strike him as *the* shepherd (26:31) intensifies its shock. He is the shepherd struck by God with suffering and death but raised again to continue as the shepherd who brings his scattered sheep back to Galilee and sends them to all peoples. Although Jesus authorizes his disciples to be his fellow shepherds, the term 'shepherd' is never explicitly applied to them. This enhances the status of Jesus as *the* shepherd upon whom they—and thus the readers—depend both as his sheep and as his fellow shepherds."

51. Saldarini, *Jesus and Passover*, 62–63, writes that in Matthew "Passover and Jesus' crucifixion go together in God's plan . . . just as the sacrifices in the Temple atoned for sins and the Passover lamb saved the Israelites from death, Jesus' self-sacrifice saves believers from sin through brining about their forgiveness." Also, Keener, *A Commentary on the Gospel of Matthew*, 624–33, explains that Jesus' mission climaxing in his death signifies a new Passover because Jesus' body and blood provide a new covenant, the ultimate act of redemption in a strikingly new way. In contrast, Brown, *The Death of the Messiah*, 1:156 considers it to be dubious to keep finding Passover motifs after the Last Supper, since Matthew seems to forget that feast once the supper is over.

day of significance commemorating God's decisive saving deed on behalf of "his people" on whom the Gospel primarily focuses.[52] Therefore, Jesus' depiction of the Passover as the opportune time (ὁ καιρός, 26:18),[53] for his own death underlines two factors: one, the death of Jesus is not only God's act of salvation but also the completion of God's καιρός through his Son, the one who carries out the saving will of his Father (1:21); and two, as the saving will of God brought about the Passover for his people in the past, the same enduring divine saving will governs his Son's redeeming death in the image of the sacrificial *Agnus Dei* (8:17; 20:28; 26:28; 27:25). By playing with these fundamental contrasts between the appearances and the facts of the story evolving around the protagonist, the Matthean passion narrative's ironist casts a soteriological tone over the Passover by depicting it as both the temporal and theological setting for Jesus' passion.[54]

The Matthean ironist depicts Jesus' death as the most fitting moment (εὐκαιρία, 26:16; καιρός, 26:18)[55] for the fulfillment of God's salvation and mercy.[56] On this note it is worth mentioning that the Gospel's implied author-ironist allows only Jesus and his disciples to call the feast by its actual name of "the Passover" (τὸ πάσχα, 26:2, 17, 18, 19) in contrast to the religious leaders' indefinite designation of it as simply "the feast" (ἡ ἑορτή, 26:5). By doing so, the ironist emphasizes that what is about to happen through the death of Jesus on the cross must be understood in the light of the Passover, which is best understood as the definite saving act of God. Perhaps, the fact that the religious leaders do not call the feast by its name but rather allude to it with an indefinite term is devised by the ironist to subtly point out their indifference to or careless treatment of God's saving presence and action in the midst of the people (11:16-24; 12:38-42; 16:1-4). In this way, the ironist exposes

---

52. Matt. 1:21; 2:6; 13:15; 15:8; 27:25.

53. Also see Matt. 8:29; 21:34.

54. Both Heil, *The Death and Resurrection of Jesus*, 24–25, 30, 75 and R. T. France, *The Gospel of Matthew* (NIBCNT; Grand Rapids: Eerdmans, 2007), 969, notes that the approach of the Passover festival provides both the historical and the theological context for the Matthean passion narrative.

55. D. Senior, *The Passion of Jesus in the Gospel of Matthew* (Wilmington: Michael Glazier, 1985), 57 notes that Judas' use of εὐκαιρία in 26:16 and Jesus' use of καιρός in 26:18 are semantically related. Senior perceives an irony that arises in the different use of καιρός employed respectively by Jesus (26:18) and Judas (26:16). In 57–58, Senior says that "ironically, both Judas and Jesus seek the same καιρός, the deliverance of the Son of God into the hands of sinful people. One does it to snatch up thirty pieces of silver; the other, to give his life on behalf of the many."

56. Besides the saving will of God, the First Gospel equally underlines the God of mercy whom Jesus' healing ministry and compassion toward the sinners represent. See Matt. 9:13, 27; 12:7; 15:22; 17:15; 20:30–31.

the false perspective of the religious leaders toward God's saving intent and their negligence, if not apathy, toward God's commitment to his people. This explains why the religious leaders set themselves against God by persecuting God's "beloved" Son (3:17; 17:5), whose person and mission are the prophetic embodiment of the saving will of God (1:21; 9:6, 13; 12:7; 23:23). Based on the evidence found in the Matthean passion narrative, the religious leaders are evidently the corporate victim of irony. Therefore, their innocence (or spiritual blindness)[57] functions as the crucial element for the Matthean passion narrative's irony because their unawareness of reality, fueled by envy (φθόνος, 27:18) propels the contrasting double-layered story phenomenon of the Matthean passion narrative: the story of Jesus vs. the story of his opponents.

From the beginning of their plot to kill Jesus, the Jewish religious leaders are determined to avert a tumult (ὁ θόρυβος, 26:5) since they think that it would be a hindrance to their deception (ὁ δόλος, 26:4) to do away with Jesus. The fabric of the narrative tells us that the religious authorities at best consider Jesus to be one of the prophets (21:11, 45-46), a threatening (21:15-16; 27:18), blasphemous, and irrelevant one (9:3: 26:64-65). The tragedy of the religious leaders begins when they perceive Jesus as their rival, stealing affection from and authority over the people.[58] The Gospel repeatedly attests to the characteristic evasiveness and unlawfulness of the religious leaders and, for that reason, Jesus criticizes them as following in their fathers' footsteps by persecuting and shedding the innocent blood of God's emissaries among the people.[59] In the same way they also attempt to persecute Jesus. The religious leaders try to prevent Jesus from gaining a favorable defense from the crowds who have, with varying degrees of certainty, regarded Jesus as a prophet (13:57; 21:11, 46), the son of David (9:27; 12:23; 15:22; 20:30-31; 21:9, 15) and one who, unlike their scribes, teaches with authority (7:29; 21:23, 27; cf. 28:18). Nonetheless, as the story of Jesus' passion progresses, what actually happens in

---

57. In "Constitution of Irony: Formal Elements of Irony" of chapter 2, we have examined the constitutive elements of irony such as an ironist, an ironically capable reader, a double-layered story phenomenon, a fundamental contrast between the two story worlds, a victim of irony, innocence, and the pleasure of irony. Among them, it has been explained that the victim of irony and innocence go hand in hand. Notice that the innocence of the victim of irony does not necessarily mean his ethical naiveté but more so self-deceptive confidence, spiritual ignorance or unawareness.

58. France, *The Gospel of Matthew*, 1054, describes the religious leaders' jealousy as coming out of their misconception of Jesus as a rival. He writes "Pilate's assessment of the situation shows a shrewd awareness of the domestic politic of his subjects. See p. 1046, n. 4, for the term I have translated 'rivalry.' Pilate's perception is valid: the purpose of Jesus' trial was not to punish a breach of the law but to get rid of a man whose claims threatened the status and authority of the current Jewish leaders."

59. For example, the prophets, the priests, the wise. See Matt. 5:12; 11:9; 13:57; 14:3-5; 23:31-37.

the trial of Jesus in Pilate's court (27:20-24) displays quite the opposite situation. In contrast to the religious leaders' effort to isolate Jesus from the people so that they may prevent the people from securing Jesus' life, which they are eager to destroy (2:3-4, 13; 12:14; 27:20), the very uproar (θόρυβος) of the people that they were determined to avoid (26:5) turns out to be their best and opportune time (ἡ εὐκαιρία, 26:16) for securing the death of Jesus. A further ironic part of the story is that the people, whose loyalty to Jesus is wrongly assumed by their religious leaders, function as the main cause motivating Pilate. Pilate is characteristically linked to the religious leaders in that both share the fear of a disturbance among the people (θόρυβος, 27:24). Hence, it is deeply ironic that the possible riot among the people, which both parties tried to avoid, marks the fittest time for God to carry out his divine saving plan through Jesus.

It would be helpful here to examine briefly who the crowds (ὄχλοι) are in the Gospel of Matthew[60] and how they function since the crowds take a distinctive role in the Matthean passion narrative. To answer these questions is by no means easy or simple.[61] Through a narrative-critical reading one thing becomes obvious that the implied author of Matthew distinguishes the crowds from the Jewish religious leaders who are chronically hostile toward Jesus.[62] Though it can be suggested that the Matthean crowds are corporately transparent,[63] they are not a flat character.[64] In fact, they exhibit both positive

---

60. Through a redactional-critical stance, J. R. C. Cousland, *The Crowds in the Gospel of Matthew* (NovTSup; Leiden: Brill, 2002), 39–43, 50–51, suggests that Matthew employs the term, ὄχλος differently from the other Synoptic Gospels. He explains that unlike both Mark and Luke, ὄχλος is the only word that Matthew uses to characterize the crowds during Jesus' public ministry and that Matthew significantly prunes and omits Mark's crowd due to the former's more exalted Christology.

61. Ibid., 5–7, finds no agreement among the New Testament scholars about the crowds in Matthew's gospel. He writes that "while a broad spectrum of opinion is not uncommon within New Testament scholarship, the case of the crowds, with their chameleon-like capacity to fit a variety of interpretations, is out of the ordinary . . . a variety of interpretation is simply that Matthew's depiction of the crowds is decidedly protean. At the root of his portrayal is what can only be described as a fundamental ambivalence or ambiguity, which makes it far from clear how the role of the crowds to be construed." The ambiguity of Matthew's portrayal of the crowds is also recognized by W. Carter, "The Crowds in Matthew's Gospel," *CBQ* 55 (1993): 54, 67. Carter suggests that the ambivalence of the crowds reflects the situation confronting the Matthean audience.

62. E. P. Sanders and Margaret Davies, *Studying the Synoptic Gospels* (London: SCM, 1989), 203–20, opines that up to the Matthean passion account, the crowds are largely described as receptive to Jesus in contrast to the Jewish religious leaders. This view stands in opposition to the positions of Jack D. Kingsbury and Anthony J. Saldarini. Kingsbury, *The Parables of Jesus in Matthew 13: A Study in Redaction Criticism* (London: SPCK, 1969), 24–28, promotes the views that the crowds along with the Jewish religious leaders comprise the "Jews," from whom Jesus turns away or that the crowds symbolize the Jewish community of Matthew's day. A. J. Saldarini, *Matthew's Christian–Jewish Community* (Chicago:

and negative traits.⁶⁵ Yet, most importantly, the crowds are not only the object of Jesus' saving ministry⁶⁶ but also they recognize in some sense that God and his wisdom are working in Jesus.⁶⁷ Regarding the ethnic make-up of the crowds, according to the First Gospel they are most likely Jewish (4:25; 7:28-29; 9:33) on the grounds that Matthew deliberately associates the crowds with Israel who is historically the people of God.⁶⁸ Nevertheless, the crowds may be comprised of a mixture of the Jews and the Gentiles (4:25; 15:23-25, 29-39), and the idea that the implied reader should envisage Gentiles among the crowds, cannot be completely ruled out. Then, what is the distinction between the technical terms used by Matthew, ὁ λαός and ὁ ὄχλος? While the former refers to people in a generic sense, and more specifically to Israel in relation to the fulfillment of the Old Testament prophecies (2:6; 13:15; 15:8; cf. 4:15-16),⁶⁹ the latter, though they are Jewish, is not synonymous with the former, yet it has a "considerable semantic overlap."⁷⁰

In the First Gospel, λαός semantically covers both the Jewish religious leaders (the leaders of the people)⁷¹ and the Jewish crowds.⁷² Unfortunately, the

---

University of Chicago Press, 1994), 38 considers the crowds to symbolize the Jewish community of Matthew's day.

63. Cousland, The Crowds in the Gospel of Matthew, 270–80.

64. While Kingsbury, *Matthew as Story*, 23–24 treats the crowds as a flat character, C. Clifton Black, "Depth of Characterization and Degrees of Faith in Matthew," in *SBL 1989 Papers* (Atlanta: Scholars, 1989), 604–23, Cousland, *The Crowds in the Gospel of Matthew*, 49 categorize the crowds as a "round" character.

65. Carter, "The Crowds in Matthew's Gospel," 64–65.

66. Matt. 9:36; 11:7; 12:15, 46; 14:14; 15:10, 30, 32-36; 19:2.

67. Matt. 9:8, 33; 15:31; 21:8-9; 22:33.

68. John Bowman, "The Significance of Mt. 27:25," *Milla wa-Milla* 14 (1974): 27; Brown, *The Death of the Messiah*, 1:58–59. If a reader takes the position that the crowds are Jewish, he must tell who these Jews are and how they are distinguished from other Jewish characters such as the Jewish religious leaders and the disciples of Jesus. Cousland, *The Crowds in the Gospel of Matthew*, 48–51, considers that Matthew's characterization of the crowds to fall somewhere midway between the Jewish religious leaders and the disciples of Jesus in that Matthew's crowds are constant, uniform, and unobtrusive as a foil to the ministry of Jesus.

69. J. A. Fitzmyer, "Anti-Semitism and the Cry of 'All the People,' "*TS* 26 (1965): 669; Cousland, *The Crowds in the Gospel of Matthew*, 78–80.

70. Ibid., 94.

71. Ibid., 77 mentions the Matthean usage of λαός in relation to the ruling body in Jerusalem.

72. Ibid., 76 explains that "in Matthew, the crowds are only mentioned after Jesus has begun his ministry, and, in the same way, once the crowds side with their leaders at 27:25, they are not mentioned again. Afterward, the leaders describe them as the λαός (27:64; cf. 26:5) and, finally, Matthew as a narrator identifies them as 'the Jews' (Ἰουδαίοις, 28:15). What this observation suggests, therefore, is that Matthew has refracted his picture of the λαός into its constituent parts during the public ministry of

Jewish religious leaders are the persecutors of the messianic Savior who has been sent to redeem Israel (his people, 1:21) and the crowds at best fit the image of lost sheep without a shepherd (9:36; 10:6; 15:24; 18:12; 25:32-33; 26:31). This explains the reason why the implied author of Matthew refers to λαός not ὄχλος in 27:25. Here, he employs the term, λαός, ironically to denote the identity of those who cry out for the blood of Jesus. This λαός at the trial and crucifixion scenes of Jesus is principally the historic Israel, encompassing both the Jewish people and their religious leaders. In this way, the Gospel's implied author-ironist presents the story of Jesus in a theological *inclusio* by addressing the same referent (λαός) who involves in both life and death of Jesus: Jesus came to save his people (λαός, 1:21) from their sins and that very people (λαός, 27:25) cries out for his blood. Certainly, it is the Gospel's depiction that Jesus the Christ Savior (1:1) has been sent primarily for the lost sheep of Israel (15:24).

Although the Matthean passion narrative's implied author meticulously links the use of λαός to the Jewish religious leaders and to those who directly demand the crucifixion of Jesus and he links the use of ὄχλος to Pilate as subjects to Rome, in the Matthean passion narrative, the "crowds" (ὄχλος) seems to be used interchangeable with the "people" (λαός), referring to the same entity opposing Jesus. Throughout the First Gospel the "crowds" (ὄχλος) function as a singly recognizable front.[73] Their plain comments on Jesus' identity such as the son of David, the prophet, and the teacher of authority provide the implied reader with substantial information regarding Jesus and thus, they influence the reader's course of reading. Despite the depiction of the positive disposition of the crowds toward Jesus in the previous narrative, in the trial scene of Jesus before Pilate, the crowds are presented as drastically susceptible to external influences and hence are unreliable. In this way, the implied author plays with irony exposing, the religious leaders' groundless fear that the people may save Jesus. Therefore, the ironic situation anticipated in 26:5 requires the implied reader to perceive the commotion (θόρυβος) of the people (λαός, 27:25) as an inevitable situation for the divinely-willed salvation to be achieved (26:42, 51-54). Despite their common determination not to stir up a commotion among the people, both the religious leaders and Pilate respectively persuade (27:20) and agitate the people (27:17, 21-24) and by doing so, eventually push

---

Jesus. The people of Israel can be divided into two camps—the 'leaders of the people' and 'the crowds.' "

73. Bowman, "The Significance of Mt. 27:25," 27 considers the Matthean ὄχλος, as a reference to the Jewish mass, to play a very significant role in the drama of salvation as one of the *dramatis personae*. Keener, *A Commentary on the Gospel of Matthew*, 671 makes an interesting point when he says that the Crowds of Matthew speak and act in uniformity and, its choric quality has some affinities with the chorus in Greek tragedy.

the people over the edge where there is no option other than invoking the death penalty for (27:25). In this ironic situation, which Pilate inadvertently notices as "getting nowhere" (οὐδὲν ὠφελεῖ, 27:24), the people (λαός, 27:25) whose salvation God has in mind (1:21) are brought together as a single, identifiable guilty party who is held accountable for the death of Jesus. Therefore, in their ignorance to the story's reality, the people surrender themselves to the forgiveness of sins for all (20:28; 26:28) secured by the death of Jesus, who has the authority to forgive sins (1:21; 9:8).

In Matthew the divinely appointed time (καιρός, 26:18) which Jesus awaits ironically coincides with this unbecoming time of θόρυβος. Further, the irony of θόρυβος reveals the veiled meaning of ὁ καιρός as the time for the death of Jesus (26:2-5, 14-16, 18) as well as a crisis for the people of God (1:21). It is a critical time challenging the people to choose between Jesus, whom they have received as the son of David (21:1-9) and as the prophet from Nazareth of Galilee (21:10-11), and their religious leaders, whom they perceived to be without authority (7:28-29; 9:33). In contrast to the empty fear of the religious leaders that the people will create a tumult by siding with Jesus, the people align themselves with their religious leaders (12:14) and bring about a riot to do away with Jesus (27:22-25). Therefore, in this ironically reversed situation of θόρυβος the impotence of the Jewish religious leaders is exposed. The story's reality involving the time of θόρυβος is that the control is not held by the opponents of Jesus, therefore, it is also not held by the evil with whom the opponents of Jesus are aligned.[74] On the surface level, the religious leaders seem to have control over the people by stimulating the very commotion (27:20-24) which they once strove to avert (26:5). This is an act of opportunism which does not differ much from their customary way of dealing with Jesus: stealth (26:4). As we have seen, the death of Jesus as the proper divine time for the forgiveness of the sins of the people (1:21; 20:28; 26:28) ironically requires the people's willing commitment to reject Jesus and shed his innocent blood. In this ironic way, God, who alone oversees and orchestrates the salvation of his people through the death of his Son, Jesus, reclaims his lost people.

CHARACTER IRONY IN THE CONTRAST BETWEEN A WOMAN AT BETHANY AND THE DISCIPLES OF JESUS (26:6-16)

This unit reveals a character irony contrasting qualities and perspectives of the characters surrounding Jesus, especially between a woman at Bethany and the disciples of Jesus as a corporate character group.[75] To illustrate this character

---

74. The Gospel of Matthew attests to the evilness of the Jewish religious leaders through their tie to the evil one. See Matt. 3:7; 9:4; 12:34, 39, 45; 16:4; 22:18, 33; 23:15.

irony (26:6-16), it is necessary to examine the implied author's characteristic use of words. For example, throughout the Gospel, the implied author characteristically employs the verb, ἀκολουθεῖν (to follow, to accompany). This verb is recognized as an important Matthean term dividing scholarly opinions regarding whether it is used literally or in a theological way.[76] In fact, instances of ἀκολουθεῖν in Matthew attest to both cases. Yet, the majority of cases are theologically employed despite the fact that some scholars consider that 4:25; 8:1, 10; 9:19; 12:15; 14:13; 19:2; 20:29, 34 and 21:9 show a plainly literary use of ἀκολουθεῖν, mostly in relation to the crowds physically following after Jesus.[77]

The Matthean use of the verb ἀκολουθεῖν is Christological, ecclesiological,[78] and salvation-historical (*heilsgeschichtlich*).[79] In the First Gospel the import of the verb ἀκολουθεῖν appears to be understood in relationship with two character groups: the disciples of Jesus and the crowds. For the disciples it is not only ecclesiological insofar as the following of the disciples establishes the example for the followers of Jesus but also Christological since their calling solely depends on Jesus' initiative.[80] For the crowds, the following of Jesus does not mean emerging discipleship or any formal commitment to Jesus.[81] It is, however, Christological as well as salvation-historical because the crowds draw attention to the person of Jesus and his ministry, especially as the son of David whose healing and mighty works foreshadow the blessed messianic age.[82] Elaborating further on the Matthean Christological use of ἀκολουθεῖν, it cannot be missed that whenever Jesus commands someone to

75. Throughout the Gospel of Matthew, its implied author depicts the disciples of Jesus as a consolidated character group distinct from other types of groups such as the Jewish religious leaders and the crowds. See Matt. 5:1; 8:23; 9:14, 19; 12:1-2; 13:10, 36; 14:15, 19, 26; 15:2, 12, 23, 33, 36; 16:5; 17:6, 13, 19; 18:1; 19:10, 13, 25; 21: 6, 20; 24:1, 3; 26:8, 17, 19, 35, 56; 27:64; 28:13, 16.

76. Kingsbury, "The Verb Akolouthein ("To Follow") as an Index of Matthew's View of His Community," *JBL* 97 (1978), 57.

77. Floyd F. Filson, *The Gospel according to St. Matthew* (HNTC; New York: Harper, 1960), 219. Specifically, Kingsbury, "The Verb Akolouthein," 61 writes that "*akolouthein* proves to be without metaphorical significance in the 'crowd passage' 4:25; 8:1, 10; 12:15; 14:13-14; 19:2; 20:29; and 21:9." Yet, for the case of 20:34 where the two blind men received sight from Jesus and then followed him, scholars like J. C. Fenton, *Saint Matthew*, Pelican Gospel Commentaries (Baltimore: Penguin, 1963), 325; and David Hill, *The Gospel of Matthew*, NCB (London: Oliphants, 1972), 290, suggest that these two men accompanied Jesus as his disciples.

78. U. Luz, *Matthew 21–28*, ed. Helmut Koester, trans. James E. Crouch) Minneapolis: Fortress Press, 2005), 424.

79. Cousland, The Crowds in the Gospel of Matthew, 172.

80. Ibid., 153–59.

81. Ibid., 36.

82. Ibid., 100, 148–52, 163–72.

follow after him, Jesus specifies that he himself is the object of ἀκολουθέιν and deliberately links the action with discipleship, requiring "cost and commitment,"[83] which are equal to the Matthean concepts of denying oneself and bearing the cross. On Jesus' command (8:22; 9:9; 10:38; 16:24; 19:21), some, such as his disciples, follow after him (8:23; 19:27-28; 27:55),[84] yet some do not, even though an invitation to follow is extended (8:19; 19:21).[85] Therefore, it is reasonable to conclude that the Matthean use of the verb, ἀκολουθέιν, readily conveys far more than the followers' physical accompaniment with Jesus. Rather, the implied author intends to employ this verb Christologically to describe the characters' meaningful association with Jesus and more narrowly to

---

83. Ibid., 58 suggests critical twin principles that mark ἀκολουθέιν discipleship: cost and commitment. Cousland writes, "It becomes apparent that, in the logia, ἀκολουθέιν connotes discipleship, for its use each time is marked by the twin factors of cost and commitment." Martin Franzmann, *Follow Me: Discipleship according to Saint Matthew* (St. Louis: Concordia, 1961), 5–7 similarly speaks of complete committal.

84. Though Kingsbury suggests cost and commitment are the key ingredients identifying the use of ἀκολουθέιν in relation to discipleship, he considers that the use of ἀκολουθέιν in relation to the female followers of Jesus in 27:55 is used in the literal and local sense of accompaniment from place to place. He downplays the appended notation that they were "waiting on him" and does not see it as a comment characterizing women as disciples of Jesus. See Kingsbury, "The Verb Akolouthein," 61. However, Matthew duly stresses the action of service or ministering (4:11; 8:15; 25:44), especially in direct link to Jesus' life of service for others (20:28). After all, is it not the fact that Jesus teaches his disciples *to serve* which essentially epitomizes cost and commitment (20:25–28)? In this conjuncture, the case of the women following after Jesus and ministering to him must be reconsidered as Matthean description of discipleship. In the same vein, France, *The Gospel of Matthew*, 1086 considers that the women followed Jesus as disciples. Also see Keener, *A Commentary on the Gospel of Matthew*, 689 who writes that "whereas the male disciples feared for their lives and were nowhere to be found, the women followed all the way to the tomb. In that culture women were relegated to a marginal role in discipleship at best, and not permitted to be disciples of rabbis . . . but these women had followed Jesus as disciples in whatever ways they could . . . , even ways that would have appeared scandalous in that culture."

85. In 8:19 a scribe voluntarily offers to ἀκολουθέιν Jesus. Jesus does not outright reject the scribe and reminds him of the requirements of cost and commitment in order to ἀκολουθέιν him. In 19:21 Jesus extends an invitation to ἀκολουθέιν him to a rich young man who wishes to be perfect. Yet, he becomes grieved at Jesus' command to give up his possessions and follow after Jesus. The implied author of Matthew implies the failure of both men to ἀκολουθέιν Jesus lies in their describing him as "teacher" (διδάσκαλε, 8:19; 19:16) because unbelievers, strangers and enemies who directly address Jesus in Matthew never use the term "Son of God," unless it be in mockery or blasphemy, but rather they use "teacher (8:19; 12:38; 19:16; 22:16, 24, 26; cf. rabbi, 26:25, 49). Kingsbury, *Matthew*, 53, 92, 115 and his article, "The Title "KYRIOS" in Matthew's Gospel," *JBL* 95 (1975): 255 point out that the title κύριος is found only in the mouth of disciples and believers, characterizing the person who utters it as acknowledging that Jesus is the one of exalted status who wields divine authority.

convey a specific theological undertone—becoming a disciple—by exclusively letting Jesus wield the command or invitation of ἀκολουθεῖν.

Another characteristic verb that the implied author uses in order to group together the characters sympathetic to Jesus and distinguish them other characters apathetic or hostile toward Jesus is προσκυνεῖν (to kneel, worship). Προσκυνεῖν is a favorite verb of Matthew. Quite a few people, either individually or in a group, *worship* him in wonder and reverence (2:2, 8, 11; 14:33; 28:9, 17) and with supplication (8:2; 9:18; 14:33; 15:25; 18:26; 20:20) as they experience the person and ministry of Jesus. The implied author employs προσκυνεῖν to describe the genuine attitude of those who experience Jesus' extraordinary person reflected through his acts which otherwise could have been performed only by God.[86] More specifically, προσκυνεῖν with the participle πεσών (prostrating, 2:11; 4:9; 18:26) stresses the act of worship exclusively reserved for God.[87] Therefore, in chapter 2, the magi's prostrating before and worshipping an infant Jesus reveals him to be a child of divine origin and majesty.[88] In fact, in his overcoming the temptation of Satan in the wilderness, Jesus proclaims that προσκυνεῖν is an act that can be rendered only to God (4:9-10). It seems that the implied author of Matthew does not intend to draw a distinction regarding the divine status of Jesus pre- and post-Easter since his disciples worship him as the Son of God before his resurrection (14:33), while the same act of προσκυνεῖν is rendered to Jesus after his resurrection (28: 9, 17).[89] Therefore, as we have examined, the implied author's characteristic

---

86. Guido Tisera, *Universalism according to the Gospel of Matthew*, European University Studies XXIII (Frankfurt am Main: Peter Lang, 1993), 57.

87. Marie-Joseph Lagrange, *Évangile selon Saint Matthieu*, 7th ed. (Paris: Gabalda, 1948), 30.

88. W. D. Davies and Dale C. Allison, *The Gospel according to Saint Matthew*, 2 vols. (Edinburgh: T&T Clark, 1991), 1:248; R. E. Brown, *The Birth of the Messiah: A Commentary on the Infancy Narrative in Matthew and Luke* (New York: Doubleday, 1977), 174.

89. Tisera, *Universalism*, 57. Also, Larry W. Hurtado, *How on Earth Did Jesus Become a God: Historical Questions about Earliest Devotion to Jesus* (Grand Rapids: Eerdmans, 2005), 141-42, explains the characteristic use of προσκυνέω in the LXX (e.g., Exod. 20:5; Deut. 4:19; Josh. 23:19) and in the New Testament (e.g., 1 Cor. 14:5; Matt. 4:9-10; Luke 4:7-8) referring to the gesture of reverence given to a deity and therefore meaning "worship." On page 145-51 and 159, Hurtado further singles out the use of προσκυνέω in Matthew and explains that the author of Matthew purposefully employs προσκυνέω to describe homage offered to the earthly Jesus. He considers that the Gospel Matthew clearly reflects the cultic reverence of the exalted Jesus in early Christian circles. On page 146, he writes that "as noted already, the term προσκυνέω is a recurrent feature of Matthew's narrative vocabulary, with thirteen occurrences, a frequency exceeded only by the twenty-four uses in Revelation among the New Testament writings. Moreover, ten of these Matthean occurrences describe homage offered to Jesus, which makes it Matthew's favorite word to designate the reverence given to Jesus by people. Of these ten uses, eight are in scenes where the earthly Jesus is given reverence (the remaining two uses in scenes

choice of words such as ἀκολουθέιν and προσκυνέιν and his regulated application of them to the characters close to Jesus is by no means aimless, but rather shows his intention to inform his reader of the typical behaviors for followers of Jesus. This is why the opponents of Jesus are described neither following nor worshiping Jesus in this Gospel.

In an attempt to expound the proposed character irony of 26:6-16, the verb, ἀγανακτέιν (be indignant) in 26:8 can be seen as another case of the implied author's specific use of a verb to present the close link between characters who share similarities that are significant for the development and meaning of the story. The verb, ἀγανακτέιν in v. 8 illustrates that the disciples of Jesus behave in a similar manner to the religious leaders. There are three incidents in which this verb is employed by the implied author. Two of them are applied to the disciples (20:24; 26:8) and one to the Jewish religious leaders (21:15). All these cases show that the two parties share a common characteristic: both have unjustifiable anger.

The case of 21:15 depicts the religious leaders' anger as unsubstantiated, therefore, unjust, corresponding to their excessive nature. Jesus enters Jerusalem in the midst of a lively welcome by a very large crowd following him and shouting exuberantly (21:8-10). Jesus proceeds to the temple, and there he reclaims the temple as a house of prayer by banning commercial activities and by driving out the money changers (21:12-13). At the same time, he also heals the blind and the lame (21:14). Watching all this, the religious leaders become indignant at Jesus. The implied author, able to penetrate the mind of the characters with Jesus, is forthright in telling why they are angry at Jesus. He bluntly clarifies that the religious leaders are incensed with hatred because they saw the wonderful things that Jesus did and heard the children acclaiming him as the son of David (21:15). This is best described as "jealousy" (φθόνος, 27:18) which in a later scene of the Matthean passion narrative, Pilate correctly identifies as the cause of the Jewish religious leaders' hatred and violence against Jesus. Based on the textual information, it is not a matter of dispute that the anger of the religious leaders at Jesus is unjust because it is due to their jealousy, conceiving Jesus as a rival who endangers their authority over the people (9:6, 8; 21:23, 27; 23:2) and therefore also their reputation and security (7:29).

Surprisingly, the disciples of Jesus also act in a way similar to the religious leaders by showing their distasteful anger when it comes to seeking power

---

where disciples reverence the risen Jesus, 28:9, 17)." Also J. R. Edwards, "The Use of Προσέρχομαι in the Gospel of Matthew," *JBL* 106 (1987): 65–74 considers the author of Matthew to also employ προσέρχομαι to explain the people's cultic or especially reverential attitude toward Jesus which means more than physical approach.

and authority. When they heard how the two sons of Zebedee with their mother besought Jesus to bestow on them a special favor by letting them to sit at the right and left hand of Jesus in his kingdom (20:21), the rest of the disciples became indignant with them (ἠγανάκτησαν, 20:24). Perceiving dissension among his disciples, Jesus teaches them about true discipleship which is epitomized as loving and humble service for others.[90] The disciples of Jesus must desert the ways that the world exerts its power and authority over men (20:25-26b). Instead, whoever would be great among the people of God must be a servant and whoever would be first among the people of God must be a slave (20:26-27), just as the Son of Man came not to be served but to serve men (8:20; 20:28a). Jesus gives his life as a ransom for many (20:28b) by humbly emptying and lowering himself.[91] As Jesus' life determinately moves toward his death in the form of a humble servant, it heavily contrasts with the glory-seeking actions of the disciples (18:1-4) and therefore exposes the ten disciples' unbecoming rage against the sons of Zebedee. Both those who ask Jesus to favor them with power and authority, as well as those who begrudge them, are no different in their failure to learn from their teacher, whose path is set on service to others and, ultimately, the salvation of mankind.[92]

Taking together the above expositions of the verb ἀγανακτέιν and its implications in revealing the characters' spiritual aptitude, the last incident that reports the disciples' anger in 26:6-16 once more points out their shortcomings. Importantly, this section harbors a character irony revealing the contrasting qualities between the disciples as a group and a woman at Bethany. While Jesus stays in the house of Simon the leper at Bethany, an anonymous woman from that region approaches Jesus with an alabaster jar of very expensive perfumed

---

90. Jesus does not overlook his disciples' digression from his teachings concerning the principles of the kingdom of Heaven. In his Sermon on the Mount in chapters 5–7, Jesus taught his disciples and the crowds the principles of the kingdom of Heaven such as being poor in spirit (5:3), being meek (5:5), being merciful (5:7), being pure in heart (5:8), being a peacemaker (5:9) and being humble and not judging one's brothers (7:1-5). The frivolous nature and the shortcoming of Jesus' disciples are further contrasted with Jesus when the implied reader considers how the latter is deeply concerned with the righteousness of God and acts on it (3:15; 5: 6, 10, 20; 6:33; 21:32).

91. David R. Bauer, *The Structure of Matthew's Gospel: A Study in Literary Design*, JSNTSup, 31 (Sheffield: Almond, 1988), 61, writes "Jesus declares that one of the characteristics of members in the eschatological community is 'meekness' (5:5), a term which Matthew connects with 'humility' or 'lowliness' (11:29); apparently, these terms are at least generally synonymous for Matthew. Jesus demands lowliness of his followers in 18:3-4 and 23:12. But Matthew presents Jesus as the prime model of meekness and lowliness. In 11:29 Jesus declares of himself, 'I am meek and lowly in heart', and Matthew reinforces Jesus' point of view then he interprets the triumphal entry with the prophetic words, 'Behold, your king is coming to you, humble and mounted on an ass' (21:5)."

92. Matt. 1:21; 8:25; 9:21-22; 14:30; 20:28; 26:28; 27:40, 42.

oil and pours it on his head while Jesus is reclining at the table (26:6-8). When the disciples see this, they become enraged (ἠγανάκτησαν, 26:8a) because they consider the woman's behavior an extravagant and pointless *waste*.[93] They complain that they would sell the woman's expensive oil for a large sum of money and use it to help the poor (26:9). With this complaint, the disciples consciously place themselves above the woman by implying her behavior is thoughtless and even selfish. It is rather an embarrassing scene to picture. While a woman pays her respects to Jesus by adorning him with a choice, fragrant oil, the disciples cannot hold their tongues and rebuke her. Their criticism of her is somewhat commensurate to chiding their teacher for permitting her action. This awkward picture raises questions in the mind of the implied reader who has been provided with information about the reality of the Matthean story of Jesus from the beginning: Is her action really extravagant? Is not the one whom she anoints after all the Christ, the Son of the living God whom the disciples previously worshipped in awe and veneration? (14:33; 16:16; 17:4-6), Are the disciples truly concerned with the poor? Do any of their actions support their philanthropic interest? Is their anger at a woman fair?

The perceptive implied reader knows all too well how the disciples repeatedly fall short of the ideal standards about which Jesus has instructed them throughout the Gospel. They are less than perfect (τέλειος, 5:48), and are men of little faith who are inconsistent and prone to doubt (ὀλιγόπιστοι, 6:30; 8:26; 14:31; 16:8). In other parts of the Gospel, the reader observes how the disciples were rather heartless toward "the least" such as children (19:13-15) and a Canaanite woman in need, who was desperately crying out to Jesus for the deliverance of her daughter who was severely possessed by a demon (15:21-23).[94] The disciples are portrayed as disregarding children coming to Jesus to receive a blessing. This is perhaps not surprising for the patriarchal society of the ancient world, with its *paterfamilias* structure, was hardly concerned with the rights of women and children.[95] The disciples are

---

93. Matt. 26:8b, "Why this waste?" (εἰς τί ἡ ἀπώλεια αὕτη;)

94. Bauer, *The Structure of Matthew's Gospel*, 61 points out that mercy is one of the essential characteristics of true disciples. Jesus taught his disciples to be merciful (5:7), implying that mercy is one of the fundamental elements of the will of God. In Matthew, Jesus not only becomes the very model of mercy (i.e. his association with the sinners and healings the sick) but also he repeatedly stresses mercy (9:13; 12:7; 23:23).

95. Ancient society is best depicted by the household and within this hierarchical societal structure, a child has no voice of right or choice along with women and slaves. In this regard, tremendously useful scholarly works have been done. See Marylin B. Arthur, "Early Greece: The Origins of the Western Attitude Toward Women," in *The Ancient World: The Arethusa Papers*, ed. John Peradotto and J. P. Sullivan (Albany: SUNY Press, 1984), 7–59.

also pictured as being annoyed by and indifferent to a Canaanite woman (15:22) persistently begging Jesus for mercy (15:23). Certainly, children and a woman fit all the criteria for "the least" and "the poor" of a society for whom the disciples claim they have a concern. Perhaps, the disciples are concerned with the actual money that the Bethany woman might have spent in purchasing a costly perfume and perceive that it had all gone to *waste*.

Sometimes the implied author subtly reveals the spiritual shortcomings of Jesus' disciples by depicting them as having taste for not only the position of power (20:20-28) but also wealth (19:16-30). For example, in chapter 19, a rich young man (19:16, 20, 22) comes to Jesus and asks him how he can acquire eternal life (19:16). Jesus advises him to sell all his belongings and *follow* him (ἀκολούθει μοι, 19:21). On hearing this, the young man becomes discouraged and sad because of his great fortunes and the difficulty of giving them up (19:22). Jesus uses this grieving young man's case to instruct his disciples that it will be harder for a rich man to enter the kingdom of heaven than for a camel to go through the eye of a needle (19:23-24). Being *exceedingly* amazed at Jesus' saying (ἐξεπλήσσοντο σφόδρα, 19:25), Peter, the representative voice of the other disciples, oddly enough asks Jesus what they will *have* for the price they have paid in forsaking everything and following him (19:27). It seems obvious Peter does not comprehend the essence of the teaching that true discipleship requires people to willingly give up their possessions and follow Jesus in total reliance and subjection. Peter's inquiry somewhat reflects his inner thought that he expects something in return as a reward for his voluntary abandonment of what he had. In addition to Peter's case, Judas serves as an extreme example of being materialistic, the worldly concern that affected all the disciples. Matthew 26:15 portrays Judas as heavily concerned with what he will get for betraying his master. At the moment when the deal is sealed, he asks his confederates "what will you give me if I deliver him to you?" (26:15a). These examples of the disciples are unflattering when we recollect how Jesus earnestly taught the disciples not to serve money (μαμωνᾶς, 6:24) and not to worry about earthly possessions (6:25-32; 13:3-9, 22), but to seek first the kingdom of God and his righteousness (6:33; cf. 3:15; 26:54). Jesus himself serves as the very example of these teachings (8:20). Given this textual information which is indispensible to a narrative-critical reading, the doubt regarding the disciples' concern for the poor seems to be inevitable.

Knowing his disciples' inner thoughts (γνοὺς, 26:10a), namely their motive for rebuking the woman at Bethany, Jesus says to them "Why do you trouble the woman? For she has done a good service (ἔργον καλόν) for me" (26:10).[96] Jesus has the power to penetrate one's inner thoughts. When the implied author describes Jesus reading the mind of the characters, the ideas or intents of the characters which Jesus perceives are always negative ones. As much as Jesus sees through the religious leaders' destructive intent (12:15) and malice toward him (22:18), he reads clearly his disciples' thoughts that are often characterized by little faith (16:8) and indiscretion (26:10). Therefore, Jesus' open commendation of a woman's work as a "good service" for him in response to the disciples' censure against the woman in their heart ironically invalidates the disciples' concern for the poor. Instead, this circumstance evolving around the contrast between these two character groups—the woman and the disciples—shows that the disciples have little regard for Jesus, in contrast to the woman's rendering her best in service to Jesus, which is an expression of her faith in and her dedication to him.

As Jesus further explains, the disciples will always have the poor with them (Deut. 15:11) and therefore they will have many chances to serve them if their concern for the poor is genuine (26:8-9). Yet, they will not always have Jesus since the days will come when Jesus will be taken away from them (9:14-15; 26:57). Therefore, it is all the more expected for the disciples to cherish the presence of Jesus with them as the wedding guests rejoice with the bridegroom as long as the bridegroom is with them (9:15a). However, this was obviously not the case for the disciples in their dealing with Jesus. If they had taken Jesus' passion prediction (26:2) to heart,[97] they would not have looked contemptuously (26:8) at the woman's earnest gesture to Jesus, who is, after all, the Son of God (14:33; 16:16; 17:4–6). The narrative in chapter 26 plainly shows that all twelve disciples possess the same shortcoming as Peter. Therefore, this circumstance makes the *good service* of the woman stands out all the more in its appropriateness and significance. The woman's devotional act to Jesus not only serves as the overture of Jesus' passion but also makes Jesus' death and burial finally feel real and immanent. For this reason the story of the Bethany woman is an inevitable part of the Matthean passion narrative. This is further strengthened by the fact that only when Jesus interprets the woman's service to him as the preparation for his impending death and burial, *then* (τότε, 26:14),

---

96. John Nolland, *The Gospel of Matthew* (NIGTC; Grand Rapids: Eerdmans, 2005), 1054 interprets that ἔργον καλὸν ἠργάσατο is "literally 'she has worked a good work', with a deliberate play between the cognate noun and the verb. Matthew probably intends an echo of the 'good deeds' of 5:16 which draw others to glorify God."

97. Heil, *The Death and Resurrection of Jesus*, 26 also points out a similar doubt that "that the disciples value giving alms to the poor as more important than this hospitable anointing of Jesus (26:9) causes the reader to wonder whether they have appreciated Jesus' pronouncement of the imminence and significance of his death during the Passover (26:2)."

Judas Iscariot, one of the twelve, goes to the chief priests and pledges to *betray* (παραδίδωμι, 26:15) his teacher and Lord (26:25) for thirty pieces of silver (26:14-15).[98]

It is crucial for the implied reader of irony to understand that the woman's anointing of Jesus is more than an affectionate gesture. As Jesus explains, her action has a theological significance in that she proleptically and timely (26:2, 16) prepares him for his burial correspondent to his final prediction of impending death (26:2).[99] She is the only character whom Jesus describes as meaningfully participating in Jesus' passion throughout the entire Matthean narrative.[100] Jesus assures (ἀμὴν λέγω ὑμῖν, 26:13) that her service to him (ἔργον καλόν, 26:10) will be remembered wherever this gospel (τὸ εὐαγγέλιον τοῦτο, 26:13), namely, the entire saving ministry of Jesus and its consummation in his death, is proclaimed.[101] Her action ironically stands in contrast with Peter's aforementioned rebuke of Jesus at the time when Jesus revealed his path inevitably leading to the cross (16:21-24). Ostensibly, one may easily consider Peter's resistance in accepting his teacher's prediction of suffering and death to be done out of affection and care. Yet, irony proves that Peter's outwardly loyal attitude to Jesus does not overcome his spiritual shortsightedness of the reality that the entire life of Jesus is divinely willed for one particular goal: the salvation of his people. The reason why Jesus says that the act of the Bethany woman is worthy of being commemorated whenever Jesus' salvific death ("this gospel," τὸ εὐαγγέλιον τοῦτο, 26:13a) is proclaimed (26:13b) is because while the woman participates in the death of Jesus in a momentous way, the disciples, despite being repeatedly informed about the reality of the passion and death

---

98. France, *The Gospel of Matthew*, 977 notes that "the devotion of the unnamed woman is sharply contrasted with the treachery of one of Jesus' inner circle, and her uncalculating generosity with his sordid bargaining."

99. W. D. Davies and D. C. Allison, *A Critical and Exegetical Commentary on the Gospel according to Saint Matthew*, 3 vols. (ICC; Edinburgh: T&T Clark, 1997), 3:447, comments that Jesus interprets the woman's action as a prophetic deed.

100. Senior, *The Passion of Jesus*, 54 notes that "the woman has 'done a beautiful thing' to Jesus (26:10) because she alone understands that the *kairos* has come." Further, on a minor scale, the magi's offering of myrrh to the infant Jesus (2:11), which the ancients used for burial of the dead, can be linked with the woman's anointing Jesus. These events point to and prepare for the eventual death of Jesus both at his birth and at the dawn of his passion.

101. Senior, ibid., 54–55. Though the exact reference of the Matthean phrase "*this* gospel" is not clear, Senior believes that it is likely that Matthew employs the term to mean the "good news" proclaimed through the story of Jesus' passion and death. Also, Luz, *Matthew 21–28*, 338 explains what "this gospel" means: "It is not inconceivable that it refers to the passion narrative. Thus for Matthew the story of the suffering of Jesus is part of the gospel."

of Jesus, fail to do. Therefore, she functions as an ironic foil for the disciples of Jesus. Her singular devotion and matching service to Jesus underlines what is missing in the disciples at the most crucial time of salvation history. Her silent, yet determined action of service to Jesus is not only proved qualitatively good (καλόν, 26:10) by her Lord Jesus, but it also makes an ironic counterpart to the disciples' empty allegiance to Jesus and their failure time and again to understand his words. Notice that Jesus speaks on her behalf. This makes her silence, even without a name, more appropriate for a character irony, because the reality of his death, as Jesus explicates, proves her character and intent valid and meaningful (26:10-13).[102] She is not a mindless woman as the disciples presumably conclude in their heart. In reality, the disciples are humiliated by their own crude thoughts when Jesus acknowledges a woman's action as valuable. Therefore, this character irony discloses the clear contrast between the disciples of Jesus full of opinions and empty promises and the nameless, unvoiced woman at Bethany. Even though she is portrayed as wordless and therefore powerless, this ironic figure speaks loudly through her sanctioned action of timely and appropriate service to Jesus in contrast to the continuing imperfection of the disciples and their disengagement in the divine saving will.

CHARACTER IRONY PERTAINING TO THE DISCIPLES OF JESUS REPRESENTED BY THE TRIO: PETER AND THE TWO SONS OF ZEBEDEE (26:30-75)

After every event essential to bringing about the death of Jesus (26:2), such as the decision of the religious leaders to destroy Jesus (26:3-5), a proleptic preparation for the burial of Jesus by a woman at Bethany (26:6-13), and Judas' seeking an opportunity (εὐκαιρία, 26:16) to hand him over to the religious leaders (26:14-16, 24-25) has been set in motion, Jesus and his disciples gather to have the Passover meal (τὸ πάσχα, 26:17–21a). In this last Passover supper, Jesus makes a covenant with his disciples which involves the offering of his body and blood (26:26-28), obviously implying his death (26:2). When Jesus takes the cup, he specifically describes it as "the blood of the covenant (τὸ αἷμά μου τῆς διαθήκης), which is poured out for many for the forgiveness of sins" (26:28). Jesus' institution of the covenant, the meaning of which is signified by blood, thematically recalls the message of 1:21 and 20:28, both

---

102. France, *The Gospel of Matthew*, 973, writes "The focus on the unnamed woman to the discomfiture of the disciples gives further expression to the gospel principle that the last will be first and the first last, and prepares us for the final act of the story, when it will be Jesus' women followers rather than the men who stay with him (27:55-56, 61; 28:1). The anonymity of this woman in Matthew and Mark is the more remarkable in that her deed is to be a perpetual memorial to her (v.13). She is to be remembered, but she has no name!"

defining Jesus' person and entire life as the Christ Savior of the people who has come to save them from their sins. It is significant that finally in 26:28, the mystery of the way of God's salvation for his people is timely exposed by Jesus himself at the dawn of his passion. While it was previously established through discussion of the meaning of the name of Jesus that 1:21 links Jesus' person and ministry directly to the divinely willed salvation and therefore serves as the story's epicenter governing the direction of Jesus' life and death, the how aspect of 1:21 is found in God's forgiveness of the sins of the people through his Son's sacrificial death. According to the logic of the narrative of the First Gospel nobody can understand the inseparable reality of the life of Jesus and the salvation of men without adopting God's point of view encapsulated in 1:21. Throughout the Gospel and the Matthean passion narrative in particular, there exists a fundamental distance between Jesus and the characters, which is created by the latter's chronic failure in understanding the revelation of the former when he reveals the salvific intent of God in his words and deeds. The opponents of Jesus always deliberately reject him before listening to his teachings (9:1-4, 33-34; 12:24; 21:15; 27:18) and the crowds are susceptible to outside influences and are capricious in their acceptance of Jesus (11:16-19; 13:13-15, 19; 15:10). The disciples of Jesus are not an exception, consistently exhibiting grave shortcomings in understanding and following Jesus' instructions (13:51; 16:12; 17:13).

After Jesus once more predicts his death and explains its meaning through the Passover meal (26:26-29), the company of Jesus goes out together to the Mount of Olives (26:30).[103] There Jesus says to his disciples that all of them will fall away (σκανδαλισθήσεσθε) because of him (ἐν ἐμοὶ, "in me") in the same night (26:31).[104] He further interprets his disciples' flight in relation to the fulfillment of the prophecy that God will strike the shepherd, and the sheep of the flock will be scattered (26:31; Zech. 13:7).[105] Previously, the implied author

---

103. Brown, *The Death of the Messiah*, 1:148 says that the Mount of Olives has scriptural resonance with the story of David's flight from Jerusalem in 2 Sam. 15. It is a reasonable exposition when we consider that Matthew reports that Jesus enters Jerusalem among the people welcoming him as the son of David.

104. Ibid, 1:127 writes that "Matt adds 'in me,' conformable to the Matthean preference for using an 'in' phrase to specify an absolute 'scandalized': 11:6; 13:57; 26:33; Cf. Mark 6:3. This clarifies that their scandal will be focused on Jesus."

105. The LXX of Zech. 13:7 reads, "'Arise, O sword, against my shepherds and against my fellow citizens,' says the Lord almighty. Strike the shepherds and scatter the sheep. And I will bring my hand upon the shepherds." Brown, *The Death of the Messiah*, 1:129-30 gives a helpful explanation about Matthew's allusion to Zech 13:7: "The context in Zech leaves the passage obscure. Earlier, in Zech 11:4-14 God had instructed someone to become a shepherd, ready to care for the sheep and be slain by

has described Jesus as a shepherd (ποιμήν)[106] who came to his people (that is, the lost sheep), to reclaim and rule over them. Yet, to achieve this, the Scripture says that the shepherd will be stricken by God and his sheep will be scattered. This seemingly disastrous picture explains the mode of the divine salvation in an unexpected way as much as the birth of the Son of God in human flesh defies the ordinary understanding of men.

When Jesus predicts that the disciples will corporately fall away from him, Peter responds with an oath, saying that although all the other disciples may fall away because of Jesus, he will never (οὐδέποτε) waver in his faithfulness (26:33). According to the Gospel, it is true that Peter frequently seems to be compelled to say or do things without investing much thought in them or without really meaning it. Therefore, Peter's confidence in his superiority to the other disciples creates an example of character irony that eventually exposes his unreliability and betrays his over-confidence in himself. Despite his leadership and courage (14:28-29), his initiative to explore and learn about important spiritual matters (15:15; 17:4; 18:21) and his positive interactions with Jesus (16:16-18; 17:4), neither his understanding of the will of God nor his dedication to doing it (12:50 cf. 6:10; 7:21) is equal to bearing one's cross since Jesus taught the disciples (10:38; 16:24) to bear actual fruits (6:30; 8:26; 16:8; 17:20; 19:27; 20:24). Most importantly, Peter explicitly stands against both Jesus' open statements regarding his death (16:21-22) and the idea of denying himself in order to bear the cross (10:38-39) which are ironically in perfect agreement with God's will.[107] In this incident Peter speaks at odds against God. So, Jesus

---

those who traffic in sheep; yet at the end of Zech 11 (vv. 15-17) God raises up a shepherd who does not take care of the sheep—thus in one chapter a good shepherd and a worthless shepherd. Zech 12 begins with a threat against Jerusalem/Judah but ends with a spirit of compassion being poured out on Jerusalem. The alternation between positive and negative seems to carry over to Zech 13:7-9, the passage that Mark/Matt. cit. In itself 13:7 is not a future prophecy but an invocative of destruction against the shepherd and the sheep; yet 13:9 describes a third of the whole as a purified remnant of God's people . . . more likely, in my judgment, of the two Zech shepherd roles, the New Testament has concentrated on the positive picture in Zech 11:4-14 for describing Jesus . . . the import of the Mark/Matt. citation is that since Jesus the caring shepherd who brought the flock into being is to be struck down, the sheep will no longer receive his care and will be scattered." Also, France, *The Gospel of Matthew*, 978 mentions that Matthew invites the reader to consider the "price" of Jesus with that of the rejected shepherd in Zech. 11:4-14, who is a paradoxical messianic figure.

106. Matt. 18:12; 25:32-33; 26:31. Matt. 2:6; 9:36; 10:6; 15:24 show that Jesus came from the Davidic line as the son of David whose primary vocation was a shepherd (1 Sam. 17:12-15; cf. Ps. 23). Heil, "Ezekiel 34," 699–702 explicates that the Gospel of Matthew describes Jesus as the fulfillment of the future Davidic leader who is God's messianic shepherd in light of Ezek. 34:23. Heil especially emphasizes both the role of Jesus as God's Davidic shepherd, fulfilling Ezek 34:30 (the promise of Emmanuel) and Jesus' expansion of the shepherding function to include his disciples and the readers.

correspondingly chides him, "Get behind me, Satan!"(Ὕπαγε ὀπίσω μου, Σατανᾶ, 16:23).

It is important to notice how the implied author presents Peter both as an individual (10:2; 14:28-31; 17:1, 4; 26:33) as well as representative of the rest of the disciples of Jesus (15:15; 16:13-28; 18:21-35; 19:27).[108] In fact, it is hard to strictly distinguish between these two portrayals because Peter is most likely an encompassing dramatic persona of the disciples as a whole. The case of Peter exemplifies that as the opponents of Jesus share similar characteristics and behavioral parameters, so also the disciples of Jesus possess coherent traits in their nature, attitudes and ideas in relation to Jesus. In fact, the voice and action of Peter not only represent other disciples' attitudes toward Jesus but also influence them, a case of which we observe in the character irony of 26:30-36 (a Bethany woman's anointing of Jesus). Therefore, an irony portrayed by the ironist in relation to a single character, Peter, may also legitimately apply to all the other disciples.

Knowing his disciples all too well, Jesus responds to Peter's pledge of unwavering loyalty (26:33) with a completely opposite prediction: Peter will deny (ἀπαρνέομαι) him three times this very night, before the cock crows (26:34). [109] It is not without meaning that Jesus specifically predicts that in such a short time his disciple's allegiance would turn into a desperate denial. Being oblivious to himself and the reality of the death of Jesus orchestrated by the divine will (1:21; 20:28; 26:28), once again Peter assures Jesus boldly, without hesitation, that even if he has to die with Jesus, he will not (οὐ μή) disown (ἀπαρνέομαι) Jesus (26:35). Moved by Peter's heroic resolution, all the other disciples likewise claim (ὁμοίως καὶ πάντες οἱ μαθηταὶ εἶπαν, 26:35) that they also will not deny Jesus, despite the prospect of their own deaths. Given the fact that Peter clearly acts as a representative figure, both his promise of solidarity to Jesus and his denial of him, which soon follows, must be seen as being done in

---

107. Kingsbury, *Matthew as Story*, 15, notes the stark contrast between Jesus' view of his passion and the disciples' view.

108. F. J. Matera, *Passion Narratives and Gospel Theologies: Interpreting the Synoptics through Their Passion Stories* (New York: Paulist, 1986), 103 describes Peter as being much more than merely "one of them." Peter is the first-called (4:28) and functions as leader and spokesman of all the disciples in the Gospel narratives. Also, Kingsbury, "The Figure of Peter in Matthew's Gospel as a Theological Problem," *JBL* 98 (1979): 71–74 discusses the Matthean portrait of the "salvation-historical supremacy" of Peter in two ways: one, Peter as the spokesmen of the disciples, and two, Peter as typical or representative of the disciples in Matthew's story.

109. Keener, *A Commentary on the Gospel of Matthew*, 634 comments that Jesus knows better than his disciples do what his disciples are made of and when Jesus predicts the disciples' fall because of him, he probably means apostasy.

a communal sense.¹¹⁰ Therefore, all the disciples are subject to corporate blame and consequence for their shortcoming.

The disciples' over-confidence in making an oath without considering the consequences and in claiming to possess qualities that they do not possess is not a new phenomenon. Earlier when the sons of the Zebedee entreated Jesus through their mother to assign them special positions of authority in the kingdom of God (20:20-21), Jesus euphemistically alluded to his death as an act of drinking "the cup" (τὸ ποτήριον, 20:22; 20:28; cf. 26:39), and questioned them as to whether they could drink the cup which he was about to drink. Without a moment of self-reflection, the Sons of Zebedee said that they could (δυνάμεθα, 20:22b), thus claiming unknowingly a participation in the death of Jesus (20:22a) on a superior level of reality (26:27-28, 39). The collective voice of the disciples in 26:35 (ὁμοίως καὶ πάντες οἱ μαθηταὶ εἶπαν), saying that they will faithfully adhere to Jesus even to death is not a different kind of voice from the voice of the sons of Zebedee saying that they could drink the cup. Whether as an individual or as a group, the disciples wear the same mask and behave in an identical way. Despite the disciples' alleged willingness to join in the mission of Jesus culminating in his death (16:21; 17:21-22; 20:18-19; 26:2), the story of the Matthean passion narrative ironically demonstrates that Jesus alone carries out this task without a single soul beside him (26:31, 40, 41, 45, 56). Therefore, each stage of the passion of Jesus inevitably put the disciples both individually and corporately to the test regarding their outspoken loyalty to Jesus. In other words, the Matthean passion narrative provides the lab test for examining the disciples' spiritual acumen and whether they understand and follow through with their words (20:22; 26:35).

To interpret the whole panorama of the character irony involving Peter (26:31-35), the implied reader must consider together the following scenes of the Matthean passion narrative: the prayer of Jesus and his arrest in Gethsemane (26:36-56) and the trial of Jesus before the Sanhedrin (26:57-75) along with the behavior of Peter that brackets the incidents. In these scenes, the way Peter deals with the violent progression of Jesus' passion breaks his previous promises (26:33-35) and therefore ironically reveals him as a person of *alazonic* (ἀλαζών) nature. Right after the disciples' allegiance to Jesus has been declared, Jesus, accompanied by his disciples, moves to a place, Gethsemane, where Jesus prepares for his final hour (ὁ καιρός μου, 26:18) with prayers just before his arrest (26:50). Just as he did on the mount of the transfiguration, Jesus once

---

110. Kingsbury, "The Figure of Peter," 74 considers the promise of solidarity made by Peter to Jesus in 26:35 to be done in a clearly communal sense since Peter's voice in this is representative. Therefore, all other disciples also share Peter's denial of Jesus.

again takes three disciples, Peter and the two sons of Zebedee (26:37) to be close to him during this time of preparation. The ironist is intentionally specific about which disciples Jesus chooses to make participants in his last hour of grief (26:37-38) and prayerful preparation for his impending death (26:36, 38). He does this for two reasons. First, Matthew's Gethsemane scene has parallels to Matthew's transfiguration story.[111] Second, these three disciples explicitly expressed their willingness to take "the cup" with Jesus (20:22; 26:35). Jesus has previously selected the trio to accompany him to his transfiguration on a mount (17:1). These three had the privilege of experiencing Jesus on a totally new and exalted level. Jesus revealed his heavenly glory before their very eyes. Because these three disciples have exclusively experienced the divine epiphany of Jesus, the reader might wonder whether they will behave differently from the other disciples in their service and understanding of Jesus. Yet, the Matthean passion narrative is uncomplicated in telling that these three are representative of the other disciples in their intentions and behaviors. The Matthean passion narrative not only depicts a striking commonness among these three in that they all publicly pledged their loyalty to Jesus on separate occasions, the sons of Zebedee in 20:22 and Peter in 26:35, but also categorizes the rest of the disciples with the trio in their partaking of the same type of vows (26:35b). Consequently, all the disciples of Jesus in one way or the other pledge that they will not disown (ἀπαρνέομαι, 26:35) Jesus even if death (that is "the cup," 20:22) will be the ultimate price. Now the proper time comes for the disciples as a corporate character to demonstrate their fidelity which they pledge to Jesus while the cloud of death is approaching fast. Jesus takes with him the same trio from the mount of transfiguration and leaves them near where he prays. With the foreknowledge of his own death making him deeply sorrowful and distressed (26:37-38),[112] Jesus asks his chosen disciples to stay awake with him (γρηγορεῖτε μετ' ἐμοῦ, 26:38), goes a little beyond them (προελθὼν μικρόν, 26:39) and falls on the ground.[113] There he begins to earnestly entreat his father (πάτερ

---

111. Anthony Kenny, "The Transfiguration and the Agony in the Garden," *CBQ* 19 (1957): 445–48; Luz, *Matthew 21–28*, 395.

112. Heil, *The Death and Resurrection of Jesus*, 43 considers the cause of Jesus' distress to be his awareness of imminent death and sorrow. Heil connects Jesus' sorrow at approaching death with allusions to the biblical psalms of lament and in accord with his portrayal as the "suffering just one" (Ps. 40:12–13; 42:9–11; 55:5–6; 116:3–4; Sir 51:6–12). Brown, *The Death of the Messiah*, 1:155–56 notes that Jesus' anguish on the Mount of Olives is due to a depth of sorrow which is produced by an awareness of imminent death (i.e. Ps. 55:5). He adds that "if Jesus is the weary prophet in Mark/Matt., in part it is because he foresees his disciples scandalized and scattered by his arrest and death, after they have betrayed and denied him. The very thought of this is enough to kill him, and he will ask God to be delivered from such a fate."

μου, 26:39, 42) to remove the cup from him (26:39), yet if the cup cannot pass away unless he drinks it, let God's will be done (26:42, 44). Jesus' demand to the three to "watch" (γρηγορέω) means more than staying physically awake, but it has a sense of vigilant togetherness which Jesus clearly stresses by saying, "watch with me" (γρηγορεῖτε μετ' ἐμοῦ, 26:38). Previously, Jesus has exhorted his disciples with the imperative "be awake" (γρηγορέω) especially in relation to the last days (the Matthean eschatology, 24:42-43; 25:13).[114] It is noteworthy that the implied author attempts to portray the death of Jesus as the beginning of the last days by emphasizing the earnest biddings of Jesus to be vigilant at the time of his approaching death. The end of the age will come with the glorious returning of the Son of Man. Yet, according to the Gospel, the death of the Son of God, the Christ Savior, is a necessary precursor to his second coming when he will bring the end of the age with him. Most certainly, the Gospel's core message (26:13) rests on the achieved salvation of men through the death of Jesus and, must be proclaimed until the end of the age (26:13; 28:18-20). Therefore, the Matthean eschatology is closely related to the death of Jesus (that is, to soteriological matters) on the grounds that his death not only launches the countdown of the last days but also the risen Jesus shall come again as the Son of Man, the judge of the World.[115]

In between the three offerings of supplication (26:38, 42, 44), Jesus returns to the trio and finds them asleep (26:40, 43, 45). According to the Gospel's presentation thus far, it is grossly improper for them to be found in laxity and carelessness at the most sinister hour of death as attested to by Jesus himself in his own words "My soul is deeply grieved, even to death!" (26:38). The contrast between Jesus facing the weighty hour of death (26:18) and the disciples at the very same time exhibiting spiritual lethargy is striking. The disciples not only have heard the repeated passion predictions of Jesus (16:21; 17:22-23; 20:18-19; 26:2) on their way to Jerusalem (16:21; 20:17-18; 21:1, 10) but also at the Passover meal, which is probably no more than several hours prior to the scene at Gethsemane (26:36). They heard more grim details from Jesus regarding the

---

113. Luz, *Matthew 21–28*, 396 provides an interesting insight regarding Jesus' falling on the ground to pray in Gethsemane. He writes that "Jesus goes a little farther in order to pray alone, as he himself has ordered (cf. 6:4-6) and also did himself (cf. 14:23). He falls on his face, not as an expression of deepest despair but in the same way Abraham did when he spoke with God (Gen. 17:3, 17; cf. Num. 22:31; 1 Kgs. 18:39; Dan. 8:17). Thus Jesus is not only desperate; he is at the same time pious."

114. Donald A. Hagner, *Matthew 14–28* (WBC; Dallas: Word Books, 1995), 783 notes that Jesus' command to "watch" later develops into a standard feature in the ethical catechism of the New Testament and refers to spiritual awareness (1 Cor. 16:13; Col. 4:2; 1 Thess. 5:6; 1 Pet. 5:8 and also as the command to pray, Eph. 6:18; 1 Thess. 5:17; 1 Pet. 4:7).

115. See Matt. 10:23; 13:41-42; 16:27-28; 19:28; 24:27-30, 37-39, 44; 25:31; 26:64.

unfolding passion such as his betrayal by one of the disciples (26:20-21) and his being deserted by the rest of them the very same night (26:31). Taking all these situations into consideration, the trio's sleeping (26:40, 43, 45) while Jesus prostrates himself alone in darkness and distress, facing the unavoidable reality of death, certainly makes the implied reader question the reliability of their words of commitment and solidarity.[116] Furthermore, as the deeds of Jesus testify to his person, the actions of the disciples likewise mirror who they are. It seems that the stupor in which the disciples are found is symbolically the best description of their inner condition. The voice of the ironist attests to this conclusion as the physical distance which Jesus removes himself from the disciples is not significant (προελθὼν μικρόν, 26:39) and the duration of his prayer should not be unrealistic for the disciples to bear.[117] Consider that when Jesus found them asleep the second time, he said to Peter in the plural, "So could you not watch with me one hour?" (οὕτως οὐκ ἰσχύσατε μίαν ὥραν γρηγορῆσαι μετ' ἐμοῦ; 26:40). Notice that the verb, ἰσχύσατε in 26:40 is second person plural imperative. The disciples' spiritually weak presence (26:41) with an alert Jesus at the hour when their pledged loyalty is duly requested leaves the impression with the implied reader that their claims that they are capable of drinking the cup (20:22; 26:27, 35, 39) cannot be trusted.

Finishing his prayers, Jesus wakes up the disciples and announces to them that he is about to be betrayed (26:46) Immediately following Jesus' announcement, Judas (ὁ παραδιδοὺς, 26:25, 46, 48), accompanied by a large crowd of armed forces, comes up to Jesus (προσελθὼν τῷ Ἰησοῦ, 26:49) [118] and hands his teacher over with a kiss (φιλέω, 26:48). This is itself an ironic act of beguilement, pretending intimacy and affection yet actually meaning separation and treachery (26:47-49).[119] Judas greets Jesus as "rabbi" (χαῖρε,

---

116. Brown, *The Death of the Messiah*, 1:156 notes that a present imperative of γρηγορέω in Matt. 26:38 demands of the three persistence and solidarity. Brown further explains historically why the three are told to watch. He says, "As part of the Passover night watch, even as Exod. 12:42 inculcates a 'watch' to be kept to the Lord for all generations."

117. Ibid., I.164 notes that μικρόν is here used adverbially which is more often temporal than spatial.

118. J. R. Edwards, "The Use of Προσέρχομαι," 67–68 provides several examples in which people approach Jesus in their implicit recognition of his exalted status as a teacher. In this article, Edwards opines that Matthew uses the term consistently to reveal the messianic or exalted status of Jesus.

119. Brown, *The Death of the Messiah*, 1:254f writes that "the Judas kiss, a sign of affection or love used to betray, entered the repertory of Christian imagery; and the evangelists were surely aware of that possibility when they described it. Already Prov. 27:6 had inculcated distrust of the kisses of an enemy, and in the flow of the Gospels the readers know that Judas is now an enemy. But on the level of history or of verisimilitude, how are we to understand Judas' use of the kiss? If it was a normal greeting that could be used by any acquaintance or a customary greeting between Jesus and the disciples, then it could

ῥαββί,, 26:49) and Jesus calls Judas "friend" (ἑταῖρε, 26:50). Previously in 23:7-8 Jesus forbids his disciples to call or greet each other with the title, "rabbi," since it is typically used by the religious leaders in their attempt to distinguish themselves from the ordinary and claim a place of honor.

Jesus used the term, "friend" (ἑταῖρε) in his teachings about the kingdom of heaven in two parables: the workers of the vineyard (20:1-16) and the wedding banquet (22:2-14). In the first parable, the workers being hired early in the morning for a denarius and who have worked in the vineyard all day long complain to the vineyard owner since he pays the same wage to the ones who were hired at the end of day and worked only one hour. The vineyard owner calls one of them "friend" (ἑταῖρε, 20:13), reminds them of their agreement regarding wage (20:13) and instructs them on his authority and generosity (20:15). In the second parable of a king's marriage feast for his son, a guest who is found without a suitable garment for the feast (22:11) is once again called a "friend" (ἑταῖρε, 22:12) by the king himself. The king ordered his servants to bind that unprepared and therefore unqualified guest for treating the king's invitation trivially (26:14), and also orders them to throw him into the outer darkness (26:13). In these parables Jesus uses the term "friend" as a typical address for a person who becomes last by falling short of grace and understanding (20:16; 22:14). By having Jesus used the word "friend" when addressing Judas (ἑταῖρε, 26:50),[120] the ironist indirectly reveals Judas' falling short of grace and his conscious separation from Jesus.

At the signal of Judas, the soldiers attempt to lay their hands on Jesus as if he is a robber (26:55). Then, one of those accompanying Jesus draws a knife and strikes the slave of the high priest, cutting off his ear (26:50-52). Yet, Jesus halts any violent resistance from his companions and allows his opponents to seize him so that the Scriptures would be fulfilled (26:54-56). This manifests that Jesus is mindful of the divine "must" (δεῖ) operating as he reveals his awareness of it in his first passion prediction in 16:21. Immediately after Jesus dejects any form of defense for him, all the disciples forsake him and flee as he announced in 26:31: "All of you will fall away because of me this night; for it is written, 'I will

---

fit into the plot of those who had paid Judas to avoid noisy resistance and hence into Judas' desire to appear disarmingly normal. If it was not a normal greeting but an unusual gesture implying special attention, then Judas was a malevolent hypocrite." Also, Luz, *Matthew 21–28*, 416 depicts the kiss as a sign of honor and affection. Yet, in the Matthean passion narrative's case, Judas evidently has misused it.

120. Brown, *The Death of the Messiah*, 1:256 similarly explains irony in Jesus' use of the term, ἑταῖρος. It is certain that ἑταῖρος is not considered a normal greeting of Jesus to a member of the Twelve. This title has nothing to do with intimate and loyal relationship. In fact, as Brown notes, there is no example of ἑταῖρος used within Jesus' discipleship in the canonical Gospels.

strike the shepherd, and the sheep of the flock will be scattered.' "At the flight of the disciples, the soldiers arrest Jesus and lead him to the high priest, Caiaphas, who is waiting along with the scribes and the elders (26:57). Meanwhile, Peter follows Jesus at a distance, enters the courtyard of the high priest, and sits with the guards to what will happen (26:58). This report of Peter's action after Jesus' arrest is filled with ironic descriptions. Earlier we examined how the implied author characteristically uses ἀκολουθεῖν (to follow) to metaphorically describe the relationship between Jesus and a disciple, implying cost (self-denial) and commitment (bearing the cross). The characters receptive to Jesus' teaching and ministry are characterized by a responsive action of following, and here Peter ironically still follows Jesus (δὲ Πέτρος ἠκολούθει αὐτῷ, 26:58), yet *from afar* (ἀπὸ μακρόθεν, 26:58) and in a *secretive* manner.[121] According to the Gospel following Jesus cannot be done properly in secret. It requires public manifestation and an open confession of faith in Jesus since Jesus taught his disciples the significance of confessing (ὁμολογέω) him before men.[122] He will acknowledge before his Father in heaven (10:32) the ones who confess him publicly. Chapter 10 further identifies confessing Jesus as bearing one's cross in spite of tribulation (10:34-42).[123] Therefore, denying (ἀρνέομαι, ἀπαρνέομαι) Jesus before men is categorically unacceptable for his followers (10:33) because public denial of Jesus is a sign of failure in bearing one's cross. In this light, it becomes clear that what the disciples pledged to Jesus at the dawn of his passion—that they would never deny him (26:33) even though they should face death (26:35b)—was none other than the promise of bearing their crosses and following Jesus to the death (that is, drinking the cup, 20:22; 26:39). However, Jesus' prediction of the disciples' denial of him (falling away, 26:33) points to

---

121. Heil, *The Death and Resurrection of Jesus*, 57–58 considers Peter's following Jesus from afar to have its origin in the Old Testament. He notes that "although all the disciples had left Jesus and run away after his arrest (26:56), Peter is still following him, but only 'at a distance' (*apo makrothen*). With its allusion to LXX Ps 37:12, 'My friends and my associates have drawn near and stand opposite me, and my companions stand at a distance [*apo makrothen*],' Peter's apprehensive following from afar contributes to the portrait of Jesus as the 'suffering just one.' Peter's distance from Jesus demonstrates how his discipleship is disintegrating."

122. Birger Gerhardsson, "Confession and Denial before Men: Observations on Matt 26:57–27:2," *JSNT* 13 (1981): 59 suggests that persecution and the public confession of Jesus in such a context have a theological significance. His view is that there is a positive divine intention behind the persecutions against Jesus' followers and the interrogations to which they are subjected because they will have an opportunity in that official place to witness or to offer testimony regarding Jesus.

123. It is worth noting that the first reference to crucifixion in Matthew is not in relation to Jesus, but to the disciples (10:38; 16:24). See Bauer, *The Structure of Matthew's Gospel*, 60.

the reality that the disciples will irrevocably fail in carrying out this particular task.

The fact that Peter secretively follows after Jesus from a distance implies that a connection still remains between the two. Yet, soon enough his threefold vow to Jesus, "I will never desert you" (ἐγὼ οὐδέποτε σκανδαλισθήσομαι, 26:33), "I shall die with you" (even though I must die with you, κἂν δέῃ με σὺν σοὶ ἀποθανεῖν, 26:35) and "I will never deny you" (οὐ μή σε ἀπαρνήσομαι, 26:35), is put to the ultimate test at an intense time and in a dangerous environment. Peter's second vow is particularly worth further examination. Here Peter's use of δεῖ, which echoes the divine necessity attached to the ministry and death of Jesus (1:21; 16:21; 26:54-56), creates a verbal irony because Peter, who once strongly rejected the idea of the suffering and death of Jesus (16:22) is now ironically stressing his voluntariness to share it. However in the moment requiring public confession of Jesus, Peter condemns himself on two levels: one, according to the divine will all the disciples of Jesus must be scattered, and two, Peter chooses to disown Jesus of his own accord.

Now the story unfolds as follows. While Peter is sitting outside with the servants in the courtyard (26:58, 69), a slave girl comes and questions him about his companionship with Jesus the Galilean (26:69). Peter publicly denies being *with* Jesus (ὁ ἠρνήσατο ἔμπροσθεν πάντων, 26:69-70)[124] as if he does not understand her statement. As he physically withdraws further from the courtyard, another maid spots him and says to the bystanders that Peter was *with* Jesus of Nazareth (26:71). The second time Peter denies her accusation with an oath that he does not know the man, Jesus (καὶ πάλιν ἠρνήσατο μετὰ ὅρκου ὅτι οὐκ οἶδα τὸν ἄνθρωπον, 26:72). At last, the bystanders doubting Peter come up to him and say with conviction that "certainly you too are one of them, for even your speech betrays you" (26:73). In fear and desperation, Peter attempts to quiet once for all the voices questioning him as a companion of Jesus by emphatically cursing Jesus (καταθεματίζω)[125] and swearing (ὀμνύω)

---

124. Gerhardsson, "Confession and Denial before Men," 54 defines the verb ἀρνέομαι that "one is denying his attachment to someone he is supposed to belong with; one does not want to know of him, one does not want to know of him, one does not acknowledge any connection with him."

125. The verb ἀναθεματίζειν is usually transitive and has an object stated. Here the object is unstated but implied. Peter's curse has been interpreted among the New Testament scholars either as Peter's placing himself under a curse or cursing Jesus as a strong denial of him. This reflects Jewish polemics directed against Jewish-Christian devotion to Jesus as seen in Acts 26:9, 11 and 1 Cor. 12:3. Interestingly, Peter's trial at the time of Jesus' trial before the Roman governor Pilate reflects Pliny the younger's *Epistulae*, 10.96.3, written in c. 110 CE, in which Pliny reports that he provided a defendant accused of being a Christian the threefold opportunity to recant (curse) the name of Jesus and offer a sacrifice to the image of Caesar as proof of innocence. A. N. Sherwin-White, *Roman Society and Roman Law in the New*

that he does not know (οὐκ οἶδα)[126] the man (26:74). In this way, Peter three times denies Jesus when he is challenged three times about his connection to the accused Nazarene.[127] In a panic, Peter, who once pledged that he would die *with* Jesus (26:35), denies his association *with* Jesus by placing himself *with* the servants, a group who has no meaning to him. Peter's three denials of Jesus correspond with his three pledges to Jesus earlier in the Matthean passion narrative (26:31-35): "Even if all desert you (fall away on account of you), I will never desert (you)" (εἰ πάντες σκανδαλισθήσονται ἐν σοί, ἐγὼ οὐδέποτε σκανδαλισθήσομαι, 26:33), "even if I have to die with you" (κἂν δέῃ με σὺν σοὶ ἀποθανεῖν, 26:35a), and "I will never disown you" (οὐ μή σε ἀπαρνήσομαι, 26:35b). These proven empty words of Peter expose an ironic inconsistency in Peter, indeed, a corporate trait of the disciples of Jesus as a whole.[128] In their blind (i.e. *alazonic*) confidence and inability to perceive reality, the disciples hastily make pledges that are easily broken despite the fact that Jesus has previously taught them not to take vows or make oaths because any religious vow in the mind of God must be fulfilled.[129] Conclusively, an irony disclosing the fundamental discrepancy between the disciples' words and their actions exposes the disciples as the *alazonic* figures of the combination of swelled confidence and little faith. However, though the Matthean passion narrative's character irony presents the disciples of Jesus as unreliable, it also communicates that the disciples have not been deserted by Jesus.[130] This is shown in Jesus' promise to reunite with them in Galilee after the

Testament (Oxford: Oxford University Press, 1963; reprint, Grand Rapids: Baker, 1978), 25–26 confirms this type of practice was an established one in Roman court at the time of New Testament. Based on ancient sources regarding the cursing of Jesus such as Justin (*Dialogus cum Tryphone* 47:4; 95:4; 108:3; 133:6) and Pliny the Younger (*Ep.*, 10.96), it is more likely that Peter is cursing Jesus rather than himself. The same view that Peter curses Jesus in the third denial is supported by Günther Bornkamm, *Jesus of Nazareth* (trans. Irene McLuskey, Fraser McLuskey and James M. Robinson; London: Hodder and Stoughton, 1960), 212; Helmut Merkel, "Peter's Curse," in *The Trial of Jesus: Cambridge Studies in Honour of C. F. D. Moule* (ed. Ernst Bammel; SBT 13; London: SCM, 1970), 66–71; Gerhardsson, "Confession and Denial before Men," 54–55.

126. The expression, "οὐκ οἶδα," is the equivalent of the verb, "to deny," ἀρνέομαι, ἀπαρνέομαι.
127. Merkel, "Peter's Curse," 66.
128. Luz, *Matthew 21–28*, 462 opines that the author of Matthew depicts Peter as the model of the Christian of "little faith," in that he is a mixture of trust and fear (14:28-31), faith and protest (16:16-20), apostasy and remorse.
129. See Matt. 5:34, 36; cf. 23:16, 18, 20-23; 26:74.
130. It must be admitted that the characteristics of the εἴρων–ἀλαζών paradigm for irony, which have been taken from the old Greek comedy and the case of Socrates, do not always square with other occurrences of irony. The εἴρων is not necessarily a dissembler or simpleton in a negative sense in the

resurrection (26:32; 28:7). It is significant to note that Jesus promises a reunion with his disciples even before the act of his betrayal and on the very same night when he is deserted by these same disciples. Jesus' promise of re-gathering the disciples who are about to go astray is, in effect, the promise that he will bring about the exact reversal of their scattering. Therefore, this particular promise implies forgiveness to his estranged disciples, something which his death actually achieves for all his people (1:21; 20:28; 26:28).

VERBAL IRONY PERTAINING TO THE INTERROGATION OF JESUS BY THE RELIGIOUS LEADERS IN HIS TRIAL BEFORE THE SANHEDRIN (26:59-68)

The Matthean passion narrative contains strings of biting verbal irony which reveal the meaning of the death of Jesus. Many of them are contained in the interrogations of Jesus and in the mockery from the opponents of Jesus in the trial scenes.[131] The level of understanding which the implied reader of these verbal ironies will obtain depends on his ability to observe of how these ironies bring about a reversal, eventually exposing the opponents of Jesus as the *victims* of their own words[132] and ironically marking them as the recipients of forgiveness which is offered through Jesus (1:21; 20:28; 26:28), their apparent victim.

Jesus is handed over to an assembly of the Jewish religious leaders (the Sanhedrin, 26:57, 59) and there he undergoes the first trial. Seeking false testimony against Jesus, the religious leaders come up with two false witnesses (18:16)[133] to condemn Jesus (26:4, 59), an incident which once again testifies to their treachery (δόλος, 26:4).[134] Also, we have previously been given literary

---

same way that the opponents of Socrates defined him. However, it is true that almost all the time he serves as a protagonistic, normative, and paradigmatic figure who establishes the superior value that overthrows the lower. It also must be recognized that there is a level of difference in evaluating ἀλαζών. For example, Jesus' disciples in the Matthean passion narrative serve as the *alazonic* figures in a corporate sense (with Peter as their representative), but not in the sense that they are utterly doomed or oblivious. The reader does not wish to follow their path but not to the same degree of rejection that he does not want to follow the Jewish religious leaders, who are the single most important corporate ἀλαζών in Matthew.

131. Keener, *A Commentary on the Gospel of Matthew*, 644, points out that the trials scenes are "heavily laden with ironies" on the ground that the trials of Jesus reveal the hiddenness of the kingdom (13:31-33). He says that "apart from those who share the correct presuppositions, the kingdom's presence remains ambiguous to those it confronts (e.g., 26:64). Ironically, the kingdom remained obscure even to many of those providing religious and political leadership to others."

132. Howell, *Matthew's Inclusive Story*, 242 notes that the Jewish leaders are the primary victims of Matthean irony.

133. According to the Jewish custom, the proper number of witnesses needed for the death sentence is mentioned in Num. 35:30; Deut. 17:6; 19:15.

evidence revealing the spiritually inadequate dispositions of the religious leaders throughout the Gospel: sly (26:4), unjust (26:59), lack of fear of God (2:1-16; 21:13), without authority (7:29; 21:23-27), hypocritical (6:2, 5, 15; 15:7; 22:18; 23:13, 15, 23, 25, 27, 29),[135] spiritually ignorant (12:3, 5; 19:4; 21:16; 22:31), envious (27:18), greedy and self-indulgent (23:25), pretentious and vainglorious (23:1-7), and most of all, evil. From the early chapters of Matthew, the implied author consistently portrays the religious leaders as a corporate character group whose dominant trait is synchronically and collectively *evil* (9:4; 12:34, 39, 45; 16:4; 22:18),[136] which corresponds with Satan. The Gospel outspokenly identifies them as a "brood of vipers" (3:7; 12:34), "serpents" (23:33), and corporately "a child of hell" (23:15) and assigns them a place in "darkness" (22:13; 25:30). Also, their lack of mercy (23:23) contrasts Jesus' manifestation of divine mercy (9:13; 12:7) as throughout the Gospel the implied reader witnesses that people in need have come to Jesus seeking mercy and they were never turned away (9:27; 15:22; 17:15; 20:30-31). When Jesus disputes the Pharisees over the law of the Sabbath such as what is lawful to do on the Sabbath in chapter 12, he predicts their unlawful treatment of him in relation to their chronic inability to understand the Words of God: "If you had known what these words mean, 'I desire mercy, not sacrifice,' you would not have condemned the innocent" (12:7). It is significant to notice that the Matthean passion narrative emphatically underscores the innocence of Jesus! (27:4, 19, 24)

The root trait of the religious leaders, that is evilness, makes the implied reader reasonably doubt whatever claims they make against Jesus. Based on the principle of the narrative-critical reading, the implied reader is privileged to possess substantial information regarding the significance of Jesus to which the characters within the story have no access. Since he is progressively instructed about the person of Jesus through the voice of the implied author and other credible witnesses such as God himself, John the Baptist, and minor characters such as the magi, he cannot miss the ironic circumstance of the trial of Jesus. A fatal combination of the evilness of the opponents of Jesus together with their spiritual ignorance, rightly labels them a corporate ἀλαζών of the Matthean

---

134. The Jewish religious leaders' treachery against Jesus further includes a lack of fear of God when doing injustice (Prov. 6:19).

135. As the implied author of Matthew employs several characteristic verbs to group together some characters homogenous in their nature and behavioral mode, he also applies typical Matthean titles to character groups. For example, if the title, "men of little faith" (ὀλιγόπιστοι), is exclusively used for the disciples (6:30; 8:26; 16:8; 17:20), and "hypocrites" (6:2, 5, 15: 15:7; 22:18; 22:13, 15, 23, 25, 27, 29) is particularly used for the Jewish religious leaders, the opponents of Jesus.

136. Kingsbury, *Matthew as Story*, 19; Powell, *Narrative Criticism*, 62–63, 66–67.

passion narrative—the prime opponents and persecutors of the normative εἴρων, Jesus. Therefore, any character within the story who willingly shares their intention to do away with Jesus is one of them, as Jesus says in 12:30, "He who is not with me is against me, and he who does not gather with me scatters."

The two false witnesses come forward and give a false testimony against Jesus that "this man said, 'I am able to destroy the temple of God and to build it in three days' " (26:61). Though the Gospel does not report that Jesus actually made such a claim, though Jesus has consistently predicted that he will be done away with at the hands of his opponents and on the third day be raised (16:21; 17:23; 20:19; cf. 12:40), this false testimony indirectly points to the profound connection of Jesus to the temple in 24:1-2. It is true that Jesus never explicitly claimed that he himself has the power to destroy the temple, though he did predict the devastating destruction of the sacred temple. Before further exposition, consider the significance that the temple of Jerusalem holds in the history of the people of God. Israel's rise and fall revolved around the temple. Israel held Jerusalem and its temple as the essential markers of their existence as a special people of God. When the Babylonians destroyed the first temple in 587 BCE, they were naturally devastated. The temple of God experienced much tribulation and was desecrated in various ways up to the time of Jesus. Some such desecrations included the Syrian ruler Antiochus Epiphanes setting up his image as a god (167 BCE) which caused the Maccabean revolt in 164 BCE, Pompey walking straight into the Holy of Holies in 63 BCE, and Herod the Great's attempt to rebuild it, far short of its original glory. Based on these historical evidences, the temple of Jerusalem always has been the object of utmost reverence, religious aspiration, and serious expectation of the ultimate restoration and vindication of Israel as the divinely consecrated priestly nation.

The testimony of the two witnesses against Jesus is fallacious. They fabricate an announcement of Jesus as if he mentioned his ability and power to bring about the actual temple destruction as well as its reconstruction within three days. This same false testimony surfaces again in the mocking of Jesus by the anonymous passers-by at the site of the cross (27:39). They taunt the crucified Jesus by saying, "You who destroy the temple and build it in three days, save yourself" (27:40). Yet ironically, what they say in a false accusation in fact points to the superior reality of what the death of Jesus actually brings about. Notice that at the very hour of the death of Jesus, the curtain of the temple was torn (ἐσχίσθη) in two from top to bottom (27:51).[137]

---

137. Hagner, *Matthew 14–28*, 849 comments that "the splitting of the curtain ἀπ' ἄνωθεν ἕως κάτω, 'from top to bottom,' together with the passive verb ἐσχίσθη, 'was split,' implying divine action, points to the event as an act of God."

It is not a trivial matter that the drastic change made in the temple at the death of Jesus is listed first among other apocalyptic and cosmological portents immediately following Jesus yielding up his spirit (27:50-53). Jesus visited the Jerusalem temple and purged the impious activities from it as his first act after his entrance to Jerusalem (21:10-13).[138] A corresponding radical completion in terms of a change in the temple occurs at the death of Jesus. The curtain of the temple covers the entrance to the Holy of Holies in the Jerusalem temple and demarcates the barrier between God and men, between the holy and the mundane. Therefore, *velum scissum* (the torn veil)[139] before the Holy of Holies at the death of Jesus theologically implies that the death of Jesus creates a new, unhindered, universal, righteous and blood-bought path to God which perfectly fulfills the central point of the Gospel and the Matthean passion narrative: the divinely-willed salvation. In other words, if the veil of the temple symbolizes its prohibition of "physical and visual accessibility to God,"[140] the person Jesus embodies the accessibility of God that corresponds to Matthew's Emmanuel Christology.

The ironic spin of a false accusation against Jesus in relation to the temple exemplifies how irony works as a powerful rhetorical device in the Matthean passion narrative. Not telling it directly, the ironist reforms the false testimony of the opponents of Jesus and uses it to reveal that the death of Jesus renews the meaning and purpose of the temple through its apparent destruction.[141] Jesus

---

138. Daniel M. Gurtner, *The Torn Veil: Matthew's Exposition of the Death of Jesus* (Cambridge: Cambridge University Press, 2007), 98–99, 124–126, points out the significance of the temple in the Matthean narrative, functioning as both a "character" and a "(deliberate) setting" which highlights Jesus the protagonist. Gurtner observes that the author of the Gospel of Matthew is intentional in his choice of location and issues in relation to the temple and its cult. Hagner, *Matthew 14–28*, 598 explains that Jesus as messianic king enters the temple to purge it. In relation to Jesus' cleansing of the Jerusalem temple, Davies and Allison, *A Critical and Exegetical Commentary*, 3:132 comments that Jesus' purge of the temple (21:12-13) anticipates Jesus' restoration of the temple.

139. Gurtner, *The Torn Veil*, 138 explains four theological implications of *velum scissum*. First, it conveys an apocalyptic heavenly vision depicting the sovereignty of God despite the tragic event of Jesus' death. Second, the torn veil implies the cessation of the function of the temple. Third, it depicts the historic destruction of the temple in 70 CE. Fourth, the rending of the veil signifies accessibility to God. For a position which relates this Matthean *velum scissum* pericope to the temple destruction in 70 CE as the fulfillment of Jesus' prophecy of destruction (27:40), see Davies and Allison, *A Critical and Exegetical Commentary*, 3:631.

140. Gurtner, *The Torn Veil*, 189.

141. In his study of the prophetic hope of Israel, Ronald E. Clements, *Old Testament Theology: A Fresh Approach* (Atlanta: John Knox, 1978), 146, writes "A further basic theme, or model, of the prophetic hope is the belief in an ultimate glorification of Mount Zion as the centre of a great kingdom of peace. Jerusalem itself becomes a place of the greatest important, with its rebuilt temple looked to as the place

witnessed the desecration of the temple by merchants and saw the purpose of the temple being frustrated by corruption and exploitation (21:12-13) and took the initiative to cleanse it. He condemned the Jewish religious leaders, for they had turned the temple, a house of the prayer (Isa. 56:7) into a den of robbers (21:13; Jer. 7:1-11). This is figuratively equal to destroying the temple which is the very charge they falsely lay on Jesus (26:61). It is not Jesus who destroys the temple, but the religious leaders and the people,¹⁴² who, in their unbelief (13:15; 15:8-9), cause the spiritual demise of the temple which Jesus bemoans. It is sharply ironic that Jesus, who is falsely accused as the destroyer-builder of the temple, is indeed rebuilding the temple through his own demise. Jesus, who is greater than the temple (12:6), renews the temple of old that has been alienated from the teachings of the law. This is the manifestation of the saving will of God (9:13; 12:7-8; 23:23).¹⁴³

Further, it is interesting to notice that Jesus treats this false accusation against him with an ironic silence (26:63) similar to how a typical εἴρων behaves in a reserved or non-committed manner in his dealing with his boisterous counterpart, the ἀλαζών. The silence of Jesus increases the intensity of the verbal irony of this false testimony which exposes the very accusers of Jesus as the victims of their own word. They speak the truth about a protagonistic-normative figure whom they accuse in their blameworthy confidence and thereby they brand themselves as guilty parties because they have accused the innocent. While Jesus is keeping silent in response to a false accusation, the high priest adjures him to tell them whether he is the Christ, the Son of God (26:63). Through the interrogations conducted by the Sanhedrin, the Matthean

---

where God's 'glory' or 'presence' would appear (cf. Ezek 48:35; Mal 3:1). To this the nations would come as an act of pilgrimage and homage, rather in the way that their representatives had done long before in the short-lived kingdom of David." When we consider the Matthean emphases on Jesus as the son of David (i.e. the King of the Jews), Jesus' journey to Jerusalem for his passion and Jesus' relation to the temple (and the law), it become evident that the implied author of Matthew portrays Jesus as the one who accomplishes the prophetic hope of the Old Testament regarding the restoration of the glory of God among Israel through the restoration of the temple. Also, regarding a close link between the restoration of the temple of God and the son of David, see Davies and Allison, *A Critical and Exegetical Commentary*, 3:636.

142. Gurtner, *The Torn Veil*, 99, notes that "Matthew is positive towards the temple in general, affirming the validity of its sacrifices and the presence of God within it. Yet the temple's destruction is imminent not because Matthew sees intrinsic problems with it, but because it is mismanaged by a corrupt Jewish leadership."

143. Ibid., 182, considers that the true identity of Jesus as the Son of God whose death is "life-giving" and "new-age-inaugurating" is revealed when the veil of the temple is torn (i.e. "the veil of the heavenly firmament is opened").

passion narrative's ironist makes it evident that the prime cause of Jesus' death is the issue of who Jesus is, especially his divine sonship.[144] It is a striking fact that both the narrator and almost all the main characters within the story make mention of who Jesus is either through a direct or an indirect means of speech such as verbal irony. The following are the representative cases where each party of the narrative speaks of who Jesus is: the narrator (1:1-19), God (3:17; 17:5), the angels (1:20), John the Baptist (3:3, 11-12), the disciples of Jesus (14:33; 16:16), the devil (4:3, 6) and his associates (8:29), the religious leaders as a corporate group (26:63, 68), the crowds (12:23; 21:11), the mockers (27:39-44), the political powers such as Herod (2:4, 8) and Pilate (27:11, 17), the marginal characters such as the magi (2:2), the blind men (9:27-28), the centurion with his soldiers (27:54) and even an object such as a written charge placed above the head of Jesus on the cross (27:37).

As far as the issue of Jesus' identity in the eyes of his chief opponents is concerned, it is striking that the scandal and the controversy of Jesus' identity actually does the reverse and exposes the identities of his opponents. In this Gospel, a link and resemblance between Satan and the Sanhedrin are shown in their mutual concern for Jesus' identity. Satan challenges Jesus' identity during the temptation in the wilderness (4:1-11) and the Sanhedrin, represented by the high priest Caiaphas, does the same thing during Jesus' trial (26:63-66).

God himself testifies to Jesus' sonship at his baptism and transfiguration. Jesus is the beloved "Son of God"[145] with whom God is pleased (3:17; 17:5). The testimony of God is the ultimate bedrock source regarding the person and mission of Jesus, the protagonist of the story. Whoever confesses Jesus as the Christ and the Son of God has had it revealed to them from God himself (16:16-17). Just as Satan challenges the identity of Jesus (4:3, 6), attempting to divert the Son of God from his devotion to carrying out his Father's will (4:3-4, 6-7, 9-10), so the chief priest condemns Jesus, saying that the defenseless victim standing before them is only pretending to be the Christ and the Son of God. However, the ridicule of the religious leaders creates a pungent verbal irony bringing three significant theological points home. One, the opponents

---

144. Erwin Buck, "Anti-Judaic Sentiments in the Passion Narrative according to Matthew," in *Anti-Judaism in Early Christianity: Volume 1 Paul and the Gospels*, ed. P. Richardson and D. Granskou (Waterloo: Wilfrid Laurier University Press, 1986), 172–73, explains that the reason for the opposition against Jesus, especially from the Jewish religious leaders, is the identity of Jesus as the Son of God. He notes that "it is evident that for Matthew the title 'Son of God,' more than any other, constitutes the point of conflict between Jesus and the Jewish opposition."

145. Jesus the Son of God (including Jesus' descriptions of God as his heavenly Father), see Matt. 2:15; 3:17; 7:21; 8:29; 10:32–33; 11:25–26; 12:50; 14:33; 15:13; 16:16–17; 17:5; 18:10, 14, 19, 35; 20:23; 24:36; 26:29, 39, 42, 53, 63; 27:40, 43, 54; 28:19; cf. 4:3, 6.

of Jesus are associates of Satan whose accusatory voice and intention resembles Satan's at the first site of the temptation of Jesus. Two, the opponents of Jesus in fact ironically utter the unassailable truth regarding the person of Jesus, that he is indeed the Christ and the Son of God (26:63) which God himself declares (16:16-17).[146] To be sure, when the religious leaders speak in words resembling Peter's confession of "Jesus as the Christ" during their interrogation of Jesus (26:63), their statements do not mean that they have received the same divine revelation as Peter had (16:17a).[147] Therefore, when the ironist puts the same words concerning Jesus' profound identity in the jeering mouth of the interrogator, it is for the sake of creating verbal irony through which he eventually intends to expose their self-victimized status, since their words betray them. Lastly, the third effect of this verbal irony regarding the person of Jesus discloses the bigger picture hidden behind the appearance. Since in the Gospel of Matthew God assumes the role of the most reliable and therefore undefeatable witness of his son, Jesus (3:17; 16:17; 17:5), when the opponents of Jesus abusively deny Jesus, the true object of their taunting becomes God himself as they unwittingly accuse him of being a liar about his son.[148] In doing so, they blaspheme God and blindly identify themselves as accusers of God.

In this interrogation by the high priest, the implied reader sees through an ironic lens a bigger conflict between God and Satan surrounding the issue of the person of Jesus. Jesus once again treats his opponents' accusation in a noncommittal manner, saying "You have said so" (σὺ εἶπας, 26:64).[149] Through

146. Brown, *The Death of the Messiah*, 1:471 notes that 26:63 is virtually identical to the confession by Peter in 16:16.

147. "Μακάριος εἶ, Σίμων Βαριωνᾶ"(Blessed are you, Simon Barjona!)

148. Bauer, *The Structure of Matthew's Gospel*, 70 also notices irony in that the religious leaders accuse Jesus of blasphemy for claiming to be the Son of God, when in fact they are the ones who blaspheme. Yet, Bauer's reasoning comes from a different angle, suggesting that the religious leaders employ false testimony to kill Jesus and that "though their proceedings are shrouded in a cloak of legality, it is an act of murder, for Jesus is innocent (27.4, 25) and indeed righteous (27.19)."

149. Heil, *The Death and Resurrection of Jesus*, 61 notes that "refusing to participate in the high priest's oath, Jesus replies with the indirect affirmation 'You have said it' (26:64), the same reply that indicated Judas' self-condemnation for his betrayal (26:25). Jesus thus turns the oath back upon the high priest, indicating that his own words have condemned him of putting God's Messiah to death." Also David R. Catchpole, "The Answer of Jesus to Caiaphas (MATT. XXVI. 64)," *NTS* 17 (1970): 214–15 summarizes a growing tendency to understand σὺ εἶπας as ambiguous or non-committal among Jewish interpretation. Through a redactional-critical reading, Catchpole, ibid., 226 concludes that Matt. 26:64 is "affirmative in content, and reluctant or circumlocutory in formation." Catchpole especially considers Jesus' answer to Caiaphas as an affirmative because the exertion of power in the temple is the Messiah's prerogative, and this view is finally confirmed by Matt. 27:40: "You who would destroy the temple and build it in three days, save yourself if you are the Son of God."

Jesus' indirect word of affirmation regarding himself, the Matthean passion narrative's ironist imports two points and effectively kills two birds with one stone. First, by letting the opponents of Jesus declare all the truth regarding their victim, the ironist reverses the moment of accusation against Jesus and makes it the moment of self-invited condemnation for his opponents. Second, the verbal irony hidden in the interrogation by Caiaphas exposes an ironic dynamic existing between the two courts and the two verdicts. This is in parallel with the scheme of the double-layered story phenomenon: the Sanhedrin vs. the court of God and the defendant, Jesus, *guilty* as an alleged pretender of being the Christ and the Son of God vs. the defendant, the religious leaders, *guilty*! as they speak against Jesus, the Son of God, with God himself as witness. Jesus' following statement to his interrogators that they will see the Son of Man seated at the right hand of Power coming on the clouds of heaven (26:64) confirms the reversal of the present court verdict which stands in opposition to the divine saving will manifested in Jesus himself. The Son of Man statement of Jesus unmistakably reflects the Old Testament prophetic tradition from the book of Daniel (Dan. 7:13),[150] denoting the Messiah's exalted status and his eschatological coming as the judge of the world. In a particular narrative-rhetorical context of this scene in the Matthean passion narrative, that is the legal-polemic context, the Son of Man statement of Jesus can also be interpreted that Jesus proclaims his future vindication and triumph over the Jewish authorities who are now condemning him to death.[151] In this case the exchange of words between Jesus the defendant and his accusers in court further reveals the reversal of the status of innocence and guiltiness under the mantle of character irony.

A string of verbal ironies continues as the events of the passion story progresses from verbal harassments to the physical abuse of Jesus by his opponents. Calling Jesus a blasphemer deserving death, the religious leaders spit in his face and strike and slap him (26:68). In their contempt they also beat Jesus, saying "Prophesy to us, oh! you Christ, who is it that *struck* you?" (26:68, italics mine). It is ironic that the Jewish leaders here unwittingly fulfill Jesus' word regarding what will happen to him as the fulfillment of the Old Testament prophecy (Zech. 13:7) that God will *strike* the shepherd and the sheep of the flock will be scattered (26:31).

---

150. LXX Dan. 7:13, "I saw in the night visions, and behold, on the clouds of heaven, one like the Son of Man coming. And he who is like the ancient of days was present and the attendants were standing before him."

151. Heil, The Death and Resurrection of Jesus, 61; Brown, The Death of the Messiah, 1:506–8.

The beleaguerment of Jesus by the religious leaders in 26:68 harbors two further instances of verbal irony which expose the defeat of the latter since they inadvertently tell the truth about their apparent victim, Jesus. First, when they taunt Jesus and call him "the Christ," they, in fact, make a true statement about Jesus whether they believe it or not. Therefore, the arrow of mockery which the opponents of Jesus launch to prick him takes an ironic turn, and comes back to wound its shooters and their credibility. Once again, the Matthean passion narrative's ironist confirms Jesus as the Christ by means of the abusive language of his opponents. The second instance of verbal irony found comes when, debasing Jesus with beatings, the religious leaders bid him to prophesy who strikes him (26:68). Right before his arrest the same night, Jesus prophesied to his disciples that "God will strike the shepherd and the sheep of the flock will be scattered" (26:31). According to the Gospel of Matthew, Jesus is the divine shepherd (18:12; 25:32–33) who rules over (2:6) and saves his sheep (15:24; 18:14), which is a metaphor for his people (1:21). In his speech to the disciples Jesus, the shepherd himself, interprets the reality of his passion encompassing all its satellite events—arrest, betrayal and death—in the image of the shepherd being stricken. A remarkable point found in this image of the dejected shepherd is that it is God himself who strikes the shepherd (26:31; Zech. 13:7) according to his will (6:10; 8:14; 26:42). Jesus subjects himself to the higher calling of his Heavenly Father by being stricken (26:67) as he willingly drinks the cup (20:22-23; 26:39) in his filial devotion to God the Father. In this light, the ignorance of the religious leaders concerning the divine reality is laid bare through irony that the Father's will to save his people is perfectly satisfied by the Son's irreproachable commitment to accomplish it. Under the reality of this overarching salvific plan of God which must inevitably brings about the death of Jesus (26:28), all the earthly authorities, including both the religious and political powers who seek to wield power over Jesus, turn out to be utterly ironic to the point of absurdity (27:1) because the death of Jesus is exactly what is necessary to fulfill the divine "must" (δεῖ, 16:21; 17:22-23; 20:17-19; 26:1-2, 24a).

Chapter 27 and Instances of Conventional Irony

Verbal Irony as Self-Criticism of the Religious Leaders (27: 4-6)

After deliberating over doing away with Jesus (27:1), all the chief priests and the elders of the people (21:23; 26:3) hand their victim over to Pilate, the Roman governor of Judea (27:2),[152] in order to legitimize the capital sentence against Jesus.[153] Then (τότε, 27:3a), Judas, seeing that Jesus is condemned, regrets (μεταμέλομαι, 27:3) handing Jesus over to the chief priests and elders and brings back the thirty pieces of silver which he took as payment for that action (26:15). Judas the betrayer (10:4; 26:15-16, 21, 23-25, 45-46, 48) in his contrition confesses, "I have sinned by betraying innocent blood" (ἥμαρτον παραδοὺς αἷμα ἀθῷον, 27:4). This concise statement of guilt characterizes Judas a tragic figure just as Jesus mentioned earlier: "The Son of Man goes as it is written of him, but woe to that man by whom the Son of Man is betrayed. It would be better for that man if he had not been born" (26:24).

The confession of Judas declaring the innocence of Jesus does not function as verbal irony which generally would overturn what the speaker says in his imperceptibility or misconception of reality. Contrarily, Judas has had a moment of self-realization (27:3) and means exactly what he says (27:4). Here Judas is a tortured figure rather than an ironic figure. He finally gets a sense of the offense he has committed against his teacher (26:18, 25, 49) and the Lord (22:42-45; 26:22). His character is irretrievably broken because his repentance ends in meaningless self-condemnation when he takes his own life (27:5).[154]

The verb, μεταμέλομαι (to rue, to regret, to feel repentance), occurs three times in the Gospel. One instance is found here, in relation to Judas (27:3). In contrast to Judas' tragic case, the other two instances of μεταμέλομαι (21:29, 32) depict the hopeful situation that one's heart can change. These examples are found in a conversation between Jesus and the chief priests and the elders of the people who are attempting to challenge the authority of Jesus (21:23). Jesus spoke in a parable of a father who had two sons in order to instruct the religious leaders in the value of changing one's heart which yields a corresponding action. In this parable (21:28-30), a father asked both of his children to go to work in the vineyard. The first one refused but afterwards he changed his mind (μεταμέλομαι) and went to work. The second son did the exact opposite of what the first son did. Jesus compared the first son, who initially failed to respond to his father's calling but later changed his heart and went to work in the vineyard (21:29), to the tax collectors and the prostitutes who inherit the kingdom of God (21:31). Contrastingly it is implied that the religious leaders

---

152. Heil, *The Death and Resurrection of Jesus*, 67, interprets Matt. 27:2 ("They bound him, led him away and handed him over to Pilate the governor") as ironic in a sense in that the same Jewish leaders who cruelly mocked Jesus' power to "prophesy" (26:67-68) take a role in confirming Jesus' detailed passion prediction in Matt. 20:18-19.

153. The execution of capital punishment was under the control of the Roman prefect-procurator, not of the Sanhedrin authorities. See Brown, *The Death of the Messiah*, 1:710.

154. Keener, *A Commentary on the Gospel of Matthew*, 656 treats the fall or apostasy of Judas and other disciples equally as the disciples' weakness and comments on the exposure of the disciples' weakness as cause for repentance (26:75; cf. 26:31-32), not sorrow unto death as in the case of Judas (27:5).

are to be identified with the second son in the parable because when John came to them in the way of righteousness, the religious leaders did not believe in his words but the tax collectors and prostitutes both repented and believed him (21:31-32).

Judas should have advanced from remorse (μεταμέλομαι, 27:3) to something constructive, such as hoping in the forgiveness of sins which Jesus himself promised to bring about (20:28; 26:28) and reminding himself of the promise of his teacher that after his resurrection (16:21; 17:22-23; 20:18-19), Jesus would reunite with his disciples (26:32-33). Instead Judas ended his repentance with self-destruction rather than bearing fruit. "Bearing fruit that befits repentance" is one of the key Matthean themes proclaimed by John the Baptist (3:8) and also, repeatedly taught by Jesus on several occasions that what one's life yields is the very indicator of the quality of the self (7:20; 12:33; 21:19). Further, given that Jesus has the authority to forgive sins (9:1-8) and that divinely-willed salvation governs Jesus' ministry (1:21; 20:28; 26:28), Judas' self-destruction sadly stands in opposition to God's willing to save his people from their sins through his Son, the appointed saving agent.

Though Judas' confession itself is not a form of irony, it promotes the reading of verbal irony in connection with the statements of the religious leaders in 27:4-6. Judas' confession regarding the "innocent blood of Jesus" coheres with the life and mission of Jesus and further, makes the reader reflect on the Matthean theme of blood. Earlier, the implied author has purposefully underlined the theme of blood in conjunction with qualities such as righteousness and innocence in the incidents such as the slaughter of innocent children in and around Bethlehem in 2:16, the beheading of John the Baptist in 11:1-9 and 14:1-13 and the murder of all the righteous blood of the prophets, the sages and the scribes in 23:29-36. By making this connection, he discloses that innocent-righteous blood has an inviolable saving effect, an idea which thematically corresponds to Jesus' interpretation of shedding his blood for the forgiveness of sins (26:28). In fact, Judas demonstrates the need that he and all other sinners have for the forgiveness that the innocent blood of Jesus will provide.[155] Therefore, Judas' confession regarding the innocent blood of Jesus is the highlight of all the Gospel's conceptual and literary mappings which are designed to communicate the most vital Matthean message that Jesus (1:21) pours his own innocent blood (20:28; 26:28) to save the people from their sins (1:21; cf. 9:5-6, 13) in keeping with the divine saving will (6:10; 18:14; 26:39, 42).

---

155. Heil, *The Death and Resurrection of Jesus*, 68.

Judas' declaration of the innocence of Jesus before the Jewish religious leaders is important to the implied reader because although his confession is a statement of truth, it does not have power on its own to amend the wrongful situation inflicted on Jesus, but rather it reinforces the murderous intent of the opponents of Jesus, as 27:4 shows. When Judas returns the thirty pieces of silver to the religious leaders (27:3) and confesses that he has sinned by betraying the innocent blood of Jesus (27:4), the religious leaders answer him indifferently, "What have we to do with that? That is your problem!" (τί πρὸς ἡμᾶς; σὺ ὄψῃ, 27:4). When Judas leaves them, the chief priests, taking the returned silver into the temple (27:5), say, "It is not lawful (οὐκ ἔξεστιν) to put them into the treasury, since they are the price of blood (τιμὴ αἵματος)" (27:6; cf. Deut 23:18). Though stubbornly being unaffected and unmoved by Judas' confession regarding the innocence of Jesus, the religious leaders cannot go without betraying themselves with their own words. Matthew 27:6 contains an instance of verbal irony that discloses the guilt of the religious leaders even as their callousness shows their indifference to conscience-stricken Judas. In 27:6, the religious leaders acknowledge in their ignorance that the money which they had paid to Judas was indeed the price of blood (τιμὴ αἵματος), which means that they bought the blood of Jesus, namely the death of Jesus. A simple question further highlights the ironic nature of their statement,[156] exposing their guilt and attacking their pretension of innocence: if Jesus is guilty as they charge him to be (26:65-66), why do they, as prosecutors, need to purchase the blood of the defendant in the first place? Purchasing the blood of Jesus once again testifies that stealth (26:4) and lawlessness are their modes of behavior (12:14; 21:33-46; 23:13-35; 26:59-60; 27:18). Ironically, when they say that it is *not lawful* (οὐκ ἔξεστιν, 26:7) for them to restore the returned money to the treasury of the temple, they incriminate themselves. Why do they consider the

---

156. The following scholars consider the religious leaders' statement, the price of blood (27:6), is ironic. See Davies and Allison, *Saint Matthew*, 978, 1041–45; Heil, *The Death and Resurrection of Jesus*, 69–70. Heil writes that "the dramatic irony heightens as they attempt to dispose of the blood money by purchasing 'the potter's field as a burial place for foreigners' (27:7). In deeming the price/value of Jesus' blood as unworthy for the temple and fit only to buy an unclean burial place for unclean people, the Jewish leaders are unwittingly disclosing for the reader the true 'value' and 'price' of Jesus' innocent blood. They show the salvific 'value' of Jesus' blood, which purchases a burial place for the 'foreigners' or 'strangers' (*xenois*) with whom Jesus identifies himself: 'I was a stranger [*xenos*] and you welcomed me' (25:35, 38, 43-44). They also show the tragic 'price' of Jesus' blood, which purchases a burial place for the 'foreigners,' who will replace the people of Israel in God's kingdom . . . the chief priests fulfill the tragedy prophesied by Jeremiah (27:9-10) as they 'took the thirty pieces of silver' (see 27:6), the paltry 'price/value' (*timēn*) with which they, as 'some of the sons of Israel,' tragically 'set a price' (*etimēsanto*) upon the Jesus they ironically reject as the truly 'valued/priced' one (*tetimēmenou*) of God's people of Israel."

returned money, which they once had paid to Judas, *not lawful* unless their intent and actions in using that money were also *not lawful*? Therefore, the religious leaders' remark regarding the blood money which they identify as unlawful is an ironic self-criticism spoken in their unawareness of the situation (that is, of reality) and lack of fear of God as Jesus diagnosed in chapter 23. Their unwitting statement exposes their lawlessness and characterizes themselves as a guilty party. This verdict is ironically hidden as they alone are oblivious to the fact that they purchased the blood of the innocent (27:4, 6) for an illegitimate purpose. Strikingly, the Matthean Jewish religious leaders as the corporate opponents of Jesus match the descriptions of the traits which God condemns in Proverbs 6:16-19: "There are six things which the Lord hates, seven which are an abomination to him: haughty eyes, a lying tongue, and hands that shed innocent blood, a heart that devises wicked plans, feet that make haste to run to evil, a false witness who breathes out lies, and a man who sows discord among brothers" (RSV). The actions of the Jewish religious leaders as they seek to bring about Jesus' death throughout the Gospel—but most intensely in the Matthean passion narrative—show them to be guilty in all seven of the above categories. Taking that fact into consideration their opposition to Jesus is not only ironic but also catastrophic because in their persecution of Jesus, the beloved Son of God (3:17; 17:5), they, in fact, stand against God himself. In this way, the ironist communicates an absurdity surrounding the death of Jesus: the innocent one has to be done away with at the hands of the guilty and the death of Jesus is *illegitimately* (unlawfully) carried out despite his accusers' attempt to seek its *legitimacy* by bringing the case to the Roman governor, Pilate.

Though Jesus is innocent (righteous in 27:19, δίκαιος) and does not deserve being condemned to death as the verbal irony of 27:6 discloses, he is not a mere victim as it at first seems on the surface level of the story. Ironically, the true power of the death of Jesus lies in his very innocence, which shows that the life of Jesus conforms to the divine purpose. It is the divine saving will that provides the *legitimacy* of the innocent death of Jesus since salvation will be proffered to God's people in the way in which he wills it. In the past, God's ways have seen the death of the just and the innocent whom he sent among the people of Israel (23:29-30). According to Matthew, the Scriptures show that God's saving work in human history through the suffering and death of the innocent fundamentally requires an ironic perspective in order to be understood. Therefore, as St. Paul characterizes it,[157] trying to make sense of the

---

157. Paul expresses that for some, who regard themselves as wise, the Christian proclamation of the innocent death of Jesus as the way of divine salvation is considered folly (μωρία, 1 Cor. 1:18). Yet, the

innocent death of Jesus based narrowly on the human cause of justice is doomed to fail because the notion that God saves mankind through the suffering and death of the righteous one sounds foolish. However, this way which seems foolish to men is God's unwavering way of achieving salvation for mankind which the Gospel describes as the divine "must" (δεῖ).[158]

CHARACTER IRONY ARISING FROM THE CONTRAST BETWEEN JESUS AS THE MESSIANIC KING OF THE JEWS (27:1-37) AND PILATE AS AN EARTHLY RULER (ʽΗΓΕΜΩΝ, 27:2)

Throughout the Gospel the implied author pays a great deal of attention to Jesus as the royal Messiah born in the house of David and as the fulfiller of the Davidic covenant in the Old Testament.[159] In the same vein, the Gospel emphasizes related themes such as the kingdom of heaven, the kingship of Jesus, and Jerusalem, which was once the capital of the Davidic kingdom and the city of the Great King (5:35) who is personified in Jesus (2:2; 21:5; 27:11, 37). In this Gospel, Jesus' title "the King of the Jews" is depicted as controversial and seems to be interchangeable with Jesus, "the son of David" in its concept and usage. The title, King of the Jews, is the dominant Christological title of Matthew and plays an important role in the Gospel.[160] It constitutes an irony when the title is misused against Jesus by a character within the story with the intent of mockery. By this title, both Jews and Romans alike revile Jesus, the commonly perceived object of trouble and impediment. The Jewish religious leaders are agitated (ἠγανάκτησαν, 21:15) to the point of jealousy (φθόνος, 27:18) which is enflamed when they witnessed that even the children received Jesus as the son of David (21:15). Likewise, the Romans, represented by Pilate's court, cast their suspicion on Jesus as a potentially rising political threat against the Roman power. This is made clear when Pilate asks Jesus if he is the King of the Jews (27:11).

Among the Jews, there exists a difference between the crowds in general and their religious leaders in their perception of Jesus as the son of David. While the disbelief of the religious leaders regarding Jesus' kingship is constant, the Jewish crowds often accept Jesus as a king who stems from David's line (9:27; 12:23; 15:22; 20:30-31; 21:9). However the Matthean passion narrative shows

---

foolishness of God is wiser than men (1 Cor. 1:25) because a seemingly foolish faith in the innocent death of Jesus ironically saves those who believe (1 Cor. 1:21).

158. Matt. 1:21; 16:21; 17:22-23; 20:18-19; 20:22; 26:28, 39, 42, 54.
159. Jesus the son of David (i.e. Jesus the King of the Jews) 1:1; 2:2, 6; 9:27; 12:23; 15:22; 18:23; 20:30-31; 21:5, 9, 15; 22:2, 42; 25:34, 40; 26:31; 27:11, 29, 37, 42.
160. Kingsbury, *Matthew as Story*, 45–49.

that the people's capriciousness allows them to be swiftly swayed. At the final stage of his messianic mission Jesus enters Jerusalem as the King of Zion, the promised royal Messiah (21:5; Zech. 9:9; Mic. 5:2) amid the people's initial welcome and shout of joy (21:9-11). However, Jesus' visit to Jerusalem and her temple is accompanied by a confrontation with the religious leaders at the temple over the issue of authority despite of the crowds' remarkable welcome of Jesus as the son of David. This instance where confrontation and adulation are oddly mixed (21:1-27) ironically links itself to the people's rejection of Jesus in the Matthean passion narrative where their shout of exaltation (οἱ ἔκραζον, 21:9) quickly turns into a clamor of condemnation (οἱ ἔκραζον, 27:23). According to the Gospel, the people shout for Jesus on two very different occasions with a totally different purpose in mind. The implied author intentionally employs the same verb, κράζω, in these two separate instances in order to mark these two groups of people as related. Clearly, the people's outcry in the Matthean passion narrative is a different sort of shout and it seals a drastic reversal of Jesus' fate: from one welcomed to one rejected.

Jesus' confrontation with the Pharisees in chapter 22 is pivotal because this incident is critical in unveiling one of the key themes of Matthew: the identity of the Christ. After the Pharisees try to test Jesus (22:34-40) by asking what the greatest commandment of the law is (22:36), Jesus redirects the issue to the more fundamental question: who is the Christ of whom the Scriptures faithfully witness (22:41-46). Considering the fact that the Gospel frequently employs Old Testament prophecies in relation to the Messiah, the Son of God, and the suffering servant in order to indicate that Jesus is the fulfillment of them,[161] Jesus' question to examine the understanding of the Jewish religious leaders regarding the identity of the Christ is quite pointed because it discloses that the root of the problem the Jewish religious leaders' experience with Jesus is based on their own ignorance. They reject Jesus because they do not know who Jesus is: the Christ[162] and the Son of God.[163] Jesus presents a theologically compact question to the religious leaders, "What do you think of the Christ? Whose son

---

161. For example, Matt. 1:1 (Isa. 9:6-7), 1:1-3 (Gen. 49:10), 1:1-16 (Gen. 12:3), 1:15 (Deut. 18:15; Hosea 11:1), 1:18 (Gen. 3:15; Isa. 7:14; Jer. 31:15), 1:23 (Judg. 13:5; Amos 2:11; Isa. 7:14; 9:6), 2:1 (Ps. 72:10; Mic. 5:2), 2:11 (Ps. 72:10), 3:3 (Isa. 40:3), 3:17 (Ps. 2:7; Isa. 42:1), 4:15 (Isa. 9:1-2), 8:5 (Gen. 12:3), 8:10 (Gen. 12:3; 2 Sam. 22:44-45; Ps. 2:7-8; Isa. 55:5, 60:3, 65:1; Mal. 1:11), 8:16-17 (Isa. 53:4), 10:34-35 (Mic. 7:6), 11:5 (Isa. 29:18, 35:5-6, 61:1), 11:7-11 (Mal. 3:1), 13:14-15 (Isa. 6:9-10), 15:8-9 (Isa. 29:13), 17:5 (Isa. 42:1), 20:28 (Dan. 9:26), 21:5 (Zech. 9:9), 21:42 (Ps. 118:22-23; Isa. 28:16, 53:3), 22:44 (Ps. 110:1), 26:15 (Zech. 11:12), 26:56 (Zech. 13:7), 26:60 (Ps. 35:11), 27:5, (Zech. 11:13), 27:9-10 (Zech. 11:12), 27:14 (Isa. 53:7), 27:23 (Ps. 35:19), 27:26 (Isa. 50:6, 53:5), 27:30 (Isa. 50:6, 53:5; Mic. 5:1), 27:34 (Ps. 69:21), 27:35 (Ps. 22:18; Isa. 53:12), 27:36 (Ps. 22:17), 27:43 (Ps. 22:7-8), 27:45 (Amos 8:9), 27:46 (Ps. 22:1), 27:57 (Isa. 53:9), 27:60 (Isa. 53:9).

is he?" (22:42), and they answer him without hesitation that the Christ is the son of David (22:42), an answer which may reflect the learned contemporary view of the Scriptures. Yet, Jesus again questions them, "How is it then that David by the spirit calls him, saying 'the Lord said to my Lord, "Sit at my right hand, till I put your enemies under your feet" '? If David then calls him Lord, how is he his son?" (22:43-45). What Jesus implies by conceptualizing that the Christ is the Lord (κύριος) of David (22:45) in a reflection of Ps. 110:1 is that the Christ is the Lord (κύριος, 3:3; 23:39) who possesses attributes and honor which are reserved only for God.[164] It is a special Matthean emphasis that Jesus Christ is none other than the Son of God as Jesus himself precisely clarifies through his dialectical questioning of the Pharisees (22:41-46), the learned of the Scriptures and those claiming authority over interpretation of the law (23:1). Consequently, the rhetorical question of Jesus achieves its end by leaving the Pharisees mute and at their wit's end. The narrative depicts them not daring to ask him more questions, perhaps more correctly, not daring to test (22:35) him with more questions.

The Gospel's deliberation of the identity of the Christ generates a verbal and a character irony in the first and the second trial of Jesus in the Matthean passion narrative respectively. In the Matthean passion narrative's report of the first trial of Jesus before Sanhedrin the high priest, Caiaphas, on behalf of the Sanhedrin, interrogates Jesus as to whether or not he is the Christ, the Son of God (26:63). Caiaphas's interrogation is ironic on two grounds: first, Caiaphas' words that link the Christ with the Son of God echo back Jesus'

---

162. Jesus the Christ (Messiah), Savior 1:1, 16-18, 21; 2:4; 11:2; 16:16, 20; 22:42; 23:10; 26:63, 68; 27:17, 22 and Jesus Emmanuel 1:23; 18:20; 28:20.

163. Jesus the Son of God 2:15; 3:17; 4:3, 6; 7:21; 8:29; 10:32-33; 11:25-27; 12:50; 14:33; 15:13; 16:16-17; 17:5; 18:10, 14, 19, 35; 20:23; 24:36; 26:29, 39, 42, 53, 63; 27:40, 43, 54; 28:19.

164. For the Matthean use of the title, "the Lord" addressing both God and Jesus, see Matt. 1:22; 2:15; 3:3; 4:7, 10; 7:21-22; 8:2, 6, 21, 25; 9:28; 11:25; 12:8; 14:28, 30; 15:22, 25, 27 (x2); 16:22; 17:4, 15; 18:21; 20:30-31, 33; 21:3, 9; 22:37, 43-45; 23:39; 24:42; 26:22. In his study of 1 Cor. 8:5-6 and Phil. 2:6-11 as the primitive sources for the Christ devotion developed in the early Christianity, Hurtado, *How on Earth*, 49–50, 94 explains that "Lord (κύριος)" as a devotional title for Jesus Christ most likely functions as the Greek equivalent of *Adonay*, the reverential alternative for the sacred Tetragrammaton in Hebrew. Also see Alan F. Segal, "The Resurrection: Faith or History?" in *The Resurrection of Jesus: John Dominic Crossan and N. T. Wright in Dialogue*, ed. Robert B. Stewart (Minneapolis: Fortress Press, 2006), 216. Hurtado further delineates that the universal acclamation, "Jesus Christ is Lord" implies that Jesus is "linked with God in ways that, rightly understood, are startling and unequaled." Therefore, in Matthew, the ideas of the Davidic Messiah and the Son of God converge in the person of Jesus and in the Matthean passion narrative, the opponents of Jesus, comprehensively covering both Jews and Gentiles concomitantly reaffirm the messiahship, the kingship and the divine sonship of Jesus in the form of taunting and abuse which ultimately betray and stupefy the scoffers themselves.

self-exposition (22:41-46) and second, Caiaphas, the representative of the entire body of the Jewish religious authority, unwittingly repeat his defendant's very same self-manifestation as the messianic Son of God whom David himself reveres as the Lord (22:43, 45). The Gospel's implied reader benefits from this type of proclamation even though it is rather indirect and therefore can be easily overlooked, since he possesses the clusters of fundamental information regarding the person of Jesus which are given to him from the beginning of the story.

In the following trial of Jesus before Pilate, Pilate's questioning of Jesus about whether He is the King of the Jews (27:1-23) is verbally ironic because Pilate declares Jesus' kingship without believing it and confirms once again Jesus' true kingship to which the Gospel unwaveringly attests. Also, Pilate's interrogation of Jesus regarding his kingship brings about a character irony that involves a reversal of the status between Jesus and Pilate. In this scene alone, the ironist frequently uses the title ἡγεμών (a ruler or governor)[165] all in reference to Pilate: seven times the noun refers directly to Pilate's office and power as the Roman governor (27:2, 11 (x2), 14, 15, 21, 27) and one time describing a judicious function of ἡγεμών as one sitting at the judgment seat (καθημένου δὲ αὐτοῦ ἐπὶ τοῦ βήματος, 27:19). Correspondingly, the personal name of the protagonist, Jesus, who is in fact the promised ἡγεμών of Israel (ἡγούμενος, 2:6),[166] also occurs with notable frequency[167] in parallel to an intense use of Pilate's official title, ἡγεμών. It is important to notice that the name of Jesus (understood as meaning "He will save his people from their sins") is repeatedly mentioned throughout the Gospel[168] and more emphatically in the Matthean

---

165. BAGD, 343 defines ἡγεμών as prince and of imperial governors in the provinces, especially of the procurators or prefects in Judea such as the case of Pontius Pilate. Merrill C. Tenney, *New Testament Survey*, rev. ed. (Grand Radpids: Eerdmans, 1985), 14, explains that "the Roman government was of two kinds. The provinces that are relatively peaceful and loyal to Rome were under proconsuls (Acts 1:7) who were responsible to the Roman Senate. The more turbulent provinces were under the authority of the emperor, who often stationed armies in them, and they were governed by prefects, procurators, or propraetors who were appointed by the emperor and answerable directly to him . . . Palestine in the time of Christ was under the supervision of the emperor, whose agent was the prefect Pontius Pilate (Matt. 27:11; translated "governor")." For the variant, see Bruce M. Metzger, *A Textual Commentary on the Greek New Testament*, 2nd ed. (New York: United Bible Societies, 1994), 65.

166. Matt. 2:6, "And you, Bethlehem, in the land of Judah, are by no means least among the rulers of Judah; for from you shall come forth a ruler who will shepherd my people Israel" (καὶ σύ, Βηθλέεμ γῆ Ἰούδα, οὐδαμῶς ἐλαχίστη εἶ ἐν τοῖς ἡγεμόσιν Ἰούδα· ἐκ σοῦ γὰρ ἐξελεύσεται ἡγούμενος, ὅστις ποιμανεῖ τὸν λαόν μου τὸν Ἰσραήλ). Translation is mine.

167. Matt. 27:1, 11 (x2), 16, 17, 20, 22, 26, 27, 37, 46, 50, 54, 55, 57, 58.

168. Matt. 1:1, 16, 18, 21, 25; 2:1; 3:13, 15-16; 4:1, 7, 10, 17; 7:28; 8:4, 10, 13-14, 18, 20, 22, 34; 9:2, 4, 9-10, 15, 19, 22-23, 27-28, 30, 35; 10:5; 11:1, 4, 7, 25; 12:1, 15; 13:1, 34, 53, 57; 14:1, 12-13, 16, 27, 29,

passion narrative.[169] This literary phenomenon is telling of the implied author's deep soteriological conviction about Jesus as the shepherd-king who will gather his lost sheep (2:6; 9:36; 25:32; 26:31) through his death. The implied author of the Gospel deliberately identifies Pilate as ἡγεμών side by side with his counterpart, Jesus, in order to create a sharp character irony. This character irony exposes Pilate's inadequacy in judging Jesus and his kingship representing the kingdom of God. To explain this, it is necessary to examine the Matthean *inclusio* that chapters 2 and 27 create.[170] These two parallel scenes in the courts of King Herod and of Pilate respectively are related to each other and provide an important insight in relation to the death of Jesus. Striking similarities exist between these two chapters and these features nicely enclose the story of Jesus as a whole. In both chapters Jesus is identified as the Christ King and his persecutors are men of high office in the political arena struggling with his kingship.

At the birth of Jesus in Bethlehem of Judea in the days of Herod the king (βασιλεύς, 2:1), wise men from the East came to Jerusalem to worship the newborn king of the Jews (ὁ τεχθεὶς βασιλεὺς τῶν Ἰουδαίων, 2:2). Herod was troubled at the arrival of the promised Christ King (1:1; 2:4-6), and all of Jerusalem,[171] a synecdoche referring to the Jews and their religious leaders, were troubled with him (2:3). Being threatened, Herod ordered a massacre, targeting all the male children in Bethlehem and its vicinity who were two years old and under in order to eliminate his assumed rival, Jesus, the King (βασιλεύς, 21:5; 25:34, 40). As chapter 2 describes, the earliest conflict between Jesus the protagonist and Herod the antagonist pertains to the issue of kingship. Therefore, this early conflict described between Herod, delegated king over Judea by the Roman emperor, and Jesus, the God-sent shepherd-king over his people (1:21; 2:6; 9:36; 25:32; 26:31) is meant to be read in relation to the later conflict of a similar kind between Pilate, another delegate of the Roman emperor, and Jesus. Although the immediate conflict between Herod and Jesus

---

31; 15:1, 21, 28-29, 32, 34; 16:6, 8, 13, 17, 21, 24; 17:1, 4, 7-9, 17-18, 22, 25-26; 18:1, 22; 19:1, 14, 18, 21, 23, 26, 28; 20:17, 22, 25, 30, 32, 34; 21:1, 6, 11f, 16, 21, 24, 27, 31, 42; 22:1, 18, 29, 41; 23:1; 24:1, 4.

169. Matt. 26:1, 4, 6, 10, 17, 19, 26, 31, 34, 36, 49, 50, 51, 52, 55, 57, 59, 63, 64, 69, 71, 75; 27:1, 11, 16, 17, 20, 22, 26, 27, 37, 46, 50, 54, 55, 57, 58.

170. The Gospels' implied author uses the technique of *inclusio*, which places the similar idea or message at the front and back of the story, so that he brings the entire story under an overarching theme. For example, he locates the promise of Emmanuel, "God is with his people through the person, Jesus," in 1:23 and resumes the same idea in 28:20 to identify Jesus as its fulfillment.

171. The Matthean use of Jerusalem implies both a place (2:1; 16:21; 20:17-19; 21:1) as well as the people of God to whom the promise of the Messiah King has been given through the prophets (2:3; 21:10; 23:37).

is resolved in the death of the holy innocents in place of Jesus, this incident prefigures a suffering-ridden path for Jesus and also forms a double-layered story world typical to irony in relation to the issue of Jesus' kingship. On the surface level of the story world Herod seems to try to destroy his rival, Jesus. However, the upper level of the story where irony anchors its meaning reveals that Herod makes a vain attempt to thwart God's will and unintentionally participates in the fulfillment of the prophecies (2:13-14, Hos. 11:1; 2:17-18, Jer 31:15) regarding the Christ King Jesus (1:1; 22:41-45; 26:64). Also, the birth of Jesus and its circumstances become more ironic when the Magi, the Gentiles, voluntarily and without reservation worship Jesus as the King while the Jews fail to acknowledge their long awaited Messiah King and disturbed at the announcement of his arrival (ἐταράχθη, 2:3). The importance of this irony involving the contrasting reactions of the people to the birth of Jesus—the worship of the Magi and the rejection of the Jews—is that it discloses early in the Gospel that Jesus' messianic kingship is not limited to the ethnic Jews,[172] but widely includes the Gentiles represented by the presence of the Magi.[173]

In a juxtaposition to chapter 2 where the kingship of Jesus is at the heart of the conflict between Jesus and Herod, so the trial of Jesus before Pilate, the governor of Judea, repeats a similar type of conflict between these two parties. Pilate interrogates Jesus "Are you the King of the Jews?" (Σὺ εἶ ὁ βασιλεὺς τῶν Ἰουδαίων; 27:11). This question reminds the implied reader of information given at the time of Jesus' birth that acknowledges that Jesus is indeed the King of the Jews who has divine origin and his kingship represents God's kingship on earth.[174] At the Gospel's birth narrative of Jesus, just as Herod the king, a political power of the day, establishes an alliance with the Jewish religious leaders, who collectively represent the Jewish people, and they together seek the life of Jesus, in the Matthean passion narrative, Pilate, another political power figure, is approached by the same enemy of Jesus, the Jews (27:15) and their religious leaders (27:20), who ask for the death of Jesus. It is important to understand that both Herod and Pilate are the delegated authorities in place of the Roman emperor, the (ἡγεμών), *de facto*.[175] If Herod began the course

---

172. Matt. 1:1; 2:6; 16:28; 21:5; 22:7, 11, 13; 27:11, 29. 37.

173. Matt. 2:1-2, 10-11; 4:15-17; 11:20-23.

174. Heil, *The Death and Resurrection of Jesus*, 71 likewise reads an irony in the interrogation of Jesus by Pilate. He notes that "the reader, who knows that Jesus is indeed 'the King of the Jews' in the sense that he is the messianic Son of God through suffering, dying, and rising as the Son of Man (26:63-64), experiences the irony that Pilate is unwittingly playing his role in establishing how Jesus is truly 'the King of Jews' precisely by mocking his kingship."

175. Both Strabo and Plutarch use the term ἡγεμών as a reference to the Roman emperor. See Strabo, *Geography*, 4.3.2 and Plutarch, *Cicero*, 2.

of pursuing the life of Jesus in order to resolve the conflict with him over the kingship, Pilate completes what was initiated by Herod by sentencing Jesus to death on the cross (27:24-26), where irony brings about a divine reversal turning the death of Jesus into the public manifestation of his divine kingship (27:54). Besides, some details involved in the procedure of the crucifixion of Jesus, such as the Roman soldiers' fake recognition of Jesus' kingship for ridicule (27:27-31) and the written charge that they placed over the head of Jesus on the cross, ("this is Jesus the King of the Jews," 27:37), are strikingly ironic because all these abuses only highlight the indisputable identity of Jesus, the King of the Jews, in an unexpected way. Therefore, through the cross, the most undesirable site of shame and demise, irony discloses that the death of Jesus is neither an end nor defeat of the kingship of Jesus but is the enthronement of Jesus the Christ King in his eternal kingdom (27:37) as the one and only ἡγεμών over his people, those who belong to the kingdom of God.[176]

The implied reader has learned of the divine kingship of Jesus in his unique filial relationship to God as expressed in the early chapters of Matthew. The reader, then, cannot miss the character irony brought forth in the dynamics between these two authoritative figures, Pilate and Jesus, in their representation of sharply different origins of power (27:1-37). Here, the divine ruler is present before an earth-bound ἡγεμών.[177] It gets painfully ironic when the narrative contrasts a very different status of the position which each party assumes. The implied author tastefully employs a spatial language in order to indicate a different level of hierarchy between these two: while Pilate sits on a terrestrial βῆμα (a judge's raised seat in the law-court, 27:19), Jesus sits on a heavenly throne at the right hand of God (19:28; 25:31; 26:64; cf. Ps. 110: 1), which clearly implies that Jesus is the eschatological judge.[178] As much as heaven is utterly remote from earth, so the power and authority which Jesus possesses is beyond a comparison with that of Pilate.

The Gospel characterizes all the earthly rulers who come into contact with Jesus—Herod the king, Herod the tetrarch, and Pilate—as a flat character group

---

176. It is worth noting that Matthew throughout the Gospel contains a significant volume of references regarding the kingdom of God and its mystery which is manifested in the person and ministry of Jesus the Christ King. See Matt. 3:2; 4:17, 23; 5:3, 10, 19 (x2), 20; 6:10, 33; 7:21; 8:12; 9:35; 10:7; 11:11; 12:15, 26, 28; 13:11, 19, 24, 31, 33, 38, 41, 43-45, 47, 52; 16:19, 28; 18:1, 3f, 23; 19:14, 23f; 20:1, 21; 21:31, 43; 22:2; 23:23; 24:7 (x2), 14; 25:1, 34; 26:29.

177. English terminology, hegemony, is a derivate of ἡγεμών.

178. France, *The Gospel of Matthew*, 1051, briefly comments regarding the *bēma* that "Jesus stands before the seated governor (v.19), an ironic reversal of the destined position of Jesus as the seated judge of the world (25:31)." Also, Davies and Allison, *Saint Matthew*, 586 notices an irony that Pilate sits as judge while Jesus, the one who is worthy of the judgment seat (25:31), stands before him.

devoid of power in any realsense. All these men sit on an earthly βῆμα and yet, their status is inconsequential in scale and is transient in comparison to the kingship of Christ and his eternal kingdom which is not of this world (20:25-28). According to the Gospel, all the human counterparts of the Christ King, in their authority and power, serve together as a corporate ἀλαζών of earthly pretension, in diametrical contrast to the one genuine figure of heavenly power, Jesus. It is ironic, therefore, when we take into account that Jesus, who is invested with God's power (26:64), will come as the judge of the world in his glory (24:30; 26:64; 28:18), the interrogation of Jesus administered by Pilate stands at odds with the reality of the story and yields a pointed question: who truly judges whom? The Gospel's implied reader is supposed to rightly answer this question since the Gospel's persistent and lucid disclosure of Jesus' kingship from its birth narrative on should enable him to perceive this character irony and also comprehend that irony unites the Matthean *inclusio* in a meaningful way to reveal one of the layers of the profoundly complex identity of Jesus.

DRAMATIC IRONY INVOLVING AN ACT OF BETRAYAL (ΠΑΡΑΔΙΔΩΜΙ)

The Matthean passion narrative reveals the how aspect of God's saving plan carried out by his Son. As the Gospel's birth narrative reveals, Jesus is "the one who will save his people from their sins" (1:21) and he accomplishes it through active passivity. In the Matthean passion narrative, throughout the course of the accusation and final conviction, Jesus remains non active, even when self-defense is called for. However, this is the very reason why the Gospel's passion story of Jesus is ridden with irony. Jesus' seeming passivity, his not defending himself in any active way, even though he is capable, is in agreement with God's way of achieving the forgiveness for his people. The Matthean passion narrative challenges its reader to sort out this colossal discrepancy between what it seems and what it meant.

Though Jesus himself is passive when it comes to his own defense, it is notable that all of the major characters involved in his passion actively participate as the events move along. As we observed earlier in this book, the implied author of the Gospel employs particular verbs, such as ἀκολουθέιν (to follow) and προσκυνέιν (to worship), in order to group some individuals homogenous in their perception of and reaction to the story's protagonist, Jesus. In addition to the cases of ἀκολουθέιν and προσκυνέιν, the narrative-critical reading of the Matthean passion narrative suggests that the verb παραδίδωμι is another theologically charged word.[179] This is the act of violence and injustice

---

179. Davies and Allison, *Saint Matthew*, 555 considers the verb παραδίδωμι to be richly connotative.

that certain characters adopt against Jesus and therefore, identifies them as a body of opponents of Jesus. The hands of these men represent the hands of sinners (17:22; 26:45) as Jesus has predicted that he would be handed over (παραδίδοται) to them.

The verb παραδίδωμι occurs most extensively in chapters 26–27 of the Matthean passion narrative, and all uses are related to the betrayal, arrest and abuse of Jesus.[180] The case of παραδίδωμι in chapter 26 relates to Judas, one of the Twelve (26:14, 21, 22, 47). The narrator identifies Judas as the betrayer early in chapter 10 (ὁ παραδιδούς, 10:4) and Judas confirms it in his actual betrayal of Jesus in the Matthean passion narrative (26:15, 25, 46, 48). In chapter 27, when Judas' initial betrayal makes Jesus' trial and suffering inevitable outcomes, the religious leaders and Pilate carry out the same act of παραδίδωμι toward Jesus despite Judas' confession that he sinned against the innocent man (27:4).

The Matthean passion narrative indicates that the religious leaders are not passive in the act of παραδίδωμι. After resolving to put Jesus to death (27:1, 20), a death which has been foreshadowed earlier in the Gospel (2:13; 12:14; 22:7), the religious leaders take an action that is similar to Judas'—*hand Jesus over to* (παρέδωκαν) Pilate (27:2, 18). Receiving Jesus handed over to him, the Matthean passion narrative depicts Pilate's struggle to deal with Jesus standing in his court not because of his defendant's resistance to the charges against him but because of the defendant's ironic passivity and, mostly, his own conviction of the innocence of his defendant (27:18, 24), which is confirmed by his wife's dream about Jesus (27:19). Yet, going against the grain of his own conscience, Pilate attempts to clear his name from the guilt of condemning Jesus by making a self-deceptive declaration that "I am innocent of this man's blood, see to it yourself" (27:24). Even Pilate's ritualistic action, washing his *hands* (27:24) as a symbolic manifestation of his innocence in causing the death of the innocent one[181] ironically connects him to the same group of opponents of Jesus since his own *hands* likewise *deliver* Jesus to those who cry out for the crucifixion of Jesus (πᾶς ὁ λαός, 27:25) to be crucified (παρέδωκεν ἵνα σταυρωθῇ, 27:26).

---

180. The verb παραδίδωμι occurs in various forms fifteen times in chapters 26–27. See Matt. 26:2, 15, 16, 21, 23, 24, 25, 45, 46, 48; 27:2, 3, 4, 18, 26.

181. See Deut. 21:1-9; Pss. 26:6; 73:13; Isa. 1:15-16 for the Old Testament references regarding hand washing ritual to declare one's innocence in causing the death of the innocent man. Scholars like Eduard Schweizer, *The Good News according to Matthew* (Atlanta: John Knox, 1975), 508; Daniel Patte, *The Gospel According to Matthew: A Structural Commentary on Matthew's Faith* (Philadelphia: Fortress Press, 1987), 380; Sjef van Tilborg, *The Jewish Leaders in Matthew* (Leiden: E. J. Brill, 1972), 93–94 consider that the purpose of reporting Pilate washing his hands before the crowd is to exonerate Pilate and the Romans.

Through the repeated action of παραδίδωμι the Matthean passion narrative's implied author identifies the corporate betrayers of Jesus. In this way, Pilate is linked to Judas and the religious leaders in shedding the innocent blood of Jesus (27:4). Although Pilate has second thoughts concerning whether Jesus' guilt is commensurate to crucifixion, his legal conscience gives in to the violent request for Jesus' life from the stirred-up crowds. Pilate chooses political expediency over justice even though he rightly perceives that the Jewish religious leaders deliver Jesus up to him out of an unlawful motive: envy (διὰ φθόνον, 27:18). Further, his suspicion of the unmerited nature of the persecution mounted against his defendant is reinforced by his wife's earnest testimony of Jesus' innocence as informed through a dream (27:19), a communication tool the Gospel portrays as an authoritative and reliable channel for God to communicate to people (1:20; 2:12-13, 19, 22). However, Pilate, a being of a powerless authority which is characteristic of other figures of power positions in the Gospel (such as Herod the king and Herod the tetrarch), becomes driven by fear of the uproar (26:5; 27:24) and consequently grants the outcry of the crowds paired with their instigators (27:20). Therefore, Pilate's self-proclamation of his innocence (ἀθῷός εἰμι, 27:24) rings with biting verbal irony: [182] Pilate is by no means *innocent* (ἀθῷός) when he in fact allows the shedding of *innocent* blood (ἥμαρτον παραδοὺς αἷμα ἀθῷον, 27:4). Pilate's claim of innocence is ironic self-exposure that he is a ἡγεμών exploited by his deceitful subjects who collectively act on stealth (δόλος, 26:4) and unjust cause (φθόνος, 27:18). It is striking that Pilate's case resembles that of Judas: although both are involved in actual betrayal of Jesus, they perceive Jesus' innocence and publicly confess it. Yet, their confessions of Jesus' innocence are ineffective to save Jesus' life but serve as a significant testimony within the Gospel that Jesus' innocence is precisely why he has to die since he gives himself as the ransom for many (20:28) in order to accomplish the divine "must" (δεῖ).[183]

While the Matthean passion narrative's ironist joins Judas, Pilate, and the religious leaders in the betrayal of Jesus through his programmed use of παραδίδωμι, he does not use the same verb to depict the involvement of other disciples of Jesus and the crowds despite the fact that they are also deeply involved in Jesus' passion. As we have examined earlier, the disciples exhibit some traits appropriate for an ἀλαζών such as empty self-confidence

---

182. From a different angle, Heil, *The Death and Resurrection of Jesus*, 75–76, observes that when Pilate tells the crowds crying out for the crucifixion of Jesus, "You see to it" (27:24), he ironically throws back upon the Jewish people the guilt for Jesus' blood that their leaders tried to ignore when they told the repenting Judas, "You see to it" (27:24).

183. Matt. 1:21; 16:21; 17:22-23; 20:18-19; 20:22; 26:28, 39, 42, 54.

and spiritual shortsightedness, which are shown in their interactions with Jesus and other characters such as the woman at Bethany. At times Jesus chastised the disciples as men of little faith (6:30; 8:26; 16:8; 17:20) who failed to keep up their enthusiasm and affection toward their Lord due to their physical and spiritual weakness (26:41). Although the Gospel's implied author does not place the disciples of Jesus on a pedestal to be celebrated, it seems that he deliberately distinguishes the disciples from the opponents of Jesus who are involved in the act of betrayal. It is important to notice that in Matthew the disciples are never portrayed as those who are hopelessly lost or without penitent hearts. Quite on the contrary, they are called "blessed" by Jesus (13:16; 16:17; 24:46). Additionally, they are the first recipients of the forgiveness of sins which Jesus establishes through the covenant of the blood (26:28). Jesus also gave them the promise of reunion with him in Galilee (26:32; 28:7, 10, 16), the honeymoon place where their love story as the master and the disciples all began (4:18, 23, 25; 15:29; 17:22; 21:11; 27:55).

Unfortunately, the initial betrayal of Jesus comes from "one of the twelve" (26:14, 21, 22, 47), despite all the faithful oaths of loyalty made by the disciples to Jesus (16:21-22; 26:22, 31-35). As we examined above, although the Gospel does differentiate the disciples from those who engage in the action of παραδίδωμι, including Judas, the Matthean passion narrative portrays them equally and plainly less than "ideal" (or "perfect," 5:48; 19:21). Although one may be more generous toward the eleven disciples' failure in keeping their word than Judas' betrayal of the innocent blood, even though he later comes to a daunting realization of the insufferable nature of that crime, in the Matthean passion narrative the disciples, represented by Peter, do "deny" Jesus (ἀπαρνέομαι, 26:34f, 75; ἀρνέομαι, 26:70, 72). This is in contrast to Jesus' teaching not to deny him publicly (10:32-33) but rather to deny themselves to take up their cross and follow him (16:24). Therefore, to an extent, all the disciples fall into sin (σκανδαλισθήσονται, 26:31, 33)[184] by rejecting Jesus (11:6; 13:57; 26:31, 33), which is exactly what Jesus has taught his disciples to be prepared to avoid in advance. In essence, the death of Jesus is the opportune time (καιρός, 8:29; 26:18) for Jesus to manifest his perfect obedience to God in public as God himself openly gives testimonies to Jesus as his beloved Son (3:17; 17:5). Furthermore, it is also the καιρός for the disciples to prove that their

---

184. BAGD, 752 defines σκανδαλίζω as "cause to be caught or to fall, i.e. cause to sin (the sin may consist in a breach of the moral law, in unbelief, or in the acceptance of false teachings." Further, it lists a case of σκανδαλίζω pass. with ἐν τινι meaning "be led into sin, be repelled by someone, take offense at someone, of Jesus; by *refusing to believe in him* or *by becoming apostate fr. him* a person falls into sin." Emphasis mine.

confession of Jesus is truthful through the public declaration of him. In contrast, in this crucial time when faith is tested, ironically they all fail by disowning him. In this regard, the Matthean passion narrative depicts the disciples as failing in both categories of faith in the person of Jesus and of understanding in the teaching of Jesus.[185]

Lastly, how does the Matthean passion narrative portray the involvement of the people in general in Jesus' passion? Do they in any way participate in the act of παραδίδωμι? The answer is affirmative, but it requires an explanation. The people are not identified as collectively carrying out παραδίδωμι. Yet, they are the very recipients of the betrayed one—Jesus is betrayed into their hands. In other words, the people are the very beneficiaries of the sacrifice of the betrayed one, Jesus. Already in chapter 1, the ironist has made an indissoluble bond between Jesus and the people, for Jesus will save his people (τὸν λαὸν αὐτοῦ) from their sins (1:21). This statement must be understood as a programmatic declaration characterizing the nature of the relationship between these two *parties*: the Christ Savior and the people who are the recipients of the forgiveness of sins. The Matthean passion narrative's suggestive language points out that he who is betrayed is entrusted into the very hands of the recipients of the "forgiveness of sins" which Jesus promised (1:21) through the ironic turn of the act of παραδίδωμι. It is poignantly appropriate and at the same time ironic that the cycle of all levels of betrayal against Jesus, which the Matthean passion narrative meticulously reports, eventually comes to its destination, into the hands of the people who Jesus came to save in the first place.

The Matthean passion narrative's dramatic irony of παραδίδωμι can be best understood when it is seen in the following circular course of παραδίδωμι which underlines the invincible tie between the Christ Savior and his people (1:21). As we have seen, the violent and unjust act of παραδίδωμι against Jesus initially has begun with Judas, one of the twelve. Judas *hands Jesus over to* (παραδίδωμι, 26:15-16; 27:4) the Jewish religious leaders, whose intent is to destroy him (12:14; 26:3-4; 27:20). Then, the Jewish religious leaders *hand Jesus over to* (παραδίδωμι, 27:2) the Roman governor, Pilate, representing

---

185. U. Luz, "The Disciples in the Gospel according to Matthew," in *The Interpretation of Matthew*, Issues in Religion and Theology 3, ed. Graham Stanton (Philadelphia: Fortress Press, 1983), 102–3, characterizes the disciples of Jesus described in Matthew. He notes that "in short, the only point at which Matthew has quite consistently 'improved' the picture of the disciples is in his elimination of the Marcan motif of their failure to understand . . . Jesus is the teacher who leads his disciples to understanding. Understanding is related to the teaching of Jesus. Faith and understanding are separated in Matthew. The disciples are men of little faith, but they do understand Faith is directed to the person of Jesus; understanding is related to his teaching."

non-Jewish authorities just as Jesus predicted that he should be handed over to the Gentiles to be mocked, flogged and crucified (τοῖς ἔθνεσιν, 20:19; 27:27-31). Pilate finally *hands Jesus over to* the people (27:26), [186] whom the Gospel's implied author specifically identifies as ὁ λαός (1:21; 27:25), despite of his reluctance to declare a guilty verdict against Jesus since he does not find any legal basis to support the people's outcry for his death. Pilate's own words, "Why, what evil has he done?" (27:23) clearly reflect this situation. The persistent demand of the people for the crucifixion of Jesus finally obtains the shedding of the "innocent blood" of Jesus (27:4, 19) as they cry out in one accord, "Let his blood be on us and on our children!" (27:25).

The Gospel's implied author never depicts the people as neutral in dealing with Jesus Christ. They willingly and consciously participate in dealing with Jesus whether their actions are initiated by their authorities or not. In both the beginning of the Gospel and its Matthean passion narrative the same people (ὁ λαός, 1:21; 27:25-26) are depicted as the key actors in Jesus' passion. As early as 2:3, the Gospel describes King Herod and all Jerusalem (represented by her religious leaders) as in sync. They are instantly threatened to the point of disturbance at the news of the birth of the Christ (2:6; Micah 5:1-3). As Herod purses a plan to eliminate Jesus, the people of Jerusalem strangely remain silent as if they are subject to Herod's intent. The Matthean passion narrative's scene of Jesus' trial before Pilate in chapter 27 strikingly corresponds to the birth scene of chapter 2. Once again the people, represented by her religious leaders (27:20) as in 2:3f, are present when Jesus' life hangs in the balance. While they were in an alliance with Herod previously, at the time of Jesus' trial before Pilate the people form an association with Pilate, another political figure and delegate of Roman imperialism like Herod. Yet, this time the people exercise the most decisive and forceful act against Jesus. Their eager and persistent cry for the crucifixion of Jesus (27:22f, 25) seals the deal: "[Pilate] delivered him to be crucified" (27:26).

As examined above, the *inclusio* between the Gospel's beginning and its Matthean passion narrative elucidates the people's connection to Jesus and also sheds a light on the dramatic irony that the chain of the action (παραδίδωμι) creates. Although the Matthean passion narrative does not identify the people as the doers of παραδίδωμι, as is the case with the disciples of Jesus (except Judas the betrayer), the collective presence of the people comes at the end of the whole cycle of παραδίδωμι and their connection to Jesus is revealed through

---

186. Timothy B. Cargal, " 'His Blood Be upon Us and upon Our Children': A Matthean Double Entendre?" *NTS* 37 (1991): 107-8, points out that Matthew does not intend to exonerate Pilate who ultimately fulfils Jesus' prophecy (27:26) and delivers him to be crucified.

the cycle of παραδίδωμι. It appears ironic on two grounds. First, we find the people (ὁ λαός, 1:21), for whom Jesus' entire saving mission exists, as active participants in securing the innocent blood of Jesus and, therefore, they give an end to the whole cycle of the act of παραδίδωμι. Second, it is to these same people (ὁ λαός, 27:25-26) that Jesus is unmistakably *handed over* (ὁ λαός, 27:25-26). This aspect is particularly chilling when we remember the opening proclamation of the Gospel that Jesus has come to save them in the first place.

In conclusion, the Matthean passion narrative's παραδίδωμι is the common *modus operandi* taken up by the major characters involving in Jesus' passion. Although apparently παραδίδωμι is an act of violence causing separation, the ironic spin of παραδίδωμι brings those who associate themselves with this offence back to the Christ Savior, whose promise is precisely to forgive the people's sins. The irony that the Matthean passion narrative's παραδίδωμι creates is dramatic in nature because the people secure their salvation by ending the cycle of παραδίδωμι when they received the *betrayed one* and deliver him unto death. The supreme ironist, God, achieves his saving will by making the people involved in Jesus' passion in ways of which they are not aware and such a condition is like fertile soil for the rise of irony.

VERBAL IRONY HIDDEN IN THE PEOPLE'S CRY FOR THE BLOOD OF JESUS (27:24-25)

Reading the Matthean passion narrative poses a challenge when trying to make sense of the people's reaction to Jesus, particularly their intense rejection of Jesus by repeatedly shouting out for his crucifixion ("Let him be crucified!" 27:22f). Further, the people's word demanding Jesus' blood on themselves and their children in 27:25 as a response to Pilate's self-acquittal from the responsibility of sentencing Jesus constructs a verbal irony. This verbal irony reveals the Matthean emphasis on universal salvation achieved through the death of Jesus and manifests how God turns things around to achieve his saving will (1:21) without men's council.

The passage that reports the people's claim on the blood of Jesus (27:24f) has been considered one of the most troubling and difficult statements of the New Testament.[187] New Testament scholars interpret the people's cry (πᾶς ὁ λαός, 27:5) either as if they voluntarily curse themselves as Judas invoked a curse upon himself (27:3-5) or as if they openly take the responsibility for Jesus' death.[188] Besides this, their cry of imprecation is often interpreted as a

---

187. Bowman, "The Significance of Mt. 27:25," 26–31; Robert H. Smith, "Matthew 27:25: The Hardest Verse in Mathew's Gospel," *CurTM* 17 (1990): 421; Cargal, "His Blood," 101.

prophecy of judgment against Israel by focusing on the people's role in Jesus' execution. For example, the people's asking for the blood of Jesus has been interpreted as the Gospel author's invention of anti-Jewish polemic[189] or anti-Jewish theme.[190] In the same vein of argument, some scholars try to explain the strange involvement of the people's posterity in shedding the innocent blood of Jesus ("Let his blood be on us and on our children!" 27:25). They suggest that although the people at the time of Jesus' crucifixion makes themselves culpable for Jesus' death, this guilt should not be passed down to the next generation because of Jesus' imminent *Parousia*.[191] However, what these critics overlook here is the verbal irony which the people unwittingly utter. The people's

188. John Dominic Crossan, "Anti-Semitism and the Gospel," *TS* 26 (1965): 189–214, examines New Testament scholarship regarding the subject. Particularly, Patte, *The Gospel according to Matthew*, 380 writes that the cry indicates that the people voluntarily put themselves under the same cursed status of Judas. From a different point of view, Davies and Allison, *Saint Matthew*, 591 considers that the people's cry out for the blood of Jesus is not a self-curse but a declaration of responsibility.

189. K. W. Clark, "The Gentile Bias in Matthew," *JBL* 66 (1947): 165–82; D. Senior, *The Passion Narrative according to Matthew: A Redactional Study* (BETL 39; Leuven: Leuven University, 1975), 257, 260; J. P. Meier, *The Vision of Matthew: Christ, Church, and Morality in the First Gospel* (New York: Paulist, 1979), 199; Francis Wright Beare, *The Gospel according to Matthew* (San Francisco: Harper and Row, 1981), 460, 531; Daniel Marguerat, *Le Jugement dans l'évanile de Matthieu* (*Le Monde de la Bible* 6; Geneva: Labor et Fides, 1981), 376; Robert H. Gundry, *Matthew: A Commentary on His Literary and Theological Art* (Grand Rapids: Eerdmans, 1982), 565; Buck, "Anti-Judaic Sentiments"; J. D. Crossan, *The Cross That Spoke. The Origins of the Passion Narrative* (San Francisco: Harper and Row, 1988), xiii, 100, 397–98; U. Luz, *The Theology of the Gospel of Matthew*, trans. J. Bradford Robinson (Cambridge: Cambridge University, 1993), 146.

190. Herman Hendrickx, *The Passion Narratives of the Synoptic Gospels* (London: Geoffrey Chapman, 1977), 143–44, mentions that Matthew as a Jewish Christian writing for Jewish Christians emphasizes the tragedy of the Jews rejecting their Messiah. He considers that the anti-Jewish theme is especially prominent in the passion narrative in contrast to the positive ecclesial theme that Matthew espouses. Likewise, Peter J. Tomson, *Presumed Guilty: How the Jews Were Blamed for the Death of Jesus*, trans. Janet Dyk) Minneapolis: Fortress Press, 2005), x, 58–76, considers the passion story of Jesus in general to stand at the center of the debate concerning what the Jesus movement has to do with the Jews or more specifically, anti-Jewish sentiment. He examines this matter in two aspects: one positive and one negative. In his preface, Tomson writes that "The positive response is that Jesus and his first followers were Jews and remained Jews. The beginnings of Christianity must therefore be understood from the perspective of Judaism. The negative response is that Christians dissociated themselves from non-Christian Jews and began to view them as hostile competitors. They even came to assume that this was Jesus' intention. After this separation, to be a Christian appears to be synonymous with being anti-Jewish. For these two reasons we cannot discuss Jesus without involving the Jews." For more references, see Meier, *The Vision of Matthew*, 200; Georg Strecker, *Der Weg der Gerichtigkeit, Untersuchung zur Theologie des Matthäus* (FRLANT 82; Göttingen: Vandenhoeck und Ruprecht, 1962), 116–17; Marguerat, *Le jugément*, 376–77.

words and their corporate actions toward Jesus must be understood under God's salvation scheme which God himself has been orchestrating along the way right up to this very moment of Jesus' death. As we examined in an earlier chapter of the book, particularly in the section where explains the literary functions of irony, every irony brings about a reversal to words, events or the dynamics of characters within the story, therefore, we expect to see the reversal which the verbal irony in 27:24f generates.

The reading of the verbal irony in 27:24f strongly suggests a re-evaluation of traditional views supporting in any way the idea that the Gospel's report of the people's cry is due to the Gospel author's anti-Semitic intent. [192] Yet, contrastingly, the narrative-critical reading of the people's cry in 27:25, "His blood be on us and on our children" (τὸ αἷμα αὐτοῦ ἐφ' ἡμᾶς καὶ ἐπὶ τὰ τέκνα ἡμῶν), discloses it as the most ironically pregnant moment within the entire Gospel of Matthew. This is the site where the implied reader of the Matthean passion narrative's irony encounters a spark of divine grace at a time of unspeakable atrocity! The people's cry incubates a hidden meaning that underlines the significance of Jesus' death and his innocent blood—the very object that the people demands in unison for themselves.

From the early chapters on, the Gospel's implied author stresses the issue of the people's estrangement from God as the result of their sins (13:15; 15:8). Jesus called them not only evil and adulterous (γενεὰ πονηρὰ καὶ μοιχαλίς, 12:45; 16:4) but also faithless and perverted (ὦ γενεὰ ἄπιστος καὶ διεστραμμένη, 17:17). After all, Jesus came to call the sinners (26:45) not the righteous (9:13) and to save them from their sins (1:21) as we examined in the case of the dramatic irony of παραδίδωμι that all sinned against God by rejecting the Christ Savior by participating in the act of παραδίδωμι in one way or another.

The Matthean passion narrative's storytelling suggests that the people's representatives, the Jewish religious leaders, are chiefly responsible in Jesus' death since they are the ones who stir up the people and led them eventually to that fateful outcry for both Jesus' crucifixion (27:22f) and his blood (27:25).

---

191. W. Sanders "Das Blut Jesu und die Juden: Gedanken zu Matt 27, 25," *US* 27 (1972), 170. Sanders argues that the Matthean author's view of the imminence of the *Parousia* prevented seeing the guilt being passed on to the next generation.

192. Bowman, "The Significance of Mt. 27:25," 26; Schweizer, *The Good News*; Cargal, "His Blood," 111 notice in common that something is not quite right with the traditional views regarding the intent of Matthew in reporting the Jewish people's crying out for the crucifixion of Jesus (27:25). Regarding irony present in 27:25, Smith, "Matthew 27:25," 428 interestingly points out that the traditional misunderstanding of 27:25, the hardest verse of the First Gospel, is because it is ridden with irony. Without full exposition, Smith briefly opines that "unlike John, Matthew trusted readers to catch the irony. Unfortunately he was overly optimistic and has suffered misunderstanding as a consequence."

Despite this, it is important to see that the Gospel's implied author unfailingly connects the people with their religious authorities: "All the chief priests and scribes of the people" (πάντας τοὺς ἀρχιερεῖς καὶ γραμματεῖς τοῦ λαοῦ, 2:4), "The chief priests and the elders of the people" (οἱ ἀρχιερεῖς καὶ οἱ πρεσβύτεροι τοῦ λαοῦ, 21:23; 26:3; 26:47) and "All the chief priests and the elders of the people" (πάντες οἱ ἀρχιερεῖς καὶ οἱ πρεσβύτεροι τοῦ λαοῦ, 27:1). In this way, the ironist intently establishes an indissoluble tie between these two parties and thereby, exposes the non-neutral status of the people in dealing with their Christ Savior.[193]

At this point, it is imperative to notice that the name of Jesus, "He who will save his people from their sins" (1:21) constantly recurs in chapter 27 at the time when the people (ὁ λαός) once again show their allegiance to their religious leaders in forming a corporate hostility against Jesus (2:3f). Also, it is necessary to discuss here about that the Gospel's implied author who functions as a divine ironist in the Matthean passion narrative purposely interchanges the crowds (ὁ ὄχλος) and the people (ὁ λαός). Are they the same group of people and the author swaps the terms once in a while in order to give the story some flavor of variety? If not, to whom does each group refer?

While some scholars view these two terms, ὁ λαός and ὁ ὄχλος, as synonyms,[194] this book suggests that the Matthean use of ὁ λαός specifically refers to the Jews.[195] It also suggests that the ironist interchangeably employs these two terms with the purpose of driving home the theme of "universal salvation" which the death of Jesus achieves through irony. In the Matthean passion narrative, ὁ ὄχλος (the crowds) are those who are persuaded by the Jewish religious leaders to ask for Barabbas but to destroy Jesus (27:20). And they shout for the crucifixion of Jesus and become a collective witness of Jesus' sentencing to crucifixion in Pilate's court (27:22-24). However, the Matthean passion narrative's implied author employs ὁ λαός in a very specific way by which he identifies the entity who specifically claims the "blood of Jesus" as ὁ λαός instead of ὁ ὄχλος. Hubert Frankemölle suggests the Gospel's author

---

193. Likewise, Buck, "Anti-Judaic Sentiments," 171 writes that "whatever may be the precise significance of the Matthean coalition of the Jewish leadership in their opposition to Jesus, it seems clear that Matthew does not simply intend to shift the responsibility for the suffering of Jesus unto the Jewish leaders and away from the Jewish people. His focus on the elders as "elders *of the people*" is calculated to draw the Jewish *people* into the limelight as well. It is as representatives of the *people* that the elders function in Matthew's passion narrative."

194. H. Strathmann, "λαός" *TDNT* 4 (1967) 51; Hans Kosmala, "'His Blood on Us and on Our Children" (The Background of Mat. 27:24–24), *ASTI* 7 (1968–9), 96–98.

195. Also, Fitzmyer, "Anti-Semitism," 669 and Schweizer, *The Good News*, 509.

meant two different entities, both represented by ὁ λαός, to appear on two separate stages of Jesus' story. He argues that while the people (ὁ λαός) in 1:21 means the new people of God (*das neue Gottesvolk*),[196] the addressed people (ὁ λαός) in 27:25 points to a collective group representing the unbelieving Jews (*kollektiv vorgestellte repräsentanten des ungläubigen Judentums*).[197] It, however, seems to be questionable because the first appearance of ὁ λαός in the Gospel immediately after Jesus' Jewish genealogy clearly suggests that ὁ λαός is none other than the people of Israel ("his people," τὸν λαὸν αὐτοῦ, 1:21). Also, throughout the Gospel ὁ λαός is described as being represented by the Jewish religious authorities (2:4; 21:23; 26:3; 26:47; 27:1) who undoubtedly embody their forefathers' tradition, Judaism. Further, it is ὁ λαός not ὁ ὄχλος mentioned in relation to Jesus' messianic fulfillment of the Old Testament prophecies in 4:16 and 15:8. Therefore, according to the Gospel of Matthew, ὁ λαός translated as "the people" in almost every English versions are most likely the historic Israel and therefore, πᾶς ὁ λαός (all the people) who collectively take up the responsibility of Jesus' blood in 27:25 logically refer to the same entity, this time, including their posterity. But what about the crowds (ὁ ὄχλος)? According to the Gospel, the crowds were drawn to Jesus and followed him during his ministry. Who are these people? The crowds (ὁ ὄχλος) in Matthew are portrayed as the recipients of Jesus' continuing mission.[198] They are a rather loosely defined group of people, likely a mixture of Jews and the anonymous ordinary followers of Jesus including Gentiles.[199] However, both the people (ὁ λαός) and the crowds (ὁ ὄχλος) are distinguished from Jesus' disciples.

The ironist of the Matthean passion narrative intends to mean the "whole nation of Israel"[200] when he shifts the subject of the cry from ὁ ὄχλος (27:20, 24) to πᾶς ὁ λαός (27:25).[201] Also, this practice of the ironist creates an *inclusio*

---

196. G. Bornkamm, G. Barth and H. J. Held, *Tradition and Interpretation in Matthew* (NTL 2nd ed.; Philadelphia: Westminster, 1971), 325, consider his people as the church, i.e., the new people of God.

197. Hubert Frankemölle, Jahwe-Bund und Kirche Christi: Studien zur Form und Traditionsgeschichte des "Evangeliums" nach Mattäus (NTAbh, NF 10, 2nd ed; Münster: Aschendorff, 1984), 218–20.

198. James M. Gibbs, "Purpose and Pattern in Matthew's Use of the Title 'Son of David,' " *NTS* 10 (1964): 446–64 emphasizes Matthew's heightened role for the crowds and a theologically interdependent link between Jesus and the crowds.

199. Frankemölle, *Jahwe-Bund und Kirche Christi*, 53, notes that the crowds can be Jewish, Gentile, both, or vary depending on the particular point in Jesus' ministry. However, Cousland, *The Crowds in the Gospel of Matthew*, 97 asserts that the crowds of Matthew are exclusively Jewish. He writes that "Matthew 4:24-25 describes the crowds as coming from a number of regions, but only the Decapolis can be regarded as a distinctively gentile territory. Even here, it is highly probable that Matthew has interpreted it as a Jewish region, given its one-time inclusion in the Davidic kingdom."

or a literary symmetry, if you will, between the beginning of the Gospel and its end. The Gospel's birth narrative functions as an epicenter for the entire story of Jesus by disclosing the divine saving will embodied in Jesus, "He who will save his people (τὸν λαὸν αὐτοῦ) from their sins" (1:21). In contrast to this, the Matthean passion narrative reveals that through the ironic turn of παραδίδωμι Jesus is given into the hands of the same people (πᾶς ὁ λαός, 27:25) whom he came to save in the first place and this time they cry out for the blood of Jesus "upon themselves and their children" (ἐφ' ἡμᾶς καὶ ἐπὶ τὰ τέκνα ἡμῶν, 27:25).

The *inclusio*, which the Gospel's front and back forms, is rather complex when we consider that this embraces "another layer of *inclusio* within" where we find the Gentiles' presence side by side with ὁ λαός in both contexts. The Gospel's implied author underlines that the Christ Savior (1:1, 21) has been primarily sent to the lost sheep of the house of Israel (15:24), whom the author deliberately identifies as ὁ λαός. Further, he reports the significance of the city, Jerusalem, in relation to Jesus' ministry. In this Gospel, Jesus exhibits a clear understanding that his public ministry will manifest itself in full in Jerusalem (16:21) and he makes an unwavering journey to Jerusalem (20:17; 21:10). Despite these strong Jewish features and inclinations which the Gospel evokes in the telling of Jesus' story, the implied author-ironist does not exclude the Gentiles from the salvation secured through the innocent blood of Jesus (26:28). As he includes both the Jews and the Gentiles represented by the Magi at the time of Jesus' birth, again he makes both parties present at the time of Jesus' death when Jesus accomplishes the divine saving will (1:21; 16:21; 20:28; 26:28), which the author metaphorically describes as "the cup" (26:39). In this way he communicates that both Jews and Gentiles encounter Jesus and profit from Jesus' saving ministry. The Gospel's birth narrative relates to the Magi who came from the East (2:1-2) in order to worship the new born King of the Jews (2:11). The particular geographical information that these men came from the East is rather ambiguous but indicates that they came from non-Jewish territory and culture. In correspondence to the Magi's presence at the beginning of the Gospel, we find the Roman centurion with his soldiers at

---

200. Beare, The Gospel according to Matthew, 531; Crossan, The Cross That Spoke, 262–63; Patte, The Gospel According to Mathew, 380; Wolfgang Trilling, Das Wahre Israel: Studien zur Theologie des Matthäus-Evangeliums (SANT 10; 3d ed.; München: Kosel, 1964), 72. Contrastingly, Saldarini, Matthew's Christian-Jewish Community, 29–32 claims that πᾶς ὁ λαός does not mean the entire Jewish people, but rather the bulk of Jews in Jerusalem. He considers that the λαός of 1:21, 2:6 and 4:16, 23 only has a theological implication.

201. Fitzmyer, "Anti-Semitism," 669–71, explains that in his own way the Evangelist wrestles with the problem of "the rejection" of Israel, with which Paul in a different way wrestled in Romans (9–11).

Jesus' crucifixion, moved by the death of Jesus and confessing him as the "Son of God" (27:54). Taken as a whole, there exist remarkable parallels between these Gentiles described in the Matthean birth and passion narratives not only in that they are found with Jesus at the most intimate and crucial moments of his life, such as his birth and death, but also in that these Gentile characters are disposed favorably toward Jesus in contrast to the hostile reaction of the Jewish population toward him in general. By playing with this sub-*inclusio* of the Gentiles' presence along with ὁ λαός within the broad *inclusio* of ὁ λαός for whom Jesus came and died, the implied author keeps a balance between the Christ Savior promised to "the historic Israel"[202] and the Christ Savior sacrificed for "many."[203] In fact, according to the Gospel, Jesus is the only true Israel (2:15, Hos. 11:1) and the people of God (1:21) to whom Jesus relates his saving ministry are meant to be defined by their relationship to Jesus beyond ethnic orientation.

As we examined earlier in this work, God himself is the supreme ironist and the Gospel's author is his ironist whose perspective is in alignment with that of God. God's path is untraveled by men and his works are concealed to men. Although his saving will, and likewise his presence, is covered with a veil from the direct understanding of men, God makes it known through his vehicle of revelation, irony, and most evidently does so at the Matthean passion narrative, such as in the case of the troublesome uproar of the people. The people's cry for Jesus' blood (27:25) appears to be troubling and begging for a meaningful interpretation since this work rejects any view that the author reports the incident with an anti-Jewish sentiment. Apparently, the cry of the people (ὁ λαός) seems to be an attempt to sever their relationship with Jesus once and for all. However, after all it is the people that Jesus initially came to save (1:21). Also, although they appear to have full control over the life of Jesus, it is God's saving will, not their whim, which governs Jesus' passion.

The people's voice precisely demanding Jesus' blood in 27:25 establishes a verbal irony in the light of Jesus' proclamation in 26:28, "This is my blood of the covenant, which is poured out for many for the forgiveness of sins." The irony lies in that all the people (πᾶς ὁ λαός, 27:25) cry out for his blood in ignorance of their relationship to it.[204] Prior to the Matthean passion narrative,

202. Matt. 1:1, 17-18, 21; 2:5-6; 15:24; 21:5, 10; 27:11, 37.
203. Matt. 8:11-12; 15:21-28; 18:14; 20:28; 26:28; 28:18-19.
204. In her study of the innocent blood of Jesus in the First Gospel in relation to the Old Testament understanding of bloodguilt and purgation, purity and pollution with particular focus to the Jewish legend of the death of Zechariah, Catherine Sider Hamilton, "His Blood Be upon Us: Innocent Blood and the Death of Jesus in Matthew," *CBQ* 70 (2008): 85, 98–100, reads irony not in the people's decision

the Gospel's implied author invokes the theme of "blood" in conjunction with qualities such as "righteousness," "innocence" and "its saving effect" as God's own work. Consider the following examples: the innocent deaths of male children in Bethlehem as Herod pursued Jesus' life (2:1-18), the beheading of John the Baptist whom the Gospel depicts as one who came to God's people in righteousness (14:1-10; 21:32) and the innocent blood of God's righteous agents, such as prophets, wise men and teachers (23:34), shed by the people throughout the history of Israel (23:29-39). The Gospel's implied author employs the cases of these righteous individuals and the shedding of their innocent blood shed to achieve God's righteousness in order to foreshadow Jesus' death. Remember that Jesus himself characterizes his saving ministry (1:21; 20:28: 26:28) as the fulfillment of all righteousness (3:15). His statement is significant on two grounds: first, in his statement Jesus explicitly equates his ministry to fulfilling God's righteousness and second, it makes the Matthean passion narrative an indispensible kernel of the Gospel since this story unit testifies to Jesus' completion of God's righteousness (3:15; the Scriptures, 26:54) and the way in which he accomplishes it through innocence, self-sacrifice and ultimately, death symbolized by blood.

Considering the fact that the Gospel steadily has implied that the innocent blood of the righteous has a saving effect, the characters' testimonies to Jesus' innocence combined with Jesus' own declaration that his blood is "for many for the forgiveness of sins" (26:28) corresponds to the Matthean paradigm that the innocent blood of the righteous saves. Therefore, the people's claiming responsibility for Jesus' blood (27:25) indicates something is odd in this picture. Here, apparently the people cry out for Jesus' blood in order to sever their relationship with Jesus. Their disproval of Jesus is so intense and unyielding that they voluntarily make the same claim even for their posterity's sake. However, it is ironic in that what is granted to them is not what they actually want but in fact, the exact opposite. The people's spiritual ignorance and disbelief in Jesus compel them to want Jesus' innocent blood with a *violent* intent to set themselves apart from him and yet, as we examined above, Jesus' innocent

for bloodshed (27:25), but in the resurrection of the holy people in Jerusalem at the moment of Jesus' death (27:52), which is faithful to the traditional Jewish hope of the restoration of Israel. In the same vein, Hamilton interprets the meaning of the covenant of the blood of Jesus in 26:28 in relation to the temple destruction in 70 CE. She writes, 100, that "as the covenant people take defilement upon themselves, the covenant is made again in the blood of Jesus. As the temple is destroyed, the temple cult is fulfilled in Jesus, in the blood poured out for the forgiveness of sins. The city is razed, but it is in the holy city that the risen ones will walk. Jesus' blood, as Matthew describes it, is poured out not only for the destruction of the covenant people and the temple but for their restoration. The restoration of Israel, however, happens in Jesus."

blood is the *inviolable* saving means of God for his people. In other words, what the people unknowingly try to *violate* is God's *inviolable* way of salvation. And, the people's attempt to *disconnect* themselves from Jesus is the very way through which God *connects* them right back to himself through his Son disowned by the people. Therefore, it is impossible to fail to see that the people's cry, "Let his blood be on us and on our children!" (27:25), is ironic because they unsuspectingly declare that they are, in fact, *under* the forgiveness of sins (26:28) which Jesus' innocent blood unfailingly produces. On the level of what it seems, the people's cry makes them responsible for Jesus' blood, and yet on the level of what it meant, they collectively assume the identity of its recipients without an understanding of the reality. They are, after all, the people (ὁ λαός,1:21) whom Jesus initially came to save (1:21).

Furthermore, the verbal irony of 27:25, together with the subsequent confession of the Roman soldiers, "Truly this was the Son of God" (27:54), reveals that the divinely-willed salvation which Jesus carried out in his death is universal, embracing both the Jews and the Gentiles.[205] It is noteworthy that the Roman centurion and his companies confess Jesus as the "Son of God" in their awe of witnessing the earthquake at the moment of Jesus' death on the cross (27:54). According to the Gospel, the apocalyptic phenomenon such as an earthquake (ὁ σεισμός, 27:54; 28:2) or storm in the sea (8:24, σεισμὸς μέγας ἐγένετο ἐν τῇ θαλάσσῃ) metaphorically indicates the divine portent or the impact of Jesus' presence among the people. For example, Matthew reports that the entire city, Jerusalem, was stirred up (Ἱεροσόλυμα ἐσείσθη, 21:10; cf. 2:3) at the time of Jesus' entrance as if an earthquake had passed through and shaken it. This expression illustrates that the people of Jerusalem strongly felt Jesus' presence among them. Likewise, the Matthean passion narrative describes the Roman centurion as existentially encountering Jesus and becoming receptive to him to the extent that he confesses Jesus. The Roman centurion's recognition of Jesus as the "Son of God," the Christological title that has been a stumbling block for the Jewish religious leaders, is a quite significant incident because, according to the Gospel, the confession of Jesus' divine sonship exclusively has to do with God's revelation and his initiative (16:17). As the Gospel's implied author shows how the death of Jesus connects all the people (πᾶς ὁ λαός, 27:25) to himself through the ironic reversal, he further extends the scope of

---

205. Heil, *The Death and Resurrection of Jesus*, 87, focuses on the Gentiles taking advantage of the ironical price that the Jewish people pay for shedding the blood of Jesus. He further opines that the Roman soldiers' confession qualifies them as representatives of the people to whom the kingdom of God will be given when it is taken from the Jewish people because of their rejection of Jesus (21:43). Also see Keener, *A Commentary on the Gospel of Matthew*, 687.

his people (ὁ λαός αὐτοῦ, 1:21) to the Romans through their uncalculated confession of him (27:54).²⁰⁶ By embracing both sides of the extended people of God, Matthew emphasizes the universal characteristic of the divinely-willed salvation,²⁰⁷ just as the entire ministry of Jesus presents his compassion and concern for both groups. It is in the Matthean passion narrative that finally Jesus' proclamation of his establishment of the Covenant through his blood gains its full sense. The Covenant which he establishes with his own sacrificial blood (26:28; Exod. 24:3-8) corresponds to the traditional Jewish belief in the New Covenant which is characterized by a universal knowledge of God and the forgiveness of sins (Jer. 31:31-34; 32:37-41). Jesus' own words describing that his blood of the Covenant is poured out "for many for the forgiveness of sins" (26:28) are crucial to understand the universal attribute of the Covenant which his blood institutes. In the past, as the blood of a sin offering was drawn out to atone for the sins of God's people, so the blood of Jesus is shed "for the forgiveness of the sins" and "for many." It is striking that "for many" is a common Semitic expression for all people and, therefore, this particular phrase that Jesus employs indicates the universal scope of his Covenant.²⁰⁸ This interpretation also sheds light on the Gospel's introduction of Jesus as the son of Abraham, the first Jewish patriarch (1:1).²⁰⁹ This Jewish Gospel

---

206. David Hill, "Matthew 27:51-53 in the Theology of the Evangelist," *IBS* 7 (1985): 76–87 interprets the inclusion of the Roman centurion's confession in 27:54 that the Gentile community has become believers and Jesus' universal mission mandate (28:16-20) is realized, proleptically, at the cross.

207. Kingsbury, *Matthew as Story*, 93 notes that "ironically, what also happens is that God turns Jesus' death to advantage for all humankind, for through his death, Jesus atones for sins and becomes the one through whom God henceforth grants salvation to all humans, Jews and Gentiles alike (1:21; 26:28)."

208. Heil, *The Death and Resurrection of Jesus*, 37 explains that "as the blood of sacrificed animals was 'poured out' by priests on the altar as a sin offering to atone for this sins of the people (Lev. 4:7, 18, 25, 30, 34), so the blood that will be 'shed' or 'poured out' by the death of Jesus represents a sacrifice for the atonement of sins 'for,' that is, 'on behalf of' (*peri*), 'many' people…that the atoning blood of Jesus will be poured out one behalf of 'many' (*pollōn*), a common Semitic expression for 'all' people, indicates the universal nature of the covenants, which brings forgiveness and salvation to all." Also see, Joachim Jeremias, "*Polloi*," *TDNT* 6. 537–38; Joachim Jeremias, *The Eucharistic Words of Jesus* (New York: Scribners, 1966), 226–31.

209. Matt. 1:1, "The book of genealogy of Jesus Christ, the son of David, the son of Abraham" (Βίβλος γενέσεως Ἰησοῦ χριστοῦ υἱοῦ Δαυὶδ υἱοῦ Ἀβραάμ). Tisera, *Universalism*, 32–39 delineates the importance of Jesus, the son of Abraham in the Gospel of Matthew. There is no direct literary contact between "the son of Abraham (Matt. 1:1)" and the Genesis texts that report God's promises made to Abraham. According to Tisera, the relationship is rather to be established in terms of ideas implied by the son of Abraham, which evokes the idea of promise to Israel and the nations. Tisera opines that the presence of Abraham in the heading gives Jesus a special weight and matches that of David. The name "Abraham" is repeatedly attested three times in the genealogy of Jesus (Matt. 1:1, 2, 7) and outside the

equally emphasizes Jesus' relationship to the prominent Jewish figures, David and Abraham. Jesus is the "son of David" (1:1), who fulfills the Davidic Covenant and ushers in his kingdom.[210] And also, Jesus is the "son of Abraham," who fulfills the Abrahamic Covenant that God's salvation (blessings) reaches to the nations through him, the true seed of Abraham.[211] The Gospel's implied author addresses the name of Abraham outside of Jesus genealogy in order to make two theological points. First, God is also the God of the nations (3:9) and second, it is through Jesus that the Gentiles' approach to God's table, in other words, the Gentiles' incorporation into the fellowship with God (8:1; 22:32), is made possible. This is why it is written "In his name the nations will put their hope" (12:28) and why the resurrected Jesus commands his disciples to carry out the mission of the Gospel to all nations to the end of the age (28:19f; cf. Immanuel, 1:23). As the Gospel declares Jesus to be the "son of Abraham," in Jesus the promise of blessings for all the nations is finally actualized and therefore, the Covenant which Jesus' blood institutes for "many" (20:28; 26:28) must also be for the nations beyond the Jewish confines.

In this way, irony is in the very nature of the soteriology of Matthew. It reveals that there is no scandal of sin that cannot be overcome by the forgiveness which Jesus' blood secures. As we have examined in the case of the people (1:21; 27:25) and their rejection of Jesus which is accelerated to the point of demanding his blood, irony brings about God-intended reversal, turning the people's cry of rejection into their unaware subjection to God's saving power which Jesus' blood embodies. In the end, the verbal irony of 27:25 revealing the ironic reversal of the people's relationship to Jesus answers a key question

---

genealogy, four times more (3:9 (x2); 8:11; 22:32). Tisera considers it a fact that Jesus takes the baton of Abraham as an eschatological figure and stretches salvation beyond the Jewish nation. The question remains, how is the nations' involvement in the idea of universalism implied in Matt. 1:1? Tisera provides several reasons to support the idea: one, the position of the son of Abraham defines the genealogy of Jesus (Βίβλος γενέσεως) which echoes the same expression in Gen 2:4, implying a universalism in largest sense, two, the position of the son of Abraham in regard to Jesus in the genealogy (1:16) determines the role of Jesus. If the promise made to Abraham moves forward along with the generations towards its realization, Jesus is not only the goal of the succession of generations initiated by Abraham (1:2) but also Jesus for the first time realizes the blessing for all nations promised to Abraham, and three, Matt. 28:16-20, with the explicit commission to go to all nations, and Matt. 1:1, with its theme of universalism, enclose the entire Gospel. Also, see Fenton, *Saint Matthew*, 37; D. A. Carson, "*Matthew*," in *The Expositor's Bible Commentary*, ed. Frank E. Gaebelein (Grand Rapids: Zondervan, 1984), 8:62; Jeffrey A. Gibbs, *Matthew 1:11–11:1* (St. Louis: Concordia Publishing House, 2006), 76–77.

210. For Old Testament references regarding the Davidic Covenant, see 1 Chron. 17:11-14; 2 Chron. 6:16; 2 Sam. 7:10-13, 16.

211. For Old Testament references regarding the Abrahamic Covenant, see Gen. 12:1-3; 15:18-21; 17:1-9; 22:16-18.

about how Jesus will save his people from their sins by demonstrating that the scandal of Jesus' cross is the sole remedy for the scandal of the people's sin. And the Romans' involvement in Jesus' death and their recognition of his profound identity shone through the cross meaningfully echoes the Gospel's proclamation of Jesus, the son of Abraham (1:1), the bearer of God's promise of blessings on the nations.

VERBAL IRONY PERTAINING TO THE MOCKERY OF JESUS BY HIS OPPONENTS (27:7-31, 35-44)

After Pilate delivers Jesus to be crucified (27:27), his soldiers take Jesus into their hands and mock his kingship (27:27-31). Yet in fact, they speak more than they know through the irony hidden behind their abusive language (27:29) which accompanies the physical abuse (27:28-31). They call Jesus "King of the Jews" and decorate him with a scarlet robe, a crown of thorns and a staff in fake honor for a helpless king.[212] As it clearly seems, their treatment of Jesus is meant for insult, not for tribute. This is in contrast to the reality regarding the person of Jesus, which the Gospel unveils in a thorough fashion: Jesus as the son of David (the Davidic king of Jews),[213] the Lord,[214] the Christ,[215] the Son of Man[216] and the Son of God.[217] In this discrepancy, irony works to bring about its aim proclaiming Jesus' kingship unequivocally through the taunt of his abusers.

---

212. Carson, *Matthew*, 573 explains that "for a crown (v. 29) the soldiers plaited a wreath of thorns from palm spines or acanthus and crushed it down on Jesus' head in imitation of the circlet on the coins of Tiberius Caesar (cf. TDNT, 7:615–24, 632f.). The staff they put in his hand stood for a royal scepter; and the mocking, 'Hail, King of the Jews!' corresponded to the Roman acclamation 'Ave, Caesar!' and capped the flamboyant kneeling." In this way, the Roman soldiers mocked Jesus' kingship in their ignorance that they were abusing a king greater than any the world had ever know.

213. Matt. 1:1; 2:2, 6; 9:27; 12:23; 15:22; 18:23; 20:3-31; 21:5, 9, 15; 22:2, 42; 25:34, 40; 26:31; 27:11, 29, 37, 42. Further, Matthew provides ample references for the kingdom of God and its mystery that is manifested in the person and ministry of Jesus the Christ King. See Matt. 3:2; 4:17, 23; 5:3, 10, 19 (x2), 20; 6:10, 33; 7:21; 8:12; 9:35; 10:7; 11:11; 12:15, 26, 28; 13:11, 19, 24, 31, 33, 38, 41, 43-45, 47, 52; 16:19, 28; 18:1, 3f, 23; 19:14, 23f; 20:1, 21; 21:31, 43; 22:2; 23:23; 24:7 (x2), 14; 25:1, 34; 26:29.

214. For the Matthean use of the title, "the Lord" addressing both God and Jesus, see Matt. 1:22; 2:15; 3:3; 4:7, 10; 7:21-22; 8:2, 6, 21, 25; 9:28; 11:25; 12:8; 14:28, 30; 15:22, 25, 27 (x2); 16:22; 17:4, 15; 18:21; 20:30-31, 33; 21:3, 9; 22:37, 43-45; 23:39; 24:42; 26:22; Jesus as the Lord of Lords 22:41-46.

215. Matt. 1:1, 16-18, 21; 2:4; 11:2; 16:16, 20; 22:42; 23:10; 26:63, 68; 27:17, 22; Jesus Emmanuel 1:23; 18:20; 28:20.

216. Matt. 8:20; 9:6; 10:23; 11:19; 12:8, 32, 40; 13:37, 41; 16:13, 27-28; 17: 9, 12, 22; 19:28; 20:18, 28; 24:27, 30 (x2), 37, 39; 24:44; 25:31; 26:2, 24 (x2), 45, 64.

217. Matt. 2:15; 3:17; 4:3, 6; 7:21; 8:29; 10:32-33; 11:25-27; 12:50; 14:33; 15:13; 16:16-17; 17:5; 18:10, 14, 19, 35; 20:23; 24:36; 26:29, 39, 42, 53, 63; 27:40, 43, 54; 28:19.

With regard to Jesus' identity as the Christ and the Son of God, the concrete examples of verbal irony appear in 27:39-44 in the form of a threefold mocking at the cross from passers-by, from the religious leaders, and from the two robbers beside Jesus.[218] The mocking by the religious leaders (that is, the chief priests with the scribes and elders, 27:41) especially exhibits full-blown verbal irony. Their derision blatantly reveals in full all three essential dimensions of who Jesus is: the Christ Savior ("He saved others; he cannot save himself," 27:42a), the King of Israel ("He is the King of Israel," 27:42b), and the Son of God ("He trusts in God. Let God deliver him now if he desires him, for he said, I am the Son of God," 27:43). In this instance of verbal irony, the ironist turns his dimmer switch to high in the expectation that the reader will not miss the revelation of irony. What can be more ironic than the chief accusers of the protagonist declaring the actual truth concerning their victim's identity at the very scene of his execution? Here, the religious leaders, who occupy the power and authority of teaching and interpreting the Word of God for the guidance of Israel ("sitting on Moses' seat," 23:2), stand against God and his proclamation that Jesus is his beloved Son (2:15; 3:17; 17:5), and in so doing, they echo the voice of Satan from the temptation of Jesus in chapter 4 (vv. 3, 6).[219] On numerous occasions, the Gospel's implied author has highlighted Jesus' intimate filial relationship with God[220] in contrast to his opponents' bond with Satan.[221] Through all these circumstances presented by the ironist, we are invited to see that he has made calculated placement of irony in the mouth of the Jewish religious authorities, the corporate ἀλαζών of the Matthean passion narrative, in order to attain two climactic ends simultaneously: the revelatory declaration of Jesus' identity at the moment of ignominy through the ἀλαζών's abusive language, and the ἀλαζών's unintended self-condemnation.

---

218. Keener, *A Commentary on the Gospel of Matthew*, 673, 682, reads that the mockery by the opponents of Jesus (27:27-44) rings with tragicomic irony

219. Ibid., 607 comments that the mockery of the religious leaders at the cross ironically reflects Satan's testing.

220. Jesus the Son of God (including Jesus' descriptions of God as his heavenly Father). See Matt. 2:15; 3:17; 7:21; 8:29; 10:32-33; 11:25-26; 12:50; 14:33; 15:13; 16:16-17; 17:5; 18:10, 14, 19, 35; 20:23; 24:36; 26:29, 39, 42, 53, 63; 27:40, 43, 54; 28:19; cf. 4:3, 6.

221. In the Matthean narrative, the religious leaders are portrayed as a single character group and they bear a common trait: "evil." Their "evil" trait corresponds to the trait of Satan ("evil," 9:4; 12:34, 39, 45; 16:4; 22:18; "brood of vipers," 3:7; 12:34; 23:33; "child of hell," 23:15; Satan is 'the evil one," 13:19, 38). Identifying the intention and attitude of the religious leaders with Satan is one of the evaluative perspectives that the Gospel's implied reader acquires through a narrative-critical reading of the Gospel of Matthew as a whole.

To give weight to Jesus' identity, the author uses the ironic leitmotif σῴζω (to save) in 27:42 to underscore Jesus as the Christ Savior. As the Gospel depicts, the divinely-willed salvation is the foundation of the entire story of Jesus, "One who will save (σώσει) his people from their sins" (1:21). Jesus carries out this foremost ministry and finally implements it through his death (20:28; 26:28). The religious leaders meant to deride Jesus' seeming defeat, hanging on the cross between two criminals, scorned to death. However, this is exactly what Jesus intends to achieve as the Gospel portrays that throughout his ministry Jesus' focus is to save others, [222] not himself. This is in harmony with Jesus' teaching that the path for Christ is to give himself and the taking of one's cross for the service of others is a manifestation for discipleship to Jesus (16:24f). Therefore, the religious leaders' contempt, "He saved others; he cannot save himself," (ἄλλους ἔσωσεν, ἑαυτὸν οὐ δύναται σῶσαι, 27:41f) imports an irony that stands at odds with the full panorama of Jesus' saving ministry with which the Gospel's implied reader is familiar. According to the Gospel's illustration of Jesus' ministry, the reason he does not save himself is not because he is unable to do so. Quite the contrary, Jesus is "able" and "mighty." He says at the time of his arrest that more than twelve legions of angels are at his disposal (26:53).[223] Yet, he willingly divests himself of his God-like power to save himself because he is fully committed to carrying out God's saving will, even to the point of subjecting himself utterly to death. He does by drinking the cup (ποτήριον, 20:22-23 ; 26:27-28, 39, 42) without making any form of resistance or self-defense.

In the end, we see that the religious authorities' mocking fails them. Their intent to display their victory and control over their seemingly helpless victim backfires. Instead, when they unintentionally confirm the identities of Jesus in full scale—the Christ Savior (27:42a), the King of Israel (27:42b) and the Son of God (27:43)—the irony operating in their words underlines their inadequate conviction regarding the person of Jesus and consequently exposes their misconceived sense of victory over him. Further, their specific mocking of Jesus' passivity (27:42), which they interpret as a sign of defeat, is precisely the way through which God's saving will is brought to its fruition. Despite his unsurpassable heavenly glory to which his transfiguration (17:1-9) testifies,[224]

---

222. See Matt. 1:21; 8:25; 9:21-22; 10:22; 14:30; 16:25; 19:25; 24:13, 22; 27:40, 42, 49.

223. The Gospel attests to the God-like power and authority of Jesus. See Matt. 3:11; 8:2-3; 9:28-32; 17:1-9; 20:21-22; 26:42, 61.

224. After Peter's confession of Jesus as "the Christ, the Son of the living God," (16:16) which had to originate from the divine revelation (16:17) according to the Gospel of Matthew, Jesus is transformed (Gk., μετεμορφώθη; Lt., *transfiguratus est*) into divine form (cf. 2 Pet. 1:16-18, "of his sovereign majesty")

Jesus dies as the cursed one (Deut. 21:23) and offers himself as a ransom for *many* (20:28; 26:28). Therefore, his passivity requires a leap of faith in order to see its true quality, not as an object of contempt but as the manifestation of his victory won by he who is irrefutably the Christ Savior (1:21).

DRAMATIC IRONY REVEALING THE CRUCIFIXION OF JESUS (27:31-36) AS THE DEFEAT OF SATAN

The Matthean passion narrative's irony presents Jesus' death as the locus where the ultimate cosmic clash between God and Satan is revealed. Earlier in the Gospel, prior to his public ministry, Jesus contends with Satan in the wilderness (4:1-11) and defeats him (4:4, 7, 10) through his reliance on God's words (4:3f) and unmatchable devotion to God as God's Son (4:5-11). Satan's three attempts to tempt Jesus identifies him as Jesus' adversary and tempter, who has clear motives of diverting Jesus' messianic ministry and planting the seed of doubt and mistrust in him. Satan reappears in other parts of the Gospel largely in the form of the accusing voices of Jesus' antagonists.

God and Satan both indirectly set different norms for conflicting interests but they vitally influence other characters within the story. The Gospel's implied author designs the narrative sensibly in the way which the voice of God can be heard through the voices of Jesus, his Son, and the narrator, who is identical with the implied author-ironist. In contrast, the voice of Satan is heard through the voices of his associates, the Jewish religious leaders. The author has depicted Satan not only as the prototype of Jesus' corporate opponents, the religious leaders (ἀλαζών), but also as the sole explicable source for this stock character group's vileness (3:7; 12:34; 13:38; 23:33).[225] Hence, the accusations raised by the religious leaders against Jesus echo the tone and implication of Satan in chapter 4. For example, in the high priest's cross-examination of Jesus

---

before three disciples, Peter, James and John, the ones who reappear as a group in the scene of Gethsemane in chapter 26. The significance of Jesus transformation is that Jesus' outward change matches his true identity. His veiled divine nature (Heb. 10:20) is substantially glimpsed in the transfiguration. According to Johannine theology, the incarnation of Jesus is a personification of the *Shekinah* glory of God dwelling among his people (John 1:14). Also, Phil. 2:5-11 witnesses the mystery of an invisible God in a visible human form that the transfiguration of Jesus lays bare before the eyes of men. A close look into Jesus' transfiguration and its circumstances further attests to Jesus' heavenly glory. In his glory, Jesus is talking with the significant figures of the Old Testament: Moses and Elijah. It was commonly believed that Moses as the prime transmitter of the law and Elijah as the most prominent prophet of the Old Testament who would reappear before the coming of the Messiah (Mal. 4). Therefore, inter-textual readings take Moses and Elijah to represent the law and the prophets respectively and their recognition of and conversation with Jesus indirectly testify to the truthfulness of the words of Jesus as Jesus proclaimed that he came to fulfill the law and the prophets (Matt. 5:17-19; Col. 2:14-17).

before the Sanhedrin, "If you are the Christ, the Son of God" (26:63), mirrors the very wording of Satan, "If you are the Son of God" (4:3, 6), in Jesus' temptation in the wilderness.

The Gospel's implied author presents several authentic witnesses of Jesus, ranging from the narrator, the celestial beings, the crowds, the demons, the minor characters being healed by Jesus, the receptive Gentiles, the disciples of Jesus represented by Peter and his voice, to most importantly, God himself. The implied author gives weight to the voice of God which authenticates Jesus' sonship to God himself as the most authoritative and reliable source of information about Jesus. Although God remains in the background of the Gospel, his presence and perspective are by no means insignificant, for he is both the conductor of his determined saving will toward men and the author of Jesus' redemptive death as its fulfillment. This is the reason why the author strategically places throughout the Gospel the voice of God which substantiates Jesus' ministry by testifying to Jesus' extraordinary filial relationship to him. While Matthean scholars have attempted to define several constituent character groups in the Gospel, including Jesus, his disciples, the crowds, the religious leaders, and other minor characters, God and Satan have hardly been treated appropriately as characters. Although both God and Satan act as invisible characters in the backdrop of Jesus' story since they are little to be seen on the physical level, they take fundamental roles as the most reliable firsthand witnesses of Jesus: God as the Father to Jesus and Satan as Jesus' primary opponent. Both have full knowledge of him.

We hear at least three attestations of God to Jesus' identity, which are key to the Gospel's theology, in both direct and indirect forms of declaration. God speaks three times in a recognizable way in the Gospel. The first voice of God attesting to Jesus' distinctive relationship to him comes early at Jesus' baptism: "This is my beloved Son, in whom I am well pleased" (3:17). The next voice of God, resonating God's first attestation to Jesus, appears in the scene of Jesus' transfiguration: "This is my beloved Son, in whom I am well pleased. Listen to him!" (17:5). While these two incidents report the direct voice of God confirming Jesus' divine origin, the following case indirectly resounds with God's testimony to Jesus. Consider Peter's confession in chapter 16 which comes between Jesus' baptism and the mount of transfiguration. Peter's confession, "You are the Christ, the Son of the living God" (16:16), must be considered to be another testimony of God to his Son as Jesus explains the

---

225. Edward M. Forster, *Aspects of the Novel* (New York: Harcourt, 1927), 65–82, 103–18, explains that a stock character is one-dimensional with a single, consistent, and predictable trait. Also, for the discussion of "character trait," see Chatman, *Story and Discourse*, 121.

source of Peter's confession is not from men but from God himself: "Blessed are you, Simon son of Barjona, for this was not revealed to you by man, but by my Father in heaven" (16:17). As the following structure features, a further close examination on the timings of God's attestations to Jesus reveals the crucial function of Peter's confession in the scheme of Jesus' saving mission which incessantly moves towards its finalization in Jesus' death. The structure does not intend to claim some sort of complete chiastic structure built in but rather help the reader to perceive how God's testimonies to his Son correspond to Jesus' passion predictions (16:21; 17:22f), which manifest Jesus' clear self-understanding as the Christ Savior.

> A. The first witnessing voice of God at Jesus' baptism (3:17), at the beginning stage of Jesus' messianic ministry.
> B. Satan's temptation of Jesus in his attempt to divert him from the path of the Christ Savior (1:21) by challenging Jesus' sonship to God (4:3, 6, 9).
> C. Peter's confession of Jesus (16:16), which functions as the second witnessing voice of God. Jesus' passion prediction immediately follows this (16:21).
> B'. On hearing Jesus' passion prediction, Peter rebukes Jesus. Jesus' response to Peter, "Get behind me, Satan!" (16:23) recalls his victory over Satan in the wilderness temptation of chapter 4.
> A'. The third witnessing voice of God at Jesus' mount transfiguration (17:5) echoes exactly the verbiage of the first witnessing voice of God (3:17). Shortly after this, Jesus predicts his passion second time (17:22f).

Interpreting the dramatic irony surrounding the death of Jesus, where God and Satan meet in conflict, paints a unique portrait of Peter. Peter, Jesus' outspoken disciple, is certainly one of a kind. God and Satan, the major hidden characters of Matthew, project their competing voices through Peter's speaking of the uncompromising principle of each side in relation to the how aspect of Jesus' saving ministry, that is, Jesus' death. In this way, Peter microcosmically embodies the struggle between God and Satan and their contrasting values and therefore, in this character, we observe that the two contrasting perspectives of God and Satan undergo a test and as a result, generate an irony. Further, Peter in his representative capacity shares a similar experience with the Jewish religious authorities: both come under the influence of Satan, the tempter.

Consider the confounding case of Peter in chapter 16, where Peter the blessed spirals down to Peter the ashamed. While the contention between Jesus and the religious leaders (the Pharisees and Sadducees, 16:1, 6) keeps growing, Peter makes a public confession of Jesus as "the Christ, the Son of the living God" (16:16), in the district of Caesarea Philippi (16:13). On hearing Peter's confession of him, Jesus declares that Peter is "blessed" by God because such a confession is only from God himself not from "flesh and blood" (16:17). Also, Jesus promises that God's church will be based on Peter's confession, that is, Jesus Christ himself which Peter's confession exclusively features. However, not long after his glorious moment of making truthful confession of Jesus, Peter slips into a ditch when he rebukes Jesus' passion prediction (16:21f). Peter's rebuke is hushed as Jesus counters him with a much stronger reproach, "Get behind me, Satan! You tempt me to sin" (16:23). Jesus' strong language in reprimand of Peter such as "Satan" (Σατάν) and "temptation to sin" (σκάνδαλον) clearly suggest that Peter crossed the line. It is important to notice that Jesus uses the term τὸ σκάνδαλον to describe the nature of Peter's attempt. Examining other cases of σκάνδαλον in the Gospel will further illumine the inference of this term. We can observe the explicit usage of the term in two places in the Gospel: here in 16:23 and 18:7 where Jesus teaches his disciples at Capernaum (7:24) regarding "who is the greatest in the kingdom of heaven" (that is, the kingdom of God). It is important to note two implications of σκάνδαλον revealed through these incidents. First, in both cases, Jesus employs the term in order to entail its close connection to sin. Second, Jesus' teaching in 18:7 particularly relates an important aspect of σκάνδαλον in that it comes from this world (ὁ κόσμος, the world of men) not from God. Therefore, we can conclude that those who cause sin belong to this world as Jesus rebukes Peter, "Get behind me Satan! You tempt me to sin *because you do not have in mind the things of God, but the things of men*" (6:23, italics mine). As Satan tempted Jesus earlier in the wilderness by enticing him with the worldly matters such as obtaining bread for sustaining life (4:3), trying God (4:6), and seeking glory (4:8), Peter's refusal to accept Jesus' announcement of his inevitable death similarly is based on his worldly interest and therefore, becomes a hindrance (σκάνδαλον) to the messianic ministry of Jesus, the Christ Savior (1:21; 20:28; 26:28). Perhaps we could give Peter some credit by interpreting his reaction to Jesus' passion prediction as a sign of loyalty because he could have meant to protect his teacher from harm rather than intend to impede his ministry. As the name, "Jesus," means, his life is meant to be given narrowly for "his people" (1:21) and broadly for "many" (20:28; 26:28). However, this very specific ministry of Jesus is out of reach of man's understanding until his death is achieved through the rejection of the people. This is why no single soul, including the entirety of Jesus' crew represented by Peter, comprehends the way through which God's saving will unfolds in the person and ministry of Jesus, despite Jesus' repeated passion predictions. Through his ups and downs, Peter bears our own image in that men are limited in perception of God's way and are also susceptible to Satan's influence.

The nature of Peter's rebuke of Jesus provides the Gospel's implied reader with insights beneficial to interpreting the dramatic irony surrounding the events of Jesus' death as the revelation of the clash of cosmic proportions between God and Satan. As the incident of Jesus' temptation reveals, Satan is an obstructive tempter of Jesus from the beginning of his ministry, embodying what is in the mind of men in diametrical contrast to Jesus' incarnation of what God wills to which the Scriptures avowedly point (3:15; 27:54). Satan's one and only intent is to divert Jesus from the path set for the Christ Savior. Satan knows the time (ὁ καιρός) of Jesus as the incident of two demoniacs in the region of Gadarenes shows. Coming out of the tombs, they cried out to Jesus, "What have you to do with us, Son of God? Have you come here to torment us before the *time*?" (8:29, italics mine). According to the Gospel, the time that the two demoniacs are concerned with none other than the time (ὁ καιρός, 26:18) of which Jesus is mindful. This is the time when God perfects his saving will toward his people through the innocent blood of Jesus, which establishes a new covenant for the forgiveness of sins (1:21; 20:28; 26:28). Therefore, Peter's rejection of Jesus' foresight that he must suffer the passion which will eventually lead him to death (16:21f) strikingly resembles Satan's scheme to avert Jesus from meeting his time and therefore, counters what God intends to achieve through his Son regardless of whether if Peter is aware of the situation or not.

However, in the Matthean passion narrative, the Jewish religious leaders, who are the associates of Satan and create a united front in opposition to Jesus, fulfill precisely what Satan wants to prevent from happening (27:31-36). Although it appears that they prevail in their conflict with Jesus, in actuality they only inadvertently assist as Jesus accomplishes the divinely-willed salvation. Previously, the Pharisees accused Jesus of driving out demons by Beelzebub, the prince of demons (9:33-34; 12:22-24 cf. 11:18). But, Jesus exposes their accusation's invalidity through his rhetorical question to them, "If I cast out demons by Beelzebub, by whom do your sons cast (them) out? Therefore, they shall be your judges" (12:27). The Pharisees' censure on Jesus' exorcism proves itself biased since on the one hand while they have been practicing the same exorcism with a conviction that it was a legitimate religious expression of faith in God, on the other hand they judge Jesus' exorcism with negativity to the extent that they label it as a demonic presentation. What is important in this scene beyond Jesus' disclosure of the Pharisees' unjust and jealous nature, which continue to work in them to the end, is Jesus' statement, "Every kingdom divided against itself is laid waste, and no city or house divided against itself will stand" (12:25). Seeing Jesus' death, which Satan initially tried to halt, achieved under the full control of the Jewish religious leaders, the associates of Satan according to the Gospel's depiction, is ironic. In other words, it is ironic because Jesus' final achievement of God's saving plan through his death tellingly indicates that the kingdom of Satan is divided (12:25) since the associates of Satan seem to frustrate the very will of Satan to divert Jesus from his messianic path (4:8-11). This scenario only further proves the incapacity of Satan on the cosmic level while every ironic situation in the Matthean passion narrative advances the victory of Jesus in his deeper conflict with Satan.[226] In the end, together with the foreseen victory of Jesus over Satan (ch. 4), Satan's total powerlessness and lack of control manifested through the ironic failure of his accomplices in the Matthean passion narrative yield a bitter laugh in the mind of the reader.

Character Irony of the Religious Leaders Accusing Jesus as a Deceiver (ΠΛΆΝΟΣ, 27:63-64)

The day after Jesus had been laid in the tomb of Joseph of Arimathea (27:57-61), the chief priests and the Pharisees gathered before Pilate (27:62) and asked him to secure Jesus' tomb until the third day (27:64), lest the disciples of Jesus go and steal him away (27:64). They support their request by recalling that they have heard Jesus, "that deceiver" (ἐκεῖνος ὁ πλάνος), say that "After three days I will rise again" (27:63).[227] Pay attention to the religious leaders' naming Jesus as "deceiver" (πλάνος). The Greek noun πλάνος is cognate to words like πλανάω (to wander, lead astray), πλάνης (wanderer, roamer), and πλάνη

---

226. Powell, *Narrative Criticism*, 48–49, likewise observes that the Matthean passion narrative is told with "tremendous irony" mainly because the religious leaders bring about the very thing Satan would prevent. On page 48, he writes that "the great irony of Matthew's Gospel, however, is that whereas the religious leaders want to bring Jesus to the cross, Satan wants to keep him from it (cf. 16:21-23). Accordingly, the conflict between Jesus (or God) and Satan is also resolved in Matthew's passion narrative, but this conflict is clearly resolved in Jesus' favor."

227. Senior, *The Passion of Jesus*, 154 notes irony hidden in the remark of the religious leaders. He says that "the leaders themselves recall Jesus' predictions of his triumph over death (" . . . we remember how that impostor said, while he was still alive, 'After three days I will rise again' "), a telling irony as the Gospel stands on the brink of the resurrection story. With another touch of irony on Matthew's part, the leaders also predict that the disciples will proclaim to the people: 'He has risen from the death,' a wary anticipation of the great missionary commission that will conclude the Gospel (28:16–20)."

(deception, fraud, digression). Although the noun, πλάνος appears for the first time in the Matthean passion narrative when the religious leaders request Pilate's order to guard Jesus' tomb (27:64), we observe that the cognate verb πλανάω is used in other parts of the Gospel. Each instance is found in Jesus' speeches, in relation to either Jesus' parabolic teaching regarding one's status of being lost by wandering away from the path (18:12f) or Jesus' warning against the deception of the false prophets and false christs (24:4f, 11, 24).[228]

In contrast to the religious leaders' characterization of Jesus as "deceiver" (πλάνος, 27:63), the Gospel otherwise shows that it is not Jesus but his accusers who fit the bill of πλάνος. For that reason, the Gospel's implied reader, who carefully follows the Gospel's story and absorbs along the way the information directly pertaining to each party, discerns that it is not Jesus but the religious leaders who adopt deception (πλάνη) as their destructive mode of behavior in contrast to the transparent and public ministry of Jesus (26:55-56). The following two cases—first, Jesus' criticism of the religious leaders' lawlessness and, second, the Matthean passion narrative's depiction of the religious leaders' plot against Jesus—support the above premise that the religious leaders' classification of Jesus as πλάνος is an example of character irony which ultimately expose the accusers, not the accused, as πλάνος.

First, prior to the Matthean passion narrative, Jesus criticizes the Jewish religious leaders' ignorance of God's law and their resulting ignorance of the will of God (τὸ θέλημά τοῦ θεοῦ).[229] According to the Gospel, the will of God stands in close relation to the law as Jesus validates God's law by fulfilling it (5:17f) and hence, conforms to the will of God as revealed in God's law and the scriptures (26:53f). Throughout the Gospel, the Gospel's implied author connects theological expressions such as "lawful" (ἔξεστιν)[230] and "bearing fruit" (καρπός)[231] to the notion of "doing the will of God" (τὸ θέλημά τοῦ θεοῦ).[232] The idea conveyed here is that the law of God should be fulfilled through the receiver's active response (9:14-17) which Jesus figuratively calls "bearing fruits." Also, according to Jesus' Sermon on the Mount, it is the will of God that to the lawful action of man a commensurate reward (μισθός) will be given.[233]

---

228. BAGD, 665 defines ἡ πλάνη as wandering from the path of truth, error, delusion, deceit, deception to which one is subject.
229. For the Matthean references to the will of God, see Matt. 6:10; 7:21; 12:50; 18:41; 21:31; 26:39, 42.
230. Matt. 12:2, 4, 10, 12; 14:4; 19:3; 20:15; 22:17; 27:6.
231. Matt. 3:8, 10; 7:16-18; 12:33; 13:8, 26; 21:19, 34, 41, 43.
232. Matt. 6:10; 12:50; 21:31; 26:42, metaphorically drinking the cup (τὸ ποτήριον) in 26:39.
233. Matt. 5:12, 46; 6:1, 2, 5, 16; 10:41, 42; 20:8.

The Gospel's focus on Jesus' fulfillment of God's law both in his teaching and deed demonstrates how "lawful" and "bearing fruit" are identical to "doing the will of God" (τὸ θέλημά τοῦ θεοῦ) as Jesus' life perfectly exemplifies this formula (3:15; 6:33).[234] In his Sermon on the Mount (chapters 5–7), Jesus reveals himself as the authoritative interpreter of God's law (7:28f; cf. 21:23; 22:33)[235] and at the same time, publicly defines his position with regard to the law as God's obedient Son. The key aspect of Jesus' teaching in this discourse has to do with his command to his disciples to pursue surpassing righteousness (5:20) that exceeds the standard of Jewish legalism (5:10, 20) because the highest standard of the law is God himself as Jesus plainly states it: "You therefore shall be perfect (τέλειος), as your heavenly Father is perfect" (5:48). Further, as regarding how to comply with God's law, Jesus instructs the disciples that God's law is to be understood with the heart, not as a code; it is mercy-oriented, not legalistic.

Considering the Gospel's emphasis on the law of God and its fulfillment, it is worth addressing Jesus' dispute with the religious leaders over the issue of "what is lawful" (ἔξεστιν) in chapter 12 (12: 2, 4, 10, 12).[236] In this chapter, we read that Jesus and the religious leaders face each other in conflict concerning the interpretation and practice of the law in the temple of Jerusalem, the center of Jewish worship and the headquarter of the Jewish religious authority. Here, the religious leaders question Jesus' authority in his interpretation of the law and judge that what Jesus teaches and does is not ἔξεστιν.[237] However, the portrayal of the religious leaders by the Gospel's implied author-ironist reveals the opposite: not only are they without authority in their teaching of God's law, but they are also without understanding of it.[238] This is demonstrated when Jesus challenges their knowledge and perception of the Scriptures with his pointed question, "Have you not read?" (οὐκ ἀνέγνωτε; 12:3, 5; 19:4; 21:16, 42; 22:31). Also, in taking counsel to destroy Jesus (12:14), they reveal the full

---

234. B. Gerhardsson, *The Mighty Acts of Jesus according to Matthew*, trans. Robert Dewsnap (Lund: GWK Gleerup, 1979), 89, notes that in everything Jesus fulfils the demands of the law.

235. In the Gospel of Matthew, Jesus presents himself as the object of *Shema* (Deut. 6) in his commandment that "You have heard that it was said to them of old time . . . but I say unto you (5:21-22)" as he actualizes the glory of *Shekinah* (1:18-21, 23; 17:1-8; 28:20) in his person and ministry as the saving agent of God. This exposition is well supported by God's own testimony at the time of Jesus' transfiguration given to the accompanying disciples of Jesus, "This is my beloved Son, with whom I am well pleased; *listen to him*" (17:5, italics mine).

236. Other than chapter 12, the term again occurs in 19:3; 22:17.

237. Matera, *Passion Narratives and Gospel Theologies*, 132, points out that in chapter 12 the opposition to Jesus comes primarily from the religious leaders (12:1-14, 24-32) with regards to the significant subject matter of the law and the Sabbath.

238. See Matt. 7:28-29; 13:54; 21:23; 22:33; 28:18-20.

extent of their lawlessness (23:28) against one who is greater than the temple (12:6), the embodiment of divine mercy (ἔλεος, 12:7) and the Lord of the Sabbath (12:8). Most importantly, Jesus' view of the will of God completely differs from that of the religious leaders in their conviction that they know the will of God expressed in his law. From the point of the story's reality, the irony, which the religious leaders corporately exhibit, is that they contest God's only beloved Son (3:17; 17:5) and therefore, vie against God himself in their full conviction that they are doing the will of God. Their zeal to fulfill the law is tainted with ill-will towards Jesus and unfortunately marks them as the *un*-doers of God's will because they are in direct opposition to the Son of God whose ministry is fulfilling God's will which the law espouses. Further, Jesus' criticism against their "lawlessness" in chapter 23 (23:1-39) and their unified perfidy in dealing with Jesus in the Matthean passion narrative (26:4; 27:3-6, 18) substantiate the fact that they practice "what is unlawful" (the opposite to ἔξεστιν).

Second, the Matthean passion narrative illustrates that the religious leaders plot to seize Jesus by trickery. This characteristically corresponds to the lawlessness of the religious leaders as Jesus points out. The way which they operate, such as trickery, indicates that they are familiar with injustice. Therefore, they are those who ironically are entitled to be called the masters of deceit (δόλος, 26:4) and the deceiver (πλάνος) in a collective sense. In contrast to their case, we do not locate a single instance in the Gospel that can link Jesus to any form of deception or indecency which would lead us to give him the label "deceiver" (πλάνος). Yet, the definition of πλάνος ironically fits one-dimensional evil nature of the religious leaders, exhibited in their thoughts, words and actions throughout their interactions with Jesus. Further, as we have identified the religious leaders as a corporate ἀλαζών of the Gospel, it is interesting to consider that ἀλαζών seems to share the close semantic undertone with πλάνος, whose main trait is characterized by πλάνη as ἀλαζών is characterized by ἀλαζονεία.[239] However, it should be admitted that defining a linking semantic origin between them is impossible

---

239. BAGD, 666 defines ὁ πλάνος as deceiver or impostor as Liddell-Scott lexicon correspondingly defines ὁ ἀλαζών as a false pretender, deceiver/impostor, or quack. As further proof, Northrop Frye, *Anatomy of Criticism* (New Jersey: Princeton University Press, 1957), 172 likewise defines the ἀλαζών as deceiver/impostor in his explanation of three types of comic characters: the ἀλαζών, the εἴρων and the βωμολόχος (buffoon). Frye, ibid., 34 explains that ἀλαζονεία has been interpreted as pretension and arrogance in word and deed or other vices such as Jewish pride in the New Testament and in other early Christian literature. Based on this evidence, considering the Matthean character of the Jewish religious leaders as a corporate ἀλαζών seems to be reasonable based on their words and deeds exhibiting ἀλαζονεία, specifically in their interactions with Jesus, the εἴρων of the Gospel.

other than their analogous implications.²⁴⁰ Therefore, the religious leaders—the story's ἀλαζών, who simultaneously also appropriate the characteristics of πλάνος—and their derision of Jesus as "deceiver" (πλάνος) together create a moment of truth about themselves which is brought forward by the character irony of πλάνος brings forward.

In summary, the Matthean passion narrative's ironist succeeds in showing why Jesus has to die from the perspective of his opponents, the religious leaders. From the perception of the religious leaders Jesus is a law breaker, ²⁴¹ a false teacher and most importantly a dangerous threat to their authority and position among the people. However, the entire Gospel attests to the opposite truth that it is not Jesus but those who sit in "Moses' seat" (23:1) are culpable for betraying God's law in their lack of understanding of it and inability to abide by it. Despite the fact that Jesus' ministry manifests his overwhelmingly profound identity as the Son of God and the materialization of the law (5:17; 7:28; 13:54; 22:33), the Matthean passion narrative ends with Jesus' death as a demon-possessed (9:34; 12:24), blasphemer (26:65) and a deceiver (πλάνος, 27:63). However, what it seems on the surface is not all there is as we find the divine reversal reasserting itself through a character irony of πλάνος. Once again, the religious leaders' final defamation of Jesus as πλάνος is nothing but a self-accusation. Consequently, it underscores the efficacy of the cross through which Jesus the Christ Savior fulfills the saving will of God amid man's lawlessness.²⁴²

---

240. Derrett J. Duncan, "Jesus as a Seducer (ΠΛΑΝΟΣ=ΜΑΤ'ΕΗ)," *Bijdragen* 55 (1994), 44–45, notes the difficulty of delineating the philological and semantic origin of the verb, πλανᾶν.

241. Charges that have been brought against Jesus in relation to the temple (26:61) and his divine sonship (26:64) reflect their concern for the law.

242. Heino O. Kadai, "Luther's Theology of the Cross," in *Accents in Luther's Theology: Essays in Commemoration of the 450th Anniversary of the Reformation*, ed. Heino O. Kadai (St. Louis: Concordia, 1967), 238, reports the understanding of Luther, the Reformer that "as Luther came to recognize the full sweetness of God's love in the cross, he realized that the cross also had an epistemological dimension. It offered clues to understanding the mysteries of divine revelation. This formed the backbone of the *theologia crucis* . . . An equally important aspect of *theologia crucis*, the cross event, was that it revealed the mystery of God's revelation and afforded insight into the secrets of God's dealings with men."

5

Theology of the Matthean Passion Narrative: The Meaning of the Death of Jesus through the Lens of Irony

To this point we have examined irony as the rhetorical device used by the Gospel's implied author, the divine ironist, for his persuasive communication. The Matthean passion narrative contains three particular types of conventional irony: verbal, dramatic, and character irony. After a careful examination of the various instances of conventional irony within the Matthean passion narrative, it is time to spell out the Gospel's theological implications of Jesus' death and its significance, which are presented through the lens of irony. Here, we will summarize the results of the narrative-critical reading of the Matthean passion narrative's ironic portrayal of Jesus' death in four categories: (i) the identity of Jesus, (ii) the saving will of God: the governing norm of the Matthean passion narrative (iii) God's universal salvation, and (iv) *Deus triumphus* vs. *Satan victus*: the outcome of the Christ-event.

THE IDENTITY OF JESUS

The Matthean passion narrative's ironic portrayal of Jesus' death gives an insight into the question of "who is Jesus?" Despite the Gospel's stress on a multifaceted Jesus as the Christ Savior, the son of David, the King of the Jews, the Lord, the Son of Man, and the Son of God, one of the major causes of conflict between Jesus and his antagonists relates to the issue of Jesus' identity. The implied author-ironist of the Matthean passion narrative particularly emphasizes three aspects of Jesus' identity: the Christ Savior, the King of Jews, and the Son of God. By means of conventional irony and its typical reversal effect, the ironist turns around the emphatic "no" into an irrefutable "yes" regarding who Jesus is.

In the hands of the Matthean passion narrative's ironist, irony is like a dimmer switch. He strategically adjusts the ironic intensity throughout the Gospel. In early chapters, he lays out the compact and straightforward revelation of Jesus (1:1, 20; 2:2; 4:1-11). Building upon this initial revelation of Jesus, the author moves into the phase of the soft intimation of Jesus as Jesus himself purposely lays aside his divinity during his ministry. Then, in the Matthean passion narrative the author once again drives the story to the glowing revelation of Jesus as the crucified Christ Savior through his rhetorical tool, irony. The revelation of Jesus disclosed through the lens of the Matthean passion narrative's irony is different from Jesus' direct divine epiphany at the time of his Transfiguration (ch. 17). The disclosure of the Matthean passion narrative's irony is covert in nature, requiring the Gospel's implied reader to read more than what meets the eyes by relying on the information about Jesus given to them from the start of the Gospel. As a result, the reader reaches the moment of enlightenment in the Matthean passion narrative as the irony concretizes the truth about the person, Jesus. This is in contrast to the victims of irony within the story world who seem to get more confounded and are persistent in their miscomprehension of Jesus.

From the dawn of the Gospel, the implied author-ironist faithfully provides his counterpart, the implied reader, with the facts about Jesus' identity in relation to God and Jewish history through means such as reliable witnesses within the story world[1] and his own direct declarations about Jesus. He does this with an intent to guide the reader's exploration of the Christ event in the way which he intends to unfold it. Entering the Matthean story world, one reads the placard displayed on the front beam of the gate, "Jesus the Christ, the son of David, the son of Abraham" (1:1) in the report of the genealogy. This announcement makes three points to which the entire Gospel relates: first, the person Jesus is the Christ (Messiah in Hebrew), the fulfillment of the Messianic prophecies of the Old Testament; second, this Jewish Messiah is intimately connected to the history of Israel and its development; and third, Jesus the Christ recapitulates the Covenants which were initially created between God and the two Jewish patriarchal figures David and Abraham in their representational capacity. Besides the Gospel's declaration of Jesus the Christ in 1:1, we read in his birth narrative that a celestial messenger announces Jesus' divine sonship (1:20) which is immediately followed by the Magi's witness to Jesus' kingship over the Jews (2:2). Jesus' unique sonship to God himself

---

1. Matt. 1:1, 17-18 (the narrator), 1:20-21; 2:13 (an angel of the Lord), 1:22-23; 2:5-6, 15, 17-18, 23 (the Scriptures, the Prophets), 2:7, 9-10 (the heavenly portent, the star cf. 27:51--53), 3:1-3, 11-14 (John the Baptist), 3:17; 17:5 (God himself, also 16:16f).

is strongly echoed in the incident of Jesus' temptation by Satan (ch. 4) and throughout the Gospel where Jesus expresses his filial relationship to God.[2] The information given of Jesus' identity by the Gospel prophetically functions in that what he is (one's identity) is in an etiological relationship to what he does (one's achievement).

Contemplating the natural correlation between what he is and what he does leads us to see that the Gospel's most important disclosure of the person Jesus comes in 1:21 where the meaning of his name is explicated: "He will save his people from their sins." The Gospel portrays that God himself bestows his Son with a name, Jesus, as a father gives a name to his son, which is common practice in ancient patriarch society. This early exposition of the meaning of the name, Jesus, is crucial because it further supplies the essential information regarding Jesus the Christ (1:1) as the Savior through whom God's will to save should be accomplished. Literally, as his name means, Jesus is an incarnation of the unequivocal divine saving will toward his people. Therefore, the Gospel's information regarding Jesus' identity given in the early parts of the Gospel, in both his genealogy and birth narrative, is substantial to indicate that Jesus the Christ is most importantly God's saving agent without an equal.[3] God himself is the Father to Jesus and Jesus alone embodies God's eternal and saving presence. Therefore, this incident where God calls his son with this prophetic name, Jesus, is full of redemptive significance and serves as an indispensible kernel for the appropriation of the Gospel which is the story of Jesus the Christ Savior (1:21).

There is an interesting parallel between the implied author's report on God's name-giving to his Son, Jesus, and the name-giving practice observed in the oriental world where paternal authority and kinship are traditionally

---

2. The Gospel's implied author does not describe Joseph as the father of Jesus in a technical expression of the father–son relationship. The author employs a verb, γεννάω ("be father of," "bear," 1:2-15) when he relates a father to a son in human biological sense. It is a clear authorial intent to show Jesus as the Son of God without an equal within the history of Israel. Therefore, when the genealogy finally reaches Joseph, a male descendant of David who takes the role of legal paternity of Jesus through an adoption, the author abandons the his characteristic use of γεννάω to describe the relationship between Joseph and Jesus. Instead, he exposes the mystery surrounding the birth of Jesus by revealing the maternity side of Jesus and leaving out the information about any human father. Yet, the essential information regarding the Father of Jesus follows soon after directly through an angel's announcement that Jesus is the divine child (1:18-25; also 2:12-15, 19-21) and God himself reaffirms this unique relationship three times at the strategic sites of the Gospel (3:17; 16:16-17; 17:5).

3. In his discussion of the early Church history regarding the devotion to Jesus as one God and one Lord, Larry W. Hurtado, *How on Earth Did Jesus Become a God: Historical Questions about Earliest Devotion to Jesus* (Grand Rapids: Eerdmans, 2005), 46–55 considers Jesus as the principal agent of God unprecedentedly exceeding many principal agent figures appearing in the history of Israel.

revered. Particularly, in the regions of the oriental world which come under the strong influence of Confucianism, a paternal name-giving is an important part of culture and is like a form of prophecy. For them, it is imperative to give a child a name with a meaning because of their belief that the child is obligated to fully live up to the significance of the name given by his father and as a result, he will honor his parents during his lifetime and afterwards through his achievements which are already anticipated in his name. The Gospel's implied author describes God as if he was an oriental father, who gives his son a special name invested with meaning, in the expectation that his son will live his life deliberately according to the meaning of his appointed name. Hence, according to the Gospel's depiction, the name of Jesus possesses a non-negotiable teleological quality which does justice to and makes sense of his entire life journey and particularly, his death. That being said, the Gospel would have been incomplete without its Matthean passion narrative because Jesus' passion climaxed in his death on the cross is the answer to the how aspect of 1:21: "How will Jesus save his people from their sins?" In other words, the Gospel's exposition of the person, Jesus, which has to do with the inquiry of what he is, will remain only half done until it finally joins with its equal in the Matthean passion narrative where we find the answer to what he does.

The Matthean passion narrative's irony makes a distinctive contribution in revealing that Jesus, "He who will save his people from their sins" (1:21), fulfills this promise through his innocent and righteous death as the Christ Savior (20:28; 26:28). As the soteriological implication of the name Jesus prophetically foresees his life in the mode of self-sacrifice, which is ultimately expressed in his cross-bearing in the Matthean passion narrative, the lives of his disciples also come in contact with the import of their teacher's name and the weight of his cross, which functions as the prolepsis of the cross for his disciples. Correspondingly, during his ministry Jesus teaches his disciples to bear their own cross (10:37-39) and follow after him, despite the persecution and suffering-ridden path awaiting them (10:24-25). Christian church history attests to the connection between the significance of the name of Jesus and the suffering of believers. For example, in his official correspondence with the emperor Trajan, Pliny the Younger, the governor of Bithynia-Pontus (c. 61–112 CE), expresses his dilemma over whether he would punish a Christian on account of the crime adhering to the name (Jesus Christ) without any other crimes involved other than their connection with his name.[4] Also the New Testament reports the actual danger and opposition that the followers of Jesus

---

4. Pliny the Younger, *Epistulae*, 10. 96

had faced due to their devotion to the name of Jesus.[5] As these examples show, for this name, Jesus, his followers throughout the centuries have walked on the foreboding path of their own "passion," lying close to the cross of Jesus.

In the Matthean passion narrative's tension-ridden context, the silhouette of Jesus' full messianic identity is once again unveiled. For instance, the contents of the interrogations and the mockery conducted by Jesus' opponents are full of ironic twists in connection with the initial proclamation of the person of Jesus in both 1:1 and 1:21. The Gospel depicts that the religious leaders are chronically ignorant of Jesus' identity and that such a tendency is in combination with their habitual rejection and hostility toward the servants of God as the history of Israel confirms (23:34-39). Amid the apparently grim situations leading up to the death of Jesus, irony subverts all of the condemnation and derision against the person of Jesus—"Are you the Christ, the Son of God?" (26:63), "Prophecy to us, Christ, who is the one who hits you?" (26:68), "Are you the King of the Jews?" (27:11), "This is Jesus the king of the Jews" (27:37), "Come down from the cross, if you are the Son of God!" (27:40), "He saved others, but he can't save himself! He is the king of Israel!" (27:42), "He trusts in God. Let God rescue him, for he said, 'I am the Son of God' " (27:43)—into public declarations that Jesus is indeed the Christ Savior, the King of Israel and the Son of God in accordance with the Gospel's strategic manifestations of Jesus in 1:1 and 1:21. The more the opponents of Jesus try to mar his reputation in their *alazōnic* ignorance and hubris, the more intensely the irony of Jesus' name increases the tragic atmosphere surrounding his passion and, thereby, exhibits irreconcilable discrepancies in will and action between God and man that bring about the death of Jesus.

Furthermore, the Matthean passion narrative reveals the theological implications of Jesus being called as the "son of Abraham" in 1:1, especially when the Roman executioners ("the centurion and those with him," 27:54) witness Jesus' death on the cross followed by nature's phenomenological reactions to it. At this they confess Jesus as the "true Son of God" (27:50-54). First, it is important to recognize the significance of these Gentiles' confession of Jesus as the Son of God because it is God's prerogative to reveal to men the nature of his Son's relationship to himself as it is manifested in the case of Peter's confession of Jesus in 16:16-17: "Simon Peter answered, 'You are the Christ, the Son of the living God.' Jesus replied, 'Blessed are you, Simon son of Jonah, for this was not revealed to you by man, but by my Father in heaven' " (NIV). Second, considering the fact that the tradition of Abraham is deeply related

---

5. For example, Matt. 10:18, 22; Acts 26:9; 1 Tim. 6:1; 1 Pet. 4:14.

to the Abrahamic covenant which epitomizes God's intent to bless the nations through Abraham's offspring (Gen. 12:1-3), these Gentiles' truthful confession of Jesus and the way through which Jesus connects himself to them at the moment of his redemptive death promised to "his people" (1:21; 20:28; 26:28) are noteworthy. The reason why we read a link between the Roman soldiers' confession of Jesus and Jesus as the son of Abraham is because just as Abraham took a unique role in the history of mankind when he, in his representational capacity (as Israel), emerged in the book of Genesis as the divine solution to the plight of men, as also Jesus, the true Israel according to the Gospel (2:15), brings that very same vision of God to its completion. Therefore, both the Magi's worshipping presence at the time of Jesus' birth and the Roman soldiers' recognition of Jesus at the cross create a semantic ground on which the Gospel's implied author is able to build the idea that the ministry of Jesus the Christ Savior encompasses God's promise to bless the nations through the offspring of Abraham. In this sense, Jesus' own passion prediction, that his life must be given as a ransom for "many" (20:28; 26:28), strikingly resembles God's promise contained in the Abrahamic covenant that "all people on earth" (Gen. 12:3) will be blessed through the "offspring of Abraham," which is equal to the "son of Abraham" in Matthean jargon.

In summary, the Matthean passion narrative's ironic portrait of Jesus' identity squares with the declaratory statements of 1:1 and 1:21: Jesus is the Christ Savior,[6] the King of the Jews (the son of David)[7] and the Son of God.[8] He is the Lord himself in perfect communion with God the Father. His total submission to God's saving will toward mankind (18:4; 20:28; 26:28, 39), which is expressed in the Abrahamic covenant, gives justice to his own name (Jesus) and proves that he is truly the divine Savior (1:21). As the son of David, Jesus is the legitimate King of the Jews, on whom Israel has waited long in anticipation that he will bring about their restoration. This messianic King ushers in the timely blessing of God to the nations at the climax of the history of Israel as the genealogy of Jesus implicates. Jesus, however, is not an ordinary human king but the Lord himself (κύριος),[9] reclaiming his original dominion and authority over his people through the unexpected means of laying down his life

---

6. Matt. 1:1, 16-18, 21; 2:4; 11:2; 16:16, 20; 22:42; 23:10; 26:63, 68; 27:17, 22, etc.

7. Matt. 1:1; 2:2, 6; 9:27; 12:23; 15:22; 18:23; 20:30-31; 21:5, 9, 15; 22:2, 42; 25:34, 40; 26:31; 27:11, 29, 37, 42, etc.

8. Matt. 2:15; 3:17; 4:3, 6; 7:21; 8:29; 10:32-33; 11:25-27; 12:50; 14:33; 15:13; 16:16-17; 17:5; 18:10, 14, 19, 35; 20:23; 24:36; 26:29, 39, 42, 53, 63; 27:40, 43, 54; 28:19, etc.

9. Matt. 1:22; 2:15; 3:3; 4:7, 10; 7:21-22; 8:2, 6, 21, 25; 9:28; 11:25; 12:8; 14:28, 30; 15:22, 25, 27 (x2); 16:22; 17:4, 15; 18:21; 20:30-31, 33; 21:3, 9; 22:37, 43-45; 23:39; 24:42; 26:22.

for the "forgiveness of sins" of his very own people and beyond (1:21; 20:28; 26:28). The Gospel's inclusion of the sympathetic presences of the Gentiles at the critical moments of Jesus' life, birth and death, which together enclose Jesus' story with noticeable similarities, suggests that in the person of Jesus, God's saving will (that is, the divine blessing) is secured for "many" (20:28; 26:28) because Jesus, the true "Son of God," as the Roman soldiers confession reveals (27:54), is the "son of Abraham," in whom all nations will see the light of salvation and put their hope.[10]

THE SAVING WILL OF GOD: THE GOVERNING NORM OF THE MATTHEAN PASSION NARRATIVE

The "saving will of God" is the *raison d'être* and *telos* of Jesus' life and ministry as the name of the Gospel's protagonist, Jesus, exclusively reflects his Father's will to save his people (1:21). It is the Gospel's message that God is the ultimate authority and key contributor to Jesus' story since his will must prevail and thus, it gives meaning to all the elements of the story. Therefore, beyond the Matthean passion narrative the various sections of the Gospel illustrating Jesus' teachings and deeds testify that Jesus is primarily concerned with the will of God throughout his ministry and that Jesus' filial obedience to God is what makes God's will reach its *telos* (6:10; 12:50; 21:31; 26:42). In the Matthean passion narrative, Jesus foresees his death as the fulfillment of God's will expressed in the Scriptures and metaphorically characterizes it as "the cup" (τὸ ποτήριον, 26:39) which only the Son of God can "drink" (26:42, 55f). Thus, the death of Jesus on the cross is where God's saving will finally transpires in perfection and constitutes the very content of the Matthean gospel (τὸ εὐαγγέλιον, 4:23; 9:35; 24:14; 26:13, 58).

One thing that is crystal clear in the Gospel is that Jesus is the Christ Savior, the solution to the sins of the world and for this end, he gives his life as a ransom for those who are in need of it (1:21; 9:6; 20:28; 26:28). As his name Jesus etiologically suggests, the course of life that he will take should be that of an extraordinary divine redeemer. Jesus unfailingly conducts his life as the living example of the saving will of God. It is not an exaggeration to say that the meaning of the name Jesus exposed in the first chapter of the Gospel (1:21) functions as the epicenter of the entire story on which the Gospel gradually builds itself to reveal how God's saving will embodied in his Son must be achieved. Jesus' passion predictions (16:21; 17:22-23; 20:17-19; 26:1-2) provide an insight to this how aspect of the Christ-event in that there is an unavoidable

---

10. Matt. 4:15-17; 12:18-21; 21:43; 24:14; 25:32; 28:19; Gen. 12:1-3; 17:1-18; 22:15-18.

correlation between the accomplishment of God's saving will and Jesus' death. In the Matthean passion narrative, the final and explicit answer to this inquiry comes through Jesus' own statements. He states that God's will is accomplished through his accepting of the assigned "cup" (26:39, 42, 55-56) to the point of the shedding of his innocent blood (26:28).

Jesus' disciples are dismayed at Jesus' passion predictions (16:21-23; 17:23) and fail to perceive its cause and effect till the end. This shows that comprehending the Jesus event and the implications of his passion culminating in his death requires more than what human reason can grant. Irony naturally thrives in the Matthean passion narrative's depiction of and emphasis on the death of Jesus primarily because there arises an immense incompatibility between who Jesus is and the cross which he bears. The Christ Savior, the King of the Jews, and, most of all, the Son of God dies on the cross, which is known as the punishment of the most slavish humiliation (*supplicium servile*),[11] under the mantle of a man of shame (*humiliores*). Also, according to the Jewish concept, the cross is a place for "the cursed" (Deut. 21:22-23). It is, therefore, the most unlikely place for divine activity.[12] Thus, the person of Jesus to whom

---

11. It is meaningful to interpret Jesus slavish death on the cross in relation to the Pauline theology in Phil. 2:6-11, especially verses 6-8 that "who, though he was in the form of God, did not count equality with God a thing to be grasped, but emptied himself, taking the form of a servant, being born in the likeness of men. And being found in human form he humbled himself and became obedient unto death, even death on a cross" (RSV). For ancient historians' comments on the cross as a punishment see Livy, *Ab Urbe Condita*, I.26.6; Seneca, *Epistola*, 101; Cicero, *Contra Verres*, 5.169; Valerius Maximus, *Historia Augusta* 2.7.12; Tacitus, *Histories* 2.72, 4.11; Columella, *De re rustica* 1.7.2. Further, the following scholars discuss the perception of crucifixion with regard to ancient people and the death of Jesus on the cross in particular: John T. Carroll and Joel B. Green, *The Death of Jesus in Early Christianity* (Peabody: Hendrickson Publishers: 1995); Ellis Rivkin, *What Crucified Jesus? The Political Execution of A Charismatic* (Nashville: SCM, 1984); Joseph A. Fitzmyer, *To Advance the Gospel: New Testament Essays* (New York: Crossroad, 1981), 125–46; R. Larry Overstreet, "Roman Law and the Trial of Jesus," *BSac* 135 (1978): 323–32; David Flusser, "The Crucified One and the Jews," *Imm* 7 (1977): 25–37; Martin Hengel, *Crucifixion in the Ancient World and the Folly of the Message of the Cross*, trans. John Bowden (Philadelphia: Fortress Press, 1977).

12. Heino O. Kadai, "Luther's Theology of the Cross" in *Accents in Luther's Theology: Essays in Commemoration of the 450th Anniversary of the Reformation*, ed. Heino O. Kadai (St. Louis: Concordia), 232–33, gives a helpful background information regarding the cross and crucifixion as a hateful punishment that "crucifixion as such does not appear in early Christian art. Probably the earliest (2d century) remaining pictorial presentation of the crucifixion of Christ was drawn during the second century by hostile hands. On the wall of the Domus Gelotiana in Rome, a building used as a school for imperial pages, one sees a drawing of a crucified ass with the Greek inscription 'Alexamenos (adores) God.' Not until the fourth century did Christians begin to represent in art form the narrative of the death of Christ. Why did the Passion narrative appear so relatively late in Christian art? Several reasons come to

the Gospel testifies with such profundity contrasts irreconcilably with the place where he is found as a dejected man.

Adopting God's saving will as the norm for the life of Jesus, the Christ Savior (1:21; 20:28; 26:28), is essential for the interpretation of the Matthean passion narrative's irony working in the circumstances leading up to the death of Jesus. It is irony which makes it possible to see, despite its tragic appearance, that Jesus' death on the cross is God's own design through which God attains his saving will and therefore, it has salutary impact on those who believe in it. Jesus' words shared with his disciples during his last meal with them nail down the fact that there is no other way to achieve God's will to free his people from their sins except the establishment of "the blood of the covenant" (26:28) through his innocent suffering and death (27:4, 19, 24).

Considering the fact that the Christian faith cannot be understood without the proclamation of Jesus the crucified, the exposé of the Matthean passion narrative's irony on the death of Jesus and its meaning sheds light on two aspect of the nature of Christianity. First, man's predicament living under the grip of sin in separation from God, to which the Christian Scriptures attest in unison, is the motivation behind God's will to save. Second, God's way is different from ours, which is best exemplified in the cross of Jesus. God saves his people from their sins through an unexpected means, the death of his own Son, Jesus, whom he loves and in whom he delights (3:17; 16:16; 17:5). The entire Jewish history, which the Matthean genealogy of Jesus symbolizes, testifies to God's saving actions for the sake of his people and the nations. What God has done through the death of his own Son, Jesus, is unprecedented since it is the realization of the divine righteousness in totality (3:15) and the sum of the Scriptures (26:54). As a tenacious disease requires a tough medicine to eradicate, the irony operating in the Matthean passion narrative reveals that the death of Jesus is the expression of God's love for his people and this engenders an inviolable remedy for man's freedom from the perilous disease, sin. In other words, the scandal of human sin requires the scandal of the cross where we find the saving God in the image of a dejected, yet innocent, Jesus. In this way, irony lies at the heart of the Christian faith. Despite the fact that irony is inherent to the nature of the cross which is not only incompatible with, but also repellent to the profoundly majestic figure of Jesus Christ, the Christian tradition sustains its vitality through a reliance

mind. Perhaps there is some truth to the conjecture that since the cross remained a sign of foolishness and a stumbling block to the Graeco-Roman world, believers found it more advantageous to stress the resurrection of their Lord rather than draw attention to His ignominious death...The lowly, suffering Jesus of the Passion story simply did not fit into the scheme of patristic Christology. The Greek fathers were more impressed by the doctrine of the Incarnation than the Vicarious Atonement."

on the saving effect of the death of Jesus (20:28; 26:28) and proclaims it as the gospel for the world (τὸ εὐαγγέλιον, 26:13).

God's Universal Salvation

In the Matthean passion narrative, the Jewish people's crying out for the crucifixion of Jesus followed by their voluntary undertaking of the responsibility for the blood of Jesus (27:24-25) yields a salient message which can only be perceived through the lens of irony. As we have examined earlier in the section dealing with the irony of the people's rejection of Jesus, the Gospel's implied author-ironist strategically uses the terms ὁ λαός and ὁ ὄχλος in order to indicate the historic Jews by the former and unidentifiable mass of people by the latter. The fact that the author always employs ὁ λαός in association with the Jewish religious authorities provides the strongest evidence for the author's particular use of ὁ λαός as an indicator of the historic Jews. At the climactic moment of the Matthean passion narrative, where the fate of Jesus seems to be in the hands of the people despite the fact that God is in fact control of Jesus' passion, the implied author-ironist of the Matthean passion narrative discloses the same identity between those who Jesus initially came to save (ὁ λαός, 1:21) and those who demand the blood of Jesus to be shed for themselves and future generation (πᾶς ὁ λαός, 27:25) by building upon the *inclusio* of ὁ λαός between chapter 2 and chapter 27.

Among the Gospel's various declarations of Jesus' identity, the exposition of the meaning of the name Jesus is especially critical since this name intrinsically signifies the indissoluble relationship between Jesus and his people. Since Jesus has come to save his people from their sins (ὁ λαός, 1:21), the restoration of the Jews back to their Christ Savior is already foreseen regardless of their willful rejection and murderous intent. Any type of surface reading is self-limited, especially when the real story is meant to be found between the lines. Such is the case with the Gospel's story of Jesus which is governed by the norms and ideas of God. An inexperienced reading of the Matthean passion narrative, particularly the incident reporting the Jewish people's active involvement in bringing about the death of Jesus, has unfortunately caused some anti-Jewish sentiments and polemics in past biblical scholarship. Nevertheless, the narrative-critical reading of the Matthean passion narrative through the lens of irony enables its intended reader to see that Jesus as the Christ Savior of his people who are on the edge of spiritual nadir.

The Matthean passion narrative's information about the nature of the blood of Jesus is fundamentally important to unlocking the irony involved in the people's simultaneous rejection and reception of Jesus. The innocence of Jesus is unequivocally testified to by Judas, the very betrayer of Jesus (27:4), and Pilate, the Roman governor of Judea, in whose hands Jesus is delivered to be convicted (27:17-19, 24). It is striking that these men both address the blood of Jesus, that is, the life of Jesus in a metaphorical sense, and confirm its innocent quality. That being said, it is important to recognize that the Gospel's implied author presents a correlation between the innocent blood and its salvific effect by reporting Jesus' criticism of the religious leaders. Jesus plainly states that throughout their history, the Jewish people have shed the innocent blood of those who were sent to them by God in order to "gather his people like a hen gathers her chicks" (23:37). It is the intent of the implied author-ironist of the Matthean passion narrative to characterize the innocent blood of Jesus as an end to the cycle of shedding of the innocent blood (23:35-39) with regard to both its significance and effect as Jesus' identity surpasses all the previous divine delegates advancing God's salvation history.

It is precisely the function of irony to make the Matthean passion narrative's implied reader see through the tragic veneer of the people's demand for the innocent blood of Jesus for the sake of destruction (27:24-25) and to realize that it is not where the story of Jesus finds its dénouement. Instead, irony brings the reader to a vantage point where he can finally identify the people's rejection of Jesus with the operation of God to save his people from their sins. As the chief rhetorical device of the Gospel's implied author-ironist, irony does conceal but also disclose. In the most unexpected way, the Matthean passion narrative's irony lifts away the cloud hovering over the answer to the question about how God claims back his people lost in sin through his Son, Jesus. The answer is hidden in the collective cry of the people which seeks the destruction of the life of Jesus: "Let his blood be on us and on our children!" (27:25). In this they claim the ownership over the blood of Jesus and unintentionally subject themselves and their future generations to the saving effect of the innocent blood of Jesus. One more thing worth mentioning here is that the descriptive language of the people brings to mind an image of the people being washed head to toe by the blood of Jesus as it reads, "Let his blood be *on* us and *on* our children!" (27:25, italics mine).

The Matthean passion narrative's irony shows that the innocent blood of Jesus that forgives the sins of the people (1:21; 20:28; 26:28) universally affects both the Jews and the Gentiles. First, God's salvation, which Jesus' innocent blood effectuates, embraces both the contemporary Jews of Jesus and all of their future generations as shown by the irony embedded in the people's cry which brings a reversal to their relationship to Jesus. This interpretation, that God's salvation is first and foremost granted to the Jews in spite of their rejection and abuse of Jesus, is in harmony with the Matthean emphases on the Jewish origin of Jesus the Christ Savior and Jesus' reverence for God's covenantal relationship to the nation of Israel, which is strongly expressed in Jesus' will to fulfill the law. Second, God's salvation achieved through the innocent blood of Jesus is also for the nations beyond the Jewish people despite the fact that Jesus comes as the Jewish Messiah (1:1)[13] and eventually dies under the charge of being the King of the Jews (27:37). Considering the fact that the Gospel's implied author-ironist subtly extends the scope of the people of God (1:21) by revealing the worshipping and receptive Gentiles at Jesus' birth and death while the historic people of God, the Jews, display attitudes quite the opposite. As the Magi rightly recognize the significance of the person of Jesus and render worship appropriate to his identity (2:1f, 11), the Roman Centurion and his soldiers confess Jesus' sonship to God ("truly, this was the Son of God," 27:54). According to the Gospel, the knowledge of Jesus' divine sonship is achieved by man's reasoning but by God's revelation as Peter's confession exemplifies it (16:16f). Therefore, the confession of the Roman soldiers reveals that God endows men, both the Jews and the Gentiles, with the gift of knowing Jesus the Christ Savior.

Further, the Gospel's testimony of Jesus as the "son of Abraham" theologically ties into the theme of Jesus and his universal salvation in that God's true Son, Jesus (3:17; 17:5), perfects the Abrahamic covenant in which God's perpetual intent to bless the nations is revealed.[14] As Jesus' entire ministry attests to his universal compassion and care for both the Jews and the Gentiles, it is truly God's intent to save "many" (that is, all, 20:28; 26:28) through his Son's innocent blood.

DEUS TRIUMPHUS VS. *SATAN VICTUS*: THE OUTCOME OF THE CHRIST-EVENT

The death of Jesus on the cross manifests God's ultimate victory over Satan. Satan (that is, the devil, ὁ διάβολος, 4:1) appears early in the Gospel at the scene of Jesus' transfiguration and continues his presence through his accomplices, the Jewish religious leaders, who collectively exhibit monochromatic evilness. The Messianic harbinger, John the Baptist, identifies them as the "brood of vipers" (3:7) and so Jesus, faced with their animosity, characterizes them in

---

13. For the Matthean references regarding Jesus the son of David (i.e. Jesus the King of the Jews), see 1:1; 2:2, 6; 9:27; 12:23; 15:22; 18:23; 20:30-31; 21:5, 9, 15; 22:2, 42; 25:34, 40; 26:31; 27:11, 29, 37, 42; for Jesus' Kingship over the Jews, see 1:1; 2:6; 16:28; 21:5; 22:7, 11, 13; 27:11, 29. 37; for Jesus the Christ (Messiah), Savior, see 1:1, 16-18, 21; 2:4; 11:2; 16:16, 20; 22:42; 23:10; 26:63, 68; 27:17, 22.

14. For the Old Testament references regarding the Abrahamic Covenant, see Gen. 12:1-3; 15:18-21; 17:1-9; 22:16-18.

the same way (12:34; 23:33). It is the intent of the Gospel's implied author-ironist to make the voices of God and Satan heard, both directly and indirectly, throughout the story of Jesus. The voices of these parties, God and Satan, can be understood in a metaphorical sense referring to their perspectives or outlooks on things. The respective voices of God and Satan grow intensively entwined with the progress of the story as it moves toward its finale.

Where Jesus' story seems to go in a fast and furious downward spiral in the Matthean passion narrative, we detect an irony hidden in the most unbecoming site of all time, that is, the cross of Jesus. The irreconcilable discrepancy between the identity of Jesus and the punishment on the cross which he bears marks his cross as the site of irony, revealing more than what it seems. Although the cross is meant to be seen as the *locus* of irrecoverable humiliation and devastating defeat, according to the Matthean passion narrative's irony, it is where the cosmic conflict between God and Satan finds its resolution in the exposure of an overpowered Satan and his impotence to vie against God.

God overturns the ordinary idea of victory and gives it a new definition through the case of the ostensible powerlessness of the crucified Jesus. Needless to say, God's ways are different from ours, as St. Paul expresses in 1 Cor. 1:27-29: "God chose the foolish things of the world to shame the wise; God chose the weak things of the world to shame the strong. He chose the lowly things of this world and the despised things, and the things that are not, to nullify the things that are, so that no one may boast before him." In this simple truth, we comprehend God as the archetypal ironist which the biblical tradition confirms.[15] Although God is invisible in the backdrop of the Gospel, his ironic stance on the circumstances of the Jesus event is adopted and expressed by the divine ironist, the implied author of the Gospel and the Matthean passion narrative.

According to the Gospel's presentation, God is the most intimate and dependable witness of Jesus. Who could be more reliable than the Father who takes a stand as a character witness of his Son in whom he is well pleased (3:17; 17:5)? By letting God's testimonies of his Son reoccur, the Gospel's implied author suggests that God's viewpoint of and intent towards his Son are the norms for the story of Jesus. In other words, understanding the *sui generis* relationship of God to Jesus and their common will, which the meaning of the name of Jesus indicates (1:21), are the interpretive keys for the proper appropriation of the meaning of the death of Jesus. God is the ultimate authority

---

15. According to the biblical tradition, God is the ultimate source of irony. His higher view of things always triumphs over the ideas and the ways of humans. The Psalmist correctly perceives the ironic nature of God and describes God as the universal victor: "He who sits in heaven will laugh" (Ps. 2:4).

over the salvation history for mankind to which the Scriptures attest. The Gospel is clear that God's saving will continues in his Son (3:17; 16:16; 17:5) and therefore, the entire ministry of Jesus the Christ Savior depends on it. Jesus satisfies every facets of the divine saving will, most radically through his selfless and innocent death. This is proven by Jesus' absolute control over the incidents leading up to his passion, which move according to his specific time table (ὁ καιρός μου, 26:18), and his prayer in Gethsemane honoring his "Father's will" for him to drink the "cup" (26:42).

The Gospel's story of Jesus can be summed up as the restoration of God's relationship with his people estranged from him due to their sins. The author describes it in various ways such as that Jesus came "to save his people from their sins" (1:21), "to gather his lost sheep like a shepherd" (2:6; 9:36; 25:32; 26:31), "to heal the sick" (9:12; 12:15; 14:14, 35-36; cf. 8:16; 10:8), "to give his life as a ransom for "many" (20:28) and "to offer the forgiveness of sins to many" (26:28). However, the characters within the story show a mixture of reactions to Jesus, widely ranging from being pliant and sympathetic to being nonchalant and hostile. Naturally, the characters on the opposite poles create a tension which must be smoothed out. The implied author-ironist of the Matthean passion narrative works well with the tension that arises between these conflicting characters since their irreconcilable conflict in ideas and values nurtures irony and intensifies its rhetorical function. Speaking of the tension that the characters generate due to their differences, God and Satan function as indispensible characters within the story world of Matthew. We observed that their voices are present in the Gospel through the voices of their associates and correspondingly, their associates respectively exhibit a distinctive pattern of thought and action in dealing with the Gospel's protagonist, Jesus.

Among the characters within the Gospel, Jesus alone fully represents God's voice as Jesus is the embodiment of God himself in flesh. Jesus plays the role of the normative, protagonistic, and paradigmatic εἴρων. He willingly takes a position of lowliness in spite of his profound identity and God-like authority in order to accomplish his Father's will to free the people from their sins. In contrast, the Jewish religious authorities, sitting in Moses' seat (23:2), comprise a collective unit taking the role of the unlawful, antagonistic, and blameworthy ἀλαζών (the Matthean passion narrative's equivalent, πλάνος, deceiver, in 27:63) and behave as unified opponents of Jesus. The Gospel's implied author-ironist underpins the fact that they are the flat character as a group, holding the single and common trait of "evilness" (9:4; 12:34, 39, 45; 16:4; 22:18). According to the Gospel's forthright characterization, their evilness originates from their association with "the evil one," Satan (13:19, 38). Thus, they are identified as "the brood of vipers" (3:7; 12:34; 23:33) and "child of hell" (23:15) in a drastic contrast to the identity of Jesus, the Son of God who is blameless in God's eyes. The Matthean passion narrative presents the collision beyond repair between Jesus, the εἴρων and the Jewish religious leaders, the ἀλαζών, which their history of agonizing conflict has been predicting along the way. Despite the fact that it seems that Jesus is passively subjugated to ignomity and utter rejection, irony, the mechanism of reversal, reveals that the exact opposite of what it seems to be on the surface is really happening.

The holistic reading of the Gospel unveils that Satan and his associates, the religious leaders, are comically pursuing the opposite end in dealing with Jesus and therefore points out that there is a crack in their bond. We learn through both Jesus' temptation by Satan in the wilderness (4:8-10) and Peter's rebuke of Jesus as a reaction to Jesus' passion prediction (16:21-23) that Satan attempts to make Jesus diverge from his Messianic path, which is equally the path to the cross, by instilling disobedience and doubt in the mind of Jesus. However, what actually transpires in the Matthean passion narrative is that the religious leaders ultimately bring about what their head (3:7; 12:34; 23:15, 33) actually strives to halt from happening. The irony of Jesus' death on the cross, therefore, causes the reversal of the status of the characters in that the seeming victim of violence, the εἴρων, turns out to be the ultimate victor through his total submission to the saving will of God, and contrastingly, the collective ἀλαζών become the victim of their own schism because of their unjust envy (φθόνος, 27:18), deception (δόλος, 26:4; πλάνη, 27:64), blind self-confidence and blasphemous ignorance (9:3; 12:24; 26:65 cf. 27:39). The Matthean passion narrative's irony surrounding Jesus' death shows a rupture within the entity forming hostility against God and his Son. In this regard, it is worth noting that Jesus' comment on the religious leaders' accusation concerning the exorcism he performs in chapter 12 functions like a prediction of the defeat of Satan and his accomplices: "Every kingdom divided against itself will be ruined, and every city or household divided against itself will not stand. If Satan drives out Satan, he is divided against himself. How then can his kingdom stand?" (NIV, 12:25-26).

The death of Jesus is where the divine perspective and the Satanic perspective clash and this clash does not mean the clash of equal powers but the defeat of the latter. The cosmic checkmate that Jesus proleptically announces through his triumph over the temptation by Satan in the wilderness (4:1-11) reemerges in the Matthean passion narrative. This is seen in the image of Satan stuck in a precipitous dilemma, neither moving forwards nor backwards while his associates make a wrong turn, by unwittingly eschewing the aspiration of their head to hinder the divine will. Therefore, on the plane of the Matthean passion narrative's irony, the ἀλαζών is by no means on par with the εἴρων, except in the sense that it constitutes diametrically contrasting qualities to the εἴρων. In essence, the death of Jesus the Son of God seen through the lens of irony imports the theology of *Deus Triumphus* (God the Victorious) because God's saving will has been climactically achieved through the offence of the cross which Jesus bore to the point of death. Consequently, the death of Jesus on the cross in its utmost disgrace and desertion yields a permanent change on the theological landscape of the Christian faith like an unprecedented earthquake. Just as we are advised not to judge the content of a book by its cover, all is not as it might first seem in the Matthean passion narrative. Through the irony of the repulsive and tragic appearance of the death of Jesus on the cross, Satan is exposed as defeated (*Satan victus*) in his impotence while God's unassailable victory (*Deus triumphus*) over sin is manifested.

Bibliography

Abrams, Meyer H. *A Glossary of Literary Terms.* 4th ed. New York: Holt, Rinehart & Winston, 1991.

Alter, Robert. *The Art of Biblical Narrative.* New York: Basic Books, 1981.

Amante, David J. "The Theory of Ironic Speech Acts." *Poetics Today* 2 (1981): 77–96.

Anderson, Janice C. *Matthew's Narrative Web: Over, and Over, and Over Again.* JSNTSup 91. Sheffield: JSOT, 1994.

Applebee, Arthur N., Andrea B. Bermudez, Sheridan Blau, Rebekah Caplan, Peter Elbow, Susan Hynds, Judith A. Langer, and James Marshall. *Literature and Language: English and World Literature.* Evanston: McDougal, Little & Co., 1992

Apuleius. *Metamorphoses.* Edited and translated by J. Arthur Hanson. Cambridge: Harvard University Press, 1989.

Aristophanes. *Clouds.* Edited by Lewis L. Forman. New York: American Book Company, 1915.

Aristotle. *The Art of Rhetoric.* Translated by H. C. Lawson-Tancred. Harmondsworth: Penguin, 1991.

———. *The Nicomachean Ethics.* Edited by T. E. Page. Translated by H. Rackham. Cambridge: Harvard University Press, 1934.

Auden, Wystan H. "The Ironic Hero." *Horizon* 20 (1949): 86–94.

Austin, John L. *How to Do Things with Words.* 2d ed. Oxford: Oxford University Press, 1975.

Austin-Smith, B. "Into the Heart of Irony." *Canadian Dimension* 27 (1990): 51–52.

Bacon, B. W. "The Five Books of Matthew against the Jews." *The Expositor* 15 (1918): 56–66.

Ball, David. "La Définition Ironique." *Revue de Littérature Comparée* 199 (1976):213–36.

Bammel, Ernst. "Peter's Curse." in *The Trial of Jesus. Cambridge Studies in honour of C. F. D. Moule.* Studies in Biblical Theology 13. London: SCM, 1970, 66–71.

——— "The Trial before Pilate." in *Jesus and the Politics of His Day.* Edited by E. Bammel and C. F. D. Moule. Cambridge University Press, 1984, 403–12.

Bar-Efrat, Shimon. *The Art of the Biblical Story*. Tel Aviv: Sifriat Hapoalim, 1979.

Bauer, David R. *The Structure of Matthew Gospel: A Study in Literary Design*. Sheffield: Almond, 1988.

———. "The Major Characters of Matthew's Story: Their Function and Significance." *Interpretation* 46 (1992): 357–67.

Bauer, Walter. *A Greek–English Lexicon of the New Testament and Other Early Christian Literature*. 2d ed. Revised and augmented by William F. Arndt, F. Wilbur Gingrich, and Frederick W. Danker. Chicago: University of Chicago Press, 1979.

Beare, Francis W. *The Gospel according to Matthew*. Oxford: Blackwell, 1981.

Beardslee, William A. *Literary Criticism of the New Testament*. Philadelphia: Westminster, 1970.

Benson, Hugh H., ed. *Essays on the Philosophy of Socrates*. New York: Oxford University Press, 1992.

Bergson, Leif. "Eiron und eironeia." *Hermes* 99 (1971): 409–22.

Berlin, Adele. *Poetics and Interpretation of Biblical Narrative*. Bible and Literature Series 9. Sheffield: Almond, 1983.

Bilezekian, Gilbert. *The Liberated Gospel: A Comparison of the Gospel of Mark and Greek Tragedy*. Grand Rapids: Baker, 1977.

Black, M. C. "The Rejected and Slain Messiah Who Is Coming with the Angels: The Messianic Exegesis of Zechariah 9–14 in the Passion Narratives." Ph D. dissertation, Emory University, 1990.

Blair, E. P. *Jesus in the Gospel of Matthew*. Nashville: Abingdon, 1960.

Boonstra, Harry. "Satire in Matthew." *Christianity and Literature* 29 (1980): 32–45.

Booth, Wayne C. *The Rhetoric of Fiction*. Chicago: University of Chicago Press, 1961.

———. *A Rhetoric of Irony*. Chicago: University of Chicago Press, 1974.

———. "The Pleasures and Pitfalls of Irony: or, Why Don't You Say What You Mean?" in *Rhetoric, Philosophy and Literature: An Exploration*. Edited by Don M. Burks. West Lafayette, Ind.: Purdue University Press, 1978, 1–47.

———. "The Empire of Irony." *Georgia Review* 37 (1983): 719–37.

Bornkamm, Günther, Gerhard Barth and H. J. Held. *Tradition and Interpretation in Matthew*. 2d ed. Philadelphia: Westminster Press, 1971.

Bowker, M. J. "The Offence and Trial of Jesus." in *Jesus and the Pharisees*. Cambridge University Press, 1973, 42–52.

Bowman, John W. "The Significance of Mt 27:25." *Milla wa-Milla* 14 (1974): 26–31.

Brandwood, Leonard. *A Word Index to Plato.* Leeds: W. S. Maney and Son, 1976.

Brewer, Cobham E. *The Reader's Handbook of Allusions, References, Plots and Stories.* Philadelphia: J. B. Lippincott Company, 1889.

Brooks, Cleanth, "Irony and 'Ironic' Poetry." *College English* 9 (1948): 231–37.

———. "Irony as a Principle of Structure." in *Critical Theory Since Plato.* Edited by Hazard Adams and Leroy Searle. 3rd ed. Boston: Heinle, 2004, 968–74.

Brooks, Peter. *Reading for the Plot: Design and Intention in Narrative.* New York: Alfred A. Knopf, 1984.

Brown, R. E. *The Birth of the Messiah: A Commentary on the Infancy Narrative in Matthew and Luke.* New York: Doubleday, 1977.

———. *The Death of the Messiah: From Gethsemane to the Grave: A Commentary on the Passion Narratives.* Anchor Bible Reference Library. 2 vols. New York: Doubleday, 1994.

Brueggemann, Walter. *Solomon: Israel's Ironic Icon of Human Achievement.* Columbia: University of South Carolina Press, 2005.

Büchner, Wilhelm. "Über den Begriff der Eironeia." *Hermes* 76 (1941): 339–58.

Buck, Erwin. "Anti-Judaic Sentiments in the Passion Narrative According to Matthew." in *Paul and the Gospels.* Edited by Peter Richardson and David Granskou. Vol. 1 of *Anti-Judaism in Early Christianity.* Edited by Peter Richardson and David Granskou. Waterloo: Wilfrid Laurier University Press, 1986, 165–80.

Burke, Kenneth. *Language as Symbolic Action.* Berkeley: University of California Press, 1968.

———. *A Grammar of Motives.* Repr., Berkeley: University of California Press, 1969.

Burnett, F. W. "Characterization and Reader Construction of Characters in the Gospels." *Semeia* 63 (1993): 3–28.

Cargal, Timothy B. "'His Blood Be upon Us and upon Our Children': A Matthean Double Entendre?" *New Testament Studies* 37 (1991): 101–12.

Carroll, John T., and Joel B. Green, *The Death of Jesus in Early Christianity.* Peabody: Hendrickson, 1995.

Carson, D. A. "The Jewish Leaders in Matthew's Gospel: A Reappraisal." *Journal of the Evangelical Theological Society* 25 (1982): 161–74.

———. *Matthew.* The Expositor's Bible Commentary 8. Grand Rapids: Zondervan, 1984.

Carter, Warren. "Kernels and Narrative Blocks: The Structure of Matthew's Gospel." *Catholic Biblical Quarterly* 54 (1992): 463–81.

———. "The Crowds in Matthew's Gospel." *Catholic Biblical Quarterly* 55 (1993): 54–67.

———. *Matthew: Storyteller, Interpreter, Evangelist.* Peabody: Hendrickson, 1996.

———. *Matthew and Empire: Initial Explorations.* Harrisburg: Trinity Press International, 2001.

Catchpole, David R. "The Answer of Jesus to Caiphas (MATT. XXVI. 64)." *New Testament Studies* 17 (1970/71): 213–26.

Chatman, Seymour. *Story and Discourse: Narrative Structure in Fiction and Film.* Ithaca: Cornell University Press, 1978.

Chevalier, Haakon. *The Ironic Temper: Anatole France and His Time.* New York: Oxford University Press, 1932.

Cicero. *De Oratore.* Edited by T. E. Page. Translated by E. W. Sutton. Cambridge: Harvard University Press, 1942.

Clark, Herbert H., and Richard J. Gerrig. "On the Pretense Theory of Irony." *Journal of Experimental Psychology: General* 113 (1984): 121–26.

Clavier, Henri. "La méthode ironique dans l'enseignment de Jésus." *Etudes Théologiques et Religieuses,* 5 (1930): 87–100.

Clay, Diskin. *Platonic Questions: Dialogues with the Silent Philosopher.* University Park: Pennsylvania State University Press, 2000.

Clines, D. J. A., D. M. Gunn and A. J. Hauser, eds. *Art and Meaning: Rhetoric in Biblical Literature.* JSOTSup 19. Sheffield: JSOT, 1982.

Cohn, Haim. "Reflection on the Trial of Jesus." *Judaism* 20 (1971): 10–23.

Combrink, Bernard H. J. "The Structure of the Gospel of Matthew as Narrative." *Tyndale Bulletin* 34 (1983): 61–90.

Conzelmann, Hans. "History and Theology in the Passion Narratives of the Synoptic Gospels," *Interpretation* 24 (1970): 178–97.

Cousland, J. R. C. *The Crowds in the Gospel of Matthew.* NovTSup. Leiden: Brill, 2002.

Crossan, Dominic M. "Anti-Semitism and the Gospel." *Theological Studies* 26 (1965): 189–214.

Crossan, John D. *The Cross that Spoke. The Origins of the Passion Narrative.* San Francisco: Harper and Row, 1988.

Crossan, R. D. "Matthew 26:47–56: Jesus Arrested." in *Tradition as Openness to the Future.* Edited by F. O. Francis and R. P. Wallace. Lanham: University Press of America, 1984, 175–90.

Culpepper, R. Alan. *Anatomy of the Fourth Gospel: A Study in Literary Design.* Philadelphia: Fortress Press, 1983.

Dahl, Nils A. "Messianic Ideas and the Crucifixion of Jesus." (Revised by Donald H. Juel) in *The Messiah: Development in Earliest Judaism and Christianity.* Edited by James H. Charlesworth. Minneapolis: Fortress Press, 1992. 382–403.

Daube, David. "The Anointing at Bethany and Jesus Burial," *Anglican Theological Review* 32 (1950): 186–99

Dane, Joseph A. *The Critical Mythology of Irony.* Athens: University of Georgia Press, 1991.

———. "The Defense of the Incompetent Reader." *Comparative Literature* 38 (1986): 53–72.

Davies, A. T. "The Jews and the Death of Jesus." *Interpretation* 23 (1969): 207–17.

Davies, W. D., and Dale C. Allison. *The Gospel According to Saint Matthew.* 2 vols. Edinburgh: T. & T. Clark, 1991.

———. *A Critical and Exegetical Commentary on the Gospel according to Saint Matthew.* Vol. 3 of *International Critical Commentary.* Edinburgh: T. & T. Clark, 1997.

Dawsey, J. M. *Lukan Voice: Confusion and Irony in the Gospel of Luke.* Macon: Mercer University Press, 1986.

Derrett, J. D. M. "'Have nothing to do with that just man!' (Matt 27, 19). Haggadah and the Account of the Passion." *Downside Review* 97 (1979): 308–15.

Duke, Paul D. *Irony in the Fourth Gospel.* Atlanta: John Knox, 1985.

Duncan, Derrett J. "Jesus as a Seducer (ΠΛΑΝΟΣ=ΜΑΤ'ΕΗ)." *Bijdragen* 55 (1994): 43–55.

Edwards, J. R. "The Use of Προσέρχομαι in the Gospel of Matthew." *Journal of Biblical Literature* 106 (1987): 65–74.

Edwards, Richard A. *Matthew's Story of Jesus.* Philadelphia: Fortress Press, 1985.

Eliade, Mercea. *The Sacred and the Profane: The Nature of Religion.* New York: Harcourt, Brace, 1959.

Ellestrőm, Lars. *Divine Madness: Interpreting Literature, Music and Visual Arts Ironically.* Lewisburg: Bucknell University Press, 2002.

Ellis, P. F. *Matthew: His Mind and His Message.* Collegeville: Liturgical, 1974.

Enck, John J., and Elizabeth T. Foster, eds. *The Comic in Theory and Practice.* New York: Appleton-Century-Crofts, 1960.

Erasmus, *Desiderii Erasmi Roterodami Opera Omnia*. 10 vols. Edited by Joannes Clericus; Leiden: Petri van. Der Aa, 1703–1706. Repr., Hildesheim: Georg Olms, 1961.

Euripides. *The Bacchanals*. Translated by Arthur S. Way. 4 vols. Loeb Classical Library. Cambridge: Harvard University Press, 1929.

Filson, Floyd F. *The Gospel according to St. Matthew*. HNTC. New York: Harper, 1960.

Finlay, M. "Perspectives of Irony and Irony of Perspectives: A Review." *Canadian Journal of Research in Semiotics* 5 (1978): 31–50.

Fitzmyer, Joseph A. "Anti-Semitism and the Cry of 'All the People' (Mt 27:25)." *Theological Studies* 26 (1965): 667–71.

Flusser, David. "A Literary Approach to the Trial of Jesus." *Judaism* 20 (1971): 32–36.

Forster, Edward M. *Aspects of the Novel*. New York: Harcourt, 1927.

Fowler, Henry W. *A Dictionary of Modern English Usage*. New York: Oxford University Press, 1959.

France, Richard T. *Matthew: Evangelist and Teacher*. New Testament Profiles. Downers Grove: Inter-Varsity, 1998.

———. *"Jesus and the Old Testament: His Application of Old Testament Passages to Himself and His Mission*. Vancouver: Regent College Publishing, 2000.

———. *The Gospel of Matthew*. NIBCNT. Grand Rapids: Eerdmans Publishing Company, 2007.

Frankemölle, Hubert. "27, 25: *pas ho laos*." in *Jahwebund und Kirche Christi: Studien zur Form und Traditionsgeschichte des 'Evangeliums' nach Mattäus*. Neutestamentliche Abhandlungen, 10. 2d ed. Münster: Aschendorff, 1984, 2–20.

Frei, Hans W. *The Eclipse of Biblical Narrative. A Study in Eighteenth and Nineteenth Century Hermeneutics*. New Haven: Yale University Press, 1974.

Frye, Northrop. *Anatomy of Criticism*. New Jersey: Princeton University Press, 1957.

———. *The Great Code: The Bible and Literature*. New York: Harcourt, 1982.

Funk, Robert W. *The Poetics of Biblical Narrative*. Sonoma: Polebridge,1988.

Gaston, Lloyd. "The Messiah of Israel as Teacher of the Gentiles: the Setting of Matthew's Christology." *Interpretation* 29 (1975): 24–40.

Gerhardsson, Birger. "Jésus livré et abandonné d'après la Passion selon saint Mattieu." *Revue Bbilique* 76 (1969): 206–27.

———. "Sacrificial Service and Atonement in the Gospel of Matthew." in *Reconciliation and Hope: New Testament Essays on Atonement and Eschatology*

Presented to L . L. Morris. Edited by R. J. Banks. Exeter: Paternoster, 1974, 25–35.

———. *The Mighty Acts of Jesus according to Matthew.* Translated by Robert Dewsnap. Lund: GWK Gleerup, 1979.

———. "Confession and Denial before Men: Observations on Matt 26:57–27:2." *Journal for the Study of the New Testament* 13 (1981): 46–66.

Gibbs, Jeffrey A. *Matthew 1:11–11:1.* St. Louis: Concordia Publishing House, 2006.

Gill, Jerry H. "Jesus, Irony and the New Quest." *Encounter* 41 (1980): 139–51.

Good, Edwin M. *Irony in the Old Testament.* Philadelphia: The Westminster, 1965.

Goulder, M. D. *Midrash and Lection in Matthew.* London: SPCK, 1974.

Gouch, P. W. "Socratic Irony and Aristotle's *eiron*: Some Puzzles." *Phoenix* 41 (1987): 95–104.

Grayston, Kenneth. *Dying, We Live: A New Enquiry into the Death of Jesus in the New Testament.* New York: Oxford University Press, 1990.

Green, Joel B. "Death of Jesus." in *Dictionary of Jesus and the Gospels.* Edited by Joel B. Green and Scot McKnight. Downers Grove: InterVarsity, 1992. 146–63.

Gundry, R. H. *The Use of the Old Testament in St. Matthew's Gospel with Special Reference to the Messianic Hope.* NovTSup 18. Leiden: Brill, 1967.

———. *Matthew: A Commentary on His Literary and Theological Art.* Grand Rapids; Eerdmans, 1982.

Gunn, D. M. "Narrative Criticism." in *To Each Its Own Meaning: An Introduction to Biblical Criticisms and Their Application.* Edited by Steven L. McKenzie and Stephen R. Haynes. Louisville: Westminster, 1993, 171–95.

Gurtner, Daniel M. *The Torn Veil: Matthew's Exposition of the Death of Jesus.* New York: Cambridge University Press, 2007.

Hagen, Peter L. *The Rhetorical Effectiveness of Verbal Irony.* Ph. D. dissertation, Pennsylvania State University, 1992.

Hagner, Donald A. *Matthew 14–28.* WBC. Vol. 33B. Dallas: Word Books, 1995.

Hamilton, Catherine S. "'His Blood Be upon Us': Innocent Blood and the Death of Jesus in Matthew." *Catholic Biblical Quarterly* 70 (2008): 82–101.

Harrington, D. J. *The Gospel of Matthew.* SP 1. Collegeville: Liturgical, 1991.

Harrison, E. F. "Jesus and Pilate." *Bibliotheca Sacra* 105 (1948): 307–19.

Heil, John P. "Matthew 27: 51–53 in the Theology of the Evangelist." *Irish Biblical Studies* 7 (1985): 76–87.

———. "The Blood of Jesus in Matthew: A Narrative-Critical Perspective." *Perspectives in Religious Studies* 18 (1991): 117–23.

———. *The Death and Resurrection of Jesus: A Narrative-Critical Reading of Matthew 26–28.* Minneapolis: Fortress Press, 1991.

———. "Ezekiel 34 and the Narrative Strategy of the Shepherd and Sheep Metaphor in Matthew." *Catholic Biblical Quarterly* 55 (1993): 698–708.

Heller, Erich. *The Ironic German: A Study of Thomas Mann.* Boston: Little Brown, 1958.

Henderson, Jeffrey. *Aristophanes: Clouds, Wasps, Peace.* Edited and translated by Jeffrey Henderson. Cambridge: Harvard University Press, 1998.

Hendrickx, Herman. *Passion Narratives: Studies in the Synoptic Gospels.* London: Geoffrey Chapman, 1984.

Hengel, Martin. *Crucifixion in the Ancient World and the Folly of the Message of the Cross.* London: SCM, 1977.

Hill, David. *The Gospel of Matthew.* London: Oliphants, 1972.

———. "Matthew 27:51-53 in the Theology of the Evangelist." *Irish Biblical Studies* 7 (1985): 76–87.

Hoggatt, Jerry C. *Irony in Mark's Gospel: Text and Subtext.* SNTSMS 74. Cambridge University Press, 1992.

Holdcroft, David "Irony as a Trope, and Irony as Discourse." *Poetics Today* 4 (1983): 493–511.

Holland, Glenn S. *Divine Irony.* London: Associated University Presses, 2000.

Hopper, Stanley. "Irony—the Pathos of the Middle." *Cross Currents* 12 (1962): 31–40.

Howell, David. B. *Matthew's Inclusive Story: A Study in the Narrative Rhetoric of the First Gospel.* JSNTSup 42. Sheiffield: JSOT, 1990.

Hurtado, Larry W. *How on Earth Did Jesus Become a God: Historical Questions about Earliest Devotion to Jesus.* Grand Rapids: Eerdmans, 2005.

Hutchens, E. N. "The Identification of Irony." *English Literary History* 27 (1960): 352–63.

Hutcheon, Linad. *Irony's Edge: the Theory and Politics of Irony.* London: Routledge. 1994.

Iser, Wolfgang, "Interaction between Text and Reader." In *The Reader in the Text: Essays on Audience and Interpretation.* Edited by S. Suleiman and I. Crosman. Princeton: Princeton University Press, 1980, 106–19.

———. *The Implied Reader: Patterns of Communication in Prose Fiction from Bunyan to Beckett.* Westport: Greenwood, 1992.

Isiodre, *Isidori Hispalensis Episcopi Etymologiarum Sive Originum Libri XX*. 2 vols. Edited by W. M. Lindsay. Oxford: Clarendon, 1922.

Jankélévitch, Vladimir. *L'Ironie*. Paris: Flammarion, 1964.

Jeremias, Joachim. "Polloi." in TDNT, volume 6. Edited by Gerhard Kittel and Gerhard Friedrich. Translated by G. W. Bromiley. 10 vols. Grand Rapids, 1968. 537–38.

Jónsson, Jakob. *Humor and Irony in the New Testament Illuminated by Parallels in Talmud and Midrash*. Reykjavik: Bókaútgáfa Menningarsjóts, 1965.

Kadai, Heino O. "Luther's Theology of the Cross." in *Accents in Luther's Theology: Essays in Commemoration of the 450th Anniversary of the Reformation*. Edited by Heino O. Kadai. St. Louis: Concordia Publishing House, 1967, 230–72.

Karstetter, A. B. "Toward a Theory of Rhetorical Irony." *Speech Monographs* 31 (1964): 162–78.

Katz, Albert N. "The Uses and Processing of Irony and Sarcasm." *Metaphor and Symbol* 15 (2000).

Kaufer, David and Christine M. Neuwirth. "Foregrounding Norms and Ironic Communications." *Quarterly Journal of Speech* 68 (1982): 28–36.

Kaufer, David. "Irony and Rhetorical Strategy." *Philosophy and Rhetoric* 10 (1977): 90–110.

———. "Ironic Evaluations." *Communication Monographs* 48 (1981a): 25–38.

———. "Irony, Interpretive Form and the Theory of Meaning." *Poetics Today* 4 (1983): 451–64.

———. "Understanding Ironic Communication." *Journal of Pragmatics* 5 (1981b): 495–510.

Keener, Craig S. *A Commentary on the Gospel of Matthew*. Grand Rapids: Eerdmans, 1999.

Kermode, Frank. *The Genesis of Secrecy: On the Interpretation of Narrative*. Cambridge: Harvard University Press, 1979.

Kierkegaard, Søren. *The Concept of Irony with Constant Reference to Socrates*. Translated by Lee M. Capel. Bloomington: Indiana University Press, 1965.

———. *The Concept of Irony with Continual Reference to Socrates*. Edited and translated by Howard V. Hong and Edna H. Hong. New Jersey: Princeton University Press, 1989.

Kilpatrick, Kirk. *Beautiful Irony, Matthew 21:1–14*. Ph.D. dissertation, Mid-America Baptist Theological Seminary, 1996.

Kingsbury, Jack D. *Matthew: Structure, Christology, Kingdom*. Philadelphia: Fortress Press, 1975.

———. "The Figure of Peter in Matthew's Gospel as a Theological Problem." *Journal of Biblical Literature* 98 (1979): 67–83.

———. "The Figure of Jesus in Matthew' Story: A Literary-Critical Probe." *Journal for the Study of the New Testament* 21 (1984): 3–36.

———. "The Figure of Jesus in Matthew's Story: A Rejoinder to David Hill." *Journal for the study of the New Testament* 25 (1985): 61–81.

———. "The Developing Conflict between Jesus and the Jewish Leaders in Matthew's Gospel: A Literary-Critical Study." *Catholic Biblical Quarterly* 49 (1987): 57–73.

———. "The Verb *Akolouthein* ("to follow") as an Index to Matthew's View on His Community." *Journal of Biblical Literature* 97 (1987): 58–60.

———. *Matthew as Story*. Philadelphia: Fortress Press, 1988.

———. "Reflection on 'The Reader' of Matthew's Gospel." *New Testament Studies* 34 (1988): 442–60.

———. "The Plot of Matthew's Story." *Interpretation* 46 (1992): 347–56.

Knox, Dilwyn. *Ironia: Medieval and Renaissance Ideas on Irony*. Leiden: E. J. Brill, 1989.

Knox, Norman. "Irony" in *Dictionary of the History of Ideas: Studies of Selective Pivotal Ideas*. 2 vols. Edited by P. P. Wiener. New York: Scribner & Sons, 1973.

———. "On the Classifications of Ironies." *Modern Philosophy* 70 (1972): 53–62.

———. *The Word Irony and Its Context, 1500–1755*. Durham: Duke University Press, 1961.

Kosmala, H. "His Blood on Us and Our Children' (The Background of Mat. 27, 24–25)." *Annual of the Swedish Theological Institute* 7 (1970): 94–126.

Lanham, Richard A. *A Handlist of Rhetorical Terms: A Guide for Students of English Literature*. Berkeley: University of California Press, 1968.

Lang, Candace D. *Irony/ Humor: Critical Paradigms*. Baltimore: Johns Hopkins University Press, 1988.

Lowe, Malcolm. F. "Who were the *Ioudaioi*?" *Novum Testamentum* 18 (1976): 101–30.

Luz, Ulrich. *The Theology of the Gospel of Matthew*. Translated by J. Bradford Robinson. New York: Cambridge University Press, 1993.

———. *Matthew 21–28*. Edited by Helmut Koester. Translated by James E. Crouch. Minneapolis: Fortress Press, 2005.

Mack, Burton. *Rhetoric and the New Testament*. Minneapolis: Fortress Press, 1989.

Marguerat, Daniel. *Le jugément dans l'évangile de Matthieu.* Geneva: Labor et Fides, 1981.
Matera, Frank. *Passion Narratives and Gospel Theologies: Interpreting the Synoptics through Their Passion Stories.* New York: Paulist, 1986.
——. "The Passion according to Matthew. Part One: Jesus Unleashes the Passion, 26:1–75." *Clergy Review* 62 (1987): 93–97.
——. "The Passion according to Matthew. Part Two: Jesus Suffers the Passion, 27:1–66." *Priest & People* 1 (1987): 13–17.
——. "The Plot of Matthew's Gospel." *Catholic Biblical Quarterly* 49 (1987): 233–53.
Meier, J. P. *The Vision of Mt: Christ, Church, and Morality in the First Gospel.* New York: Paulist, 1979.
Merkel, Helmut. "Peter's Curse." in *The Trial of Jesus.* Edited by Ernst Bammel. Cambridge Studies in Honor of C. F. D. Moule. SBT 13. London: SCM, 1970, 66–71.
Meyers, Alice R. "Toward a Definition of Irony." in *Studies in Language Variation: Semantics, Syntax, Phonology, Pragmatics, Social Situations, Ethnographic Approaches.* Edited by Ralph W. Fasold and Roger W. Shuy. Washington: Georgetown University Press, 1974, 171–83.
Miller, Walter. *Cicero, De Officiis.* Translated by W. Miller. London: William Heinemann LTD, 1928.
Morris, Leon. "The Biblical Use of the Term 'Blood.'" *Journal of Theological Studies* 3 (1953): 216–27.
Muecke, Douglas C. "Images of Irony." *Poetics Today* 4 (1983): 399–413.
——. *Irony and the Ironic.* London: Methuen, 1970.
——. *Irony: The Critical Idiom.* London: Methuen, 1970.
——. "The Communication of Verbal Irony." *Journal of Literary Semantics* 2 (1973): 35–42.
——. *The Compass of Irony.* London: Methuen, 1969.
Natanson, Maurice. "The Arts of Indirection." in *Rhetoric, Philosophy and Literature.* Edited by Don M. Burks. West Lafayette, Ind.: Purdue University Press, 1978, 35–47.
Nolland, John. *The Gospel of Matthew.* NIGTC. Grand Rapids: Eerdmans, 2005.
Oates, Whitney J., and Eugene O'Neill, Jr., eds. *The Complete Greek Drama: All the Extent Tragedies of Aeschylus, Sophocles and Euripides, and the Comedies of Aristophanes and Menander, in a Variety of Translations.* 2 vols. New York: Random House, 1938.
O'Day, Gail R. *Revelation in the Fourth Gospel.* Philadelphia: Fortress Press, 1986.

Olson, Elder. *Tragedy and the Theory of Drama.* Detroit: Wayne State University Press, 1961.

Otto, Rudolf. *The Idea of the Holy: An Inquiry into the Non-Traditional Factor in the Idea of the Divine and Its Relation to the Rational.* Translated by John W. Harvey. New York: Oxford University Press, 1950.

Patte, Daniel. *The Gospel According to Matthew: A Structural Commentary on Matthew's Faith.* Philadelphia: Fortress Press, 1987.

Perelman, Chaim. *The New Rhetoric: A Treatise of Argumentation.* Translated by John Wilkinson and Purcell Weaver. University of Notre Dame Press, 1969.

Perrine, Norman. "The Use of (para)*didonai* in Connection with the Passion of Jesus in the New Testament." in *Der Ruf Jesu und die Antwort der Gemeinde.* Edited by E. Lohse. Göttingen, 1970, 204–12.

Petersen, Norman R. *Literary Criticism for New Testament Critics.* Guides to Biblical Scholarship. Philadelphia: Fortress Press, 1978.

Plato. *Apology, Crito, Phaedo, Symposium, Republic.* Edited by Louise Ropes Loomis. Translated by B. Jowett. New York: Walter J. Black, 1942.

Pliny the Younger, *Epistulae.* Translated by William Melmoth. Revised by W. M. L. Hutchinson: William Heinemann, 1931.

Porkorny, Julius. *Indogermanisches Etymologisches Wörterbuch.* Band I. Bern: Francke, 1959.

Powell, Mark A. *What is Narrative Criticism?* GBS. Minneapolis: Fortress Press, 1990.

———. "The Plot and Subplots of Matthew's Gospel." *New Testament Series* 38 (1992): 187–204.

———. "Toward a Narrative-Critical Understanding of Matthew." *Interpretation* 46 (1992): 341–46.

———. "Expected and Unexpected Readings in Matthew: What the Reader Knows." *The Asbury Theological Journal* 48 (1993): 31–52.

Quintilian, *The Institutio Oratoria of Quintilian.* Translated by H. E. Butler. Cambridge: Harvard University Press, 1920–1922.

Reinhartz, Adele. "The New Testament and anti-Judaism: A Literary-Critical Approach." *Journal of Ecumenical Studies* 25 (1988).

Reiss, Edmond. "Medieval Irony." *Journal of the History of Ideas* 42 (1981): 209–26.

Rhoads, David M. and Donald M. Michie. *Mark as Story: An Introduction to the Narrative of a Gospel.* Philadelphia: Fortress Press, 1982.

———. "Narrative Criticism and the Gospel of Mark." *Journal of the American Academy of Religion* 50 (1982).

———. "Narrative Criticism: Practices and Prospects." Page 264–85 in *Characterization in the Gospels: Reconceiving Narrative Criticism*. Edited by David M. Rhoads and Kari Syreeni. JSNTSup 184. Sheffield Academic, 1999.

Ribbeck, Otto. "Über den Begriff des eirōn." *Rheinisches Museum* 31 (1876): 381–400.

Richter, D. H. "The Reader as Ironic Victim." *Novel* 14 (1981): 135–51.

Ricoeur, Paul. "Interpretative Narrative." Page 237–57 in *The Book and the Text: The Bible and Literary Theory*. Edited by R. M. Schwartz. Cambridge: Basil Blackwell, 1990.

Rieckert, S. J. P. K. "The Narrative Coherence in Matthew 26–28." *Neotestamentica* 16 (1982): 53–74.

Rivkin, Ellis. *What Crucified Jesus? The Political Execution of a Charismatic*. Nashville: SCM, 1984.

Robert, Andre de. "L'ironie et la Bible." *Études Théologiques et Religieuses* 55 (1980): 3–30.

Robinson, J. M. "The Gospels as Narrative." in *The Bible and the Narrative Tradition*. Edited by Frank McConnell. New York: Oxford University Press, 1986, 97–112.

Saldarini, Anthony J. *Jesus and Passover*. New York: Paulist, 1984.

Sanders, E. P., and Margaret Davies. *Studying the Synoptic Gospels*. London: SCM, 1989.

Sanders, W. "Das Blut Jesu und die Juden. Gedanken zu Matth. 27, 25." *Una Sancta* 27 (1972): 1968–71.

Scholes, Robert and Robert Kellogg. *The Nature of Narratives*. London: Oxford, 1966.

Schweizer, Eduard. *The Good News According to Matthew*. Translated by David E. Green. Atlanta: John Knox, 1975.

Sedgewick, Garnett G. "Dramatic Irony: Studies in Its History, Its Definition, and Its Use Especially in Shakespeare and Sophocles." Ph.D. dissertation, Harvard University, 1913

———. *Of Irony: Especially in the Drama*. Toronto: University of Toronto Press, 1935.

Senior, Donald. "The Passion Narrative in the Gospel of Matthew." in *L'Évangile selon Matthieu*. Edited by Michel Didier. BETL 29. Gembloux: Éditions J. Duculot, 1972, 342–57.

———. "The Death of Jesus and the Resurrection of the Holy ones (Mt. 27:51-53)." *Catholic Biblical Quarterly* 38 (1976): 312–29.

———. *The Passion of Jesus in the Gospel of Matthew.* Wilmington: Michael Glazier, 1985.

———. "Matthew's Special Material in the Passion Story: Implications for the Evangelist's Redactional Technique and Theological Perspective." *Ephemerides Theologicae Lovanienses* 63 (1987): 272–94.

Sharpe, Robert B. *Irony in the Drama: An Essay on Impersonation, Shock, and Catharsis.* Chapel Hill: University of North Carolina Press, 1959.

Shipley, Joseph T. *Dictionary of World Literature, Criticism, Forms, Technique.* New York: Philosophical Library, 1943.

S'hiri, Sonia. "Literary Discourse and Irony: Secret Communion and the Pact of Reciprocity." *Edinburg Working Papers in Linguistics* 2 (1991): 126–42.

Smith, Robert H. "The Hardest Verse in Mt's Gospel." *Currents in Theology and Mission* 17 (1990): 421–28.

Spencer, Aida B. "The Wise Fool (and the Foolish Wise). A Study of Irony in Paul." *Novum Testamentum* 23 (1981): 349–60.

Stanton, Graham A., ed. *The Interpretation of Matthew.* Edinburgh: T. & T. Clark, 1995.

States, Bert O. *Irony and Drama: A Poetics.* Ithaca: Cornell University Press, 1971.

Sternberg, Meir. *Poetics of Biblical Narrative: Ideological Literature and the Drama of Reading.* Bloomington: Indiana University Press, 1985.

Strathmann, H. "λαός." in *TDNT* 4. Edited by Gerhard Kittel and Gerhard Friedrich. Translated by G. W. Bromiley. 10 vols. Grand Rapids, 1964–76, 51.

Strecker, Georg. *Der Weg der Gerichtigkeit, Untersuchung zur Theologie des Matthäus.* Göttingen: Vandenhoeck und Ruprecht, 1962.

Suleiman, Susan. "Interpreting Ironies." *Diacritics* 6 (1976): 15–21.

Syreeni, Kari. "Between Heaven and Earth: On the Structure of Matthew's Symbolic Universe." *Journal for the Study of the New Testament* 40 (1990): 3–13.

———. "Peter as Character and Symbol in the Gospel of Matthew." in *Characterization in the Gospels: Reconceiving Narrative Criticism.* Edited David M. Rhoads and Kari Syreeni. JSNTSup 184 (1999). 160–52.

Tanaka, Ronald "The Concept of Irony: Theory and Practice." *Journal of Literary Semantics* 2 (1973): 43–56.

Tannehill, Robert C. *The Narrative Unity of Luke-Acts: A Literary Interpretation.* 2 vols. Philadelphia: Fortress Press, 1986/1990.

Tenney, Merrill C. *New Testament Survey.* Rev. Grand Rapids: Eerdmans, 1985.

Tindale, Christopher W., and James Gough. "The Use of Irony in Argumentation." *Philosophy and Rhetoric* 20 (1987): 1–17.
Thirlwall, John Connop. "On the Irony of Sophocles." *The Philological Museum* 2 (1833): 483–537
Thompson, Alan R. *The Dry Mock: A Study of Irony in Drama.* Berkeley: University of California Press, 1948.
Thomson, J. A. K. *Irony: An Historical Introduction.* London: George Allen and Unwin, 1926.
Thrall, William F., and Addison Hibbard, *A Handbook to Literature.* Revised by C. H. Holman. New York: Odyssey, 1960.
Uspensky, Boris. *A Poetics of Composition: The Structure of the Artistic Text and Typology of a Compositional Form.* Translated by Valentina Zavarin and Susan Wittig. Berkeley: University of California Press, 1973.
Uwe, Japp. *Theorie der Ironie.* Frankfurt am Main: Vittorio Klostermann, 1983.
Van Tilborg, Sjef. *The Jewish Leaders in Matthew.* Leiden: Brill, 1972.
Vlastos, Gregory. "The Socratic Elenchus." in Vol. 1 of *Oxford Studies in Ancient Philosophy.* Edited by Julia Annas. Oxford: Clarendon, 1983, 27–58.
———. "Socratic Irony." *Classical Quarterly* 37 (1987): 79–97.
Vellacott, Philip. *Ironic Drama.* Cambridge: Cambridge University Press, 1975.
Weaver, Dorothy J. "Power and Powerlessness: Matthew's Use of Irony in the Portrayal of Political Leaders." *Society of Biblical Literature* 31 (1992): 454–66.
Weimann, Robert. *Structure and Society in Literary Theory.* Charlottesville: University of Virginia Press, 1973.
Wilcox, Max. " 'Upon the Tree': Deuteronomy 21:22-23 in the New Testament." *Journal of Biblical Literature* 96 (1977): 85–99.
Williams, James G. "Irony and Lament: Clues to Prophetic Consciousness." *Semeia* 8 (1977): 51–71.
Witherup, Ronald D. "The Cross of Jesus: A Literary-Critical Study of Matthew 27." Ph D. dissertation, Union Theological Seminary in Virginia, 1985.
Wood, J. A. "The Anointing at Bethany and Its Significance." *Expository Times* 39, no 10 (1928): 475–76.
Worcester, David. *The Art of Satire.* Cambridge: Harvard University Press, 1940.
Wright, Nicholas T. *The New Testament and the People of God.* Minneapolis: Fortress Press, 1992.

Index of Names

Alter, Robert, 8n33, 92, 95n61
Amante, David, 64, 64n231, 71n280, 87
Anderson, Janice, 11n45, 12n50
Apuleius, 21, 79, 83, 85; *Metamorphoses*, 21, 79, 80n2, 83, 83n11
Aristophanes, 21, 27, 31–38, 42, 59–60, 79; *Nubes*, 21, 31, 31n34, 32–37, 59, 79
Aristotle, 4, 27, 32, 37n71, 39–42, 44–46, 49, 60, 76, 93; *Ars rhetorica*, 4, 4nn15–16, 34n54, 39n80, 44n113, 46n126; *De caelo*, 94n60; *Ethica nichomachea*, 39, 40, 40n88, 41, 42, 49, 49n145, 60; *Poetica*, 2n5, 88n38, 89n47, 93n54, 103n12

Booth, Wayne, 1n1, 4, 4n17, 7n28, 10, 11n42, 15n68, 16, 16n71, 17, 17n74, 18–20, 25n3, 26, 27n14, 28n24, 53, 53n174, 54, 56, 64n225, 64n229, 68n253, 69, 72, 77, 110–11
Brooks, Cleanth, 55, 58n211, 87
Brown, Raymond, 107, 107n24, 108–9, 115n51, 119n68, 124n88, 132n103, 136n112
Brueggemann, Walter, 5n20, 8n33, 63n227, 98
Burke, Kenneth, 4n14, 43–44, 45n121, 56n194, 69, 96n67

Cargal, Timothy, 9, 11n47, 168n186, 171n192
Carter, Warren, 9–10, 10n41, 13n59, 97n70, 103n11, 104n16, 118n61, 119n65
Catchpole, David, 8n34, 149n149

Chatman, Seymour, 1n2, 11, 11n44, 13n59, 66n245, 102n5, 103n9, 184n225
Chevalier, Haakon, 53, 73n288
Cicero, 27, 30, 32, 42–46, 48–49, 60–61, 63, 76–77, 96; *Academicae quaestiones*, 45n123; *Catalinam*, 18n83; *De officiis*, 30n32, 43, 43n105, 96n68; *De oratore*, 43n98, 44n111, 44n114, 46n126, 51, 61n216, 62n220, 77n315; *In verrem*, 45n121; *Prof Caecina*, 45n122
Clark, Herbert, 62n219, 69, 69n266, 71n280
Clavier, Henri, 58n21
Combrink, Bernard, 13n60, 103n9, 111n37
Cousland, J. R. C, 118n60, 119n63, 123n83, 173n199
Crossan, Dominic, 158n164, 169n188, 170n189, 174n200

Dane, Joseph, 19n92, 32n42, 38n75, 40
Dawsey, James, 8n33, 12n48
Duke, Paul, 8n33, 13n59, 16, 57n200, 65n234, 68, 73n291, 74n294
Duncan, Derrett, 192n240

Edwards, Richard, 8n34, 13n58, 109, 125n89, 138n118
Eliade, Mercea, 4, 4n18
Euripides, 7n29, 21, 52, 59n213, 93n55, 94; *Bacchae*, 21, 79, 93

Fitzmyer, Joseph, 119n69, 172n195, 174n201, 200n11

France, Richard, 112n43, 116n54, 117n58, 123n84, 130n98, 131n102, 162n178
Frankemölle, Hubert, 172, 173n197
Frye, Northrop, 30n. 31, 95n65, 191n239

Gerhardsson, Birger, 8n34, 140n122, 141n124, 142n125, 190n234
Gerrig, Richard, 62n219, 69, 69n266, 71n280
Gill, Jerry, 8n33
Good, Edwin, 7n28, 8n33, 80n3
Gough, James, 27n12, 63n222, 65n236, 67, 71n277, 77n311, 81n9, 88n34

Hagen, Peter, 29, 29n25, 64n233, 71n279
Heil, John, 9, 107n23, 115n50, 116n54, 129n97, 133n106, 136n112, 177n205
Hoggatt, Jerry, 5n20, 8n30, 17n78, 43n110, 58n211, 66, 69, 72n281, 74n294, 87, 91n51, 96n67
Holdcroft, David, 4n12, 87
Holland, Glenn, 5, 5n22, 6, 18–19, 58n211, 64n221, 66n242, 69, 70n271, 78, 90n48
Horace, 60n215, 63; *Ars poetica*, 60n215, 63n221

Isidore, 50; *Etymologiae*, 50n155

Jónsson, Jakob, 8n33, 43, 96n67

Kaufer, David, 51, 51n165, 64n230, 65, 65n237, 69–70, 87n29, 88n34
Kierkegaard, Søren, 7n28, 32, 54–55, 57n196, 70n271
Kingsbury, Jack, 8, 8n31, 12n48, 97n72, 102, 102n5, 104n17, 105, 109, 118n62, 122n76, 134n108
Knox, Dilwyn, 28, 29n26, 49n146, 49n148, 51n163

Knox, Norman, 31, 31n38, 32, 33n44

Lanham, Richard, 63

Matera, Frank, 13n60, 102n9, 103n9, 104, 111n38, 134n108
Michie, Donald, 2, 8, 8n31
Muecke, Douglas, 7n28, 16, 26, 28, 54–55, 56n196, 62, 66, 75–76, 87, 89, 90, 95

Natanson, Maurice, 18n87, 63n221

O'Day, Gail, 5n20, 69, 69n261
Otto, Rudolf, 4, 4n18

Petersen, Norman, 8, 8n31
Plato, 6, 27, 32, 35–36, 38–39, 42, 45, 48, 60; *Apologia*, 6, 6n25, 35, 35n56, 36n62, 37, 60; *Phaedo*, 37; *Respublica*, 35n55, 36–37, 37n65, 37n70; *Sophista*, 35, 35n55; *Symposium*, 36–37, 37n65, 38, 39n77, 60
Porkorny, Julius, 28, 28n18
Powell, Mark, 2, 9, 11n42, 12n48, 14n61, 71n275, 74n294, 102, 189n226

Quintilian, 3, 27, 32, 37, 42, 46–51, 53, 60–61, 78; *Institutio oratoria*, 3n6, 3n9, 4n13, 37, 37n68, 46n127, 46n142, 50n157

Rhoads, David, 2, 8, 8n31
Ribbeck, Otto, 7n28, 27n11, 29n29, 44, 79n1
Rivkin, Ellis, 200n11

Sedgewick, Garnett, 2n5, 7n28, 25n1, 37n71, 42n96, 52, 53n170, 57n200, 63n227, 65n240, 73n286, 76n309, 77, 90

Senior, Donald, 9, 108–9, 116n55, 130n100, 170n189, 188n227
Sharpe, Robert, 7n28
Shipley, Joseph, 74n297, 88n39
Smith, Robert, 9n38, 169n187, 171n192
Socrates, 6–7, 21, 29, 31–36, 36n63, 37, 37n69, 38–40, 42–49, 51–54, 59–61, 73, 95, 95n64, 143n130
Sophocles, 21, 52, 59n213, 79, 89, 90n49; *Oedipus Rex*, 21, 79, 90

Tanaka, Ronald, 57n202, 70n270, 111n39
Thirlwall, John, 52, 52n166, 57n200, 65, 88–89
Thompson, Alan, 34n51, 43, 56, 57n198, 65n239, 78, 81n8, 86n23, 95–96

Tindale, Christopher, 27n12, 63n222, 65n236, 67, 71n277, 77n311, 81n9, 88n34

Uspensky, Boris, 11n46

Vlastos, Gregory, 32, 32n43, 39, 44, 95n64

Weaver, Dorothy Jean, 8n32, 9, 10n40, 17, 57n200, 74n294, 85, 97, 97n70
Williams, James, 6, 6n24, 8n33, 73n286, 74n298, 80n3
Worcester, David, 7n28, 37n72, 57, 58n211, 78n319, 96n66

Xenophon, 27, 31–32; *Memorabilia*, 32n40, 35n59

Index of Subjects

blasphemy, 97, 123n85, 149n148

character irony, 21, 57, 79–80, 95–96, 98–99, 111–12, 121, 125–26, 133–35, 142, 150, 158–63, 188–89, 192–93
Christ-event, 10, 22, 193–94, 199, 204
conflict, 2, 9, 22, 30, 63–64, 72–74, 78, 96–97, 106, 109, 149, 160–62, 185, 187–88, 190, 193, 205, 207; ἀγών, 30, 63, 73
conventional irony (or ironies), 2–3, 10–11, 19–21, 79, 110, 114, 151, 193
cross, 2, 3, 7, 22–23, 106–8, 114–16, 123, 130, 133, 140, 145, 148, 162, 166, 177, 180–82, 192, 196–201, 204–5, 207–8; bearing one's cross, 22, 132, 140; centrality of the cross, 7; message of the cross, 3; *supplicium servile*, 200
crowd, ὄχλος, 119, 172–73, 202

deception, 33, 40, 45, 49, 59, 76, 117, 189, 191, 207
divine irony, 6; divine ironist, 3, 12–13, 110n35, 111, 193, 205; implied-author ironist, 17, 22, 85, 101, 120, 174, 183, 190, 193–94, 202–3, 206
double-layered story phenomenon, 63, 74, 112, 114, 117n57, 161; dualistic story phenomenon, 2, 74; two levels of story, 63, 72n283
dramatic irony, 18n70, 52, 57, 57n200, 58n209, 58n. 210, 63n227, 80, 88, 88n37, 89–91, 91n50, 92–94, 154n156, 163, 167–68, 171, 183, 185, 187

figures of speech, 3, 86; trope, *tropos*, 3, 3n9, 4, 25, 47–51, 53, 61, 81; scheme (figure), *schema*, 3–4, 61
forgiveness of sins, 107, 121, 131, 153, 166–67, 175–78, 187, 199, 206
formal elements of irony, 20, 64; constitution of irony, 63, 117n57

identity of Jesus, 21, 148, 162–63, 193, 205, 207; normative figure, 30, 47; protagonist, 30, 59, 85, 96–97, 105–6, 114, 116, 143n130; Christ Savior, 105–6, 114, 120, 132, 137, 167, 169, 171–75, 181–83, 185–87, 192, 196–202, 204, 206
ignorance, 7, 22, 30, 36–37, 39, 45, 73, 75, 84–85, 89, 91, 93–94, 96, 114, 121, 144, 151, 154, 157, 175–76, 189, 197
inclusio, 120, 160, 160n170, 163, 168, 173–75, 202
Implied author, 1–19, 22, 64, 66, 85, 97, 101, 103–4, 107, 109, 110–13, 118, 120, 122–23, 128–29, 132, 134, 137, 140, 144, 153, 156–57, 160, 163, 165–66, 168, 171–72, 174–79, 181, 183–84, 190, 193–98, 202–6
implied reader, 1, 10–11, 13, 14–15, 18–20, 66, 75, 77, 104, 110–11, 119–20, 127, 130, 135, 138, 143–44, 149, 154, 159, 161–63, 171, 182, 187, 189, 194, 203
impostor, 40–41, 73, 188n227, 191n239
innocence, 22, 63, 75–77, 94, 117, 144, 150–55, 164–65, 176
interpretive community, 13, 69; confederacy, 66, 71, 87

ironic reversal, 81, 85, 162n178, 177, 179
irony: ἀλαζών, 29–30, 33–34, 34n51, 40, 40nn89–90, 41, 42n95, 59–60, 73, 75–76, 85–86, 95–97, 97n72, 112, 135, 142n130, 144, 147, 163, 165, 181, 183, 191, 191n239, 192, 206–8; ἀλαζονεία, 39–40, 40n89, 41, 60, 191, 191n239; εἴρων, 28, 28n20, 30–34, 34nn51–52, 35, 38–40, 40nn89–90, 41–43, 43n105, 44, 46, 48, 48n140, 59, 64, 66, 75–76, 85, 95–97, 112, 142n130, 145, 147, 191n239, 206–8; εἰρωνεία, 1, 21, 25, 29–47, 49, 59–60, 80, 95; ὕβρις, 76, 94; *alazōn*, 29; *alazonic*, 94, 135, 142, 143n130, 197; *allegoria*, 47, 50, 61; *dissimulatio*, 28–29, 42–47, 61, 76; *eirōn*, 7n28, 27n11, 29, 29n29, 30n33, 31n37, 39n79, 79n1; *eirōneia*, 1, 21, 25, 29; *ironia*, 28–29, 42, 44, 46–51, 61; ironist, 1, 3, 6–7, 10, 12–13, 16–19, 22, 28, 43–46, 48–49, 54–56, 62–72, 75–79, 81–82, 84–85, 87–88, 91, 93, 101, 110–13, 116–17, 120, 134, 136, 138–39, 146, 148–51, 155, 159, 165, 167–68, 172–75, 181, 183, 190, 192–94, 202–6; over-confidence, 133–35; working definition of, 20, 27, 62–63
ironic intent, 19, 64, 67

Jewish religious leaders, 9, 102, 115, 117–21, 125, 143, 147, 154–57, 161, 165, 167, 171–72, 177, 183, 187–89, 204, 207; antagonists, 22, 97, 183, 193; corporate opponents of Jesus, 155; Jewish religious authorities, 173, 181, 185, 202, 206

lawlessness, 154–55, 189, 191–92

literary-rhetorical device, 1, 15, 29; rhetorical strategy, 45, 66

mockery, 45, 59, 81, 107, 143, 151, 156, 180, 197; mocking pretense, 33

name of Jesus, 101, 105, 107, 132, 159, 172, 196, 200, 205
narrative criticism, 10–13, 13n60, 14n62, 15–16, 19–21, 64n229, 101–2, 110, 110n36, 111; narrative-critical reading, 9–10, 16, 19, 21, 110, 118, 128, 144, 163, 171, 193, 202
New Criticism, 7, 55, 55n184

obedience, 22, 108–9, 112, 166, 199, 207

Passion of Jesus, 108, 112, 135; blood of Jesus, 154, 165, 168–70, 172, 174, 175n204, 178, 187, 202–4; cup, τὸ ποτήριον, 22, 38, 112, 131, 135–38, 140, 151, 174, 181–82, 199–200, 206; death of Jesus, 22–23, 63, 101, 107–13, 116, 118, 120, 130–31, 134–35, 137, 141, 143, 145–46, 151, 154–56, 160–62, 166, 169, 172, 175, 177, 185, 192, 197, 199, 200–2, 204–5, 207–8; innocent blood, 9, 22, 101, 107, 117, 121, 152–54, 154n155, 156, 165–66, 168–71, 174, 175n204, 176–77, 187, 200, 203–4; innocent blood of Jesus, 9, 22, 153–54, 165, 168–70, 174, 187, 203–4; passion predictions, 137, 185, 187, 199–200; price of blood, 154; ransom for many, 101, 126, 183
Passover, πάσχα, 108, 113, 115–16, 131, 137; feast, 113–14, 116
people, λαός, 119, 164, 168–69, 172–75, 177–78, 202; πᾶς ὁ λαός, 164, 169, 173–75, 177, 202

pleasure of irony, 117n57; reward of irony, 76

Romanticism, 51–54, 54n176, 55, 57, 62; romantic irony, 7, 16n70, 54n176, 55, 56n196, 58n211

Socratic irony, 31, 35, 37, 39, 49n149, 51, 57, 60, 73n288
Sophoclean irony, 51–52, 57, 89
stable irony, 10, 16–17, 17n83, 18–19, 19n92, 20, 64n229, 65n237, 68, 76–77, 110–11; tamed irony, 16; unstable irony, 16–17, 18n83; untamed irony, 16, 18

tumult, θόρυβος, 114, 117, 121
tragic irony, 57, 89, 89n40, 90

universal salvation, 22, 169, 172, 193, 202, 204

verbal irony, 28nn24–25, 57, 57n200, 58n211, 64n233, 71n80, 80n4, 81–86, 86n23, 87–88, 95, 111, 141, 143, 147–53, 155, 165, 169, 170–71, 175, 177, 179–81; indirect means of speech, 148

victim of irony, 63, 68, 71, 71n273, 75, 117, 117n57

will of God, 6, 22, 108, 112, 127n94, 147, 189, 190–91, 199; divine must, δεῖ, 139, 141, 151, 156, 165; divine perspective, 1, 5–7, 14n62, 112, 207; divinely-willed salvation, 2, 104, 120, 146, 153, 177–78, 182, 187; governing norm, 21–22, 193, 199; saving will of God, 21, 110, 116–17, 147, 192–93, 199, 207

www.ingramcontent.com/pod-product-compliance
Lightning Source LLC
Chambersburg PA
CBHW071156070526
44584CB00019B/2812